ACCOUNTANT'S GUIDE TO THE INTERNET

Second Edition

ACCOUNTANT'S GUIDE TO THE INTERNET

Second Edition

ERIC E. COHEN

John Wiley & Sons, Inc.

NEW YORK • CHICHESTER • WEINHEIM • BRISBANE • SINGAPORE • TORONTO

I would like to dedicate this book to my God and my family.

This text is printed on acid-free paper. ∞

Copyright © 2000 by John Wiley & Sons, Inc.

All rights reserved. Published simultaneously in Canada.

This publication is designed to provide accurate and authoritative information in regard to the subject matter covered. It is sold with the understanding that the publisher is not engaged in rendering legal, accounting, or other professional services. If legal advice or other expert assistance is required, the services of a competent professional person should be sought.

Library of Congress Cataloging-in-Publication Data
Cohen, Eric E.
    Accountant's guide to the Internet/by Eric E. Cohen.—2nd ed.
      p. cm.
    Includes index.
    ISBN 0-471-35834-7 (pbk.: alk.paper)
    1. Accounting—Computer network resources. 2. Internet (Computer network) I. Title.
    HF5625.7.C64 2000
    025.06'657—dc21
                                    99-40253
                                      CIP

Printed in the United States of America

10 9 8 7 6 5 4 3 2 1

Contents

Introduction   ix

Chapter 1   **The Internet: What It Is and Why It Is Important**   **1**

What Is the Internet?   1
Why Is the Internet Relevant to Accountants?   6
What Is the History of the Internet?   18
What Are the Benefits for Accountants?   19
Where Is the Internet Going?   21
Interview: Rich Walker, Intuit   29

Chapter 2   **What You Can Do on the Internet**   **33**

Mail   33
Mailing Lists and List Servers   47
Mailing Lists   48
Newsgroups   53
FTP   72
Live Chat   77
Finger   80
Whois   80
Ping and Trace   81
World Wide Web   81
Other Clients   84
What's Not so Hot on the Internet?   86

Chapter 3   **Accessing the Internet: Getting Connected**   **93**

Types of Connections   93
Types of Services   101

Software   104
Places to Access with a Modem   106
On-Line Services   107
Internet Service Providers   111
Other Sources for Internet Access   113
Moving Beyond Traditional Internet Tools: Unified Messaging   114

Chapter 4   Software for the Internet   119

Web Browsers   119
File Management and Manipulation   127
Design Tools   134
Utilities   139
Internet-Integrated Products   141
Interview: John Patrick, IBM   143

**Chapter 5   Marketing Tips for Accountants:
               Establishing a Marketing Presence   147**

Introduction to Internet Marketing   147
Marketing Process   148
Marketing Sites   164
Other Aspects of an Internet Presence   165

Chapter 6   Research and Search Tools   171

Introduction   171
Web Searches   173
What's New and What's Like New?   183
Non–Web-Oriented Searches   186
Places to Research and Search   190
New and Unusual Tools   194
Putting It All Together   196

Chapter 7   Electronic Commerce   203

Introduction to Electronic Commerce   203
Electronic Storefronts   204
General Advertising   207
Accountants   207
Auctions   208

Automobiles   209
Banks   210
Books   212
Computer Sales and Support   212
Credit   214
Investments   215
Postage   217
Travel   218
Procurement   220
Underlying Technologies   221
Ordering on the Web   222
Accounting Solutions   224
Storefronts in a Box   226
Issues Paving the Way for Electronic Commerce   228
Interview: Great Plains   240

Chapter 8   Security and Privacy   245

Security   245
Privacy   258
Assurance   268

Chapter 9   Productivity Ideas for Professionals   277

Internet and Productivity: An Introduction   277
Internet, Productivity, and Accounting: An Introduction   278
Aiming Toward the Goal   286
Meeting the Mission   286
Standardization and Policies   294
Sites of Special Interest for Office Productivity   296

Chapter 10   Accounting-Oriented Electronic Resources   311

Introduction   312
Author's Pet Pages   312
Accountants—CPE   313
Accountants—Miscellaneous Resources   314
Accountants—Individuals and Listings of Listings   315
Accounting—Profession   317
Accounting Software—Dealers   318
Accounting Software—Developers for CPA   319

Accounting Software—Developers of Commercial Products   320
Accounting Organizations   322
Accounting—Tax and Law   325
Bar Code   325
Publishers of Books and Magazines   326
Business and Reference   328
Computers   330
Databases   331
EDI, ISO, Manufacturing, and Electronic Commerce   332
Government Resources   333
Internet—General   335
Internet—Oddities   337
Internet—Security   337
Internet—Winsock and World Wide Web-Specific Resources   338
Investments   339
Law   339
Mailing List Archives   340
Diversions (After Tax Season)—Movies, Television,
   Entertainment   340
News and Magazine Search Tools   340
On-Line Services and National ISPs   342
People and Business Listings (White and Yellow Pages)   343
Software—Shareware   344
Software—Commercial   344

Chapter 11 International Issues   347

Professional Society Use   347
Internet and Communication   350
Leads and Financing   350
Coming to an Understanding   351
Getting Down to Business   353
Electronic Commerce   354
More Links   354

Appendix A
Glossary   355

Index   361

Introduction

OVERVIEW OF THE BOOK

This book is a tour guide for accounting professionals who are interested in learning more about the Internet, how to use it, how others are using it, and how to find accounting-specific resources. The book is divided into this introduction, 11 chapters, and an appendix.

Chapter 1, "The Internet: What It Is and Why It Is Important," provides a perspective on where the Internet came from and where it is going.

Chapter 2, "What You Can Do on the Internet," discusses the types of services offered for those accessing the Internet, such as e-mail, file transfer, discussion groups (USENET), and the World Wide Web.

Chapter 3, "Accessing the Internet: Getting Connected," covers the various methods of accessing the Internet: commercial on-line services, Internet Service Providers, and direct connections.

Chapter 4, "Software for the Internet," outlines the tools you will need to get the most from the Internet.

Chapter 5, "Marketing Tips for Accountants: Establishing a Market Presence," covers how to complement your traditional marketing with an on-line presence.

Chapter 6, "Research and Search Tools," discusses the different search tools available for auditors and accountants, such as search engines and commercial databases.

Chapter 7, "Electronic Commerce," deals with issues relating to business and conducting business on the Internet.

Chapter 8, "Security and Privacy," highlights issues relating to real and imaginary hurdles on the Internet.

Chapter 9, "Productivity Ideas for Professionals," provides examples and descriptions of how other financial professionals have used electronic resources.

Chapter 10, "Accounting-Oriented Electronic Resources," discusses the resources available to accountants, auditors, and financial professionals, such as listserves, newsgroups, and World Wide Web sites.

Chapter 11, "International Issues," provides information for conducting business outside of the United States.

The appendix consists of a glossary of Internet-related terms.

WHAT ARE THE BENEFITS OF USING THIS BOOK?

The Internet has become a vital part of how business does business, how people spend their time at work and at play, and how organizations, governments, and the media reach out. In this second edition, we again try to capture the core topics of the Internet that the CPA and financial manager should be aware of. We highlight the trends, postulate on what will be important tomorrow, and offer a single resource for finding out more on these topics. Whereas three years ago, the message was "Climb aboard!" now the message is "Be part of shaping the future." Where three years ago we said to get e-mail and a Web site, now we say find the resources to deal with e-commerce.

You can come up to speed on what the Internet is and what it means for you, your career, and your firm. Most accountants in public practice have a large body of information with which they need to keep current. Keeping up with accounting and auditing rules, tax changes and opportunities, new versions of tax and write-up software, and management and marketing skills is already a full-time job for the practitioner.

Enter the Internet, an area that undergoes an evolutionary change every three months. Newspapers and trade magazine trumpet the latest resources available on the Internet. Clients are being showered with sales pitches about it. Business is being conducted electronically through it.

This book will help you learn the basics of the Internet, its relevance to accountants in public practice and industry, and how it will impact the profession in the future.

You can learn what resources are available specifically for financial professionals and how to find new resources that become available after this book was written. The Internet has been likened to being placed in the New York

City Public Library, without a card catalog or signs on the shelves, and being told to find *Moby Dick*. With appropriate direction, you can find your way to the fiction section. Without guidance, you will find excellent books and worthless books—but you probably will not complete your task.

This book contains the guidance of a CPA who has devoted six years to finding resources on the Internet for both a CPA firm and its clients. The author has worked with experts in the accounting, software, and publishing fields. You can benefit from thousands of work-hours spent learning the Internet and evaluating its relevance to the accounting profession.

The Internet is a rich storehouse of resources. There are so many resources available and the technology changes so quickly that understanding what is available is an overwhelming task. Many of those resources are aimed at the accountant, designed to make keeping up with the rest of the profession easier—if you can find them.

This book helps you find those resources. Although there is more information available than any person or firm can use in the course of a day, relevant information is not easy to find initially. However, when you know what is available and how to explore on your own efficiently, you will find resources that will make you more efficient, more effective, and more valuable to your clients or company.

You can find out how other CPAs are using the Internet. CPA firms that have embraced the Internet have found it invaluable for communicating internally, with clients, and with referral sources. They have found resources to run their practices more efficiently. Many have found it an invaluable marketing tool.

You can find out how the changing business information transfer environment will affect you, your firm, and your clients. More people are choosing to buy through the Internet, 24 hours a day, seven days a week. CPA firms are taking tax return information in over the Internet. CPAs are even accepting bids for audit work on the Net (http://www.cpaauction.com).

The CPA must understand the American Institute of Certified Public Accounting's Auditing Standards Board Statements (No. 31, No. 55, and No. 78).

HOW CAN YOU USE THIS BOOK?

This book can be used in a number of different ways. It can serve as a general overview of the Internet: what it is, its benefits, and its affect on society as a whole. However, because of the book's focus on the accounting profession, many of the basics will be covered only in summary form. If you find topics of particular interest, you will want to refer to other excellent titles that deal with those topics in more detail.

This book can be used as a basis for determining the areas of the Internet of immediate benefit to accountants and as a guide in developing a firm strategy for internal implementation and consulting services.

In addition, this book offers many listings of Internet resources that will be of interest to accountants as well as instructions on how to access other lists that are constantly updated on the Internet itself.

CAPTURING THE INTERNET IN PRINTED FORM . . . NOT! (A WARNING)

Hitting a Moving Target

Reading written material about the Internet is like having a letter in hand describing your baby granddaughter at birth and then seeing her eight months later. There is some resemblance to the original description, but a lot of growing up went on in between. The letter was timely and accurate, but the subject changes daily.

The Internet is not only growing and changing but also nearly impossible to describe. To some, it is e-mail, a pipeline from their company's mail system to the world. To others it is the World Wide Web. To others it is the files or databases they can access. It is also a point-of-sale terminal in the customer's den for 24-hour-a-day banking and buying—in your jammies.

Almost every day an evolutionary new standard, revolutionary new technology, counterrevolutionary business alliance, or cautionary salvo from the news of some security breach hits the newspapers. This book is a balance sheet of the Internet: a picture in time, obsolete by the time ink goes to paper.

"Obsolete" Is Not the Same as "Useless"

Like the computers you just bought, this manual will be obsolete by the time you are done reading it. Things are changing so fast that you can keep up only by getting into the habit of checking the headlines and Internet regularly. Similar to a computer, the fact that newer technology is out there does not decrease the value of having resources now. This manual provides the foundation so you can understand and follow these changes.

Warranty on the Owner's Manual Is Shorter Than on the Purchase

In the world of the Internet, three months represents a generation and three years, a lifetime. Although I have done my best to make sure the information you see and hear is complete and up to date, resources will have changed or disappeared, corporate direction will move in paths other than originally announced, and references to the locations of computer resources may no longer work. If you find the links don't work, try again later to make sure it wasn't just busy when you tried it. Remove pieces from the reference name, moving right to left, to see if some part of the site is still up. If that does not work, use one of the indexes mentioned in Chapter 6, searching on the general topic. This should return related information, even if the original site has ceased to exist. The author's home page, found at (http://www.computercpa.com), provides an up-to-date list of accounting resources and lists.

The good news is that as more firms gain their own domain names, offering portability as they move from ISP to ISP, sites that disappear completely seem to be on the fall. By the same token, a site may not have been updated for years, even though it has a high ranking on a search engine. Roadside Rubbish on the Information Superhighway—is it a problem?

Final Exhortation

With this apology then comes the exhortation—get to know more than e-mail and Yahoo! You can't keep up with everything on the Net, but you can find resources that can lead you there. Yesterday I helped a client close a deal by finding a small piece of information on the Web. If knowledge is power, the Internet can be best friend or chief tormenter. Back in the 1980s, each Novell documentation package came with a book about the books. Keep up, and keep up with those who keep up on your behalf.

COMMENT ON THE SECOND EDITION: HOW MUCH HAVE THINGS CHANGED?

Two Years

Two years have gone by from 1997 to 1999. The changes on the Internet landscape bear as little resemblance to the predictions as jet cars and robopet dreams of the 1950s resemble today's crowded freeways and airports. Yet the changes are substantial, and they may reflect more a change in people than ongoing changes in technology. Has the Internet become an integral part of your life? For many, the answer is yes.

As you wake you put on the coffee and check the news. You spy e-mail with the answer to your computer question you posted just before going to bed. Responding to Uncle Bill's catching-up e-mail will happen later. You map out your daily travels, put in a few bids for some equipment (your high bid, anyway—it will bid for you while you're out). You write some thoughts for a few colleagues to ponder for a meeting tomorrow, order some books and a tape for your niece's birthday, and reserve some library books. Is it really a good thing that you can do all this between 6 A.M. and 7 A.M.?

The price is right. What does $20 a month buy you? About 200 minutes monthly on a cell phone; basic charges on a Web site, a virtual assistant, and an AOL account, perhaps even basic cable TV? Cable TV brings you entertainment and news on its schedule. Cellular offers you voice communications anywhere, anytime—slow data access. AOL and Internet ISP—they give you anywhere, anytime communications, news, entertainment on your schedule. Where else can you find date-sensitive information so readily available, and sign up right there? Where can you fill out forms, have roundtable discussions—move from one topic to the next, or even handle multiple things simultaneously—as freely as on-line?

The Internet and the Profession

- When The Accountant's Guide to the Internet was first published, the Internet had become an important topic.
- Almost one-half of CPAs interviewed had e-mail.
- Netscape Navigator and Microsoft Internet Explorer 3 were battling for supremacy.
- Electronic banking had its first champion with Security First Network Bank (http://www.sfnb.com,the first FDIC-insured Internet bank).
- Digital payment schemes were trying to gain a foothold.
- Cable Internet access was being tested as ISDN tried to move out and ADSL was up and coming.
- The AICPA had just established its Web presence while carefully maintaining its CompuServe presence.
- CompuServe, MSN, and Prodigy were reinventing themselves.

How much has what we have seen and done changed!

- Most CPAs have individual, if not corporate, e-mail.
- IE 5 stands triumphant as America Online seeks to keep Netscape alive.
- Banking on the Internet is big. So is retail, computer sales, security trading, insurance, hotels and airline tickets, real estate—the service businesses are in turmoil. Stock brokers, travel agents, car salespeople, computer marketers, book sellers (who faced the dreaded "Amazonian basin" with the popularity of Amazon.com)—all have seen traditional channels erode as buyers flock to the Web. Even the auditing profession is touched

by an on-line site promoting the posting of needs for accounting services with the chance for CPA firms to bid on-line for the work. Digital payment schemes were still trying to gain a foothold.

- Cable Internet access is rolling out.
- The AICPA prepares to roll out its first major makeover in three years, but struggles in other Internet attempts.
- CompuServe is owned by AOL, MSN and Prodigy are Internet Service Providers and portals.

Major Changes

In 1999 hardware had doubled in capacity and performance (thanks, Moore's Law!) while dropping in price even more drastically. An exception—modem speeds have not changed to match. IE 5 and Windows 98 have integrated the Internet with the desktop (to the dismay of the Department of Justice). Web commerce has seen most banks, brokerage firms, mail order chains and retail firms, and even bookstores go on-line, with new competitors Amazon, Price-line, E-Trade carving out and leading the on-line niches. Dell and Cisco have found the Web to be huge marketplaces, and software vendor Egghead reinvented itself as a web-only entity.

People Changes

The audience may be the biggest change over the last two years. Few professionals have no e-mail addresses, and many have multiple addresses. Many companies have their own domain name. Informal surveys of accountants show that more than half have purchased goods from the Internet. In fact, in contradiction to some surveys that people fear putting their credit card numbers on the Web, the lure of cheap buys has elevated the Internet auction—at sites like eBay—to some of the most popular sites on the Net. These offer no assurance, no reputation, no e-cash, and no warranty.

Some practitioners are still waiting for this Internet thing to pass by, like CB radios. The AICPA joins the chant of many that every CPA needs to become a computer expert or the industry will pass the profession by, making the CPA obsolete. The interest in the Internet, gauged by attendance at technology seminars and the purchase of Internet books aimed at the profession, has decreased markedly as people say, "I have e-mail and know how to Yahoo! What else would I need to know?"

Others have had their lives transformed by the Net: finding friendships, marriage partners (often to the dismay of current partner), e-mail to keep in touch, and more. And client/server has given way to web front-ends.

The Web as user interface has changed the face of corporate computing and personal finance alike. The use of the Net as a knowledge and communication tool has led to the desire for constant contact. Hotels have had to add charges for phone use over 30 minutes as travelers have set up mobile offices and tied up the hotel PBX. Wireless e-mail, phone-based e-mail, browser-based e-mail, cell-phone-based e-mail abound. Palm VII personal digital assistants now come with e-mail everywhere.

Business and the Web

Businesses crave all Web, all the time. Presales support, sales, customer service, knowledgebases, self-service for on-line lookup of availability and order status: An e-presence not only can offer business efficiencies, but the bar has been raised in an 24-hour a day seven day a week availability—or at least virtual availability. Want a CD now? Need to check when to make a trip?

In contrast, many people are still humming along on Netscape 3 with their 28.8 modem to visit Yahoo (now a portal), Alta Vista (now accepting advertising), or the IRS and AICPA.

WebTrust was developed to promote assurance services (as were BBBOnline and TRUSTe), but who cares? Slow pipes, minimal security, naive users: This is a powder keg waiting to blow. The biggest change in Internet hardware is the nut behind the keyboard. Forget speed, security, and standards—if there is a Beanie Baby or Furby out there, I have cash *now*!

Technology

Microsoft has made NT a popular platform for "Internet in" (proxy server) and "Internet out" (IIS, site server). Apache (server) and Linux (operating system)—free products—have grown in corporate acceptance. Hosting services (IBM/Great Plains) may signal the resurgence of outsourcing accounting. Y2K brought additional impetus to the move away from DOS to the "friendlier" Internet climes of Windows 95/98/NT.

Tools

Tax research sites have grown and matured and audit and accounting sites have started to spring up. Government sites have matured while society sites seek their role (ranging from Microsoft-sponsored to spokeperson/resource/marketing tool). Search tools are integrated with the browser, while search engines add more power. Audio and video are still largely secondary to text and graphics, although some voice over IP gains corporate favor. Instant messaging and ICQ grow among some, and cascading style sheets, Java and Javascript add flash. XML may extend the Web to be a better provider of structured information transfer.

Business Use

Intranets have grown in popularity, and standard tools, such as Office 2000, have changed to reflect that the documents on the Intranet need to be easily accessible by non experts. Internet projects often are developed on an individual basis and not a corporate plan; Internet marketing is not integrated in marketing plans, on business cards, part of the overall strategy, but something done so as not be left behind.

Business-to-business (B2B) formalized systems are still coming together. Digital certificates or virtual passports have not taken hold to eliminate password overload. Corporate policies and e-mail as part of corporate communications are still developing. Application Service Providers (ASPs) now offer to host all of a business' applications, not just their website.

A Wild Ride

Yogi Berra said, "If they don't want to come, you can't stop them." E-auction sites prove that individuals will buy from complete strangers if there is a bargain, and a community grows to support it. Amazon.com grew larger than its traditional competitors, Barnes & Noble and Borders. Available money from venture capital investors hoping to seed the next billion-dollar buyout have sent the value of Internet stocks through the roof—even companies that have never shown a profit.

If it can be done on a computer, there is venture capital for it. Text gives way to graphics; static gives way to dynamic; islands give way to integration. It must be mainstream if CPAs are trying to make a buck from it . . . if the Federal Trade Commission and the Department of Commerce are involved . . . if Russia is planning on it (http://www.gov.ru). Two years later the burden is on the vendor to integrate.

Obsolete?

By the way: Most tools and sites from 1997 still work fine.

TIME LINE OF EVENTS

Here a brief calendar of major events between the first and second editions.

1997

PC prices fall below $1,000. At the time of this writing, they are below $500.

The Social Security Administration temporarily puts personal information on-line for all to see. Privacy has escalated to become a major issue.

America Online cannot keep up with subscribers, must "selectively" offer refunds to customers who call and complain they aren't getting the services they subscribed to. AOL overcame their service problems to blow away their competition.

Representative Christopher Cox (R-Calif.) and Senator Ron Wyden (D-Ore.) propose the Cox-Wyden bill, banning new taxes on electronic commerce and calling for a clear national Internet policy. In 1999 the issue rose again.

U.S. Robotics beats Motorola by shipping the first 56 Kbps modem.

Thirty-nine members of the Heaven's Gate cult committed suicide. As the cult did Web design work to pay bills, many in the mainstream press were quick to blame the Net.

Microsoft acquired WebTV Networks Inc. for $425 million. TVs and PCs grew closer.

Millions used the Internet to follow a historic chess match in which Deep Blue, IBM's supercomputer, defeated world champion Garry Kasparov, the first time a machine had beaten a grand master at this level. Kasparov blamed his defeat on human interference. Kasparov in 1999 conducted a similar game—this time against everyone on the Internet.

Netscape upped the ante in the browser wars and launched Netscape Communicator.

The Supreme Court slapped down the 1996 Communications Decency Act with a ruling that the government's attempt to censor cyberspace "abridges the freedom of speech protected by the First Amendment."

The Nevada state legislature signed Senate Bill No. 13, the first law of the land on spam, which "prohibits sending certain unsolicited electronic mail under certain circumstances." In 1999 spam escalated anyway.

Microsoft announced that 1 million copies of its new browser, IE 4.0. were downloaded during its first 48 hours of availability. It later claimed the same for IE 5.0 but said the earlier figure was based on partial, not full, downloads.

The Justice Department took Microsoft to court for threatening computer manufacturers who remove the Internet Explorer browser from the desktops of systems sold with Windows preinstalled. The stage for a protracted court battle was set after a federal judge ordered Microsoft Corp. to halt its practice of requiring personal computer makers to distribute its Internet browser with the company's Windows 95 operating system. In 1999 the trial was supposed to be wrapping up.

AOL, the biggest on-line service, is now bigger than all local ISPs combined.

1998

PC prices fall below $600.

Portals begin to deliver personalized news and ads.

Merger mania begins, a precursor to billion-dollar IPOs, including MCI-Worldcom, America Online-Netscape, and Compaq-Digital.

XML is declared a standard by the World Wide Web Consortium.

General Electric said it would require its partners to join its Web procurement network in an initiative that could save it as much as $200 million per year by 2003.

The Clinton/Lewinsky scandal sends 830,000 visitors to MSNBC daily.

Microsoft begins to give away Internet Explorer for free.

MSN ceases being an on-line service.

San Francisco federal appeals court makes it illegal to use a trademark as an URL and sell it to the trademark owner.

In April 1998 Priceline launched its service enabling consumers to name their own price for leisure airline tickets. In less than a year, it is worth $10 billion.

U.S. Senate outlaws net gambling.

The iMac is introduced, becoming the number-one selling personal computer in December, and Apple's stock rebounds.

MIT's Sloan School requires applications over the Internet.

The Starr Report hits the Internet.

Clinton's video testimony is available on-line, searchable through Alta Vista.

Network Solutions' contract to oversee and hand out domain names expired at the end of September, but two weeks later government officials, still not ready to make the change, extended it for another two years. The Internet Corporation for Assigned Names and Numbers, the group that has been formed to create the new registration system, calls on the government to speed up the process.

Iridium offers communications anywhere, then faces major problems in start-up.

AOL is honored by the film *You've Got Mail,* starring Tom Hanks and Meg Ryan.

Linux gains popularity as an operating system—and it's free.

1999

Vice President Al Gore proclaims that he invented the Internet. In response, former VP Dan Quayle announces that he invented the dictionary.

Internet Explorer 5.0 ships, with XML support. IBM, Lotus, Microsoft, Oracle, and every other major software developer declare that their products will embrace XML.

CHAPTER 1

The Internet: What It Is and Why It Is Important

This chapter provides a perspective of what the Internet is, where it came from, and why it is important to accountants. It covers what the Internet is, its relevance, its history, and its benefits.

The following outline summarizes the contents of this chapter:

- *What is the Internet?* This section answers the question: "What is the Internet?'
- *Why is the Internet relevant to accountants?* This section discusses the importance of the Internet to our clients and the profession.
- *What is the history of the Internet?* This section provides a brief time line of the development of the Internet, showing that its roots are old but its popularity is recent.
- *What benefits are there for accountants?* This section provides a taste of how learning about the Internet can help accountants.
- *Where is the Internet going?* This section offers a glimpse at emerging issues that may transform the Internet and business.
- *Interview:* Rich Walker, director of the professional partner programs for Intuit, offers his views on CPAs and the Internet.

WHAT IS THE INTERNET?

If you ask a roomful of businesspeople to define the Internet, you will get a variety of answers. In Internet seminars around the country I have heard answers like:

> *"It's e-mail."* For years, technology companies have used computers to keep in touch, with electronic addresses like eric@computercpa.com, cyber-cpa@technologist.com, and CyberCPA@sprynet.com (all ways to get in touch with the author).

"It's the World Wide Web." Newspapers, magazines, and commercials all say to type their address into software designed to read their electronic content. If you know their URL (uniform resource locator), such as <http://www.microsoft.com>, you type in the contents between the brackets to access text, graphics and multimedia content, in this case, Microsoft Corporation's site.

"It's global communications." Whether by e-mail, Web, or otherwise, you can communicate with someone in Kishinev, Moldova, as easily as in Kansas City, Missouri.

"It's information exchange." Electronic newsgroups, bulletin boards, and chat areas are a few of the ways people on the Internet share advice, plan projects, and promote agendas.

"It's an ever-expanding database of information." From the great literature of the ages to the history of commercial advertising, the Internet stores and makes available information on almost any topic imaginable.

"It's electronic storefronts." Dell Computer Corporation, Priceline.com, Amazon.com, Lands End, L.L. Bean, and businesses small and large are all marketing, collecting orders, and even taking payment on the Internet.

"It's the bumper sticker of the 1990s." The Internet is all that, and more. You can spend hours chatting with others using your keyboard (Instant Messaging) or using your computer's built-in microphone and speaker (with Microsoft's NetMeeting or Excite Chat). You can spend the day surfing the World Wide Web with Microsoft's Internet Explorer using Yahoo! (http://www.yahoo.com) as your tour guide. You can access Deja (http://www.deja.com) or RemarQ (http://www.remarq.com) to filter through the contents of USENET or using the latest Netscape Navigator version 6 extensions that adds enhanced Java-enhanced XML Smell-O-Vision. The Internet is far more expansive than all of that. Yahoo! is not the Internet; neither is the USENET or e-mail.

What is the Internet, really?

The Internet

The Internet is the world's largest computer network, a network of networks, providing instant access to a wealth of information and services. Estimates vary widely, but it is estimated that tens of millions of computers are hooked together with 100 million plus current participants worldwide, with an additional million new participants joining monthly.

The Internet is not a centrally administered commercial service like America Online. Started 25 years ago by the Defense Department, the thing that has become the Internet has grown to encompass universities, research organizations, businesses, and homes. If you are affiliated with a major university or corporation, you can probably get inexpensive or free access. Otherwise, local and national services can link you to the Internet, and telephone companies also offer access in most areas.

The Internet was developed to provide a means for military messages to find their way from one computer to another computer no matter what happens to the connections between them. Over the last decade, commercial use has grown considerably.

With expanding popularity and commercialization, the Internet's infrastructure (its basic pipeline) and its resources are being taxed. In addition, new users unfamiliar with Internet etiquette litter the cyberwaves, and pranksters take advantage of free access, much to the dismay of many of the Internet's older citizens. Some of these disgruntled Interneters have let their displeasure be known by causing havoc on the Internet. Other newcomers have taken advantage of the gullible nature of Internet newcomers to *hack* (gain illegal access into) computer systems, spread viruses, and move traditional scams onto the net.

The Internet's resources are mind-boggling. Users can access the computer systems of governments, major libraries, try out the software in computer departments of major universities, and converse with experts in almost any field. In addition, if more than 100 people are interested in talking about any topic, you can find a discussion group about it. Lyrics of popular songs, transcripts of popular movies and television shows, and the (other) great literature of the world can all be beamed to an individual's computer. Users can listen to the radio, check how cold the soda is in a soda machine at the Rochester Institute of Technology, talk to people's cats, and view NASA's astronauts in space through a computer.

Accountants will find the American Institute of Certified Public Accountants (AICPA) and most state societies online as well as support from the software and hardware companies with which they do business. The Internal Revenue Service is there, as is the Securities and Exchange Commission, tax and accounting resources, and other practitioners.

Network of Networks. Technically, the Internet is a "network of networks." A network is two or more computers that communicate with each other. Computers connected to each other in close proximity and through a company's own wiring and cabling are known as a *local area network,* or *LAN.* Computers and LANs connected to each other over a wide geographic area and over public communications are known as *wide area networks,* or *WANs.* The Internet is the primary connection backbone for LANs and WANs around the world. Its infrastructure is scaleable (portions can be added to or replaced with more powerful equipment easily) and technically sound.

Practically, the Internet is a pipeline through which companies can communicate and offer services from their own computers for free or for profit as well as the home to the World Wide Web, called the Web, for short. All of the major on-line services are connected to the Internet and use it to transfer electronic mail (e-mail) from service to service.

To enter that pipeline, a computer (or the computer on which a user shares time) must be recognized officially as being on the network known as the Internet. This is accomplished by the assignment of a network address, known as an *IP (Internet protocol) address.* Packets of data move at the speed of light across this network using these IP addresses as their routing slip. IP addresses, four-segmented numbers like "149.174.211.5", are hard for people to remember; thus a system that lets users assign easier-to-remember words, such as "sprynet.com", was developed, and is known as the *Domain Name System.* A special relationship with an Internet service provider is necessary to have a unique IP address assigned to an organization; we will discuss later why this is important.

Electronic Wild, Wild West.   Realistically, the Internet is a new frontier, filled with opportunity, and also a changing landscape, with resources coming and going daily and desperadoes who take advantage of unknowing newcomers. With the right tour guide, users can find their way around, get settled, and start doing business. Even then, the Internet is sometimes inefficient and unreliable. Many of the resources the author has enjoyed have disappeared since the beginning of his research, and others will be gone by the time you read this.

Companies bear a risk when they rely on the Internet, as the Internet quickly teaches users two great things: patience and disappointment. An Internet site may be impossible to connect to; the Internet can be so overloaded that response time becomes interminable; the information may not be kept up to date. Why should it be? Many Internet resources are noncommercial, and there is no overriding reason to maintain them. Others are advertising driven and offer no assurance of reliability.

E-mail is sometimes unreliable. The best commerce sites, from eBay to Charles Schwab, go down. Using the Internet for business is, therefore, like investing in penny stocks or starting a business in the former Russian Commonwealth. The rules and standards are constantly changing. What is set up today may be obsolete tomorrow. However, incredible financial rewards are available.

In addition, traditional, more reliable proprietary access to databases and support is quickly disappearing, as companies move their support to the Internet and online services abandon their traditional services for the Web. In addition, the Internet has major governmental and educational resources not found on other services.

Different from On-line Services. The Internet is different from traditional online services. An online service, such as America Online, has a central administration and clear ownership. One group is accountable for its content, direction and support. A call to a toll-free number gets you started with centralized billing for the services you use from their service.

The Internet is not centrally administered. As a potential user of Internet resources, the subscriber enters into an agreement with another firm that already has a link to the Internet. That firm may be an on-line service, an independent company, or one of the telephone companies, and may provide Internet access only or other services.

The Internet is not American. Access worldwide makes controlling and legislating the Internet impossible.

If It Is Not Centrally Administered, Then Who Is in Charge? Who is in charge? Despite the efforts of U.S. government legislators to date, no one is officially in charge of the Internet. The Internet community has set up some organizations as coordinators, such as the Internic (http://www.networksolutions.com), the organization responsible for maintaining domain name registrations. However, from that point on, the services, support, and responsibilities, including network cabling and wiring, are distributed among many organizations. The services are dependent on people who want to let others access their computer. If it is illegal to have something on my computer in Rochester, New York, I can manage a site in the Cayman Islands from home instead. Netscape and Microsoft race to add features to their software so that it will become the de facto standard—even if there are de jure standards in place.

Users of America Online will use America Online's software, call America Online's telephone system, and hook into America Online's services. With the Internet, there are an incredible number of hands in the pot, including:

A worldwide user community

Networks

Standards groups

Public interest and policy groups like the Internet Society (ISOC) and the Internet Engineering Task Force (IETF)

Access providers

Software providers

Content providers

Hardware vendors

Infrastructure sector

Investment community

Service providers

Governments

Who is paying for all this? One of the first questions people ask when they see the resources available on the Internet is "Who is paying for all this?" The Internet pools finances from taxes, access fees, advertising, and the voluntary efforts of the Internet community.

WHY IS THE INTERNET RELEVANT TO ACCOUNTANTS?

The Internet is generally important for its popularity and presence and for the resources it makes available. It is especially important for financial professionals due to client expectations, the changing business information transfer environment, resources specifically for accountants, and marketing opportunities.

Internet Is Popular and Showing Up Everywhere

There was a time when people saw the Internet as a plaything for computer-friendly and socially challenged young adults and scientists. No more. No longer is the Internet the domain of early adapters, who readily grab every new electronic toy and try out every new technology. From the Land of the Nerds to the homes of the affluent, the Internet has taken hold.

The Internet phenomenon has hit, and hit fast. With the popularity of the user-friendly Web, the landscape of the Internet has changed quickly. On-line services such as CompuServe, America Online, and others, first made Internet access available to the general public in 1995. Software and services sprang up quickly. Companies like Microsoft announced one month that the Internet was a fad to the general public; the next month it was reorganizing its entire business to make way for the Internet.

Users who want to wait to find out more about the Internet are too late. The Internet has become a part of everyday life. *USA Today* and other newspapers regularly review Web sites and include listings of Internet activities with radio and television schedules. Web addresses are becoming as commonplace as toll free (800 and 888) phone numbers in advertisements.

AT&T, MCI, and Sprint have gotten into the Internet business. Access is given away for free in return for demographic information, and computers are given away free with contracts for access. Internet service providers, Web page designers, and HTML (Hypertext Markup Language, the language of the Web) consultants are making cold calls. Accounting software that uses the Internet for order entry can be purchased off the shelf. Clients get offers to start new storefronts on the World Wide Web for free.

The Internet has become a way of life. It is standard equipment on new computers, incorporated into Microsoft's Windows 98 and the latest operating systems. You get free Internet access with Intuit's latest versions of the popular Quicken home finance software. Microsoft thought the idea of an inexpensive home Internet computer was so good that it bought the company (http://www.webtv.com). That way, anyone who can afford a television can afford access to the Internet. Of course, the rush of under-$500 computers hasn't hurt either.

Does explosive interest translate into staying power? CB radio and Cabbage Patch Dolls were important at one time. However, until something better comes along or the Internet crashes down on itself due to its phenomenal popularity, the Internet is a land of opportunity.

Internet Makes Valuable Resources Available

A vintage commercial for Apple Computers starts with a young lad on the way to school and a better life. It ends with the dejected lad sent back home, defeated, because his family had not made an investment in an Apple computers. Today the Internet has come to replace (or at least greatly reduce our reliance on) expensive encyclopedias, newspapers with yesterday's news, and television. The U.S. Government, newspapers and magazines, and countless other organizations and individuals have made information, documents, programs, and their own expertise available for the taking from the Internet.

Clients Expect Us to Use and Understand the Internet

Are certified public accountants (CPAs) known as technology risk takers? The CPA profession is one marked by a distinctive past. Objectivity, independence, and integrity are the watchwords of the profession. Yet over the years the profession has undergone a transformation. Once the keepers of the attest function, CPAs have branched out into consulting, personal financial planning, and a number of potentially questionable activities—activities that may bring their objectivity, independence, and integrity into question.

As a whole, we are not the most proactive occupation in the world. Accountants are not known as risk takers. We gravitate toward proven methods and technologies. We want to make safe recommendations to our clients to limit their dissatisfaction with us. This leads to silence in areas outside of our expertise. At the same time, we can lose clients to competitors who provide recommendations in these areas.

Many times CPAs who were forced into adopting some new technology or practice find it is to their advantage. Many CPA firms bought fax machines only when their clients begged them or embarrassed them into it. Accounting software, like Intuit's Quicken, frightened many partners as they mediated on the loss of bookkeeping and write-up revenue. Likewise, clients have dragged CPAs into the Internet.

Clients are on the Internet. The government says so. The National Telecommunications and Information administration, in its regular *Falling Through the Net* series, keeps track of who is on-line and who isn't (http://www.ntia.doc. gov/ntiahome/fttn99/contents.html). Our clients say so. After working from 7 A.M. to 7 P.M., clients go home, eat dinner, and sit down to *Forbes, Fortune,* or the *Wall Street Journal.* How will that new tax law affect their business? Should they invest in that new XML firm? They want CPAs to be on e-mail, so they can write a quick note at their convenience. They also want Web-based updates on business topics. When they can buy books, trade stocks, and buy a car at 3 A.M., why can't they contact their CPA?

Clients are now interested in a new business frontier—the Internet. The changes in that world are so quick that Gary Trudeau satirized it in a comic strip. His characterization of Bill Gates ("Bernie") is facing a downturn in business. He made a mistake unlike any in 15 years—he went to lunch. By the time he had returned, the whole industry had changed. (Check it out at <http://www.doonesbury.com>.)

Tax laws can change, often retroactively; CPAs must advise clients about the alternatives and the possibilities. Technology also changes rapidly. Unfortunately, clients' impressions of changes brought on by government fiat are different from those based on the whims of commercial acceptance and Microsoft's marketing power. CPAs are not comfortable with responding to clients whose hardware and software decisions have become obsolete due to a shift in the computer industry.

Clients and firms want to make money, and if they can do that by conducting business, advertising, or posting the results of business operations on the Internet, where will the CPA profession fit in? If CPAs cannot act as business interpreters or guides, who will be leading clients into new ways of doing business?

The Internet touches every area of accounting. From original entry to financial statement presentation, it is on the Web. Tax preparation is pushing toward electronic filing and investment firms are giving filing and tax preparation away. Bookkeeping is facing the "Biz Dial tone"—online accounting systems. Auditing techniques have to change. Personal financial planning departments face competition from e-Trade and online brokers. You can do business of all kinds online. What advice do we give regarding online banks, insurance, travel, purchases of everything from cars to caskets, airline tickets and computers. Reaction time is measured in minutes, not months.

The Internet changes voice and data transfer by becoming phone lines and data network. The Internet is a broker, a binder, and a breaker of marriages. Software updates and support, computer-based training and delivery of training, and opening up governmental resources change the skill sets looked for in new hires.

Are you ready to advise clients on the business advantages of the net? Can you tell them how to move into electronic commerce without compromising a clean audit? Other firms are doing it! If you cannot provide services to your client, someone else will.

Some areas you can be involved with your client:

- Preparation for embracing change
- Education in the availability and use of technology
- Goal setting to help in measuring success
- Planning and project design
- Designing systems
- Implementing and testing systems
- Deployment of systems
- Promoting and marketing of Internet presence
- Monitoring and maintaining systems.

As for your firm:

- How has your firm changed in the last three years?
- Are you offering resources on the Internet?
- Do you use Internet travel and planning tools?
- Do you offer competitive research analysis?
- Are you prepared for lawsuits around misuse, harassment, and intercepted client-privileged matters?

- Can you deal with viruses, break-ins, or natural and man-made disasters?
- Are you marketing your services? Providing superior client service?
- Are you finding and maintaining the best employees?
- Are you reaching new markets?
- Are you cashing in on the billions of dollars of venture capital available?
- Are you making sense of it all?

The Changing Business Information Transfer Environment

We live in a computerized society. News is quicker electronically. Transferring updates to stock prices, checks that clear the bank, accounting information—anything that needs to be typed, entered, posted, analyzed, tabulated, or otherwise reported—is better, faster, and more efficient if done electronically. That includes business and accounting information and means there will be plans to defraud and to take advantage—and that means CPAs should know what online services are: their advantages, disadvantages, and schemes. Electronic cash is an area of great concern. It has no reporting engine or any accountability, and is under a lot of scrutiny from the government. The sales and income tax ramifications are just beginning to be worked out.

CPAs have been a vital link in relationships among banks, investors, and companies for many years. In most cases, however, they have had little to do with the computerization that has sped up business decision making. Now technology has become integrated into the business process, leading to smaller, faster decisions. Enterprise resource planning (ERP) systems provide links among vendors, companies, and customers and enable them to act as one; the system is more efficient, but the potential for security and control problems is great. From mail, to Express Mail, to fax, to instant access to the computer, business has felt the need to disseminate information, programs, and data as quickly and as cost effectively as possible.

The Internet is a major part of the way business will conduct itself in the near future. MasterCard, Visa, Verifone, and many newer companies, such as Cybercash and qPass, are providing digital, secured cash for buying on the Internet. Electronic Data Interchange (EDI), the international standard for business-to-business data transfer, will be transacted using the Internet instead of high-cost value-added networks. As CPAs, we will be responsible for auditing and explaining these new types of transactions. In addition, many companies now present their financial statements on the Net. Does the Internet have any consequences in financial statement preparation and presentation?

E-mail: Electronic mail has become a business requirement, similar to a phone number or a fax line. Imagine the following scenario: As you prepare to purchase office furniture from the representative who has visited your office, you say you will call with some color preferences. They offer you a business card, write down a phone number, and say, "If you call this number after noon, the guy in the bakery will come upstairs and get me." (You quickly consider canceling the order to find a more stable company with a phone.) To be without access to e-mail puts a company in a similar predicament.

Whether keeping up with other members of the firm within the office or while traveling, or keeping in touch with clients, prospects, vendors, or others, e-mail is inexpensive and convenient. It is now part of every task we accomplish on the computer. E-mail is everywhere. How is business information transferred? Whether within an organization only or to the rest of the supply chain, e-mail is how information is transferred. Like the old pneumatic tube used in banks, information of all kinds is placed into e-mail and magically arrives. There are other ways to move information, but when it comes down to it, few things have the immediacy of "You've Got Mail!"

From Microsoft Word 6 on, there has been a menu option in Word to send the document by e-mail. This turned the file into an attachment to be carried along by the messaging system. Now the "mail me!" button beckons from every application. Popular report writer Crystal Reports and financial reporter FRx are designed to let users send their reports to an e-mail recipient. Lucky recipients can get more than static reports; they get to work with the actual data, ready to be resorted, filtered, and printed.

Goldmine Software's contact manager, Goldmine, and other contact management applications treat e-mail as a more-than-equal option to calling, printing a letter, or showing up in person. Goldmine incorporates e-mail, see Exhibit 1.1, as a normal part of doing business, including filing incoming and outgoing e-mail with the contact record. Sending e-mail isn't limited to the desktop. From the days of cc: mail and Lotus 1-2-3 on the DOS-based Hewlett Packard 200LX to Palm III successors, the option to compose anywhere and send when you get back to home base has helped make the person on the go get his or her work done more efficiently. Wireless personal digital assistants like the Palm VII and its successors transform e-mail to anytime, anyplace, send-and-receive tools. Inexpensive, pure e-mail units like the PocketMail systems sell for less than $200, offer unlimited e-mail for $10 a month, and offer e-mail sending and receiving using an 800 number and a device that fits most hotel and pay phones. (You shouldn't be sending from a plane anyway!).

While there are a number of other options for two-way text messaging, and while most wireless units are limited to text mail (no shipping spread-

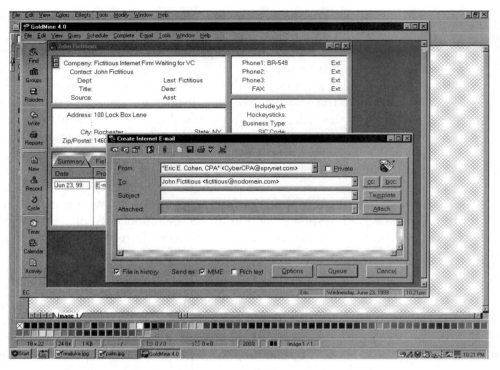

Exhibit 1.1   Goldmine incorporates e-mail as a normal part of doing business.

sheets here!), e-mail is a great way to pass along information to people when you think about it, not just when they are available.

Fax machines: Facsimile (fax) machines are equally important. Clients won't think much of a company they have to call before sending a fax so the company can pick it up at the local Kinko's Copy Center. Unlike the telephone, which has been around for as long as anyone in business can remember, fax machines have been popular for only a decade. Federal Express introduced their service, Zap Mail, in the mid-1980s, only to have businesses buy the technology behind Zap Mail—the fax machine—rather than use FedEx's service.

Word Processors, Spreadsheets, and the Internet: The Internet is part of the operating system and the software. Office 2000 is so integrated with the Internet that users can open word processing documents and spreadsheets from within Internet Explorer as shown in Exhibits 1.2 and 1.3. You can do this without having to know what program created the document in the first

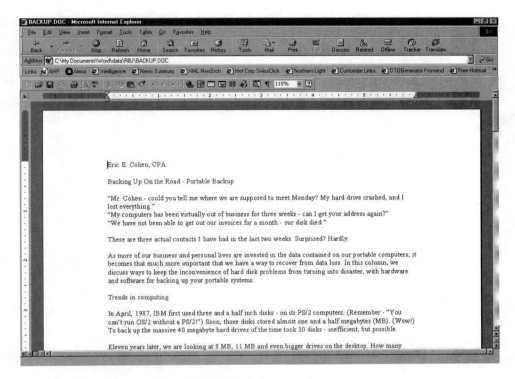

Exhibit 1.2 Sample Office 2000 Word document.

place. Software is going from applicationcentric to documentcentric. If you want to get away from Office 2000, you can get an Office 97 suite called StarOffice as shown in Exhibit 1.4; that is almost free. Where? Of course, on the Internet, at <http://www.stardivision.com>.

Audits and the Internet: SAS (Statement on Accounting Standards) No. 78 amended SAS No. 55, effective for audits of financial statements on or after January 1, 1997, by replacing the definition and description of the internal control structure that auditors must understand and document. Among the new requirements of SAS No. 78 is one that the auditor must obtain knowledge of the activities management uses to monitor internal control over financial reporting. Electronic commerce bypasses traditional methods of internal control. CPAs must plan on how to help clients prepare for these changes. Otherwise, how will CPAs be able to audit their systems, document their procedures, or protect them? When everything is said and done, how will CPAs make sure that clients have not opened themselves up for internal or external exposure to fraud and untraceable transactions? How can CPAs reduce the

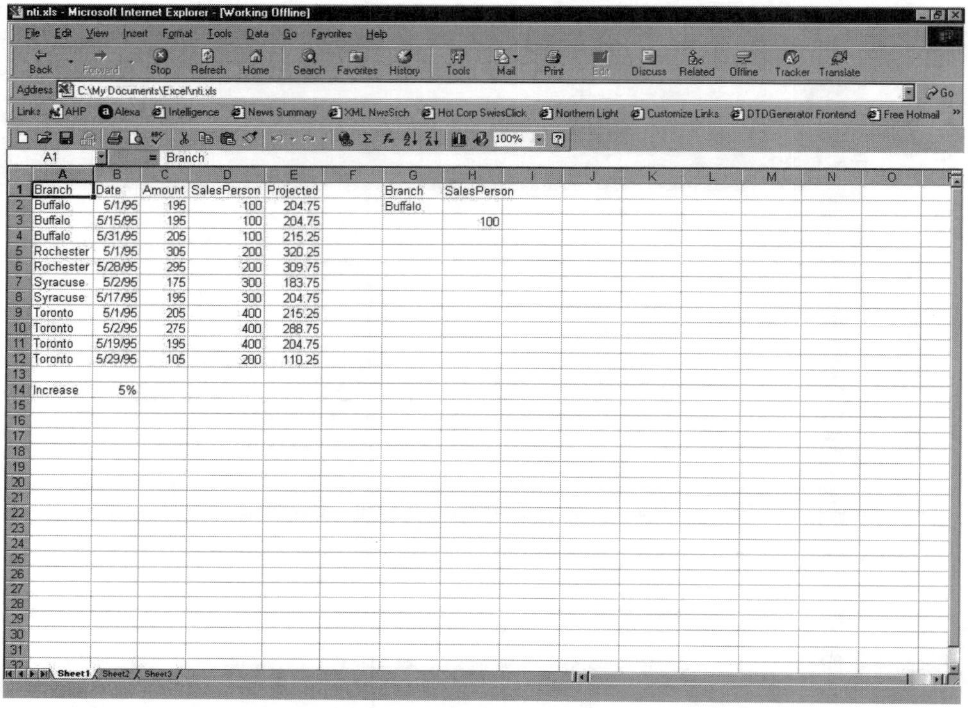

	A	B	C	D	E	F	G	H
1	Branch	Date	Amount	SalesPerson	Projected		Branch	SalesPerson
2	Buffalo	5/1/95	195	100	204.75		Buffalo	
3	Buffalo	5/15/95	195	100	204.75			100
4	Buffalo	5/31/95	205	100	215.25			
5	Rochester	5/1/95	305	200	320.25			
6	Rochester	5/28/95	295	200	309.75			
7	Syracuse	5/2/95	175	300	183.75			
8	Syracuse	5/17/95	195	300	204.75			
9	Toronto	5/1/95	205	400	215.25			
10	Toronto	5/2/95	275	400	288.75			
11	Toronto	5/19/95	195	400	204.75			
12	Toronto	5/29/95	105	200	110.25			
13								
14	Increase	5%						

Exhibit 1.3 Sample Office 2000 Spreadsheet.

possibility that clients will move to another CPA who can help them take advantage of technology?

In 1996 the AICPA issued an audit guide to EDI, a decade after EDI became popular. At the 1996 AICPA Computer and Technology Conference, speakers mentioned efforts to guide the industry in evidence (SAS No. 31) with regard to electronic commerce. In addition, the AICPA established a task force, the Impact of Electronic Transactions on Financial Statements and the Accountant's Report Task Force, to assess the impact of information technology on financial data and accountants' reporting responsibilities. In 1999, the AICPA has responded to new technologies like XML with projects to capitalize on change. The world changes so quickly that the AICPA is struggling to keep up with the flood of technology. No wonder CPAs find change so difficult.

CPAs are concerned with things like separation of duty, audit trails, security, reliability, protection of assets, and proper reporting. The Internet is famous for hackers, lack of documentation, lack of control—and now digital ordering, electronic cash, and nontraceable international sales. So much for proper authorization!

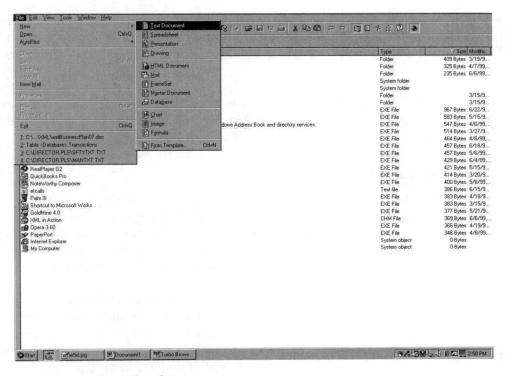

Exhibit 1.4 StarOffice Suite.

Auditability has gone down the drain, because e-cash can go anywhere. The U.S. Treasury Department has established a task force to create "toll booths" on the Internet so it can make sure cybertransactions are in tax compliance. Credit card numbers, even with security algorithms, are fairly free picking for hackers. Although there are no reports of a credit card being misused when transferred using Secure Socket Layers (SSL) encryption, the vendors' computers are open doors to enterprising hackers. Is this any way to run a business? Do we ignore the opportunities or try to equip our clients on how to best do business while carefully noting the risks that come with the rewards?

CPAs need to be aware of what goes on on the Internet. Not everyone will be comfortable with taking an active role in this area, of course. For those who resist, certain areas of practice will be closed to them. Others will stretch the boundaries. Most will find out how to take advantage of the most popular features. Some will bring in the Internet but will have secretaries or administrative assistants print out their e-mail and dictate their responses. The pervasiveness of the Internet and businesses embracing its technology will happen nonetheless, and some firms will benefit from being on the forefront. The CPA Vision Project, the AICPA's account of where the profession sees itself in the next decade calls for CPAs to be interpreters and knowledge managers of the future.

Sales Tax and the Internet: Sales tax in the day of mail order was hard enough; now we have the Web. Many issues come into play when the Internet is used to buy and sell.

Resources for Research

The Internet offers research tools that can search through and isolate important information from the field of education, the government and commercial businesses. This information is vital for understanding the businesses and industries with which CPA's work. There are tools for searching through current and potential law and tax statutes from the federal government and many states.

As CPAs and businesses go online, the Internet becomes an excellent source for industrial espionage, as firms offer up information about themselves that was impossible to find before. Need a heavy senior with experience in manufacturing? Check out your competitors' Web sites! They will let you know whom they have who might fit your requirements.

Marketing Opportunities

The Internet provides marketing opportunities to meet clients' needs more efficiently and expand your client base. It offers the opportunity to enter new markets, offer new services, and receive better feedback on performance.

Many CPA firms have brochures. They are expensive to produce and go out of date quickly as partners and staff leave and new services are added. With an Internet presence, that same quality material can be made available to view all day, every day, without printing and mailing charges or long-distance phone calls. How often do you have to give directions to your office? Put them online!

Corporate Accounting

Corporate accountants face many of the same issues as CPAs in public accounting: internal auditing issues, electronic commerce, distributing financial information electronically, dealing with the financial and tax reporting issues that come with new markets and foreign business, making sure the books and records are still auditable. Never before has sound internal control been so important. The publication of the COSO (Committee of Sponsoring Organizations of the Treadway Commission) Report has brought a new standard and framework for sound internal control, and SAS No. 78 conforms to this new definition and expands on what auditors will be expecting from internal management.

Should You Be on the Internet? 10 Questions to Ponder

Do you need any electronic connections at all?

- Do your clients want to contact you on e-mail? If so, you need to be on the Net somewhere. Juno is free, and America Online is easy to use.
- Do you or your people do much out-of-town travel? E-mail provides a way to be contacted and contact others inexpensively and quickly when you are on the road.
- Do you have multiple sites where e-mail or group chat would help? These services can keep groups up-to-date with each other.

Do you need Internet access?

- What is the downside of being dragged kicking and screaming into the information age? (phone, fax, Internet—the next business requirement)
  Note: Internet use is not easy yet—the "manual" does not always exist! However, rewards come to those who are willing to invest in learning technology and to be on the "bleeding" edge of technology.
- Do you rely on PCs in your own business? Support and fixes available on the Net pay for themselves.
- Do you have a computer consulting department (internal/external)? The Internet provides connections to every major computer-oriented company for news, fixes, and support. Even if you just help your clients with Quick-Books, you will benefit greatly.

How can you take advantage of the Internet?

- Can people buy your services sight unseen?
- Would you like a 24-hour-a-day literature fulfillment service?
- Can you benefit from up-to-the-minute news on your industry?
- Can your firm benefit from a 24-hour hot line to the government for tax and business laws and resources?

When Shouldn't You Be on the Internet? When Does the Internet Fall Short?

When the power goes out and you can't go online

When connecting is too expensive (long distance) or impossible (outside of range for wireless)

When connections are unreliable or the software or equipment insufficient (wrong version of browser, too little encryption)

When users are too uncomfortable with technology

When there is no trust

When service is denied

Remedy the situation, and then come on board!

WHAT IS THE HISTORY OF THE INTERNET?

History of the Internet—How Did We Come So Far So Fast?

The Internet has taken the United States by storm, but it is not new. It has been around a while. It was born with roots in the government, military, and education, and grew into the business field in the beginning of the 1990s. It has matured and reached general acceptance within the last five years. Now everyone is trying to get in on the act.

In Development for Over 20 Years.   In 1969 four computers were networked together as a precursor to the Internet. Bolt Beranek and Newman (BBN) had devised a technology called *packet switching.*

In the early 1970s, the Internet challenge was issued: Develop a network that can withstand partial outages and still function. The idea was to create an environment where messages would be able to go from one computer to another, no matter what happened in between them. At this point, 40 sites were attached to the research and defense network ARPAnet (U.S. Advanced Research Projects Agency) created by the Department of Defense (DoD). Meanwhile, the TCP/IP (Transmission Control Protocol/Internet Protocol) concept was developed by Vinton Cerf and Robert Kahn. TCP/IP is the elemental core of the Internet. IP, or *Internet protocol,* is the "envelope" with the address where the information is supposed to go; TCP, or *transmission control protocol,* breaks up files into workable chunks.

Bitnet started in 1981 and gained popularity in 1983, the "Year of the Network."

ARPANet adopted TCP/IP 1982, and in 1983 TCP/IP the conversion was complete

The National Science Foundation (NSF) established supercomputer centers around the country on the structure of ARPAnet. The NSFNET was a backbone network with 56K transmission speed. (Most individuals now have this capability—it was fast then but is woefully insufficient now.)

In 1993 a front-end to the Web, called Mosaic, was born, and the Internet has not been the same since. This friendly front-end made the Internet available to those not comfortable with archaic UNIX commands. In 1995 all major online services made graphical access to the Internet available to their subscribers.

New Technologies.   From a simple tool to navigate the Web, software like Internet Explorer has grown in complexity and function. Newly integrated into the Web are *wallets*—resources for maintaining and exchanging credit card information and electronic currency in a secure fashion. In addition, multimedia features, such as sending streaming audio and video, including watching television shows, teleconferencing and workgroup computing tools, and virtual reality are becoming popular.

WHAT ARE THE BENEFITS FOR ACCOUNTANTS?

What Is in It for Me?

You have been inundated with advertisements, commercials, and well-meaning friends urging you to get an on-line service. You may have asked, "What can I do with it?"

There are many benefits of on-line computer information systems. You can research almost anything you would look up at a library more efficiently on an on-line service. For example, on the Web you can get:

- Instant access to news
- Inexpensive advice on legal, accounting, and computer-related issues
- Help for searching through governmental, financial, business, and computer-related periodicals
- Access to software fixes, shareware programs, and graphics

You can download marketing information, prospectuses, and financial newsletters, view real-time Standard & Poors data, and download disclosure information such as SEC filings, analyst reports, financial statement data, and earnings data on various industries. You can find almost anything on the

Internet, and most of it is free (except for accounting pronouncements, for the time being).

Personal Uses

Anyone in any walk of life will find interesting and helpful information on the Internet. In the United States, most businesspeople begin to tour the Information Superhighway at home and later bring their knowledge of the available resources to work. In other countries, such as Canada, computers do not have the same presence in the home; on-line access has taken off more slowly without time to play.

Adult Use: The Internet has information on entertainment, lifestyles, personal growth, news, and hobbies and can be used to find a new career or a new love. You can track your investments, go shopping, and learn about anything that interests you. You can research your family's health, compare parenting notes with other parents, and keep in touch with a child away at college.

Kids: Kids will find tools for school, such as dictionaries and computer games, and electronic magazines for fun. They can talk with friends and make new ones around the world. They can learn new skills, follow their favorite television show or movie, or set up a Web site of their own.

Major Business Uses

Communications: You can instantly communicate with your organization's customers and clients. Decrease your organization's postage costs and improve customer responsiveness by using e-mail. Dramatically reduce your company's long-distance telephone charges using on-line communications. Conduct business meetings with participants around the globe—at a moment's notice—using on-line communications channels. You can combine phone, fax, and e-mail, and receive them all over the Internet.

Information Access: You can get up-to-the-minute financial quotes, instantly access vital business statistics, and monitor important emerging industry activity. You can access public and private databases and obtain essential business data in seconds. You can gain access to your customers' purchasing decision makers and leverage your present marketing plans.

Marketing: You can build your organization's image through on-line newsletters, reports, and low-cost interactive on-line publicity programs. You can let potential clients access information about your organization without tying up valuable personnel resources. You can get feedback from clients quickly and cheaply by conducting market research and informational surveys.

Personal and Firm Productivity: You can improve your personal productivity by subscribing to an electronic clipping service that monitors business journals and key newspapers. You can get up-to-date world, business, and political news delivered to your desktop. You can access telephone and e-mail directories to find anyone in the United States. You can discuss professional issues and challenges with experts and senior-level colleagues around the world. You can expand the effectiveness of your organization's limited budget by accessing shareware, freeware, commercial software, and graphics at no cost. You can receive computer support when you need it at no charge from the company itself and from others who want to help. You can keep up with the latest federal, state, and local regulations that impact your organization's operations. You can access hotel, airline, and travel information from anywhere.

Accounting Service Areas

Auditing: You can subscribe to mailing lists with discussions of the latest issues in auditing. You can access exposure briefs and keep up with changes through your state society and the AICPA. You can exchange audit plans.

Consulting: You can find out what software or techniques other companies are using to be successful. You can find and receive information on companies that provide products and services your clients need. You can pull down the latest fixes and updates from accounting software vendors.

Taxes: You can access governmental agencies and receive help. You can get advice from practitioners in other states or countries. You can get free updates from publishers in the tax and accounting-reporting field. You can download forms and publications anywhere, anytime.

WHERE IS THE INTERNET GOING?

Power to the People!

The Internet is a great leveler. Is the store not open when you want to shop? Do you despise certain businesspeople, such as those in insurance sales, brokers, and car sales? Do you want to transact business at your convenience, at your price, at your time?

Welcome to the Internet. Stores are open when you want them to be open. The phrase "Call back during normal business hours" normally does not apply. Are you concerned about prices? If the business does not promise the lowest prices on the Internet (http://www.buy.com, one of many sites where you can buy goods below cost), you can send a price comparison tool (like MySimon: http://www.mysimon.com) to check out better pricing for you.

Feel like you have no power if you are taken advantage of? A posting in the newsgroups or on a Web page can have incredible results. If you would like to make your voice known directly to visitors of a Web site, there's Third Voice (http://www.thirdvoice.com). Within the Third Voice community, Web sites can be annotated with comments that are separate from, but associated with, the sites. Like a Post-it Note, Third Voice users can share their opinions, good, bad, and perverse, on a Web site—much to the dismay of the company hosting the site.

Communicate with People in the Manner They Prefer

Some people love e-mail. Others like the urgency of a fax. Direct mail makes the most sense in other organizations. How can you keep track of who wants to receive information in which media?

Larger companies are finding a solution at (http://www.vignette.com), the home of Diffusion. Diffusion technology will enable Vignette customers to manage the distribution and delivery of personalized information across any delivery channel, including the Web, e-mail, fax, pager, and telephone, regardless of the channel the communication originates from or is routed through. The result is multichannel information delivery solutions for automating personalized, closed-loop interaction between an enterprise and its clients. For example, through this integration, a financial services company could immediately and proactively alert a client, via the client's preferred method, when trading events, such as confirmation of block trades, buy/sell decisions, initial public offering filings, and stock price changes take place. If the customer cannot be reached through the primary channel, the communication will be escalated to the next level, until the customer receives the message. The company then receives confirmation of delivery, an additional benefit in mission-critical business situations.

XML Is Ready to Transform Business and Accounting

Welcome to the XML revolution. The World Wide Web Consortium first declared XML a standard in February 1998. In a little more than a year, every major software developer rapidly and avidly declared the importance of

XML. IBM, Lotus, Microsoft, Oracle, SGI (Sun Microsystems)—all have said that XML will be at the core of their products. In March 1999 Microsoft's Internet Explorer 5 Web browser became the first consumer product to support XML.

What Is XML? XML is a platform-independent, self-describing, expandable, standard data exchange format that can be used either independently or embedded and used within other solutions. An XML file contains all of the data and the entire context necessary to understand the contents. It doesn't matter what computer, what operating system, or what application creates an XML file. XML is a markup language. You start out with the basic content then put instructions around the content to tell readers or software what that data is. Based on that context, users can filter, sort, and include the data in templates defined by external presentation files or with relatively simple programming techniques. XML separates presentation from content. Unlike HTML, the Hypertext Markup Language, XML does not hard-code the formatting instructions along with the actual content. The same XML file can be printed for manual inspection; filtered, sorted and formatted for presentation on the Internet; turned into Braille; read by a text-to-speech engine; incorporated into a search engine; and transformed from an accounting product to a write-up package.

Also unlike HTML, XML does not limit what its instructions, or tags, are. HTML may limit you to bolding, indexing, and other formatting options, whereas XML lets you create your own database by making up your own starting and ending tags. Which of these provides more information, or context, to you:

<h1>990801</h1>

or

<please-remit-by>990801</please-remit-by>

Extensibility is one of XML's greatest strengths. (In other words, users can make up the names that go inside those tags.) When a group or industry can agree on those tags, the effect is powerful.

XML's coworkers. XML files can be supplemented by other files, which further define data and let users sort, filter, and present the data in an unlimited number of ways. For example, you can create a file called a data type definition (DTD) file to help make sure that any XML files you create are properly organized. Other files transform, format, and manipulate the XML files.

The standards for these other files are still being hammered out. Microsoft is pushing for definition files called schemas and formatting templates called XSL—the eXtensible Stylesheet Language. Where there is peace and certainty in the issue of XML, XSL is another story.

XML's Role.   If you have ever had the responsibility for transferring data between systems or even creating a report with a report writer, you understand why many people feel retyping is a better alternative than trying to transfer the data by computer. Depending on your software, you have a limited number of choices, each with advantages and disadvantages. A dBase format is as close to a universal database as any; a Lotus or Excel spreadsheet format will probably lose column headings. Plain or comma-separated text has to be parsed into a new system. XML has the potential to make data transfer between two systems or multiple organizations as simple as "export to XML" and "import from XML".

XML is being hailed as the great "data hub." Although databases based on pure XML do not have the same performance and tools as proprietary databases, data turned into XML is easily portable from system to system. XML has been embraced by AT&T for new voice technologies, by wireless Internet device manufacturers as the way to transmit Web information to wireless Internet devices, and by publishers as a means of developing one set of content that can be printed or displayed on the Internet in a multitude of ways—because XML separates content from presentation.

XML's role as data hub has led to major efforts to adapt electronic data interchange (EDI) to XML. If the standards involved are accepted, EDI using XML will be far easier for small companies to use than the present alternatives.

XML's time has come. Businesses increasingly rely on disparate systems, but it is difficult to get the systems to talk. There is information overflow everywhere but few tools to organize that information. The Internet makes a great research tool, but getting 30,000 hits from your favorite search engine accomplishes little; we need tools that search content in context.

XML in Accounting.   From the accounting viewpoint, the needs are equally strong.

If you are a CPA, you may want an easy answer to the question, "How do I get data from my clients' systems into my write-up system?"

If you are responsible for corporate accounting, you may be looking for a way to get accounting information into your general ledger from your payroll provider or a separate operations system, such as manufacturing or job costing.

Perhaps you are looking for a way to consolidate accounting records from multiple sites, or wish you had a better way to get data into a budgeting and forecasting tool and back—without needing to pay a programmer to custom-develop an interface for each system.

Dell Computer Corporation recently announced that it has embraced XML as the tool for tying its customers' procurement systems into its order entry system.

If the software developer community accepts XML, accounting data can be transferred easily from any accounting-oriented system—payroll, manufacturing, and ERP—to any other accounting-oriented system—such as budget and forecasting tools, a CPA's tax or write-up product—and back again.

It is possible that XML will even be part of tax filing in the near future. UWI.Com is developing the XFDL (eXtensible Forms Definition Language) protocol for InternetForms for the secure and self-standing filing and submitting of forms. XFDL offers content, context, and structure in digitally secure and signed archives, and offers data verification, user help, automation, and precision layout and printing. The Internal Revenue Service has been taking a close look at this technology.

XML as Information Tool.   The concept behind XML—developing a hierarchical view of the data in a firm—will be important for nontechnicians as the core of future knowledge management efforts and business process design. Consultants who help their clients get more use from accounting software by accessing the data directly will find that XML holds great promise. Internet research is going to be impacted, on the Internet or searching for information on your local intranet. XML search tools combine the best aspects of hierarchical categorizers, such as the search engine Yahoo!, and indexing search engines, such as Alta Vista. Hierarchical categorizers let you search through a manually maintained hierarchical category tree but not the content of the pages. Indexers let you make elaborate searches on their content but leave you in the blank where context is concerned. New search engines that understand XML offer both context and content, making searches more meaningful, focused, and relevant.

Software developers are all making plans to incorporate XML. Monarch, from Datawatch, is a popular tool for extracting data from report files. Datawatch sees XML as a natural extension for its products. FRx, the financial statement reported that is a de facto standard for off-the-shelf accounting, also has begun it move toward XML.

The best-known data conversion product is Data Junction Corp.'s Data Junction. The right version of Data Junction can understand almost any data format, from EBCDIC to COBOL—more than 150 formats in the Enterprise Edition. Data Junction can then sort, manipulate, and export the data into almost any other data format. It is available in Windows and UNIX versions. Data Junction has XML capabilities available today as shown in Exhibit 1.5. It lets you map fields from any of the database files it can read to an XML file structure. Then it creates an XML file that can be read by any XML browser, such as Internet Explorer 5.0. (See Exhibit 1.6.)

AICPA.   The American Institute of Certified Public Accountants has been involved in a project to determine the profession's role in the establishment of XML and associated standards. Its findings agreed with what others are saying: XML can be used to significantly decrease audit costs, facilitate continuous auditing, improve data movement into write-up and tax software, and offer new methods of financial analysis and reporting. An article on the project first appeared in the May *Journal of Accountancy.* The AICPA project Web site is currently at http://www.xfrml.org.

Understanding XML should not be left to the technologists. It is a tool for organizing information for easy retrieval, for presentation in an unlimited number of forms, for creating a common understanding of business, and for integrating disparate systems. Businesswide involvement is needed to catego-

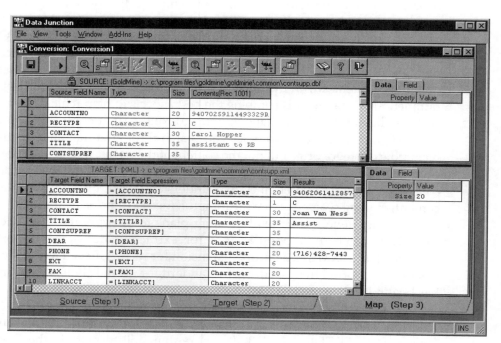

Exhibit 1.5   Data Junction has XML capabilities.

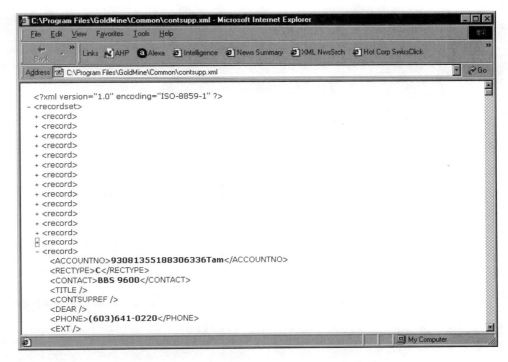

Exhibit 1.6 Data Junction file can be read by Microsoft Explorer.

rize that data for easy retrieval. The standards for creating the files that define, transform, and present XML files are in flux. The tools to work with XML are just coming out, or XML is being added to the tools used today. XML will have an impact today and for years to come. The author's Web site with information about XML for accountants is found at <http://www.computercpa.com/xml2.html.> (See Exhibit 1.7.)

Continuous Auditing

Data Junction is just one tool that the accounting profession will have to cope with the explosion of data sent through the Internet and its kin. Continuous auditing—or as it is now practiced as "far more frequent auditing"—will be required as financial information will be flying fast and furious.

Data extraction and analysis tools will grow in importance as a tool in the auditor's toolkit. The classic audit tool for working with external data is the data extraction and analysis tool. This tool combines many of the capabilities (data conversion, text mining, database and report writer) in one product that

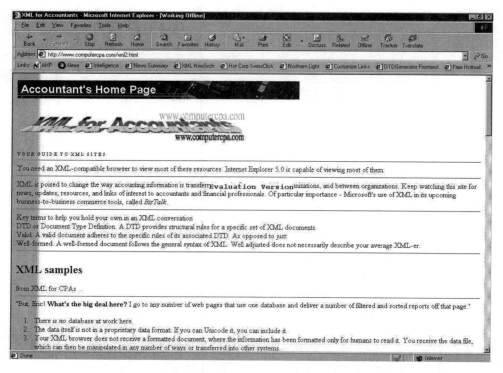

Exhibit 1.7   The author's Web site with information about XML for accountants.

is highly refined for the audit function. A data extraction and analysis tool give users the power to take an external file, select records that match chosen criteria, create a statistical sample, stratify data for a bird's-eye view, check file totals and extensions, look for gaps in numerical sequences or duplicate documents and records, and re-create aging reports.

The best-known data extraction and analysis tools are the CICA's WinIDEA (for Windows) and ACL Software's ACL (for Windows, DOS, Macintosh, UNIX, and MVS). Both products are powerful audit tools that incorporate the best features of each other's functions with each new release. The latest release of IDEA—(http://www.cica.ca)—has narrowed the gap between it and ACL—(http://www.acl.com) with a (Visual Basic for Application) VBA-like scripting language to automate processes. ACL has had a batch command, or scripting, language for some time.

IDEA is a Windows-only program. If that is not too much of a limitation, the user enjoys a product that acts like an Office product, including right-click support for functions and a consistent look and feel. Wizards lead the user through many tasks. ACL's interface is not as intuitive for the novice. However, both systems employ a very easy-to-use data import assistant, similar to those found in Excel, and ACL can read files directly from computer tape.

Open Source

An Office 97–compatible suite of software called StarOffice is available over the Internet free for individual, noncommercial use. The concept of offering software on the Internet for free is continuing to gain momentum. The Open Source Movement offers the programming code for free on the Internet so organizations can use, improve and share programs. Visit <http://www.opensource.org> for more information.

One of the best-known products is an operating system called Linux. This UNIX derivative is quickly gaining acceptance in businesses small and large due to its reliability, speed, and price. Used with another free product from the Internet, the Apache Web Server, powerful Web servers can be put together on the thinnest possible budgets.

Yes, there is open-source accounting software under development. Will it be able to compete with the commercial products for power, support and reliability? The future of computing and accounting systems may be driven by the answer.

INTERVIEW: RICH WALKER, INTUIT

Interview with Rich Walker, director of the professional partner programs, Intuit

How did Intuit first get involved in the Internet for its own use?

Having pioneered the use of connectivity in on-line banking in its Quicken and QuickBooks products, Intuit early on recognized the value of Internet-based customer communication and support, e-commerce, and providing financial information. Quicken.com, for example, has quickly become one of the leading personal finance sites on the Web.

How did it begin offering Internet-oriented services to its customers?

Intuit's initial foray into Internet services was the launch of Quicken.com, aimed at providing consumers with information and tools to manage their financial lives. Subsequently Intuit introduced Web-based products, including QuickenMortgage and InsureMarket, both of which are one of the top providers of mortgages and insurance on the Web.

For the small business owner who uses QuickBooks, the QuickBooks Online Payroll Service provides a 24-hour-a-day connection to Intuit's payroll center, for immediate processing of the payroll and local printing of checks or direct deposit stubs.

All of our tax preparation products, including ProSeries, Lacerte, and TurboTax, provide for electronic filing of individual and business returns. Web Turbo Tax allows complete processing of individual federal and state returns from the Web, with over 350,000 returns filed in this manner for TY98.

What is your impression of CPAs and their Internet use?

[The] CPAs' primary use of the Internet is for e-mail (70 percent of Quick-Books professional advisors have e-mail accounts), and for publishing "brochure-ware" sites on the Web.

How about their clients?

Small business owners are flocking to Internet usage. In a 1999 study of QuickBooks users, we found that:

- 87.7 percent of QuickBooks users accessed the Web for business or personal use in past three months, not including e-mail.
- 15 percent of these have high-speed access.
- 75.2 percent have used e-mail for business purposes in the last three months.
- 40 percent use the Internet for business purposes at least four times a week.

What makes your Internet offerings unique?

The wide array of financial information, data exchange with financial institutions (into Quicken and QuickBooks), connected services such as payroll, and remote entry into Quicken and Web TurboTax are a few of the differentiating factors for Intuit's Internet-based products and services.

What is your vision for accountants' use of the Internet?

In the short term, accountants will increasingly use the Internet to transmit accounting data files back and forth from their office to the client's office. In the long term, however, accountants will use the Internet to access and monitor clients' financial data and, consequently, provide real-time analysis and consulting.

For your own firm?

The first "wave" of technology was enterprise computing, with an emphasis on automating the back office. Intuit was a leader in the second wave of PC computing, which focused on automating the customer, or user, of information. Now, in the third wave of connected computing, Intuit is a leader in automating the communication of financial data among the individual or small business owner and his or her constituencies, such as banks, accountants, government, suppliers, employees, and customers.

Do you think the Internet has had a profound effect on accounting and accounting practice?

Not yet. There will be a migration from desktop-based A&A software to applications that use the Internet to draw from a variety of information and data sources in a real-time manner.

Corporate?

Obviously, the Internet has had a tremendous impact on the way in which businesses offer their products and services, communicate with their customers and potential customers, and interact with their legacy systems. Consumer expectations demand that businesses offer informational sites, e-stores, and operational back-ends such as order tracking.

Education (continuing and preparatory)?

While just beginning, Web-based training will quickly become the standard for self-study CPE (continuing professional education) courses. Lack of bandwidth [limit on the amount and speed of data being exchanged] currently limits the amount of true interactivity of the training course, but strides in communication hardware and the methods that Web applications use to deliver screens will alleviate this issue.

What should accountants be doing to keep up and prepare for the future?

Don't scrimp on technology—but up-to-date hardware and high-speed communication devices, such as DSL [digital subscriber lines]. Don't designate one person in the office to be the "IT guru"—it should be everyone's responsibility to learn about the application of technology.

What do you see as the greatest challenges still to be faced?

Bandwidth. Privacy of financial data. Resistance to using the Internet to transmit financial data.

Do you have favorite Internet resources and software?

My favorite search engine is AskJeeves.com, a natural-language engine. As you might expect, Quicken.com is my favorite financial Web site. I track my portfolio on Quicken.com, and use the Quicken 99 Web Entry tool to remote-enter transactions for later downloading onto my Quicken desktop.

From Here . . .

Chapter 2 discusses where you can go to get some of these benefits.

What You Can Do on the Internet

This chapter provides an introduction to the basic services for which the Internet can be used. It discusses the types of services offered for those accessing the Internet, such as e-mail, file transfer, discussion groups (Usenet), and the World Wide Web. The following outline summarizes the contents of this chapter:

- *What's Hot On the Internet*
  Mail: The foundation of the Internet
  Mailing lists and list servers: News and views delivered to your e-mail
  Newsgroups: Public bulletin boards covering every topic you can imagine
  FTP: Moving files around the Internet
  Live chat: Instant messaging in print and voice
  Finger: finding out about a user
  Other clients: Multimedia, telephones and more
  Whois: Finding out about users and companies
  Ping and Trace: teChnical tools for the Internet
  World Wide Web: The hottest spot on the Internet
- *What's Not So Hot On the Internet*
  Gopher: A menu-driven interface to the Internet, the old way
  Telnet: Acting as a terminal on a remote computer.
  Others gone by the wayside...

MAIL

E-mail: Introduction

Everyone needs an e-mail address. It is the electronic in-box that has become as necessary as a telephone or facsimile machine in business. It is the very foundation of the Internet and is designed for one-to-one and one-to-many direct transfer of information or questions. Where other resources wait on the

Internet for you to go to them, e-mail comes to you. E-mail can link people together in an office, across the country, or around the world.

E-mail is enabling. Large companies have had internal e-mail systems for some time. Internet e-mail provides a similar set of tools to smaller firms and individuals. E-mail offers a link for small companies to be more powerful and for large companies to orchestrate their efforts better.

E-mail is an inexpensive way to keep in touch. Free offerings, inexpensive offerings, and more expensive offerings make communication within an office, company, or organization, among people with similar interests, or with potential business relationships easier, transcending time and geography. Each e-mail message is, to all intents and purposes, free; you never run out of stamps or need to stay up to 11 P.M. to keep the cost of the collect call down.

E-mail is asynchronous. Just as the VCR enabled people watch television whenever they want, e-mail lets people communicate whenever they want. Messages can be sent to staff and managers on the road, at home, or in the office, at any hour, in whatever level of detail is necessary. Spreadsheet and word processing files can be transferred along with a message about their use.

Advantages of E-mail

The convenience of sending messages at any time has made e-mail a popular method of communication. Long-distance charges and time differences are eliminated. Messages are easily archived, the information reused, and large bodies of information transferred. E-mail can be used for purposes other than sending simple messages you type, including being used as the foundation for electronic commerce (receiving orders) and collecting information for marketing purposes (forms).

There are many ways to communicate. You can send a letter or a fax. You can place a phone call and leave a message with a receptionist, answering machine, or voice mail. However, in many situations e-mail is a better tool.

E-mail is much faster than mail.   E-mail lets a businessperson send a note to a client on the weekend or an advisor at 11 P.M., and the recipient can read and acknowledge the message whenever it is the most convenient. E-mail can find its way to the recipient's electronic in-box in a manner of seconds, so thoughts and plans are communicated at the speed of light. E-mail messages can contain graphics, spreadsheets, and music. However, not everyone has e-mail, but everyone can receive a letter.

E-mail is in a computer-readable format.   Information sent by e-mail does not have to be retyped to be reused. E-mail can be sent concurrently with other e-mail messages, so there is never a busy signal, unlike a fax machine. Messages are not as easily mishandled by others or lost. Fax machines are better suited for documents already on paper.

E-mail can be prioritized. People can conduct only one phone call at a time, while they can receive, scan, and prioritize many e-mail messages simultaneously. Phone tag is the bane of people who spend their life talking with others. "Let John know I returned his call returning my call returning his call." With e-mail, you can get the message across no matter what the other person is doing or where he or she is. Phone mail limbo is also avoided; most phone mail directories are limited in the functional grouping capability. On the receiving end, you can control which messages you want to read and respond to, by the sender and the subject line. However, you will seldom e-mail someone where an immediate response or negotiation is preferable or necessary, such as the message "Your house is on fire." Messages do not come through garbled, as on an answering machine or voice mail; they are not misinterpreted, as they sometimes are by a message taker; they do not require the recipient to be always available, as with a phone.

In summary, you can use e-mail for communicating information whenever desired—there are no time constraints. E-mail is useful where an immediate response is not necessary; the phone is still better for persuasion and where an instant response is necessary. E-mail can be anonymous and untraceable but is relatively unsecure, although encryption with security tools like PGP (http://www.pgp.com) help. It is ideal for technical information, writing, and collaboration; no retyping is necessary. E-mail lets you read and respond to some messages while ignoring others, allowing more control. For good and bad, it lets you send a message to a thousand as easily as a message to one.

Getting E-mail

Their domain name: *Free E-mail:* Juno. E-mail accounts are available for free (if you do not mind a little advertising when you send and receive your messages) from companies like Juno (http://www.juno.com). In exchange for filling out a detailed demographic survey, you get an e-mail account at no cost. You will need a computer, a modem, and a phone line. You do not require Internet access. You access your Juno mail through Juno software and special dial-in numbers. Juno has overcome most of the limitations of its e-mail software and is now offering Internet access services as well.

You will find free and fee-based e-mail services that are relatively inexpensive. These can serve many people well, but lack the advantages of a personalized domain name.

MyTalk.com: Another interesting e-mail option is a service that lets you receive e-mail without a computer—MyTalk.com. With MyTalk.com, you receive a free e-mail address and a toll-free number. When people e-mail you, you call your toll-free number and pick up your messages using text-to-speech synthesis. You can reply with a voice attachment or send traditional mail through their Web site.

Free E-mail-Web-based: If you don't want to give up quite as much information about yourself, and you already have Internet access, you can get free e-mail accounts that are accessible through the World Wide Web. Most of the portal services, such as Yahoo! (http://www.yahoo.com), Netscape (http://www.netscape.com), and Excite (http://www.excite.com) offer free access to e-mail accounts. Hotmail, owned by Microsoft, has powerful e-mail that integrates with the Microsoft Outlook Express mail product. By signing up at <http://www.hotmail.com>, you get an e-mail address such as yourname@hotmail.com. Lycos offers a number of interesting addresses, such as yourname@technologist.com.

Excite's e-mail service offers a lot more than free e-mail, a trend that should become widespread. Excite is also offering a free voice-mail service, where people dial a toll-free number to leave you messages and faxes, which you pick up through your e-mail account.

Business and individuals can sign up with an on-line service, such as CompuServe (http://www.compuserve.com) or America Online (http://www.aol.com). Each America Online account actually offers five e-mail addresses, one for each screen name. That way you can have an e-mail address for each member of your family and keep business mail separate from personal.

You will get an e-mail account when you sign up with an Internet service provider, such as MindSpring (http://www.mindspring.com). As with other accounts of this type, your e-mail address will be in the form yourname@ mindspring.com.

Your domain name: You can enter into a special relationship with an Internet service provider to open the door for your own domain name. Although there is usually an additional fee for this relationship, there are many benefits. Without your own domain name, you are known as <username@service.com>, such as CyberCPA@sprynet.com. With a domain name, you could be known as <username@yourcompany.com>; my domain name is computercpa.com. This offers two primary advantages:

1. It looks more professional. When you or your staff hand out business cards and they share a domain name, it makes it easier to get in touch

with your firm—and what will your clients think if they have to get in touch with Partner Sam at Sam@bigfoot.com and Manager Sally at Sally@juno.com?

2. It is portable; if you move to another e-mail provider, you can file for a change of address.

Domain names tell you about the type of organization with the domain identifier:

com = commercial
edu = educational
gov = governmental
mil = military
net = infrastructure, network
or = other organizations.

They may tell you the country of origin, such as:

au = Australia
de = Germany
uk = United Kingdom

Note that domain names may or may not properly represent the organization's name or purpose.

There is no forwarding service for e-mail sent to an account you no longer maintain. However, domain names can be transferred from your account at one ISP to your account at a different ISP, so you don't have to worry about losing e-mail, contacting all your contacts, or changing your stationery. This is possible because the domain names are maintained in a database, most likely at an organization known as the InterNIC (http://rs.internic.net or http://www.network-solutions.com). However, in most cases you must have an agreement with an ISP for a static (dedicated) IP address to be associated with your domain name. This is not included in a standard dial-up account, although you can get a relationship like this for less than $20 per month.

Note: If money is a problem, for a yearly fee of $24.95 plus a $25 setup fee, services like NameSecure.com offers you three features:

Web Site Forwarding: Web site forwarding conveniently forwards visitors to your personal or business Web site or to a noneditable "under construction"

Web page. You maintain your current Web account, but users are transferred to your site.

E-mail Forwarding: E-mail forwarding transfers all your e-mail to one existing address, anywhere on the Internet.

URL Gripper: URL Gripper holds your domain name in the browser location box while visitors surf your site.

Which service should you pick?   An e-mail account lets you send messages to and receive messages from anyone else who has an e-mail address, even if it is on a difference service from the one you subscribe to. Sometimes it is easy to send a message to someone on a different service, sometimes it is more difficult. The biggest problem is when sending attachments—binary files such as word processing documents or spreadsheets—between services. Sometimes there is no charge to compose and transmit e-mail, other times there are charges for composing on-line, sending, receiving, and storing your messages.

Often the software you must use is prescribed by your service provider, but you can use many tools to get the job done. Some of the tasks associated with e-mail are: creating and maintaining an e-mail address list; composing and editing messages; sending and receiving messages; reading messages, responding to messages, and storing/archiving them.

Using E-mail

E-mail accounts can be used to send a message to one person or a group of people. E-mail software has an address book feature where you can store the names and e-mail information for people you contact regularly; you also can type in the e-mail address on a one-time basis. You can send e-mail messages to many people by identifying each person individually; most e-mail software also lets you define multiple identities or groups and assign individuals to those groups. Then, if you want to send a message to everyone in a group, say the board of directors of a company or your top 20 clients, you can identify the group as the recipient of the e-mail. If you will be sending messages to the same group of people repeatedly, by setting up a group once you will avoid a lot of typing later.

Attachments are files you send along with an explanatory e-mail message. Because the Internet e-mail system is inherently ASCII-oriented, you cannot easily send binary (nontext) files. Software must convert binary files to ASCII and then arrange for the person on the other side to have software that can turn the converted ASCII back to its original binary format. The standard for the ASCII/Binary translation in the Unix world were uuencode and uudecode. On the Mac, Binhex is used regularly. MIME-compliant software can take care of the conversions automatically. Most e-mail software today has no problem with attachments, although some users still have difficulties with these files.

Uses of E-mail

As the partner comes into the office, she boots up her PC and checks her incoming e-mail. A senior is checking on some additional information needed for a tax return; a fellow partner is asking about her availability for lunch; a client asks if the tax-planning idea he heard on the radio affects his business. She sends an e-mail to her tax client asking for additional information, tells the staff person to follow up in three days, lets the other partner know her availability, and forwards the radio tax tip to the tax partner in charge for his staff to follow up on, which sends an acknowledgment on a standard form back to the client. Before she is done, a mailing that summarizes some new consulting tips from her peers comes through, as does a note from her college-age daughter asking for a cash advance.

Yes, e-mail can provide an efficient channel for communications between CPA practitioners and accountants in industry, with clients, customers, vendors, coworkers, peers and employees.

Anything can be sent within an organization, including spreadsheets, databases, word processing files, video, and programs. Questions and information can be left for another without waiting in line to catch the other person, leaving pink "while you were out" notes, or sticking Post-it notes on people's desks, papers, computers, and walls. When staff is away from the office, audit workpaper files can be sent back to the office for review, and paperwork received at the office, like confirmations, can be scanned and sent out on-site.

In multibranch offices, between business partners, and in establishing new relationships, e-mail can provide a quick way to share a thought or ask a question. When starting a purchasing project, for example, a document can be quickly communicated to many organizations for their review.

Between organizations, messages can be sent at the sender's leisure to the appropriate person at another business and followed up when possible. E-mail is more easily administered and tracked than phone or fax, automatically, with an archive of messages sent and received; it is self-documenting. E-mail lets you transfer CAD drawings, spreadsheets, and business documents electronically. EDI using e-mail allows businesses to transfer the files needed for EDI commerce at a relatively low cost.

Financial managers are responsible for collecting financial information and communicating the results to others. Managers must communicate with their subordinates. Practitioners need to communicate with authorities. E-mail makes it all possible. Sending financial statements via e-mail provides a quick way to distribute the information. Users can immediately put e-mail in spreadsheet form to work in their own spreadsheet program.

E-mail Software

Many software options are available for the different aspects of e-mail: composition, address books, sending, tracking, responding, archiving, and following up.

Features.   While millions of new users join the electronic world each month, the software and corporate policies used for e-mail, the most basic of Internet tasks, has not kept up with that of a similar tool: the word processor. Word processors accomplish a similar task—composition of messages—but put their end result on paper instead of sending it off over the phone wires. Word processors do not need to receive messages, as e-mail software does. Some word processing capabilities, such as columns, embedding graphics, and indexing, do not have an immediate place in the largely text-only world of e-mail. However, many word processing features are starting to show up in e-mail programs and vice versa. What should you expect to see in an e-mail package? Some basic features are described in the following sections.

Composing Messages.   In the simplest form, the sender goes through six steps to compose an e-mail message.

1. Address
2. Subject
3. Additional recipients
4. Composition
5. Spell check
6. Transmission

First, the sender types the recipient's e-mail address when prompted, then adds a subject line summarizing the message that follows. Next, the sender indicates whether, as on normal business correspondence, anyone should be copied or blind copied. (CC and BCC come from the good old days of "carbon copy" and "blind carbon copy"; this should become xerographic copy and blind xerographic copy soon.) The greatest time is then spent preparing the actual message. After spell-checking, the message is sent on its way.

Most e-mail software lets you maintain an e-mail address book, where you can keep and retrieve e-mail addresses of people you correspond with repeatedly. Many let you classify some of those names into groups, so you can more easily send a common message to groups, such as "all managers," "second shift employees," or the board of directors.

The electronic equivalent of letterhead is the use of a *S/G* (signature), a predefined block with your company name, address, phone, and other important information. Most mail packages let you save a personal SIG, which can be included automatically with your mail as you compose it.

Most e-mail packages also let you attach additional files, such as word processing, spreadsheet, and other binary files, and control the necessary steps of preparing the files for e-mail transfer.

Finally, the software can transfer the composed messages to the computer system for sending.

Retrieve Messages.   Likewise, e-mail software can go to your service provider to get the messages waiting for you. A list of the messages appears in a window, which you can sort through by sender, date, or subject, and then view the contents. Once you have read the message you may wish to reply to the sender, send a copy of it on to someone else, place a copy in an e-mail folder, or print out the message.

Extra Features.   While most e-mail software can do the preceding tasks, some have additional functionality that may be important for your business.

E-mail can be sent and received using the same Hypertext Markup Language that makes Web pages so attractive. The use of graphics that makes the pages attractive also increases the time to download mail and can make off-line reading more difficult.

Additional tools for making the composition of mail more effective include word processing–like style sheets and templates to help ensure that documents are more likely in accordance with firm policies; mail merge, so customized messages can be sent to groups more easily; and tools for writing in non-English text.

Add to that the basic premise that correspondence sent by e-mail is about as secure as that written on the back of a postcard. Built-in encryption (making the message unreadable without a code) can broaden the scope of what you can safely discuss by e-mail. Unlike Web browsers, where the SSL standard makes credit cards and other information being transferred between two computers safe, the encryption standard for e-mail is still not fully in place. Using PGP or other encryption tools can help.

For receiving mail, some e-mail packages let you set up automated filters, to file, forward to another user, or delete messages based on from whom the messages come and their contents. You can set a filter to delete junk mail, while you can direct mail from clients or customers automatically to the appropriate recipient.

In addition, an integrated Virus Checker, such as McAfee Vshield (http://www.nai.com) can add some peace of mind to what you are downloading.

Examples: Basic E-mail

Where do you get e-mail software? Your on-line service provider probably included a mail client with the software you received when you enrolled.

How does your e-mail software rate? Do you wish it could do more? Take a look at some of the e-mail packages we reviewed. Most of the products are free or inexpensive, and the features can make a big difference. Some examples of e-mail software follows.

Proprietary mail software

- Juno (http://www.juno.com) is proprietary e-mail with its own software, and now lets you do the basics other products do, such as send and receive attachments.

- CompuServe offers many software front-ends to their software, including WinCIM; America Online also has a proprietary user interface. Both incorporate e-mail software to send and receive messages to other users on the same service and to any service or users connected to the Internet.

Unix

If you are using a dial-up account, you probably are calling into a UNIX system, where you can use reliable but somewhat outdated mail software including elm and pine ("Pine Is Not Elm"). Unix dial-in accounts are becoming rarer, but are still found at institutions like libraries and colleges.

Windows

If you use Microsoft's Office products, you have one of their own e-mail clients. Microsoft Exchange shipped with Windows 95 and includes tools for encryption as well as easy integration with Word and other Office products. See Exhibit 2.1 for an example. Outlook Express, which shipped with later versions of Windows 95 and with Windows 98, is available for free from the Microsoft Web site at <http://www.microsoft.com>. If you use Netscape Communcator to browse the Web, Netscape includes its own e-mail client, Netscape Messenger: http://www.netscape.com. (See Exhibit 2.2.) These provide similar functionality but are better integrated to their browsers and other software.

Many other e-mail products are available for a fee or for free, and most software products now incorporate some e-mail functionality built in.

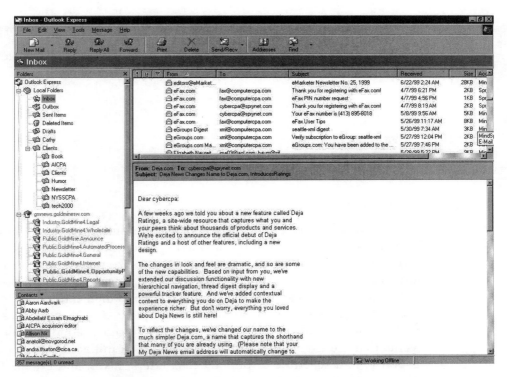

Exhibit 2.1   Outlook Express is available for free at the Microsoft Web site.

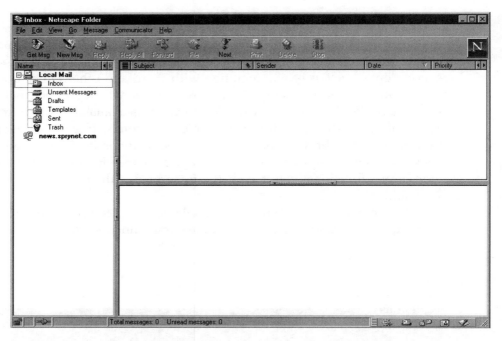

Exhibit 2.2   Netscape includes its own e-mail client, Netscape Messenger, with its browser for the World Wide Web.

Examples: Advanced E-mail

Are you looking for some additional capabilities?

Contact Management

*   To really supercharge e-mail, take a look at Goldmine 4.0 from Goldmine Software (http://www.goldminesw.com). Goldmine integrates e-mail into a complete contact management system. You can maintain e-mail addresses with your complete contact background, create mail merge and other correspondence for paper, fax, or e-mail, and track e-mail received by the company from which you received it. You can receive e-mail messages and incorporate the sender into a predefined series of events that are triggered automatically, from an initial automatic e-mail response, to a schedule of phone calls, letters, faxes, and e-mail. Goldmine can create new prospect records or attach incoming e-mail to pre-existing contact records for complete tracking of all correspondence.

Goldmine 4.0 incorporates e-mail into normal business activities rather than keeping it off on its own.

- Microsoft's Outlook, Novell's GroupWise, and other workgroup software are also working to provide a central solution to communications. These packages promote their ability to let you send and receive messages, faxes, pager messages, and more. This is covered in more detail in Chapter 3, under "Unified Messaging."

Problems and Issues with E-mail

E-mail is great and an integral part of people's lives. Yet there are a number of issues that remain to be resolved fully.

Business communications are almost out of control. What used to take weeks has accelerated: from traditional mail, to two-day and overnight express, to the fax machine. Now business communications can be instantaneous. Some people receive so much mail that a response like "Eric, you are right!" has no meaning. This has led to the need to "quote" the most important part of the original message; most often these quotes are set apart from the response by a ">" in front of each line of text. Many software products can be configured to do this automatically.

Junk mail is easier to send. Many organizations have begun to take advantage of the easily accessible in-box and the opportunity to disseminate a message to hundreds or thousands of people at no cost by sending advertising and other solicitations to whatever e-mail address they can get their hands on. This is very annoying but unavoidable. Good e-mail software uses a function called *filters* to let you manually ignore the messages or remove them from sight before you have to consider them, if desired.

Checking for e-mail can become a compulsion. As popularized in the Cathy comic strip, many people can hit the button to check for their mail too often. When the network is connected to the Internet, a mail message can show up automatically on the computer screen (or a signal that new mail as been received); however, e-mail has to have its proper place. It is not a method to get a quicker response than a phone or fax. It is a different medium, to express short or detailed messages or questions to be handled in a batch mode when the recipient chooses.

E-mail is only beginning to be accepted as a means to send important or legal documents. You have to consider the legality of business documents delivered via e-mail. Digital signatures are in place throughout the country, but no one overriding law unifies the laws in place by each state.

E-mail addresses are not centrally maintained and administered. How do you find someone's e-mail address? Well, the best thing to do is ask for it. E-mail addresses are assigned and tracked by each individual service provider and not by a centrally administered group, so there is no one official place to find the information. However, there are many tools for tracking down a person's postal and electronic addresses. Yahoo (http://www.yahoo.com), Lycos (http://www.lycos.com), and many other sites let you search for e-mail and postal mail information. Internet Explorer 5 has a people search included in its search function.

E-mail makes firms forget the commonsense reasons they came up with procedures for traditional mail. E-mail should be composed with all the seriousness of a standard business letter.

Security is a major issue with e-mail. Some people say you should write in e-mail only what you would send on a postcard. There is no commonly embraced standard for e-mail security. However, with the proper tools, e-mail can be very secure: You know that only the recipient can read the mail you send, the recipient knows that you sent the mail, and you have the assurance that the message has not been altered in the process. However, between known partners, security can be established easily. PGP (Pretty Good Privacy) and other methods of security are necessary to ensure that privacy, authentication, and other issues are properly dealt with for commerce and secure business information transfer. PGP uses private and public key encryption to help promote the safe passage of data. A CPA can hold the public keys of 100 partners in a partnership, encrypt their K-1s or other sensitive data, and have confidence that the data sent will properly be received.

E-mail is not the U.S. Postal Service – no change of address form exists. Mail does go to the wrong places (because of the nut loose behind the keyboard) with some unusual results, but faxes are no different. The United States Postal Service is discussing an e-mail cancellation service with all the authority of a traditional postmark.

E-mail is a gray area. Within a business, e-mail can be abused. Can the employer view it, or is it private? Can employees use encryption without the employer's permission? Can e-mail create legal problems for the employer under agency law? Few firms have drafted e-mail policies to guard, guide, and promote the efficient use of internal systems.

E-mail cannot convey emotion. If someone says on the phone, "I hate you, get out of here!" he or she may be conveying anger or playfulness. The words lose their true meaning in print. This has led to the use of symbols known as *emoticons*, or *smileys*.

E-mail involves more typing than many people care to do. For this reason, many phrases that are used often have standard abbreviations. As traditional mail uses "PS" to add a thought at the end of a letter, e-mail uses the shorthand of BTW, IMHO, and LOL for "by the way," "in my humble opinion," and "laughing out loud," respectively.

OTHER SMILEYS AND EMOTICONS

:-)	Basic smiley	BRB	Be right back
;-)	Winky smiley	BTW	By the way
:-(	Frowning smiley	IMHO	In my humble opinion
:-|	Indifferent smiley	LOL	Laughing out loud
:-o	Uh-oh!	OTOH	On the other hand
:-P	Sticking out your tongue	PMJI	Pardon me for jumping in
(-:	Left-handed smiley	RTFM	Read the _ _ _ manual
8-)	I wear glasses	RSN	Real soon now
%-)	I've been on the Net too long	TIA	Thanks in advance
:~)	I have a cold	TTFN	Ta ta for now
:-#)	I have braces	TTYL	Talk to you later
:-{)	I have a mustache		

MAILING LISTS AND LIST SERVERS

As already discussed, e-mail lets one organization send messages to one recipient or many, either by typing in the recipient's e-mail address(es) at the time the e-mail is to be sent or by using a name or a group from an address book. However, sometimes that procedure can become ungainly.

For example, say your firm decides to send a new weekly electronic newsletter to clients and prospects. You set up all of the clients and prospects in an address book, set up a group named "Newsletter," assign the list members to that group, and mail out the newsletter to everyone in that group. As clients and prospects come and go, you maintain the list manually. Soon a client indicates she would like to be taken off the list for a month while she and her husband vacation in the Caymans. Another client asks to get the newsletters monthly instead of weekly. Pretty soon, maintaining the list becomes a full-time job. When administration of e-mail becomes ungainly, it is time to look at mailing lists, or listserves.

MAILING LISTS

Mailing lists are e-mail with an automated subscription service. You subscribe by e-mail, make changes to your type of subscription by e-mail, and receive your materials by e-mail.

Special software at the server tracks who wants to subscribe and what type of subscription they would like. (Recipients do not need any special software other than traditional e-mail software.) Some software lets subscribers choose how often they want to receive postings, as individual messages or compiled into one mailing, in brief or in detail. In addition, the software allows users to temporarily remove themselves from a list.

Mailing lists can be used as simple address-book replacements, when you wish to have a one-way exchange. In this case, your newsletter or other information goes from your firm to its employees, clients, or prospects. In some cases, the lists are used to deliver electronic versions of traditional periodicals as well as new electronic magazines (e-zines) that point out the unique nature of the Internet—it lets anyone become a publisher for next to nothing. The costs of assembling content and making the publication available to the world are minimal.

In addition, mailing lists can be used for two-way (or many-way) communications. They can be used to set up round-table discussions, where all who are interested can receive the submissions made by others and contribute as well (with the list owner's permission). Brown University and the University of Pennsylvania are among colleges offering long-distance learning using mailing lists. The schools send the class material to class members, who reply and carry on a discussion about what they have studied.

Using Mailing Lists

To use a mailing list, you must join (or subscribe to) the list. Lists of lists can be browsed at a number of sites, including Liszt (http://www.liszt.com) and Neosoft (http://www.neosoft.com/internet/paml/paml.htm1). These sites provide instructions for getting information on over 90,000 lists.

Normally two e-mail addresses are used in conjunction with mailing lists. The first is the e-mail address used to send subscription-oriented commands, such as subscribe or unsubscribe. It is an automated service, so users must type commands to the address precisely as instructed. The second is the e-mail address used to distribute submissions to all subscribed. Sending subscription-oriented commands to this address is annoying to subscribers and does not accomplish the change to the subscription desired.

Some mailing lists let users change from a detailed subscription, where every submission shows up when sent, to a digest mode, which either combines all messages for a desired period into one message or just lists part of the messages. By controlling the number of entries into your e-mail, you can better identify the messages and control them for reading and responding at your leisure.

If you miss messages, some submissions are archived and available as part of newsgroups (discussed later) or accessible through the Web. Others are not archived unless a member chooses to do so.

Some limit submissions to a select group of people; others limit those who can subscribe; and others moderate (edit where appropriate) the submissions.

Materials Available on Mailing Lists

Mailing lists are a way to keep up with the latest news in special areas, have an ongoing discussion with others on important topics that arrive in your e-mail, and simplify the process of letting those who are interested take in as much or little of the information as necessary.

Many mailing lists are helpful to those in the accounting profession. A few major groupings, available from the ANet, an educational accounting consortium, and from FinanceNet, a federal government site, are specifically accounting related. There also are groups for various aspects of consulting, like business process reengineering. You can get accounting and finance abstracts, news on Canadian accounting technology, and the latest news on Internet security.

Mailing lists are very focused. They can handle sensitive issues, like self-help, nicely. Advertisers who get hold of a mailing list know that subscribers are interested in a topic. Mailing lists can be closed, can be free or for fee, and can be for business, personal, or wild.

Start Your Own Mailing List

Chapter 5 covers starting your own mailing list. Mailing lists can be profitable tools for marketing, customer support, and employee communications.

Participating in Mailing Lists

As stated above, two organizations currently provide a number of mailing lists of interest to accountants in particular: ANet and the U.S government's FinanceNet site. Here is more detail on their offerings.

ANet Mailing Lists. One of the major services provided by ANet is more than 30 mailing lists in a range of areas. The principal mailing list is ANews-L, which provides information on a variety of coming events, new publications, and important developments on the Internet. You can find out more at <http://www.csu.edu.au/lists/anet/>.

Some of the lists you can subscribe to include:

ANews-L (News)   This low-volume but high-quality mailing list concentrates on news of journals, conferences, seminars, and other matters of interest to the academic accounting community.

AAcrdn-L (Accounting Program Accreditation)   This list provides an open forum for the exchange of ideas, concerns, questions, or comments by individuals involved with their department/school/unit's efforts to obtain either American Assembly of Collegiate Schools of Business (AACSB) first-time accreditation or reaccreditation of their school's accounting programs.

     The primary focus of the list is AACSB accounting accreditation in the United States, but general business school accreditation items that relate to the accounting accreditation process are welcome. General issues of accreditation that might encompass accounting programs in other countries are welcome on the general ANet teaching and curriculum list, ATeach-L.

AAccSys-L (Accounting Information Systems)   This list discusses all matters concerned with accounting information systems theory and practice. Archives of the list are maintained.

AAudit-L (Auditing)   This list discusses all aspects of external and internal audit. Archives of the list are maintained.

ABooks-L (New Books)   This list allows authors and publishers to advertise the arrival of new books in the discipline. Comment: Be warned— unashamed advertising is allowed in this mailing list. Archives of the list are maintained.

AEthics-L (Ethics)   This list discusses the ethical dimension of accounting and auditing. Archives of the list are maintained.

AEthnog-L (Accounting Ethnography)   This list discusses the ethnographic dimension of accounting and auditing. Archives of the list are maintained.

AFinAcc-L (Financial Accounting)   This list discusses all aspects of financial accounting. If the demand warrants, this may need to be supplemented by country-specific mailing lists. Archives of the list are maintained.

AGvNFP-L (Governmental and Not-for-Profit Accounting)   This list discusses accounting for government and not-for-profit organizations. Archives of the list are maintained.

AIntAcc-L (International Accounting)   This list discusses all aspects of international accounting. Archives of the list are maintained.

AIntSys-L (Intelligent and Expert Systems)   This list discusses the application of intelligent and expert systems to accounting and management. Archives of the list are maintained.

AJobs-L (Academic Positions)   This list carries academic job announcements. Contact the ANet team for information. Archives of the AJobs-L list are maintained.

AMgtAcc-L (Management Accounting)   This is the management accounting list. Archives of the list are maintained.

AOilAcc-L (Extractive Industries)   This list discusses accounting for extractive industries, including oil and gas. Archives of the list are maintained.

AProfsn-L (Academic/Profession Interface)   This list discusses the nexus between academia and the accounting and auditing profession with particular emphasis on improving the relationship and cooperation between the two areas. Archives of the list are maintained.

ASocial-L (Social Accounting)   This list discusses all aspects of accounting in its behavioral and sociological context. Archives of the list are maintained.

AStdnt-L (Accounting Student List)   This list enables student-to-student contact around the world. Archives of the list are maintained.

ATax-L (Taxation)   This list discusses all accounting and other tax-related issues. Archives of the list are maintained.

ATeach-L (Teaching and Learning)   This list discusses developments in the teaching, learning, and curriculum design of accounting and auditing. Archives of the list are maintained.

ATwoYear-L (U.S. Two-Year College System)   This list is devoted to teaching and learning in the U.S. two-year community college system. Archives of the list are maintained.

Miscellaneous Lists

Double Entries.   A spin-off from ANet is Double Entries, a list containing information about what is in accounting journals and other news of note. The management of the list is now the responsibility of AccountingEducation.com [previously undertaken by ANet at (http://www.csu.edu.au/anet)]. This is a website for the academic accounting community (http://www.accountingeducation.com).

To receive this list, register your name and e-mail address via the Register option on the AccountingEducation.com Web site. Go to <http://www. accountingeducation.com>.

Insite Direct. Insite Direct is a regular publication from CPAOnline.com. Subscriptions are free. To subscribe or unsubscribe, visit <http://www.cpaonline.com/insite/direct> or send e-mail to:
Subscribe: insite-request@cpaonline.com with "Subscribe" in the body.

Unsubscribe: insite-request@cpaonline.com with "Unsubscribe" in the body.

Canadian Accounting Technology One active site is largely focused on Canadian technology but has subscribers throughout North America who regularly share their insights about accounting-oriented hardware and software. You can join Can-AccTech by sending an e-mail message to majordomo@morochove.com and, in the e-mail message body, state: subscribe can-acctech.

CISACA-L This is a list for accountants interested in internal audit and systems issues. To subscribe to CISACA-L, send e-mail to listserv@vm.cc.purdue.edu with "Subscribe cisaca-l" in the e-mail message body. The Institute of Internal Auditors has a more complete list of IA-related sites at (http://www.theiia.org/tech/iserve 1.htm).

FinanceNet Mail Lists. FinanceNet proclaims itself the largest government Internet administrative network in the world with a presence on all service platforms. It was first established at the National Performance Review in March of 1994 and is operated by the National Science Foundation. Its mission and goals include improving accountability and stewardship of public financial assets by:

- Providing rapid access to pertinent electronic information
- Establishing electronic communication links between FinanceNet Mail staff and taxpayers across all geopolitical government boundaries for sharing information, ideas, lessons learned, and successes
- Providing an electronic clearinghouse for information on the sale of government assets to the general public

FinanceNet is the only clearinghouse for the electronic sale to the general public of all government assets and surpluses, federal, state, and local. FinanceNet's GovSales mailing list is one of the largest government mailing lists in the world. "GovSales" is FinanceNet's fastest-growing segment.

FinanceNet is also the Internet home for:

Association of Goverment Accountants (AGA)

Association of Government Leasing and Finance (AGLF)

Auditor General of Rhode Island

Federal Accounting Standards Advisory Board (FASAB)

Government Accounting Standards Advisory Board (GASB)

Government Finance Officers Association (GFOA)

International Consortium for Government Financial Management (ICGFM)

International Institute of Municipal Clerks (IIMC)

Joint Financial Management Improvement Program (JFMIP)

Latin American and Caribbean Regional Financial Management Improvement Project

National Association of State Auditors, Comptrollers and Treasurers (NASACT)

National Council for Public/Private Partnerships (NCPPP)

New York City Comptrollers Office (NYCComptNet)

Public Risk Management Association (PRIMA)

A current listing of their mail lists is available at (http://www.financenet.gov/financenet/start/news.htm). (See Exhibit 2.3).

Each mailing list topic is matched by a corresponding newsgroup to encourage intergovernmental discussion and dialog on each topic.

NEWSGROUPS

Introduction to Newsgroups

We move from e-mail–oriented services to services that require special software to access them. The first of these services is known as USENET, network news, or newsgroups.

Newsgroups are global bulletin boards, where people post public messages for others to reply to and comment on. The adage "If there are more than 10 people in the world interested in a topic, there is a Newsgroup available to talk about it" is not far from the truth. More than 30,000 topics from around the world on professional, business, personal, entertainment, lifestyle, and downright silly topics occupy people's hearts and minds.

Newsgroups are a clearinghouse for ideas, offers of help, graffiti, and cries for help. Anyone can come and contribute, agree, or disagree. Some groups

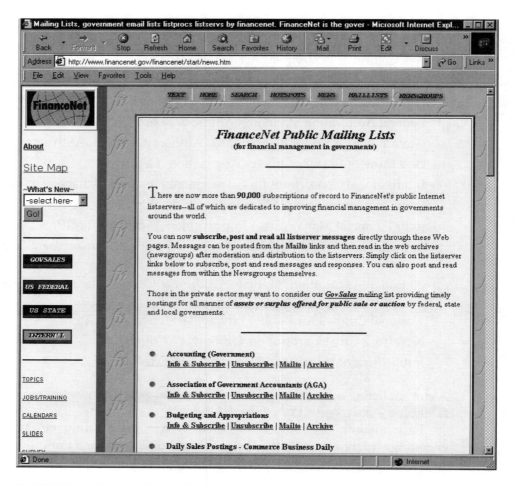

Exhibit 2.3   FinanceNet mailing lists.

are moderated; others are unmoderated, as befits the Internet's role as highway for the free interchange of ideas. Important note: Unlike e-mail, the contents of the messages in newsgroups are archived and available, so think twice before posting in the wrong place and the wrong manner—a human resources professional may someday scour the newsgroups for your name and your submission.

On-line services such as CompuServe, America Online, and Microsoft Network offer their own versions of the newsgroups, called forums or special interest groups. In the accounting profession, CompuServe's accounting-oriented forums are among the most active and diverse, with the Accounting Forum <GO ACCOUNTING>, the Accounting Vendor Forum <GO ACCTVEN>, and many more. [A more complete list of on-line discussion groups can be found at (http://www.computercpa.com/disc.html.)] Most of the on-line services maintain personal finance and tax forums. The Internet's newsgroups include groups for accounting software, taxes, business, import/export, and many more.

The newsgroups serve many very important purposes to business, to accountants, and to auditors specifically. No area related to the Internet has as much interaction, give and take, and back and forth as newsgroups. Where e-mail and mailing lists are directed at the in-box, newsgroups are a compilation of knowledge. If you need to find out what people think about a company, an industry, an idea, or a trend, you will be able to find it in the newsgroups. If you want to leave a cry for help and find someone who is willing to pass on information that would be otherwise be expensive or perhaps even impossible to get, you can do it on the newsgroups.

Many companies have found their trade secrets quickly distributed because their employees love the Internet, like to help others, and like to think they have a reputation for knowledge. The Internet community fosters getting and giving help; big egos enjoy the opportunity to display their knowledge in a public forum. A request for help with a software package or the best use of technology often results in replies from people around the world that may be worth more than the best local expert can provide. Sometimes a request goes unanswered.

Of course, there is nothing to stop the ignorant from chiming in, but sometimes you get what you pay for. Advice gained from the newsgroups should be taken with care, if not suspicion. There are those who take advantage of the newsgroups to advertise improperly, setting up the same schemes you would see by phone or mail (MAKE MONEY FA$$$$$T!). Items may be listed for sale, but be no more authentic than a newspaper ad—and it costs nothing to post to a newsgroup.

For small companies, newsgroups provide a panel of experts to query on topics of business. It's up to you to weigh the value of their responses and determine how best to follow up. There are places to announce job requirements, seminars, your Web page, and seek help with internal systems, often getting free help from others who have gone through similar problems in far less time than it takes the vendor to reply.

There are also groups discussing EDI, not-for-profits, training, and education. There are groups with news, announcements about everything and anything, and very sophisticated, technical computer issues.

You can ask for help with your Novell network, learn how to make Excel do Pivot tables, compare and contrast word processors, and find the latest news in any industry, locally or internationally. You can take part in the obscure, the obscene, and the obsessive.

Newgroups are a great place to see information about new technology, new resources, and events, just like a traditional bulletin board. You can offer and find jobs. You can get the news. You can find people talking about your favorite hobbies from around the world and share tips and tricks. You can find the perverse and the religious.

CPAs and financial managers need to keep up with information relating to accounting, computers and the Internet, as well as general news and personal interests. Here is a list of the more serious groups, which may be worth reviewing regularly.

Practice
 misc.taxes

 misc.taxes.moderated

 soc.org.nonprofit

Computers—Accounting Software/Systems
 alt.computer.consultants

 bit.listserv.edi-I

 biz.comp.accounting

 comp.os.ms-windows.apps.financial

 misc.business.records-mgmt

Consulting
 misc.business.consulting

 sci.engr.manufacturing

FinanceNet has its own newsgroups that offer instructions for using its news server as shown in Exhibit 2.4. They also offer tools for finding the information in their archives as shown in Exhibit 2.5.

Examples of newsgroups available include the following. Moderated newsgroups are specified in text. An asterisk indicates a hierarchy under which are other hierarchies and groups.

 gov.org—Organizations related to international government/public activities

 gov.org.admin—Organizations related to government administration

 gov.org.admin.financenet—FinanceNet information on public financial management (moderated)

 gov.org.g7—G7 group of nations

 gov.org.g7.announce—Announcements on G7 activities (moderated)

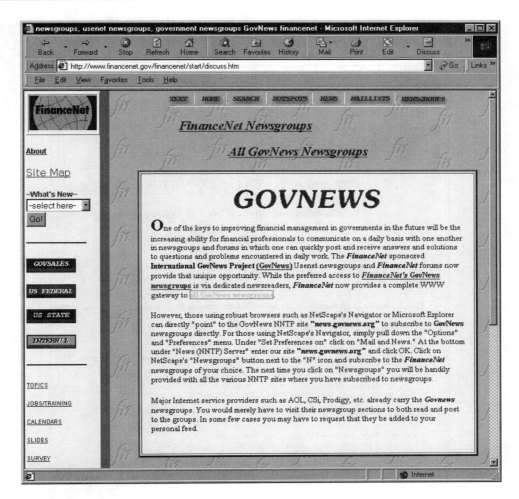

Exhibit 2.4 FinanceNet news server instructions.

gov.org.g7.environment—G7 Environment and Natural Resources Project (moderated)

gov.org.g7.misc—General G7-related discussions (moderated)

gov.topic—Topics of international interest

gov.topic.admin—Government administration, management

gov.topic.admin.finance—Financial management within government

gov.topic.admin.finance.accounting—Public accounting (moderated)

gov.topic.admin.finance.asset-liab-mgt—Asset-liability management (moderated)

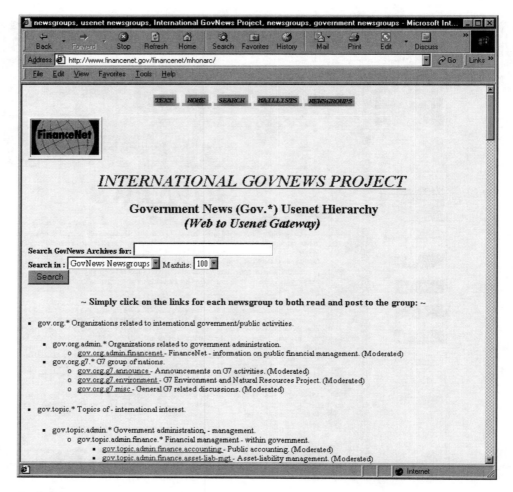

Exhibit 2.5   FinanceNet search engine for its archives.

gov.topic.admin.finance.audits—Financial audits of government agencies (moderated)

gov.topic.admin.finance.budgeting—Appropriations and budgeting management (moderated)

gov.topic.admin.finance.calendar—Calendar of public finance events (moderated)

gov.topic.admin.finance.int-controls—Internal financial controls (moderated) gov.topic.admin.finance.legislation—Discussions of public finance legislation (moderated)

gov.topic.admin.finance.local—Local financial issues (moderated)

gov.topic.admin.finance.misc—General public finance topics (moderated)

gov.topic.admin.finance.municipalities—Municipal financial issues (moderated)

gov.topic.admin.finance.news—General government finance news (moderated)

gov.topic.admin.finance.operations—Government financial management operations (moderated)

gov.topic.admin.finance.payroll—Government payroll issues (moderated)

gov.topic.admin.finance.perf-measures—Financial performance measures (moderated)

gov.topic.admin.finance.policy—Government financial policy (moderated)

gov.topic.admin.finance.procurement—Procurement management (moderated)

gov.topic.admin.finance.reporting—Financial statements and reporting (moderated)

gov.topic.admin.finance.state-county—State and county financial issues (moderated)

gov.topic.admin.finance.systems—Financial software and hardware systems (moderated)

gov.topic.admin.finance.training—Financial personnel and training (moderated)

gov.topic.admin.finance.travel-admin—Travel administration (moderated)

gov.topic.admin.privatization—Privatization of government, public/private partnerships (moderated)

gov.topic.finance—Topics related to money and the financial system

gov.topic.finance.banks—Banking, monetary supply, currency exchange (moderated)

gov.topic.finance.securities—Securities, commodity futures, etc. (moderated)

gov.topic.forsale—Sales of government equipment/property/assets

gov.topic.forsale.misc—Miscellaneous government asset sales (moderated)

gov.topic.info—Information, information—policy, systems, libraries

gov.topic.info.systems.epub—Government use of electronic publishing (moderated) gov.topic.info.systems.year2000—Accommodating dates after the year 2000

gov.topic.telecom—Telecommunications: telephone, radio, TV, Internet

gov.topic.telecom.announce—Telecommunications-related announcements (moderated)

gov.topic.telecom.misc—Telecommunications: telephone, radio, TV, Internet (moderated)

gov.topic.transport—Transportation and shipping

gov.topic.transport.air—Aviation, aircraft, travel by air (moderated)

gov.topic.transport.misc—General international transportation (moderated)

gov.topic.transport.navigation—Navigation systems (moderated)

gov.topic.transport.rail—Railroad transportation (moderated)

gov.topic.transport.road—Transportation over roads, auto safety, mass transit (moderated)

gov.topic.transport.shipping—International shipping and package delivery (moderated)

gov.topic.transport.water—Maritime-related issues, transportation over water (moderated)

gov.us—U.S. national hierarchy

gov.us.fed—U.S. federal government

gov.us.fed.cia.announce—Central Intelligence Agency announcements (moderated)

gov.us.fed.congress—U.S. Congress and legislative branch agencies

gov.us.fed.congress.announce—Announcements about Congress (moderated)

gov.us.fed.congress.bills.house—Bill text from the House (moderated)

gov.us.fed.congress.bills.senate—Bill text from the Senate (moderated)

gov.us.fed.congress.calendar.house—House calendar of activities (moderated)

gov.us.fed.congress.calendar.senate—Senate calendar of activities (moderated)

gov.us.fed.congress.discuss—Follow-up discussions on Congress (moderated)

gov.us.fed.congress.documents—Congressional documents

gov.us.fed.congress.gao—Government Accounting Office

gov.us.fed.congress.gao.announce—Announcements about the Government Accounting Office (moderated) gov.us.fed.congress.gao.decisions—Decisions from the comptroller general (moderated)

gov.us.fed.congress.gao.discuss—Discussion on the Government Accounting Office (moderated)

gov.us.fed.congress.gao.reports—Reports from the Government Accounting Office (moderated)

gov.us.fed.congress.record—*Congressional Record*

gov.us.fed.congress.record.digest—Digest from the *Congressional Record* (moderated)

gov.us.fed.congress.record.extensions—Extension of remarks in the *Congressional Record* (moderated)

gov.us.fed.congress.record.house—House pages from the *Congressional Record* (moderated)

gov.us.fed.congress.record.index—Index to the *Congressional Record* (moderated)

gov.us.fed.congress.record.senate—Senate pages from the *Congressional Record* (moderated)

gov.us.fed.congress.reports—Congressional reports

gov.us.fed.courts—U.S. Federal Courts

gov.us.fed.courts.announce—U.S. Courts announcements (moderated)

gov.us.fed.dhhs—U.S. Department of Health and Human Services

gov.us.fed.dhhs.announce—Department of Health and Human Services announcements (moderated)

gov.us.fed.dhhs.fda.announce—Food and Drug Administration announcements (moderated)

gov.us.fed.dhhs.ssa.announce—Social Security Administration announcements (moderated)

gov.us.fed.doc—U.S. Department of Commerce

gov.us.fed.doc.announce—Department of Commerce announcements (moderated)

gov.us.fed.doc.cbd—*Commerce Business Daily*

gov.us.fed.doc.cbd.awards—Contract awards in *Commerce Business Daily* (moderated)

gov.us.fed.doc.cbd.forsale—Surplus property sales in *Commerce Business Daily* (moderated)

gov.us.fed.doc.cbd.notices—General notices in *Commerce Business Daily* (moderated) gov.us.fed.doc.cbd.standards—Foreign standards notices in *Commerce Business Daily* (moderated)

gov.us.fed.doc.census.announce—Census Bureau announcements (moderated)

gov.us.fed.doc.noaa.announce—National Oceanic and Atmospheric Administration announcements (moderated)

gov.us.fed.dod—U.S. Department of Defense

gov.us.fed.dod.announce—Department of Defense announcements (moderated)

gov.us.fed.dod.army.announce—Department of the Army announcements (moderated)

gov.us.fed.dod.army.reserve—Department of the Army Reserve (moderated)

gov.us.fed.dod.navy.announce—Department of the Navy announcements (moderated)

gov.us.fed.dod.usaf.announce—Department of the Air Force announcements (moderated)

gov.us.fed.doe.announce—Department of Energy announcements (moderated)

gov.us.fed.doi.announce—Department of the Interior announcements (moderated)

gov.us.fed.doj.announce—Department of Justice announcements (moderated)

gov.us.fed.dol.announce—Department of Labor announcements (moderated)

gov.us.fed.dot—U.S. Department of Transportation

gov.us.fed.dot.announce—Department of Transportation announcements (moderated)

gov.us.fed.dot.faa.announce—Federal Aviation Administration announcements (moderated)

gov.us.fed.dot.nhtsa.announce—National Highway Traffic Safety Administration announcements (moderated)

gov.us.fed.dot.uscg.announce—U.S. Coast Guard announcements (moderated)

gov.us.fed.ed.announce—Department of Education announcements (moderated)

gov.us.fed.eop—Executive Office of the President of the United States gov.us.fed.eop.announce—Executive Office of the President announcements (moderated)

gov.us.fed.eop.white-house.announce—President and White House staff announcements (moderated)

gov.us.fed.epa.announce—Environmental Protection Agency announcements (moderated)

gov.us.fed.fcc.announce—Federal Communications Commission announcements (moderated)

gov.us.fed.fdic.announce—Federal Deposit Insurance Corporation announcements (moderated)

gov.us.fed.fema.announce—Federal Emergency Management Agency announcements (moderated)

gov.us.fed.ferc.announce—Federal Energy Regulatory Commission announcements (moderated)

gov.us.fed.fmc.announce—Federal Maritime Commission announcements (moderated)

gov.us.fed.frs.announce—Federal Reserve System announcements (moderated)

gov.us.fed.gsa.announce—General Services Administration announcements (moderated)

gov.us.fed.hud.announce—Department of Housing and Urban Development announcements (moderated)

gov.us.fed.nara—U.S. National Archives and Records Administration

gov.us.fed.nara.announce—National Archives and Records Administration announcements (moderated)

gov.us.fed.nara.fed-register—*Federal Register*

gov.us.fed.nara.fed-register.announce—Announcements about the *Federal Register* (moderated)

gov.us.fed.nara.fed-register.authoring—Discussion for *Federal Register* authors (moderated)

gov.us.fed.nara.fed-register.contents—Contents and indexes of the *Federal Register* (moderated)

gov.us.fed.nara.fed-register.corrections—Corrections to the *Federal Register* (moderated)

gov.us.fed.nara.fed-register.presidential—Presidential documents in the *Federal Register* (moderated) gov.us.fed.nara.fed-register.proposed-rules—Proposed regulations for the *Federal Register* (moderated)

gov.us.fed.nara.fed-register.rules—Rules and regulations for the *Federal Register* (moderated)

gov.us.fed.nasa.announce—National Aeronautics and Space Administration announcements (moderated)

gov.us.fed.nasa.ksc.announce—NASA Kennedy Space Center specific announcements (moderated)

gov.us.fed.nrc.announce—Nuclear Regulatory Commission announcements (moderated)

gov.us.fed.nsf.announce—National Science Foundation announcements (moderated)

gov.us.fed.nsf.documents—National Science Foundation documents (moderated)

gov.us.fed.nsf.grants—National Science Foundation grant information (moderated)

gov.us.fed.opm.announce—Office of Personnel Management announcements (moderated)

gov.us.fed.sba.announce—Small Business Administration announcements (moderated)

gov.us.fed.sec.announce—Securities and Exchange Commission announcements (moderated)

gov.us.fed.state.announce—Department of State announcements (moderated)

gov.us.fed.treasury.announce—Department of the Treasury announcements (moderated)

gov.us.fed.treasury.irs.announce—Internal Revenue Service announcements (moderated)

gov.us.fed.usaid.announce—U.S. Agency for International Development (moderated)

gov.us.fed.usaid.pib—USAID Procurement Information Bulletin (moderated)

gov.us.fed.usda.announce—Department of Agriculture announcements (moderated)

gov.us.fed.va.announce—Department of Veterans Affairs announcements (moderated)

gov.us.org—Organizations related to U.S. government/public activities gov.us.org.admin—Organizations related to government administration

gov.us.org.admin.aga—Association of Government Accountants (moderated)

gov.us.org.admin.fasab—Federal Accounting Standards Advisory Board (moderated)

gov.us.org.admin.gfoa—Government Finance Officers Association (moderated)

gov.us.org.info—Organizations in government/public information

gov.us.org.info.ace—Americans Communicating Electronically (moderated)

gov.us.org.info.ala—American Library Association (moderated)

gov.us.topic—Topics of U.S. national interest

gov.us.topic.agri—Topics in agriculture

gov.us.topic.agri.farms—Farming: growing crops, raising livestock (moderated)

gov.us.topic.agri.food—Food production and distribution, food nutrition. (moderated)

gov.us.topic.agri.misc—General agricultural issues (moderated)

gov.us.topic.agri.statistics—Detailed statistics on crops, livestock, and food production (moderated)

gov.us.topic.ecommerce—Electronic commerce/services with government

gov.us.topic.ecommerce.announce—Government electronic commerce infrastructure announcements (moderated)

gov.us.topic.ecommerce.misc—Discussions concerning government electronic commerce (moderated)

gov.us.topic.ecommerce.standards—Standards for government electronic commerce (moderated)

gov.us.topic.emergency—Natural disasters, recovery, prevention

gov.us.topic.emergency.alerts—Important bulletins for immediate broadcasting (moderated)

gov.us.topic.emergency.misc—Natural disasters, recovery, prevention (moderated)

gov.us.topic.energy—Generation and delivery of energy

gov.us.topic.energy.misc—Generation and delivery of energy (moderated)

gov.us.topic.energy.nuclear—Nuclear power and radioactive materials (moderated) gov.us.topic.energy.utilities—Regulated utilities providing gas and electricity (moderated)

gov.us.topic.environment—Topics related to environmental protection.

gov.us.topic.environment.air—Air quality, ozone, greenhouse gases, noise (moderated)

gov.us.topic.environment.announce—Announcements on environmental protection (moderated)

gov.us.topic.environment.misc—General environmental protection (moderated)

gov.us.topic.environment.toxics—Hazardous material use, disposal, cleanup (moderated)

gov.us.topic.environment.waste—Waste disposal, recycling (moderated)

gov.us.topic.environment.water—Water issues: drinking, irrigation, sewage (moderated)

gov.us.topic.finance—Topics related to money and the financial system

gov.us.topic.finance.banks—Banking, monetary supply, currency exchange (moderated)

gov.us.topic.finance.securities—Securities, commodity futures, etc. (moderated)

gov.us.topic.foreign—Topics on foreign relations, trade

gov.us.topic.foreign.news—Selected news media reports from outside the United States (moderated)

gov.us.topic.foreign.trade—Issues involving foreign trade, importation, customs (moderated)

gov.us.topic.foreign.trade.leads—Information on trade opportunities collected by U.S. governments (moderated)

gov.us.topic.foreign.trade.misc—Issues involving foreign trade, importation, customs (moderated)

gov.us.topic.foreign.trade.statistics—detailed statistical reports on import/exports (moderated)

gov.us.topic.gov-jobs—Topics on employment within government

gov.us.topic.gov-jobs.employee.issues—Discussions on government employee issues (moderated)

gov.us.topic.gov-jobs.employee.news—News of interest to government employees (moderated)

gov.us.topic.gov-jobs.hr-admin—Human Resources administration (moderated) gov.us.topic.gov-jobs.offered—Announcements of new job offers

gov.us.topic.gov-jobs.offered.admin—Administrative job opportunities in government (moderated)

gov.us.topic.gov-jobs.offered.admin.finance—Jobs in public financial management (moderated)

gov.us.topic.gov-jobs.offered.admin.ses—Senior Executive Service job opportunity (moderated)

gov.us.topic.gov-jobs.offered.announce—Announcements on job hunting in government (moderated)

gov.us.topic.gov-jobs.offered.clerical—Clerical job opportunities in government (moderated)

gov.us.topic.gov-jobs.offered.engineering—Engineering-related job opportunities in government (moderated)

gov.us.topic.gov-jobs.offered.foreign—Federal job opportunities located outside the United States (moderated)

gov.us.topic.gov-jobs.offered.health—Medical and health-related job opportunities in government (moderated)

gov.us.topic.gov-jobs.offered.law-enforce—Law enforcement job opportunities in government (moderated)

gov.us.topic.gov-jobs.offered.math-comp—Math- and computer-related job opportunities in government (moderated)

gov.us.topic.gov-jobs.offered.misc—Unclassified public sector job opportunities (moderated)

gov.us.topic.gov-jobs.offered.questions—Questions and answers on job hunting in government (moderated)

gov.us.topic.gov-jobs.offered.science—Physical sciences job opportunities in government (moderated)

gov.us.topic.gov-jobs.offered.technical—Technical job opportunities in government (moderated)

gov.us.topic.grants—Grant opportunities

gov.us.topic.grants.research—Grant opportunities for research (moderated)

gov.us.topic.info—Information, information—policy, systems, libraries

gov.us.topic.info.abstracts—Abstracts of new publications

gov.us.topic.info.abstracts.cdrom—Abstracts of new CD-ROM releases (moderated)

gov.us.topic.info.abstracts.epub—Abstracts of new publications available electronically (moderated) gov.us.topic.info.abstracts.infosystems—Abstracts of new on-line systems and services (moderated)

gov.us.topic.info.abstracts.print—Abstracts of new publications available in hard copy (moderated)

gov.us.topic.info.libraries.govdocs—Government documents libraries (moderated)

gov.us.topic.info.libraries.technology—Library information technology discussion (moderated)

gov.us.topic.info.policy.announce—Announcements on government information policy (moderated)

gov.us.topic.info.policy.misc—Discussions on government information policy (moderated)

gov.us.topic.law—Topics on law and the legal system

gov.us.topic.law.pub-contract—Lawyers discuss federal public contract law (moderated)

gov.us.topic.nat-resources—Natural resources

gov.us.topic.nat-resources.forests—Forestry, logging, and wood production (moderated)

gov.us.topic.nat-resources.land—Other uses of public land, such as grazing, wetlands, watershed (moderated)

gov.us.topic.nat-resources.marine—Fishing, aquaculture, marine sanctuaries (moderated)

gov.us.topic.nat-resources.minerals—Extraction and transportation of minerals (moderated)

gov.us.topic.nat-resources.oil-gas—Extraction and transportation of oil and gas (moderated)

gov.us.topic.nat-resources.parks—Public land for recreation and tourism, museums (moderated)

gov.us.topic.nat-resources.wildlife—Wildlife management, hunting (moderated)

gov.us.topic.statistics.announce—Brief announcements on economic and demographic statistics (moderated)

gov.us.topic.statistics.reports—Detailed reports on economic and demographic statistics (moderated)

gov.us.topic.telecom—Telecommunications: telephone, radio, TV, Internet

gov.us.topic.telecom.announce—Announcements on general telecommunications policy issues (moderated) gov.us.topic.telecom.misc—Discussion on general telecom policy issues (moderated)

gov.us.topic.transport—Transportation and shipping.

gov.us.topic.transport.air—Aviation, aircraft, travel by air (moderated)

gov.us.topic.transport.misc—General transportation in the United States (moderated)

gov.us.topic.transport.rail—Railroad transportation (moderated)

gov.us.topic.transport.road—Transportation over roads, auto safety, mass transit (moderated)

gov.us.topic.transport.shipping—International shipping and package delivery (moderated)

gov.us.topic.transport.water—Maritime-related issues, transportation over water (moderated)

gov.us.usenet—Topics about the U.S. government usenet news system

gov.us.usenet.admin—Discussion of gov.us news administration

gov.us.usenet.announce—Administration announcements (moderated)

gov.us.usenet.answers—FAQs and periodic articles (moderated)

gov.us.usenet.control—Control messages for U.S. government newsgroup changes (moderated)

gov.us.usenet.groups—Discussion of gov.us management

gov.us.usenet.lists—News-related statistics and lists (moderated)

gov.us.usenet.questions—Questions and answers for users new to gov.us newsgroups

gov.us.usenet.software—Discussion of gov.us-specific software

gov.us.usenet.test—Use in testing news software setups

gov.usenet—Topics about the international government usenet news system

gov.usenet.admin—Discussion of government news administration

gov.usenet.announce—Administrative announcements (moderated)

gov.usenet.answers—FAQs and periodic articles (moderated)

gov.usenet.control—Control messages for top government newsgroup changes (moderated)

gov.usenet.groups—Discussion of government hierarchy management

gov.usenet.lists—News-related statistics and lists (moderated)

gov.usenet.questions—Questions and answers for users new to government newsgroups gov.usenet.software—Discussion of government news specific software

gov.usenet.test—Use in testing news software setups

Using Newsgroups

Newsgroups seem to have much in common with mailing lists. There are tens of thousands of topics on moderated and unmoderated groups. With mailing lists, you subscribe to the list, and group contributions wind up in your mailbox. With newsgroups, you subscribe in a different way: You are telling your software to make it easy for your to review the groups you are interested in and to keep track of the last message in each group that you have read. Unlike a mailing list, you must start up your news software to read the postings in the groups you choose; with a mailing list, the postings are delivered to your e-mail automatically.

Let's say you are interested in the five-string banjo (alt.banjo), the "old-timey" method of playing the five-string banjo (alt.banjo.clawhammer), or any other topic. With the right software, and if your Internet Service Provider subscribes to that group, you will find a newsgroup on which people have started topics of discussion, responded to others about the matter, and written back and forth until there was no more to say. The discussions are not real time. You go to the newsgroup, read the messages that have been left there, and then respond, either adding to the responses there or by sending a message back to someone who left a message on the group. To find a newsgroup by word or topic, you may want to use <http://www.liszt.com/>, which is a search enquire for mail lists and news groups.

Some packages (like Microsoft's Internet News) help you identify the groups you are interested in by letting you type in part of the topic in which you have interest, such as "account" or "star trek", and then narrowing down the 15,000-item list to those containing the text you have entered, for you to select for subscription. From that point, you tell the software to bring down the headers (the name of the subscriber, the subject, the date and size, as well as if it is part of a series of discussions—a thread—or stands on its own). Then you can select a message or thread, and the software will display the message.

Often the messages are at the end of a very old topic and have completely diverged from the original topic, like a bad case of the game of telephone. However, if it is pertinent, you can choose to add your thoughts to the thread or reply directly back to a sender. This often leads to flames: When people are so incensed by what someone said or did, they respond back, often violently, to tell the sender how wrong he or she was. This happens most often when someone not fully aware of the social rules in a newsgroup violates them, asks a question handled in the groups FAQs (frequently asked questions archive), or commits some other infraction of the unwritten and written laws.

Many newsgroups have been around well before America Online and other services provided access and were developed for a particular reason. Then the computer newbies came in and started causing problems. One group, for example, was set up for the sole purpose of discussing UNIX's X-windows, but people who had problems with Microsoft Windows started making postings. Another group is for records management (as in accounting) but was flooded with questions related to the round 33-rpm kind. Jokesters with nothing better to do than bother each other crowd out discussions on accounting issues.

Finding Information in Newsgroups

With more than 30,000 groups, there is no way to read every message in every group. Fortunately, there are tools to sift through the listings. One pundit has said that the entire collection of human knowledge is transferred over newsgroups every four days (especially if your world revolves around *Star Trek*). Others say that humans use only 10 percent of their brains, and with some of us that is more obvious than others.

Few Internet Service Providers are willing to dedicate the hard disk space to archive more than a few weeks of these postings. Some services maintain posting archives for months or longer, in particular Deja (http://www. deja.com) and RemarQ (http://www.remarq.com). Both services make it easy to read and contribute to newsgroups without having to learn the special software needed to access newsgroup submissions.

The Reference.com site (http://www.reference.com) is a powerful clipping service that scours newsgroup messages each day and sends abstracts of contributions that match search requirements. Unfortunately, the service has been down for a long time, and whether it will be active when you read this is open to question. Other newsgroups scanning services include TracerLock (http://www.peacefire.org/tracerlock) and The Informant (http://www.informant.dartmouth. edu).

Software

A newsreader is incorporated into Netscape Composer for Windows, and Microsoft integrates news software into Outlook and Outlook Express. Windows users also can use Forte, Chameleon, and Trumpet News Reader; Macintosh users can use Newswatcher. There are some standard newsgroup-reading software packages for dial-up Unix accounts, in particular nn (network news) or trn (tiny reader for news).

Newsreaders let you choose the groups to be presented each time (subscribe) as well as select groups that are of interest to you only sporadically, so you must identify them specifically. With subscribed groups, your software keeps track of the last messages you read, making it easier to pick up where you left off.

Net Etiquette (Netiquette)

An important part of getting along with others on the Internet is understanding the culture and ways of those who have been using the Internet for a while. The regular denizens of the group enforce these rules, known as net etiquette (or netiquette) often fiercely.

Some of these rules:

- Do read the list of frequently asked questions (FAQs) before posting messages.
- Do read a few days' worth of messages before contributing. Reading but not participating, also known as *lurking*, sounds like spying but is expected and appreciated.
- Do consider whether it is more appropriate to respond to someone directly instead of to everyone on the group.
- Do not write messages all in uppercase.
- Make sure your message is appropriate to the group.
- Do not send a message to multiple groups unless appropriate.
- Do not directly solicit business unless that is the purpose of the group.
- Be careful before you act defensively, insult someone, or call him or her names.
- Be careful before you respond to someone who seems to clearly be off point or off the wall. The person may be doing it on purpose to be controversial.

FTP

Introduction to FTP

If you want to be able to access a huge storehouse of programs, fixes, and updates, find graphics and clip art for your Web and desktop publishing projects, and most important transfer files back and forth between computers (necessary for publishing your own Web pages), you will want and need FTP.

FTP stands for file transfer protocol. It is the oldest (1971), quickest, and cleanest way to copy files between computers on the Internet. Newer tools have begun to eat at FTP's popularity, but it probably will be around for a while.

FTP is used for transferring information between two sites. For example, if you have accounts on two systems, you may use FTP for tasks like uploading HTML documents for your home page or transferring documents for mailing and collaboration.

Unfortunately, FTP requires more basic computer knowledge than almost any other Internet task because users need to know how to find their way around a computer. In an environment like the Internet, where computers sharing information seems to happen so easily, FTP seems anachronistic. It requires a bit of knowledge about computers, like the difference between text and binary files, how to navigate around the file structure of Unix and DOS computers, and the limitations of file names in various systems.

When challenged with a vendor's claims that software was so easy "Even your mother can use it!" *Wall Street Journal* reporters took up the claim. The reporters and their mothers met with the developers. One major roadblock for the mothers was their computers' subdirectory structure. Where was that file, anyway? The software did not live up to its claims.

For the average Web user, getting files from other computers and bringing them to their computer is fairly intuitive: Whenever you run around the Web, you will see attractive graphics saying "Click here to download the latest version of the software." Often you will be presented with a list, highlight an item on it, and respond to a dialogue box telling where to put the file on your own computer. For example, when you go to Microsoft to pick up the latest version of their Internet Browser or use the IRS Web site to download forms, you are using FTP but are guarded from its complexities. The hardest part is figuring out where the software deposited the file in your own machine and what to do with it.

This relative ease of use hides the fact that these transfers are using FTP. These transfers happened so easily because other people made decisions on your behalf. FTP lets you get at files that cannot be accessed through carefully cataloged Web pages. In addition, this easy FTP is one-way only—from the host computer to your own (unless you count sending e-mail and attachments as uploads). The only way you can get files from your computer to a host is through FTP. If your only goal is to surf around the Web and collect a few graphics, the complexities of FTP are not worth your time. If, on the other hand, you may need to update your business's Web page on your ISP's computer, FTP is vital. The on-line services have tried to get around the complexity of FTP by automating the process of uploading your files to your Web site, but this method is limited.

Using FTP

Logging In.   The first step in using FTP is to log on to an FTP server. This may be a server that offers public access or one on which you have an account.

Public access servers offer *anonymous FTP,* where "anonymous" is the login name you use to access remote computers. (Your e-mail address is normally requested as the "password" for this public access login so the host sponsors can know who is using the service.) Popular FTP sites are often overcrowded, and attempts to log on as anonymous may be denied. The most popular FTP sites have *mirrors,* duplicates of their sites at less popular sites.

When you update your own Web site, you will need to log on to your host computer.

The Internet address you use to contact an FTP site is sometimes the name of the main site itself (http://uhura.cc.rochester.edu), or sometimes a special address (most often beginning with the prefix "FTP") is established, such as <FTP.microsoft.com>. If you are starting FTP from a command line, typing "ftp ftp.microsoft.com" may seem strange, but you must separate the command "FTP" from the name of the site that starts with "FTP" to distinguish it from other resources. Within a Web browser, you would type <ftp://ftp.microsoft.com>. Here ftp:// is the protocol, and ftp.microsoft.com is the computer name.

Once you have established an FTP connection, your software will probably display both your file system and the remote computer's. There is one big hitch—you can use a limited number of commands while in FTP mode, and they are not the same ones you normally use. FTP is set up to let users move around and transfer files, not manipulate them.

Finding Your Way Around.   Although Macs and Windows PCs have file managers that make sorting through files and moving them around easy, Unix is a very difficult environment to work in. (See the Unix cheat sheet at the end of this chapter.) A graphical tool like the shareware FTP client ws_FTP lets you move around Unix and other file systems more easily, limit the files to the ones you want (such as only the files annotated as text files, with the .TXT extension), and view text files, such as indexes of directory contents or README files describing what different files represent. See Exhibit 2.6. Once you select the files you want to transfer individually or in groups, you can copy them back and forth with a keystroke.

Along with the commands to tell the computer what type of file you are working with (binary or text) and instruct it to send or retrieve files, there are a few other commands to move around the Unix file structure, change the type of reporting on the screen as activity takes place, and get into and

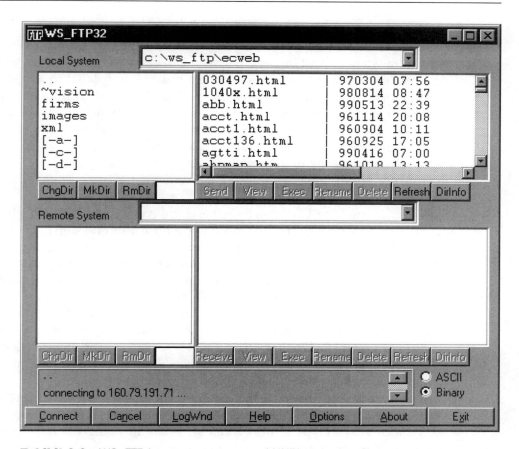

Exhibit 2.6 WS_FTP lets you move around UNIX and other file systems more easily. Copyright 1999 Netscape Communications Corporation. All rights reserved.

out of a site or the FTP program. (See the FTP commands at the end of this chapter.)

Transferring files. If you set up a Web site on an off-site computer, you will need a way to transfer the files from your computer to the other site. The files you need includes the text file that is the foundation of your pages (the HTML coding, most often with the extension HTM from DOS or Windows computers and HTML from Unix computers). There also are the binary files: any graphics (.GIF, .JPG), sounds (.AU, .WAV, .RA), video (.QT, .MOV, .AVI, .MPG), and whatever other files you will have available for download from your site. Sometimes you will offer files for users to download, most often in a compressed form (.ZIP, .EXE) to speed the transfer from the host to the end user.

Note that binary files must be transferred in binary mode, so no changes are made in the file between computers; for text (ASCII) files, on the other hand, a translation must be done between Unix and DOS computers, as they terminate each line of text differently. Text must be translated to appear correctly in text editors and word processors. Transfers for text and binary must be done separately, and the computer must be told which mode, binary or text, to do the transfer in. HTML code should be transferred in text mode, whereas graphics and other multimedia should be transferred in binary mode. The commands to get one (get) or multiple files (mget) and upload one (put) or multiple files (mput) are not difficult and are hidden by the use of ws_FTP.

If you are running FTP from a shell account (your computer is not directly attached to the Internet), you may need to perform a second step to get the file you just FTP'd from the remote computer. It is probably now sitting on the host computer. Therefore, you need to transfer it from the host computer to your local PC using the telecommunications program's file transfer capabilities. One of the most popular methods of transferring files from a host to a terminal is using Zmodem. On a Unix computer, the Zmodem transfer is begun by typing "sz filename", where filename is the name of the file you wish to send to your own PC. Once again, the binary/ASCII issue comes to play: You would type "sz -a filename" to transfer an ASCII file using Zmodem. Other options include sb (Ymodem), sx (Xmodem), and kermit -s (kermit).

If you are dialing into a shell account, you are using a terminal emulation software package, not a Web browser. Some terminal emulation programs, like Windows 95's Hyperterminal, can sense an incoming file transfer automatically. Other programs make you tell your PC that it should prepare for an incoming file (often pressing the "Page Down" key).

Favorite sites

A number of sites have large collections of shareware and other files available at no cost. These include

CICA: FTP.cica.indiana.edu

Walnut Creek FTP: FTP.cdrom.com

Washington University at St. Louis: wuarchive.wustl.edu

Software

ws_FTP, a shareware FTP client from lpswitch, Inc., is considered one of the best packages. An FTP client is included with most Internet software. Sometimes you can use a Windows File Manager—like interface to move around directory structures, select one or multiple files, and move those files between your local workstation and the remote computer. Sometimes you will be using the more stark command-line approach. Netscape Navigator version 3.0 and later lets you drag and drop files to an FTP server, a little-known feature of the browser.

Basic FTP Commands for Command-line Use

Pwd	Print working directory—"where am I?" (Unix)
Ls	List of directory contents—names only (Unix)
Dir	List of directory contents with details (FTP only)
cd	Change directory
(a)scii	Instructions to prepare for an ASCII transfer
(b)inary	Instructions to prepare for a binary transfer
get	Get a single file
mget	Get multiple files
put	Send a file to the remote computer (from your computer)
mput	Send multiple files to the remote computer
quit	End the FTP session

Unix Cheat Sheet for DOS Users

	DOS	*UNIX*
Copy files	copy	cp
Rename files	ren	mv
Delete files	del	rm
List files	dir	is
Type file (list to screen)	type	cat
Separator	\	/
Go to Eric's directory	cd\Eric	cd/Eric
What directory am I in?	cd	pwd

LIVE CHAT

Instant Messenger

Wouldn't it be great to know if your coworkers, friends, and associates are on-line and be able to send them a message instantly if you needed—

or wanted—to? That idea is behind the America Online Buddy list, which is also freely available to anyone and included in the latest versions of Netscape Communicator. Instant Messenger lets you set up the people you want to keep in contact with, as shown in Exhibit 2.7. When they are on-line, it lets you know . . . and makes it easy to send and receive quick messages.

For many businesses and organizations, this has been a powerful tool. You can instantly contact the people you need to come up with background information for a call you are on; a secretary can convey important information to the boss wherever the boss may be; groups can coordinate without the chaos of international Relay Chat (see below).

It also means that you can be checking your e-mail, minding your own business, when Mom, or Aunt Sue, or some chatty friend decides it is time to bring you into an extended conversation—another example of time-wasters run amok.

Exhibit 2.7 Instant Messenger lets you identify the people you want to keep in contact with.

NetMeeting

You can talk and videoconference. You can share a whiteboard for drawings, a chat window for quick typing, send files back and forth, and collaborate with shared applications. The software is free and has powered away the competition. Microsoft NetMeeting is free and permits virtual meetings. (See Exhibit 2.8.)

IRC (International Relay Chat)

It is three in the morning, and you decide to catch up on some research, but something is wrong with new software you set up. Where can you find someone to help you right away? Welcome to International Relay Chat (IRC), a gathering spot for discussions on any topic at any time.

IRC is a real-time conferencing tool where you type messages to a single person or a group. They can respond in real time as well. IRC is inexpensive, spontaneous, and often bawdy or a waste of time, like shouting "Who wants to buy a used car?" in a crowded theater. It was instrumental in the 1993 Per-

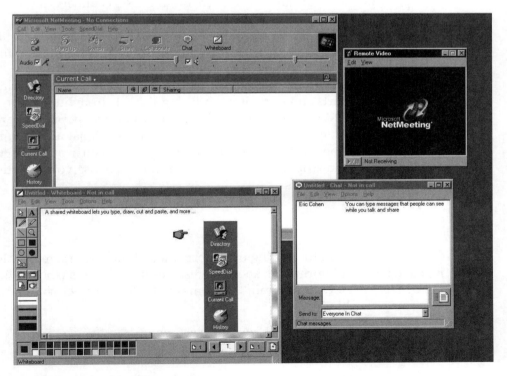

Exhibit 2.8 Microsoft NetMeeting is free and permits virtual meetings.

sian Gulf War and the Russian coup and is purportedly used by the militia groups in the U.S. Users are identified by screen names of their choice; someone going by the name "bgates" is as likely to be Englebert Humperdink as he is to be Bill Gates.

IRC has made the news repeatedly with sad stories. The media can be addictive. Families are being torn apart by a husband or wife who meets the mate of their dreams. Others fall for con artists out to fool a lonely visitor into parting with their money.

Various servers provide lists of IRC channels. They are topical, often very crude, and typically poorly managed. When you connect to an IRC server with your IRC software, you will find hundreds or thousands of channels, which are similar to forums, rooms, or topics. There are channels for lifestyles, hobbies, languages, and areas of the world, TV shows, and support. Some are always there, with regulars who visit daily and visitors who wander through. Others are temporary, used for a teleconference or other informal meeting.

If you are looking for people interested in chatting real time on a topic, IRC is a far more mature technology than areas where people communicate using audio tools, like NetMeeting. IRC software has tools for finding groups by topic, category, and number of users on-line. IRC channels can offer communication in many different languages.

You can start new private groups for your own purposes and meetings or join groups already in progress. With a moderator, IRC can be useful for conferences and meetings. An unusual feature of IRC is the use of "bots," computer robotic responders that act as helpers or tormentors, responding like human counterparts and sometimes indistinguishable from humans.

Software for Windows includes Microsoft Chat and popular shareware packages irciiwin, winirc, ws_irc, and mIRC. Microsoft Chat adds fun to IRC by letting you choose a cartoon character to represent you as your discussion turns into a comic strip. (See Exhibit 2.9.) You can choose your emotions to better convey your points.

FINGER

Finger is a program for finding out information about a user; are they logged in; have they left information about themselves that displays when you finger them? Finger is a DOS program that comes with Windows 95; shareware versions are available.

WHOIS

Whois is a program that lets you query the InterNIC database to find out who has filed for domain names. WinWhois is a shareware program for this purpose.

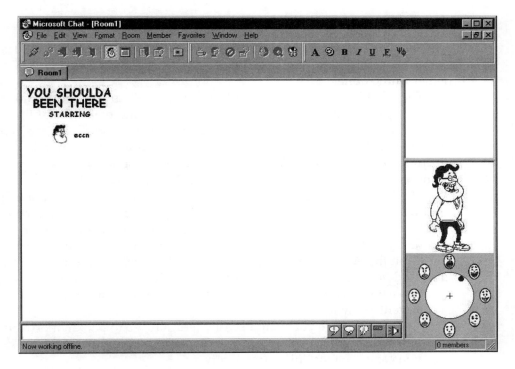

Exhibit 2.9 Microsoft Chat adds fun to IRC by letting you choose a cartoon character to represent yourself.

PING AND TRACE

Ping is a program used to see how long it takes for a packet of data to go from your computer to its destination. Trace is used to follow the path of data from your site to its destination, reporting on which networks it travels along the way. WSPing32 from Ipswitch, Inc., is an excellent tool that includes both Ping and Trace.

WORLD WIDE WEB

The hottest part of the Internet is the World Wide Web, made popular by graphical front-ends to the Web, Web browsers. These front-ends work only with a special kind of connection to the Internet, one where your computer is assigned an IP address by the service you call in to. The on-line services all offer this type of connection, although your computer may require some special setting changes if you accessed your on-line service before the Web software became available.

What It Is

The Web is client/server systems providing access to multimedia information across the Internet, through the use of services including Network News, FTP, telnet, and Gopher.

The World Wide Web (www, W3, or "the Web") is an effort to link all the various and dissimilar resources on the Internet into one "web" of interconnected information. Web documents are known as "pages" and may contain multimedia (graphics, photographs, sounds, video) as well as links to other documents, telnet sites, FTP sites, WAIS servers, gopher servers—almost any resource available on the Internet can be linked into the Web.

Moving around the Web is easy. *Search engines* are Web sites that help you find what you are looking for. Once you have found an interesting page, you look for underlined blue words, which typically are links to other Internet resources and Web sites. Even pictures and graphics can take you to other places on the Web when you click on them. If you click on something by accident and you want to stay where you are, you can hit the escape key, click on the stop icon on your browser, or use the "back" button to come back as if you never went anywhere.

If you find a page you want to easily return to, go to Bookmarks (Netscape) or Favorites (Internet Explorer) in your browser menu, click "Add Bookmark" and you can save that link permanently.

Its History

Tim Berners-Lee of CERN (the European Laboratory for Particle Physics in Geneva) is credited with developing the technical foundation of the Web, which first became operational in 1991.

MOSAIC, a graphical interface, started the graphical revolution. Web users no longer had to know Unix to find their way around the Internet.

Traffic on the Web has increased tremendously through the 1990s. In 1992 the traffic for the entire year was 500 megabytes. For the first quarter of 1993, it increased 10-fold over the entire prior year, to 5 gigabytes. In September 1994, three times that volume passed through the Web in a six-hour period.

America Online has recently purchased Netscape. The shining glory of the Internet, whose cast of characters brought us the Web browser, as we know it, succumbed to the pressures of Microsoft and its own admitted lack of innovation. Netscape was almost singly responsible for concept of "Internet time," where three months brought entirely new innovations and changes. Netscape did a spin-off of some of the development to the open development organization Mozilla.org before the acquisition. This move was meant to breathe new life into the browser; unfortunately, outside contributions have been few. What will we say about Netscape in 2001?

Important terms

The following three acronyms are used constantly in reference to the Web.

HTTP (Hypertext Transport Protocol)   These letters in front of an Internet listing mean that the service being offered is a Web site.

HTML (HyperText Markup Language)   HTML is the text that is sent from the server to the Web client that defines what will show on your screen. HTML consists of the basic text that appears on your screen as well as sets of tags, simple codes that tell the Web browser what to display and where.

HTML files do not appear exactly the same in different browsers. Some browsers do not have all features available and cannot display files that take advantage of those features. Even with the latest browsers, differences in default fonts can make pages look very different.

URL (Uniform Resource Locator)   The address of a Web site, most often consisting of the Web identifier <http://> followed by the computer's domain name on which the HTML is located and the name of the HTML file to bring up first.

For example, the URL of the author's Web page used to be http://www.servtech.com/re/acct.html. This translates to: A Web page (http://)

at the Service Tech commercial organization, whose computer offers web services (www.servtech.com)

in the "re" subdirectory (/re/) (that stood for "Rochester Everywhere," a daughter site for "Downtown Anywhere," a popular national mall)

and the HTML file called acct.html <acct.html>

Now it is http://www.computercpa.com

A Web page (http://)

Registered to some computer somewhere that has been registered to recognize ComputerCPA <www.computercpa.com>

in the default subdirectory and using the default startup file.

Web Compared to Gopher

Gopher (see below) had many features in common with the Web. It offered an easy-to-use, predesigned interface with hypertextlike links to get at other Internet resources.

Gopher and the Web are also very different.

- System administrators developed gopher menu systems. The Web lets anyone put their HTML code up, with hypertext links pointing anywhere the designer wants. Instead of system administrators selecting resources, anyone can set up a page of links and pointers to resources. Gopher menu items are there because of the administrators.

- Gopher search tools are limited to searching the so-called "gopherspace", made up of gopher menus; search tools on the Web do their best to transverse the widespread and chaotic Web.

- Gopher pages are simple menus; Web pages look like published documents and appear very different on different Web clients; sometimes they are unusable.

Browsers

To access the content of the Web, you need a Web browser. (See Chapter 4 for more information on browsers).

Text Browsers: lynx, www.   If you do not have an account that assigns an IP address to your computer, you are more limited in the multimedia you can experience on the Web. Many colleges and businesses still offer shell accounts (time-shared usage of their text-based systems) on Unix-based systems. For those of us with shell accounts, Lynx is a text-based browser that lets users gain much of the information (text and hyperlinks, with the capability to download the multimedia components) without the graphics. In 1995 the number of text-only browsers dropped from an estimated 80 percent of the marketplace to less than 20 percent. An earlier text-based browser, www, is still found on some sites; the links are chosen by number, instead of moving with the cursor keys and selecting hypertext links.

OTHER CLIENTS

Other Clients: Introduction

When telephone, television, radio, and computer all come together—sometimes called convergence—one tool will be all we need to know everything and be connected to everyone. For those willing to deal with the current weaknesses of groundbreaking offerings, Internet access already makes many of these capabilities available—but do not throw away your cellular phone, cancel your cable television, and give up on your newspaper subscription quite yet.

RealPlayer

Your Winsock connection to the Internet opens up some fantastic new capabilities. You can listen to radio stations live, access libraries of speeches, or catch the latest news and views using RealPlayer. RealPlayer (http://www. real.com) delivers streaming audio (you do not have to download the audio file to your computer before you listen to it—just enough at a time to listen to). You can develop customized radio broadcasts by finding the resources that make audio snippets available of newsmakers, music, speech, and archives of radio broadcasts. If you are far from home or want to listen to catch the flavor of another city, or want to hear a favorite sports team's game being broadcast, you can do it with RealPlayer.

Shockwave and Plug-ins

A number of features can be added to your Web browser with software called plug-ins. These are helper applications that work with Netscape Navigator. (At the time of this writing, Microsoft was adding the capability to Internet Explorer). They let you do tasks such as read Adobe Acrobat files (http://www.adobe.com), browse through virtual reality worlds, and work with multimedia more effectively, all without having to start a second program. One of the most popular add-ins is the ShockWave (http://www. macromedia.com). It lets you develop a multimedia slideshow, which requires less resources on the user's end than a video; the slide show is created with presentation graphics programs instead of a recording studio. You can then show that animated slide presentation on the Internet. Slide presentations require less bandwidth than streaming video, making transmission over a 28.8k connection more feasible; because the "brains" necessary to understand the instructions in the slide show are included in the plug-in to the browser, only the text and graphics need to be downloaded. There are no true standards in this area, and with all of the competing presentation graphics packages, you need a special plug-in for each tool. Competitors Macromedia, Asymetrix, Microsoft, and others are spicing up the information that can be portrayed on Web pages, both with enhancements for their graphics packages and with automation tools like Java, ActiveX, and others.

Push Isn't Dead: Excite@Home's Excite Assistant

This free software allows users to download customized content automatically from their My Excite portal start page to a desktop client. Users will be able to browse through stock quotes, sports scores, horoscopes, and other content without having a browser open or even being on-line.

The program notifies users when they have received Excite Mail. It also enables them to listen to over a dozen channels of audio content, using Real-Networks' RealAudio technology. The company plans to upgrade the product with features such as several new channels of audio. The 1.3-megabyte program downloads information in the background, much like an earlier push product, PointCast. The program is set up to conserve bandwidth. It stays out of the way when the user is browsing the Web or using e-mail, downloading information when the Web connection is idle. It's based on XML, by the way.

Faxing on the Internet

You can do everything else for free; why not send faxes on the Internet? Larger companies are using their sophisticated communications lines to send faxes within their organization and to the phone systems with which the communications lines are connected. With a little help from your friends, you can send faxes throughout the United States and into many foreign countries for free. More later on eFax.com, PeopleFax.com, and HotCorp.com's Swissclick.

WHAT'S NOT SO HOT ON THE INTERNET?

Where did they go? Some had great promise but never realized it. Others shouted their arrival but whispered their departure. Still others tried but failed. Others went out in a blazing departure.

Gopher

The Internet was difficult to use in the early 1990s. Some folks at the University of Minnesota thought, "Wouldn't it be great to come up with an easy-to-use tool that lets the user choose all the different Internet resources from an easy-to-use user interface?" The answer was . . . no, not the Web. The answer was . . . gopher. System administrators set up menu systems that could lead the user to text, graphics, file downloads—just like the Web. Those folks from Minnesota just lost this one. Good-bye, gopher.

Looking for information from the government or an educational institution? Instead of firing up your Web browser, you may want to spend a few minutes in gopherspace. Although gopherspace sounds like you took a wrong turn off the Information Superhighway and wound up in a corn field, it is actually the domain of information you can access using "gopher".

Gopher is a client/server, menu-driven, information location and retrieval tool to get at resources on the Internet. It offers hypertextlike links to resources that system administrators of gopher servers feel would be helpful to users.

Gopher originated at the University of Minnesota; no definition of it would be complete without a reference to the furry rodent that is the U of M's mascot.

Gopher is a *client/server* system. A gopher client sends requests to a gopher server to get the information from it. The system administrator determines what to offer you.

Gopher is a *menu-driven* system. These requests are made through the use of menus, where each menu item can lead to another menu, text, a database search, or one of the other Internet services. These menus and the information they link to are known as gopherspace.

Gopher was designed to make the Internet easy to use. Although gopher is losing favor to the more popular Web, it is still the main tool for getting at the resources of many organizations, such as educational institutions, the government, and not-for-profit organizations that have not moved their resources to the Web.

Before the Web was popular, system administrators considered the resources their users might want access to and developed a menu-driven interface to those resources. Unlike the Web, you could not develop a desktop-published interface that looked like a corporate brochure or sales piece. However, the menu could lead you off to those sites that various systems administrators had determined would be helpful. Selecting a menu choice can lead to another menu, a Web site (text based), a telnet site, a text file, a graphic, a video and other multimedia content, or a dead end.

You can bookmark favorite gopher sites to return to them easily. Gopher provides a common interface so that the vagaries of system design do not make finding information on one gopher site more difficult than another.

As the capabilities of gopher have been taken and enhanced by the Web, the number of gopher sites has not increased to the same extent as Web sites.

A good Gopher software choice is wsgopher from EG&G Idaho, Inc. Unlike a line-oriented gopher client, you can use wsgopher to keep many windows open to trace your way through the menus, do searches, and keep the search windows open as you are looking through the contents of a selected site.

Telnet

You have an account on a computer in Rochester, New York, but you are in California. Do you make a long-distance phone call to check in? Not with Telnet. Telnet lets you log into your own system from another computer using the Internet as your long-distance provider. After you have connected with telnet, your interactions with the computer are just like they would be if you had dialed directly into your computer, on site or through a phone call.

Telnet is a protocol and program that lets you access other computers as if you were logging in to that computer from a terminal. It makes the system that you are calling think you are a dumb terminal.

Once you have connected via telnet, you do not need to run any more programs on your own computer: you run them on the computer you are connected with, but your keyboard sends its keystrokes to the other computer and your screen "echoes" what is happening on the other end. You can capture information to your hard disk or printer, if you wish, to use at a later time.

The strengths of telnet include the strengths of a multiuser computer system: As a terminal, you would have access to the programs and resources on the remote computer, such as data, printers, and outgoing connections. You can process at the speed of the remote computer, and have access to the Internet at the speed the host is connected to the Internet. Telnet can be convenient: If you have shell access to other accounts, you can tie in to the Internet on one account and check in to the other accounts through telnet, so you do not have to make multiple phone calls.

The weaknesses are largely the same as those of a multiuser system. As a terminal, you are not actually connected to the Internet, so files you download go to the host, not to the computer you're using. You need to run special software to get files to that computer. In addition, telnet's performance is often slower than a direct phone connection.

Telnet is not as important as it was in 1996. The Web and graphical user interfaces have changed the use of the Internet greatly. Twenty dollars for unlimited Internet access has been the level for many people going graphical, and the use of dial-in, shell accounts has become almost passé. Internet access is split among inexpensive local access, inexpensive national access, and access through on-line services. For students and others whose e-mail accounts are on systems that can only be reached by a long-distance phone call, telnet is very practical. You would need to have an account to access these systems.

In addition, organizations that have not made their databases and other resources available to the public by way of the Web may make their systems available for anyone to access using telnet. Library systems are an excellent example. Companies with legacy systems (minicomputers and mainframes without Web software) also make telnet access available to their users. The research and library information available on the Internet that is available only using telnet can be helpful to financial professionals. Many of these offer guest accounts for public access. Some organizations offering telnet access include the Library of Congress and many public libraries, NASA, and other governmental and educational resources.

A telnet client comes with Windows 95. Shareware telnet clients are also available, with varying abilities. Some telnet programs also include file transfer capabilities to facilitate up- and downloading between your computer and the host computer.

Internet Phones

Why Internet Phones?   While most radio and television broadcasters are not openly hostile to the hundreds of radio stations and Internet-only broadcasters, the telecommunications industry is in an uproar over Internet phone services. With Internet phones, you can talk to and hear others speak over the Internet. That means you can call anywhere in the world for the cost of two local phone calls.

Free long-distance calling through the Internet? "Free" requires some explanation. Both parties need to have a multimedia computer—Internet phones use the built-in microphone and speakers (or those on the sound card) of your computer. You both need a modem and an available phone line. You both need a true connection to the Internet. These phones are limited.

- The sound quality is not necessarily as good as a traditional phone. Most conversations begin with an exchange of callers inquiring whether the other can hear them well.

- You cannot call a traditional phone for free, other than 800 (toll-free) systems and a few areas where someone has set up a server for this purpose.

- The person on the other end has to have the same software package (until the standards proposed by Intel and others come into full play) and be available to speak. However, a short traditional phone call or a prearranged time determined through e-mail can set up an Internet phone call.

If long-distance charges restrict your calling, these packages can be very helpful—and it is a lot of fun to speak to people around the world at no charge. The Federal Communications Commission has been petitioned to stop people from using these packages. Telecommunications companies point to the inconveniences of Internet phones and indicate they are "concerned" that Internet phones will slow down the Internet for everyone else. The FCC has indicated that it does not plan to regulate the software and services at this time.

In the meantime, Internet phones provide an inexpensive means for two branches of an office to connect by an intercom even though they are 1,000 miles apart and lets families or business partners hear each others' voices as they work together.

Examples of Phones.   For the consumer, NetMeeting has preeminence. Many large companies are doing Voice over IP, but on the consumer front, no one wanted to pay for phones like Internet Phone from Vocaltec Ltd. (http://www.vocaltec.com). Vocaltec is a pioneer in the area with Internet Phone.

Net2fone (http://www.net2phone.com) is one of the first attempts actually to hook an Internet phone into the phone system, using the services of IDT. It offers reduced cost billing through IDT's phone system. The advantages of calling a toll-free number through the Internet are limited but may come into play where an 800 number is blocked or unavailable from your calling district.

For the security conscious, PGPPhone is available from the MIT download site for PGP (Pretty Good Privacy): http://www.mit.edu/network/pgp.html.

Internet Phones: Suitable for Business?   Is it worth it for a business to spend time setting up laptops for staff to try to understand each other over tinny speakers to save a few bucks on an engagement? Probably not. But for longer calls, long-term collaboration, and international relations, Internet phones can be an efficient tool.

Internet Video

CU-Seeme.   Moving from audio to video, CU-SeeMe lets you teleconference using ordinary modems and phone lines. CU-SeeMe was developed at Cornell University (the CU of CU-SeeMe) and a commercial version is offered by White Pine Software, Inc.: http://www.cu-seeme.com.

With the addition of a digital camera, such as the inexpensive Connectix QuickCam, two users or multiple users can talk and see each other, although not at full speed with a 28.8K connection. The video is more jerky, like a Max Headroom cola ad. However, CU-SeeMe lets you see the person you are working with, which helps to build relationships and share visual information more easily. The CU-Seeme product isn't obsolete, as it is being incorporated into new products. But it couldn't compete with NetMeeting for consumer and business acceptance.

VDOPhone and VDOLive.   VDOPhone is another teleconferencing software package (http://www.vdo.net). VDOPhone comes from the makers of VDOLive, a standard on the well-dressed Internet computer. From two-way communication back to one-way, you can watch television shows over the Internet. VDOLive (http://www.vdo.net) has been showcased by Public Broadcasting

(PBS) (http://www.pbs.org) by letting people watch the current episode of some of its shows, especially *Life on the Internet*. The picture, at 160 by 120 pixels, only fills up a small section of your computer screen, especially at 800 × 600 mode or higher and the action is jerky. But you can watch television shows at your convenience using your Internet connection. A minimum 28.8K connection is necessary for good performance. VDO is doing little these days.

Pointcast Network

Information aimed at one; the Pointcast Network, <http://www.pointcast. com/>, provides free software, a free service, and running, animated advertising that resembles the ads played on the scoreboards at sports stadiums: silent and often clever. The Pointcast Network (PCN) works as an application or as a screen saver. Why would you want to download something that plays constant commercials on your computer as a screen saver? Because of the content. You can bring news and finance information to your computer for display on the screen saver or your more detailed reading.

- Among the options for your personal customization: PCN can collect news and present the latest from *Money* magazine, *Time* magazine, and *People* magazine.
- You can choose from a list of nearly 100 industries, and PCN will present the latest news about the industry for you. For example, if you have clients in advertising, publishing, and mining, PCN will keep you in touch with what is hot in those industries.
- You can identify the ticker symbols of up to 25 publicly traded companies and have PCN display stock information and collect news about those businesses.
- Local weather and your favorite sports teams' results can all be collected and displayed.

PCN is an excellent service, and Pointcast hoped to market the technology for companies to disseminate information internally. PCN was so popular within large companies that its ongoing drain on internal networks has prompted network administrators to ask users to update it on demand instead of continuously. The success of PCN brought a series of competitors who also generally failed to make a name for themselves.

Pointcast is a former shining star now on its last legs. It was slow, and Internet portals like Excite, as well as new applications like Excite Assistant and Yahoo! Messenger offered similar capabilities with less stress. Now they have been bought by Launchpad Technologies, Inc. and will be incorporated as a minor tool in their Entry Point, part Pointcast and part eWallet.

PointCast has come full circle, from one of the hottest companies in the Internet space to a minor piece in someone else's e-commerce puzzle. Bon voyage, Pointcast. You were a great service.

From Here . . .

Chapter 3 covers how to get on-line.

Accessing the Internet: Getting Connected

The purpose of this chapter is to describe the options available for business and individuals to access the Internet.

The following outline summarizes the contents of this chapter:

- *Types of Connections:* When you say you are on the Internet, are you really on the Internet? Different types of connects are discussed in the section.
- *Software:* The technology is old, but the software is just out of the wrapper; this section covers the software you need to make the most of your connections.
- *Places to Access with a Modem:* People have been using modems for more than Internet access. Here are some places they have been dialing.
- *On-line Services:* Which proprietary on-line services offer compelling content? The on-line services offer you their services and links to the Internet, at a price.
- *Internet Service Providers:* These provide pure Internet access, often at a fixed fee, or sometimes free. Here you can learn where to sign up.
- *Other Sources for Internet Access:* This section discusses some other ways to get on the Net.

TYPES OF CONNECTIONS

Speed, Connectivity, Price—Pick Two

So you want to be on the Internet? That phrase—*on the Internet*—means different things to different people before. To some, it means hooking a company's e-mail system into the Internet so messages can be sent within the organization and around the world. To others, it means letting people call into their Unix-based computer system to access the Internet. With the popularity of the Web, most companies are promoting services including the most complete kind of Web access. However, some companies are using a bait-and-switch ploy, as they offer incomplete access. How can you be on the Internet without being *on the Internet?*

When connecting to the Internet, you have a number of choices to make. The first is the type of service you will require. The second is the physical connection you make to get that service.

Each type of connection has trade-offs. Some offer blazing speed but will not serve you away from the office. Others offer you access anywhere with limits on speed. For the right price, you can get almost anything, of course.

Welcome to the Internet! You need a computer, a modem, a phone line, and an account to get started. (Yes, you can go to the library, use your neighbor's computer, or hook in using the office's Internet connection through the network, or if you can convince your spouse, you can get an ISDN line or cable modems, but we are talking about simply signing in!) America Online (AOL) is a popular way to get started because it is simple to load and go. Using an ISP (Internet service provider) may require a little more help in configuring your software, but if you know what you are doing, it is a 5- to 10-minute task.

Let's assume you have a nephew who gets your computer up and going. Now what? Inventory: Browser. Check. It came with your machine. We can pick up Netscape later. Adobe Acrobat. Need to get it if it isn't on your computer. It lets you read tax returns and a slew of other documents that you'll find up at your professional association's Web site. You'll need an unzipper (PKZIP) to let you work with files that have been shrunk and archived on the Net. You'll be able to get just about anything else later. More in the next two chapters.

Physical Connections

First you will need to figure out the physical connection you will be making. Your choice will largely depend on where you will need to access the Internet from and the duration of your sessions.

If your computer is on an internal network, your network administrator may be able to provide network-based access for you and the other network users. If you are on the road or at home, you will need to connect personally.

Dial-up Connections—Ordinary Phone Lines.   Most individuals and smaller organizations use dial-up connections to get to the Internet. That means they use an ordinary telephone line to call into their service provider.

Your access will be affected by the amount of information that can go between your computer and the host. Ordinary phone lines can be temperamental, and you may not be able to use the full speed of your modem. (A *modem* is a device that turns computer bits and bytes into the sounds a phone line requires and then it converts those sounds back into the computer bits and bytes.)

Many people are using modems that transfer 28,800 bits per second, with some more up-to-date users running so-called 56K modems. These operate at a maximum of 53K from the ISP to the computer and 28.8k from the computer to the ISP. The speeds are currently limited by law. For more information on relative modem speeds, see Exhibit 3.1.

Depending on your local telephone company, you may be paying a fixed fee for business service or a per-minute charge.

Dial-up Connections: ISDN. Many phone companies also offer ISDN (integrated services digital network), which provides a digital connection using your present phone lines and ISDN modems (more correctly, terminal adaptors). The cost of an ISDN modem is comparable to other modems, and the price of ISDN service is also dropping rapidly. ISDN connections offer two to four times the speed of standard high-end modems over normal phone lines.

Do not get too spoiled by ISDN access at your home or office. When you hit the road, it is unlikely that you will find ISDN in your hotel room or at your clients' offices.

Most ISDN providers charge a per-minute fee for ISDN usage, and ISPs often charge a premium for ISDN access.

Dial-up Connections: Other

A number of companies are offering satellite or cellular access to the Internet. For example, the cellular providers know that there is dead air time even in the

Modem relative speeds			
Year	Speed	Relative to 28.8K	Time to transfer 1 MB
1983	300 KB	.010	8 hours
1985	2,400 KB	.083	1 hour
1989	9,600 KB	.333	15 minutes
1993	14,400 KB	.500	10 minutes
1994	28,800 KB	1.000	5 minutes
1996	56,000 KB	2.000	2 minutes
ISDN	128,000 KB	4.444	1 minute
T-1	1.54 MB	53.472	5 seconds
ADSL	2 MB	69.444	4 seconds
Cable Modems	10 MB	347.222	<1 second

Exhibit 3.1 Modem relative speeds.

middle of the average phone conversation. Computer data can be sent during that time at little additional cost to them using a technology known as *cellular digital packet data* (CDPD). Small home satellite receivers can receive Internet data at 400,000 bps (bits per second), in conjunction with a 28.8 modem to send information to the Internet; this can provide much faster response.

Most of these special providers charge for time or data transferred over their service.

Permanent Connections: Leased lines.   Along with dial-up connections, many organizations choose to lease a line with a full-time connection to their Internet provider. Special equipment is necessary to hook your internal network to those connections, known as *routers* and *CSU/DSUs* (channel service unit/digital service units). *Firewalls* protect your network from the outside and *gateways* connect your networks together. Networks based on Unix or Windows NT are relatively simple to attach to the Internet. Networks based on Novell NetWare prior to Version 4.11 are another story. They used IPX, a competitor to IP.

A 56K (kilobit) line provides better response than ordinary phone service and modems, and is relatively inexpensive.

T-1 lines are expensive, but offer very fast (1.54 MB or megabits per second) access, the speed of a slow internal network.

Frame relay offers a guarantee of a 56K chunk of a T-1 line, with the possibility of sharing any unused portion with others. This offers speeds ranging from 56K on a bad day to 1.536 MB on a good day.

New and emerging technologies include ADSL (asymmetric digital subscription line) and cable modems (using the resources of your cable television connection), which will offer speeds of 640K to 2 MB from your machine to the host, and 6 MB to 10 MB in, respectively. Other options, far more expensive, can offer increased access speeds: AT&T offers arrangement of up to 45 megabits per second known as T-3 lines.

For example, consumers are seeing Digital Subscriber Line service in Chicago using Telocity's (www.teleocity.com) InterChange service, offering 1 megabit-per-second Internet access for $49.95 per month. Their Residential Gateway includes a modem and can be installed by the consumer. Telocity plans to be in 30 cities by the second quarter of 2000. The InterChange residential gateway can be attached to a PC by the consumer, using a parallel port, a Universal Serial Bus interface, or an Ethernet Network Interface Card. Unlike ADSL or even ISDN, this makes the service customer-installable. Most DSL deployment thus far has been to businesses, although Bell companies that have FastAccess will see residential deployment when G.Lite technology becomes commercially available. G.Lite is a standard that is designed to make home installation of ADSL easy. The G.Lite version of ADSL is still 8 to 10 times faster than the ISDN services offered for Internet access, capable of providing 1.5 Mbps downstream and 386 Kbps upstream. ADSL is always on, so you do not have to connect to receive your e-mail, unlike ISDN.

Note: Cable modems will provide speeds of 10 million bits of information a second, 350 times the speed of a standard modem. However, that high-speed connection is only between your PC and the cable company's head-quarters. The rest of the computers on the Web still use slower lines and are crowded with traffic. A cable modem moves the bottleneck from your modem back to the Internet infrastructure.

Success of Connections

The CompuServe service is venerable and accessing its forums can be an exercise in patience. However, even the newest sites can seem reeeeaaaallll sssslllooow. As we said before, the Internet is a teacher of patience. You type in the URL of your favorite site and sit, waiting for a Web page to appear or wondering why the site isn't responding. The Internet is a speed demon one second and slow as molasses the next. Your browser gives you little indication of which inconsistencies and performance problems are slowing you down. Would you like to know why the problems occur in the first place—and maybe even how to solve them?

We became familiar with Net.Medic (www.vitalsigns.com, 1-888-9VITAL9) back when the name of the company was VitalSigns Software and closely matched the URL and 800 numbers; now the company's name is INSoft. (INSoft is the new product division of International Network Services.) Net.Medic is a browser companion—software that works with your Internet browser to monitor, isolate, diagnose, and correct problems that affect your Internet connection. (See Exhibit 3.2.) The number of links in the chain that can slow things down is surprising. We have experienced CPU load performance problems and low memory issues (our test PC was the weak link), modem configuration issues, router problems at our Internet Service Provider, plain old slow traffic on the Internet, and really slow remote Web site servers. Net.Medic identifies the problems quickly and offers recommendations for solving them. In certain cases, it automatically fixes them for you. Net.Medic offers two levels of service: The free downloadable utility offers enough reporting to let you diagnose your basic problems, while paying the reasonable fee to unlock the rest of the functionality offers a great deal more. You can try the full features of the software for 30 days before it disables its advanced functionality.

Net.Medic identifies performance problems and isolates them to a specific component of your unique Internet path—PC, modem, ISP, the Internet itself, or a remote Web site. Net.Medic animates the end-to-end connection, a little like the America Online login process, showing you exactly what is occurring across the Internet, including traffic jams and bottlenecks. Is the problem in

Exhibit 3.2　Net.Medic works with your Internet browser to monitor, isolate, diagnose, and correct problems that affect your Internet connection. Use with permission from Net.medic.

the network or at a specific server? Is the network congested or the connection slow? Green, yellow, and red indicators highlight the responsiveness of each component. If there are problems, an icon on your toolbar can alert you to check out the Net.Medic dashboard.

When you start up Net.Medic, you will see only the Net.Medic icon in the system tray—a gray plus sign. Right-clicking on the icon gives you access to the Net.Medic dashboard; the most important logs and reports; modem, Internet and network Control Panel applets; and WINPCFG, the Windows program for determining the IP number assigned to your computer. As your Internet work begins, the icon will turn green as long as things are running relatively smoothly, yellow if there are warnings, and red if there are problems.

Opening the dashboard offers the graphical view of the connection, graphs of incoming and outgoing traffic (throughput statistics are always helpful, especially with threats like BackOrifice around—why is my PC sending twice as much as it is receiving?), retrieval statistics, and session times. The dashboard can be configured to show any or all of these components, and the components can float on the desktop or be attached to the browser.

Because Net.Medic reports your throughput, retrieval time, the Web server load and efficiency as well as network delays and congestion levels, it is helpful to evaluate Web site performance as it gauges the size of the page it is downloading, the time it takes, and whether any delays are due to the Web site itself or the Internet connection. Net.Medic also monitors your PC and modem, helping ensure optimal configuration. If you have ever sat and watched "Server contacted. Waiting Reply" and wondered if it is really true,

Net.Medic can help by identifying a hung server condition way before your browser admits it exists. When this happens, Net.Medic can automatically reinitiate your server request, eliminating long waiting times, manual retries, and time-outs. Net.Medic will keep track of how often you visit particular sites and track statistics about their performance. Most of Net.Medic's History Reports are part of the paid version; they include the ability for monitoring and reporting your ISP's performance, logging busy signals, call completions, disconnects, average connect rates and other data about the service levels you actually experience. If you have guaranteed service agreements with your ISP, this program be very helpful.

You can purchase Net.Medic directly from INSoft via the Web (http://www. vitalsigns.com) or by phone (1-888-984-8259) (from the United States and Canada) 916-859-5209 (from other countries) for less than $50. It works with Windows 95, Windows 98, or Windows NT 4.0 and with version 3.0 or above of Internet Explorer or Netscape.

NetMonitor is a free utility designed to get you to purchase a suite of products called Modem Wizard 4.0. NetMonitor allows you to check under the hood of the Internet and see exactly what is going on. (See Exhibit 3.3.) Like Net.Medic, it offers Internet statistics like the URL you are viewing and its associated IP address, the number of Internet hops along the information superhighway, your user IP address, connect speed, transfer rate (and red, green, yellow light graphics to help you determine if you are going slow, medium, or fast), and a graphical visual display (like an oscilloscope) of bytes coming and going across your Internet connection. Is it as good as Net.Medic? Not quite. The graphic display is limited and the statistics and reliability are poor. It is available from <http://www.kissco.com>.

DeMon 4.40 is billed as "the $5.00 Internet tool you can't be without." It is a dial-up networking monitor and POP3 e-mail system. DeMon is a simple easy to use powerful little monitor utility that works in conjunction with Microsoft's Dial Up Networking Adapter. It provides a clean and customizable interface (designer apps!) and keeps tabs on the incoming and outgoing bytes from your current connection. The program also monitors idle times, providing an alarm if a certain time limit is reached allowing you to check either your connection or your download. The program also provides highly accurate throughput information for both ingoing and outgoing information, allowing you to get raw transfer speeds instead of averaged ones. It provides a modem histogram that shows how much of your current connections speed you are using. The program also features a nice powerful little POP3 and SMTP e-mail client to allow you to check your email, read it, and send e-mail all from within the program in 4 MB of system RAM. Available from: http://www.ycis.com/~rkx/rkxsoft/demon/index.html.

Exhibit 3.3   Net Monitor allows you to check under the hood of the Internet and see what exactly is going on. Used with permission from Kiss software.

Net.Medic continues to be the superior alternative, offering more for free and much more for a fee. You can get all three and try them for yourself.

Citrix and Microsoft Terminal Server

Many companies have begun using the Internet as a conduit between their branch offices, a way to transfer data inexpensively. No matter which type of connection you choose, products from Citrix (http://www.citrix.com), such as those licensed by Microsoft in its Terminal Server product, turn an NT Server into a multiuser computer. Even over POTS lines, remote computers of almost any vintage can call into the Citrix-based server and compute at whatever speed the server and load permit. The Internet is a network of networks and some people are embracing it as the connection of choice.

TYPES OF SERVICES

E-mail Only

An e-mail account lets you send and receive e-mail. Of course, e-mail is the primary reason many businesses use the Internet. E-mail is included as a standard feature with most on-line services.

Many companies have set up e-mail gateways to the Internet. Their employees can send e-mail through their internal system and direct their e-mail to the Internet.

Although e-mail accounts are meant to provide e-mail services, you can use e-mail to take advantage of other resources on the Internet, although it is rather awkward. This e-mail access to other services is important when Web access is limited, but offers little of benefit to North American businesses.

In today's mobile world, however, e-mail services are different. Wireless is coming. Cellular connections are growing in popularity. Small, wireless Internet units may be the next big thing. But these connections are slow.

U.S Robotics has started showing off its Palm VII unit. Available at press time, it has an integrated wireless modem, powered by an independent battery and offering multiple-month battery lives. Expected to cost between $600 and $800, the unit will offer e-mail and limited HTML support. Data transfer speeds will be in the area of 8 Kbps. The Palm will use the familiar Palm software to send and receive e-mail.

The Nokia 9000 Communicator series is already available, offering access at a whopping 9.6 Kbps—although 56 Kbps speeds may be available by the end of 1999.

Less ambitious but possibly useful is PocketMail (1-800-POCKETM), a $9.95-per-month service that offers access to e-mail from any analog phone via an 800 number, using a lightweight, $200 handheld device specifically for e-mail. Although the service lets you send and receive an unlimited amount of mail, the contents are limited in size, graphics, and attachment capability.

As cell phone/computer combos and personal communication devices emerge, users should evaluate e-mail with embedded voice, graphics, and PGP signatures, and the use of heavy Java and Javascript, cascading style sheets, and moving GIFs.

Shell Accounts

A shell account lets you share time on another computer known as a host, often a Unix-based computer system. Many universities make this type of account available. Because you are acting as a terminal into their computer system, you will be able to run whatever Internet software you have permission to run on the host.

Shell accounts have their advantages and disadvantages. They reflect the difference between running a multiuser operating system and being part of a network. With a shell account, you have access to Internet resources, but the host is the computer on the Internet, not yours. Processing and data transfer happen at the host; the host simply exchanges keystrokes and screens with your computer. Your performance is enhanced and limited to matching your modem with the speed of your host, but you are only sending keystrokes and a small amount of text for screen updates most of the time. Your modem will become a problem only when you are transferring programs or other large files from the host to your computer. However, you have storage space allotted to you on the host, so you can bring programs to the host and download them at your leisure.

Advantages: The host is usually connected to the Internet with a very fast connection, faster than the average home or business. That means that most functions will happen more quickly than if you did them from your own computer. Reading mail, checking through newsgroups, and other basic tasks happen very quickly. In addition, you can access the host from almost any computer or terminal, with no need for fast equipment or specifically configured software. That means that you can do your work from almost any computer or terminal, which is handy when you are away from the office and do not want to set up your system on-site. Also, because professionals maintain the host, users do not have to be technically inclined to get the benefits, use updated versions of software, or do backups. Shell accounts tend to be less expensive than more sophisticated accounts as well.

Disadvantages: You will not be able to run popular Web browsers on your own machine or other programs, such as the multimedia tools that require that your own computer be attached to the Internet. Downloading files from the Internet is a two-step process: first getting the file to the host and then from the host to your own computer. In addition, you will probably have to learn a little Unix to take advantage of a shell account.

Although you cannot run the latest Web browsers on your own computer, most shell accounts let you use a text-based Web browser called Lynx to visit Web sites. Lynx running on a host is very fast compared to using a Web browser on your own computer. Lynx does not download or display the graphics; graphics take far longer to download than the basic text components of a Web page. However, more and more Web sites assume you have a graphics-based browser, and many Web sites cannot be viewed or used at all with Lynx, as the designers built their design entirely around their graphics. The use of Lynx as a browser has gone from 80 percent in early 1995, to 20 percent at the end of 1995, to 5 percent in the middle of 1996. In 1999 Lynx usage is very limited. Lynx usage probably decreased so quickly due to the introduction of graphical Web access by the online services in late 1995.

You can access a shell account with any terminal emulation software. For those who can only get shell access but want to see the graphics on the Web, some special communications packages are available. These packages, particularly shareware packages TIA and Slipknot, let you use your shell account and your PC to emulate a pseudo–graphical Web browser. A small program is loaded on the Unix system, which works in concert with a larger program on the PC. However, many organizations do not permit the use of these programs on their accounts.

PPP/SLIP

If you want to run Netscape Navigator or Microsoft Internet Explorer to see the graphics and hear the sounds of the Web, you will need a more sophisticated account. With PPP (point-to-point protocol) and SLIP (serial line Internet protocol) access, your computer dials into a host and becomes part of the Internet. You are on the Internet; your host assigns you an IP address, so the packets of information come directly to your computer. This type of account shines where the shell account falls down.

Advantages: With a PPP or SLIP account, your computer is on the Internet. You can take advantage of every capability available: graphics, multimedia, and talking with people with your voice around the world at no charge. When there is a new program to access news, watch television, or exchange electronic business cards, you can do it . . . if you have taken the time to set up your equipment properly, loaded and configured the software, and worked out the technical bugs.

Disadvantages: You must have a powerful computer to take advantage of this type of account—the faster and the more memory and storage, the better. You can run only those programs you have loaded on your computer. Accessing your account and your mail from anyone else's computer is nearly impossible. The speed at which you access the Internet is limited by your modem, so everything you do will be slower than on a shell account.

Because of the relative strengths and weaknesses of shell and PPP/SLIP access, you may want to find a provider who will let you do both. Then you can use PPP/SLIP for more intense use and shell for checking your mail when you are on the road or in a hurry.

Each Internet service provider has a series of IP numbers they can assign to PPP or SLIP dial-in accounts. It is something like handling a deck of playing cards. Each time you dial in, you are given a card with an IP number.

When you hang up, the card goes back to the deck and is reshuffled. You may or may not get the same IP number the next time you dial in. However, you can pay your ISP extra and have a card set aside for you. Each time you dial in, you will get the same IP number. Although this relationship costs more, it is helpful for filing for a domain name. When you file for a domain name, the InterNIC or other authority requires an IP address to go with the name. Then, when someone types your domain name, the IP address can be found and attached to the data packets, so they can find their way to your computer. Your ISP can assist you in filing, or you can do it yourself at rs.internic.net or (http://www.networksolutions.com). We recommend choosing a domain name and filing soon. Domain names are being taken quickly.

SOFTWARE

You have now determined what type of service you want and how you will physically connect to the Internet. Next you will need to start planning the software you will need to connect to the Internet. With a shell account, you need only a basic telecommunications program. Otherwise, you will need to begin to assemble, or purchase preassembled, the building blocks of packages you will want to take advantage of the Internet.

Basic Communications Software

When you dial into a Unix host, you need a simple telecommunications package. Windows 3.1 shipped with a very weak application called Terminal, windows 95/98 comes with a stronger accessory called HyperTerminal. Most computers that come with modems ship with additional communications software that can act as a terminal, send faxes, and sometimes provide voice mail capabilities.

There are three main functions of a terminal emulation package:

1. Establishing a session with the host (dialing into your host).

2. Emulating a terminal the host can support (most often vt100 or ANSI).

3. Coordinating file transfers between your computer and the host, most often using a protocol called Zmodem. Windows's Terminal only supports the Kermit and Xmodem protocols, which are much slower than Zmodem. Other helpful features include being able to capture what is displaying on your screen to a disk file or to the printer.

The ability to download software from the Internet is important, because so much Internet software is available only there. Many companies use their terminal emulation software as a starting point to find other software and download it to their own computers.

Once you have dialed and logged into your host, you will be running the programs made available to you by the host. We will be discussing these products in more detail in Chapter 4.

Internet Enabling Software—Winsock and TCP/IP

If you plan to have full access to the Internet, your computer has to speak TCP/IP. On a Windows-based computer, that means using a software program known as *Winsock*. Winsock comes with Windows for Workgroups or Windows 95/98 but must be acquired separately, as shareware or as part of commercial packages, for Windows 3.1. It will come with the startup disks offered by many service providers, which are designed for those who do not want to have to earn their way onto the Internet by their sweat and intelligence. Macintosh computers also come with TCP/IP capabilities. DOS users can get PPP or SLIP programs as well.

Setting up TCP/IP on a computer is not a trivial matter, unless you receive preconfigured software from your service provider. Windows 95/98 does an admirable job of providing wizards to lead you through the process of preparing your computer for access, but some technological expertise is recommended.

Dialer

If you are physically connected to a network on the Internet, TCP/IP will get you rolling. Otherwise, you need a dialer to call up your Internet host and exchange the appropriate information to get you logged on and on-line. Once again, Windows 95/98 does an admirable job of making this painless with its dial-up networking and dial-up scripting tools. Your preconfigured software also will have these capabilities.

Once you have TCP/IP going and have dialed and logged on to your service provider, you are ready to take advantage of the Internet's software.

Winsock-compatible Software

In Chapter 2 we covered the services and software you can use with your TCP/IP connection to the Internet (using your Winsock-created pipeline to the Net). Internet startup kits it come with Web browsers, through which you can easily acquire any other software you may need.

PLACES TO ACCESS WITH A MODEM

Now that your computer is in place and you have some communications software, such as HyperTerminal, a modem, and a phone line, you can begin to explore the resources made available to you. You may already be using a computer to dial a bulletin board system (BBSs) or to exchange EDI (electronic data interchange) documents with your trading partners. More likely, you have a subscription to one of the on-line services. In any case, it will be most cost effective to subscribe to an Internet service provider who can provide more inexpensive and powerful links to the Internet.

Non-Internet Sites

Bulletin Board Systems.   Before the computer-oriented spent their free time exploring the Internet, they spent their time setting up and calling bulletin board systems. A BBSs is a computer set up to receive phone calls from other computers and provide a menu of options, including message bases, file areas, and distribution of news using bulletins. BBSs often provided games, price lists, and other resources, depending on their purpose.

To access the BBSs, you called the phone connected to the computer. A business might install multiple lines dedicated to the BBSs so that many people could access it. Hobbyists often set up BBSs to operate during their bedtime hours, so they could use their home phone line as the access line to their BBSs. The systems were often repositories for shareware programs and viruses, and contained the gossip for the local community or guesses about the season opener for *Star Trek.*

Local BBSs were set up for special segments of society—for example, those interested in religion, hand-held computers, or teaching. Software companies would set up a BBSs to receive support questions and provide software fixes and updates. The government set up BBSs to provide a distribution point for publications. Few businesses dared set up a toll-free number for their BBSs, as that invited lengthy long-distance calls to their site.

With the advent of the Web, many system operators have moved their bulletin boards to the Internet. The Internet allows many more people to access the system and can be started up without dedicated computers or phone lines.

Some of the remaining BBSs provide a valuable service, especially where inexpensive Internet access is not available. For example, one network of these systems, known as FidoNet, lets its users send and receive Internet e-mail.

Value-Added Networks.   Many retail or manufacturing businesses have been asked by a large client or vendor to transmit business documents using EDI (electronic data interchange). Doing so has meant acquiring software to perform the interface between the EDI data and the accounting system as well as software to communicate with an intermediary known as the VAN (value-added network).

The VAN provides many services, but the most basic is providing electronic mailboxes where the two businesses can leave the EDI documents for each other. The VAN maintains the computer, provides security so others cannot access the business data, and makes sure the data are available to the subscribers when needed. For that privilege, subscribers are charged what many consider a large fee. However, the total cost of doing business with EDI was much lower than manual input, and it broke time, geography, and language barriers, opening up international business.

Private Networks.   Many companies with networks in their offices use modems to communicate between their offices or for their employees to access when they are away from the office, at home or on the road. This is what is known as a wide area network (WAN). Sometimes that connection makes the calling computer an additional node on the network, and sometimes that connection has the caller take over a local computer for additional processing speed.

With private networks, as with the Internet, you can have dial-in and direct connections. However, since most private networks require a long-distance call to access from other cities, many businesses are examining the Internet as a less expensive way to hook their offices together. In addition, other organizations hope to provide that link.

ON-LINE SERVICES

Traditional on-line service providers are commercial firms offering a variety of services.

Common Features to On-line Services

Connections
> Phone numbers to dial directly into their computer system
>
> Gateways so you can access the Internet through their systems (and on their meter)
>
> Limited access to their services directly through the Internet

Content
> News

Financial information

Weather

Entertainment

Education

Games

Discussion

Special interest groups (like a bulletin board for messages)

Real-time chat

Hardware and software support

Cost

$10 a month with five hours of free time

E-mail

An e-mail address that you can use to contact anyone on any service

Ease of Use

Software that makes calling easy

Many phone numbers so you can call when you are traveling (without a long-distance phone charge)

Support for any problems you may be having

A common interface to all of their features

Graphical Access to the Internet

Web access

Software for designing Web pages

Web site hosting

Central Administration

Centralized support

Centralized billing

CompuServe

CompuServe (800-827-6364) is one of the oldest and most venerable of the on-line services, with a strong business bent but a stodgy reputation. CompuServe offers many Internet services and offers access to the Web as part of its standard CompuServe service. A failed WOW! service for kids and a spun-off dedicated Internet subsidiary (SpryNet) once served other needs. CompuServe is now owned by America Online.

CompuServe is one of the most flexible services (if only for the moment). Unlike its closest competitors, you can access CompuServe many ways:

- Through its own CompuServe Information Manager for Windows (WinCim), DOS, or Macintosh software
- Through other commercial and shareware front-ends designed especially for CompuServe
- Through standard terminal emulation software (for many services)
- Through a proprietary phone number
- Using your Winsock connection to the Internet
- Using telnet on the Internet

With these options, you can use the resources of CompuServe from any computer with no special software or setup other than knowing CompuServe's phone number. This is especially important when you need to send mail or download a software fix and are miles away from your own computer.

This flexibility is not true for CompuServe 2000, CompuServe's migration to a Web service. However, CompuServe announced plans to keep the proprietary service for as long as necessary, with the intent of letting subscribers come in through the Internet.

CompuServe makes many resources available to the subscriber. It has the best corporate support among the on-line services, so hardware and software companies will more likely be represented on CompuServe than on any other service (other than the Internet itself). CompuServe has made much of the Internet available to its users for years, adding in 1995 full graphical Web access.

As part of CompuServe, you pay an hourly rate for any of its regular services, including Internet access, past an initial five hours of services. In addition, CompuServe acts as a gateway to many private databases, which come at an additional fee.

CompuServe has undergone a facelift after being acquired by America Online. CompuServe 2000 will be marketed as an Internet service "for grown-ups." It will be offered at an introductory discount price of $9.95 a month for 20 hours of content and Web access. A $19.95 flat-rate plan is also available. The new CompuServe is being pitched to business and professional users as well as consumers.

Longtime CompuServe subscribers have seen a number of CompuServe efforts come and go, including a limited Internet service for families and a universal passport for single-login access to multiple Internet sites (with a built-in billing mechanism that might have changed the face of the Internet if it succeeded).

The $9.95 for 20 hours of CompuServe and Internet access may be very attractive to practitioners who can use access to CompuServe's accounting-oriented discussion groups but will not spend large amounts of time on the Internet. The redesign—boasted to be faster, simpler to navigate, more powerful, and with easier e-mail—also may be specifically designed to appeal to older users, consistent with the current 35- to 55-year-old demographic of the typical CompuServe subscriber.

CompuServe has expanded its news sources to include the *New York Times*, CBS Sportsline, and other popular Web content providers. CompuServe also has entered into agreements with MCI WorldCom and will be developing customized versions of its software for them.

Many of the changes are bringing CompuServe more in line with the rest of the industry. Their "State-of-the-Art E-Mail Features" include spell-check and the ability to format and send pictures and multiple attachments in e-mail messages. Users expect this in Internet e-mail.

The Integrated Contact List and Instant Message™ features come from AOL and are included in recent versions of Netscape. Customizable Toolbars have been in Internet Explorer for the last three versions.

The New Main Menu is more like one of the popular Web portals, offering a continuously updated news ticker with headlines from the Associated Press, market analysis from CBSMarketWatch.com, personalized news folders, and links to CompuServe's information, content, and services channels.

Like AOL, CompuServe will now offer five member names per account; each member name represents a separate e-mail address and has its own password for privacy. No more morning greetings from junior wondering what a net operating loss is.

The domain name has been shortened to cs.com. This is a very long time coming. There is a new, alphabetized address book. Also a long time coming. Switch Member Names Without Disconnecting is a nice feature for workgroups and families. CompuServe E-Mail Scheduler makes it possible for members to schedule the automatic downloading and sending of e-mail messages as well as newsgroup articles periodically throughout the day.

CompuServe has been through a lot over the last few years. These efforts show that AOL is putting some money into keeping CompuServe floating for a while longer.

Microsoft Network

Microsoft introduced the Microsoft Network (MSN) to the horrors of the other on-line service providers and under the scrutiny of the Justice Department. When a user installs Windows 95/98, an icon for MSN appears on the screen, beckoning them to try it. MSN quickly grew to a million reported users after August 24, 1995, when Windows 95/98 was introduced. Interestingly, at that time it could only be used by Windows 95/98 users. In 1999 MSN stopped offering proprietary content.

America Online

At almost 20 million users, America Online (800-827-6364) is handsome, elegant, and considered easy to use. It also offers $ 21.95 per month unlimited use, but at the price of ads, ads, and more ads. User of DOS, Windows, and the Mac can access America Online, although you must use their software to do so.

New users of on-line services have flocked to America Online due to its ease of use, features, and CD-ROM disk every home and business receives from them every month. Up to five people can share an account and receive their mail separately through the use of separate "screen names."

America Online provides one of the easiest methods of setting up a Web page in the industry. Each screen name has 2 megabytes of disk space for Web pages that can be created by filling out a simple questionnaire or uploaded by those more familiar with the language of the Web, HTML.

Prodigy

Prodigy (800-776-3449, 800-PRODIGY) became a popular on-line service when it cost $9.95 per month for unlimited use, despite heavy advertising on every screen. The traditional service was scheduled to stop in 1999. Prodigy offers Internet access at an hourly or monthly rate.

Other Services

Although a number of other services exist, old and new, and have their faithful subscribers, America Online stands alone as the most vital on-line service. CompuServe has resources of the greatest importance to accountants and financial managers.

INTERNET SERVICE PROVIDERS

In 1993 there were no Internet Service Providers (ISPs) in Rochester, New York, a city with a population of 400,000 and a greater metropolitan area of 900,000. Now there are a number of independent ISPs, and the phone company (Frontier Corporation), long-distance carriers, and on-line services all hope you will become their annuity.

An Internet Service Provider offers TCP/IP access to their computer, which is on the Internet. They normally offer no proprietary additional information content (that would otherwise be unavailable from the Internet) but always offer technical support, often provide software preconfigured to make access easier, and sometimes provide training.

Depending on the size of the ISP, it may offer dial-up services or offer direct connections. Direct connections are especially valuable when you can hook a whole network or business to the Internet, not just one station.

Local ISPs have a limited number of access phone numbers in regions outside of area. Some offer toll-free access numbers for travelers, but will charge a surcharge for their use. That means that accessing the Internet can be more costly if you do a lot of out-of-town travel.

National ISPs have many more areas in which you can dial a local phone number to access your account. People who regularly travel will want to consider a national ISP to keep their phone and on-line service bills affordable.

The standard charge in the United States for unlimited, dial-up Internet access is $19.95 per month. Some services charge more, and some less. Your choice will depend on availability, speed, and reliability in your home city and where you will be traveling, the type of connections you will be looking for, and the support you will require.

You can find lists of ISPs in your area at http://www.thelist.com. You also can search for them at http://www.ispcheck.com, http://www.barkers.org/online/index.html, and http://ispfinder.com.

Some major ISPs include:

America Online, $21.95 per month for unlimited usage. America Online Inc., Dulles, VA; 800-827-6364, 703-265-2120; <http://www.aol.com>.

AT&T WorldNet, $21.95 per month for unlimited usage. AT&T WorldNet, Basking Ridge, NJ; 800-967-5363; <http://www.att.net>.

Earthlink $19.95 per month for unlimited usage, plus a $25 setup fee (waived if you sign up on-line). EarthLink, Pasadena, CA; 800-395-8425; <http://www.earthlink.net>.

Mindspring, $19.95 per month for unlimited usage, plus $25 setup fee (waived if you sign up on-line). MindSpring Enterprises, Atlanta; 888-877-7464; <http://www.mindspring.net>.

Also consider:

IBM: http://mypage.ihost.com

Sprint: http://www.sprintbiz.com

UUNet: http://www.us.uu.net

OTHER SOURCES FOR INTERNET ACCESS

There are a number of options available for gaining access to the Internet, especially if you are satisfied with dial-up accounts.

Colleges and businesses

If you are an alumnus of a local college or an employee of a business with Internet access, you may be able to obtain low-cost or free access to the Internet through the organization's account. Colleges do not always offer PPP or SLIP access; shell accounts are more the norm. Accessing your account from outside of your local area will require a long-distance call or connecting (telnetting) from another account.

If you live near a college, it may be worth your time to use the Internet there. When researching sites for this book, the author took a five-minute walk to the college library, where Web sites come up much quicker (four times or so) than over his dial-up account.

Free ISPs

No monthly charge to surf! Sound too good to be true? Perhaps. That's why this section comes with a major caveat.

You need to be careful with "free" Net access. You may need to buy software up front. There is no guarantee the site isn't going to disappear in a couple of months, leaving you with useless software and no Net access. Free ISPs have little motivation to offer good technical support, if any, and may offer unreliable connections. If you are ready for no help and lots of busy signals, charge ahead.

There are many options, including some where you pay an up-front fee, while others offer free surfing, usually if you complete a detailed demographic survey. Check out NetZero at http://www.netzero.net or Net Marketing's site at http://www.freewwaccess.com. Netzero is subsidized by banner ads. The service is reportedly fairly good, and it is available nationwide. Would you prefer to pay a little up front and then surf? Try Freewwweb at http://freewwwebusa.com. These services are very busy, and making a connection at peak hours can be difficult. Try it—it's free. Then determine if free Internet access is worth the price.

Freenets

Freenets are attempts to make the Internet available to the community at little or no cost. Often the people who would most benefit from the Internet, such as those looking for work, are those who can least afford access. With a

Freenet account, you have a limited amount of time each day to access the Internet, send and receive mail, and perform research. Freenets are always looking for volunteers to help with technical support. You can sign up for Freenet accounts across the country. However, if you need to dial your Freenet long distance, the charge will nullify whatever cost savings you may have hoped for compared to commercial services that offer local access. A list of FreeNets is maintained at <http://y4i.com/freeaccess.html>.

Libraries

Many public libraries offer access to the Web. While a trip to the library to use the Internet may not be as convenient as a home connection, it has many advantages. It requires no computer purchase or software configuration and comes with ready support. Library Internet connections are often very quick compared to a home connection. The downside is that you probably will not be able to set up your own Web page or have a personal e-mail account (for receiving e-mail). However, a library Web site in conjunction with a Freenet account or a free Web-based e-mail account can combine the benefits of both.

MOVING BEYOND TRADITIONAL INTERNET TOOLS: UNIFIED MESSAGING

Voice on the Internet

The popularity of the Internet has spurred on the development of not only e-mail but voice through the Internet. Internet voice systems, like those bundled with Microsoft Internet Explorer, are becoming more reliable and standardized.

Internet phones go beyond computer-to-computer communications. Companies can tie the Internet into their internal phone systems to allow Web sites visitors to click on a link and speak directly to a salesperson or technical support. The customer uses the computer microphone, speaker, and sound card, but the support person would answer the phone as if the call were placed more conventionally.

The quality of voice through the Internet does not approach standard service. However, companies have embraced the technology behind the Internet, TCP/IP, and voice over IP technology has found a cost-saving and reliable home. Large companies can now bypass the traditional phone companies and communicate and fax through the Internet within their company—and through the Net. Vocal'Net Server, from Inter-Tel of Chandler, Arizona, is a call server that manages phone calls, sending them through the Internet, your intranet, or the traditional phones, whichever is most expedient.

Perhaps you would like to access your voice-mail through the Internet. NexPath Corporation of Santa Clara, California, offers the inexpensive but powerful Nexpath NTS Server. At less than $4,000 for an 8-port system, you get computer telephony, Internet-accessible voice mail, and Web-based administration.

Phone as Computer Terminal

Many times telephone entry of data into a system can be helpful. Companies hoping to gather survey information or feedback for their customers can have real-time access when end users can complete the survey with their touch-tone phone. Interactive Voice Response systems ("Press or say `One'") open the door to those of us who have not moved to touch-tone or for whom it is not available.

Moving to the next step, Applied Language Technology of Cambridge, Massachusetts, specializes in phone systems that respond to your voice to enter information into and access computer databases—automatic speech recognition (ASR). You can, for example, ask for the latest price for a stock by saying the company name or ticker symbol, instead of wallowing through a huge menu system, memorizing codes, or spelling it out on the phone. Speaker verification capabilities ensure that users have the authority to access information.

Unified Messaging

What if you could retrieve all the messages being sent to you—voice, fax, e-mail, alphanumeric pages, Web pages—from either a computer or a telephone, whichever is more convenient? The world where messages are data, no matter where they come from, is the world of unified messaging (UM).

COM2001 NTX, from COM2001 Technologies, Inc. of Carlsbad, California, is arguably the most heralded, flexible, and esoteric of the products available. From a single-user on a laptop to a network-based solution, COM2001 offers traditional and IP-based communications, Web, fax, mail and conferencing servers, and the unique Personal Assistant, which can respond to verbal commands to place and receive calls, access Web pages, send and receive e-mail—all from a phone. This feature is similar to the fascinating Wildfire (800-WILDFIRE; http://www.wildfire.com), a speech-driven service that tracks you down, takes voice commands, screens and announces calls, creates conference calls on the fly, and announces callers during calls . . . no additional equipment necessary.

Getting Practical

Buffalo, New York-based Voice Technologies Group, Inc., is another leader in the CT industry and proponents of UM. They offer practical advice about who should consider implementing these systems and their expected benefits.

What type and size of company is the best candidate for a unified messaging system?

- Companies of 50 to 500 employees with highly mobile sales, support, and executive teams
- Companies with internal management of their e-mail, LAN, and telephone resources.
- They run their businesses on a LAN (vs. a mainframe)
- Their "road warrior" types are already laptop-equipped and literate, and are already using remote access to their home office's LAN network
- Companies that run their mid-sized offices with "friendly" telephone systems

How Does a Unified Messaging System Make a Company or User Money?   It allows people to be more effective in their job and handle more communications faster with fewer errors; key employees (information workers and road warriors) can manage more information and communication per day in less time.

The only commodity that any of us has that is of any value is our time. We sell it for hard dollars. In a unified world, (almost) all of your messages are in a single place.

Virtual Assistants

We are not about to tell you to fire your receptionist to save on overhead costs. However, you may be willing to hire a new assistant who will work 24 hours a day, seven days a week, for $20 a month and long-distance charges. When that $20 means one more sale, one more client service rendered, one more opportunity to be in touch when it is otherwise impossible, it is money well spent. The Internet has become the focal point of the Virtual Office, and every Virtual Office needs a Virtual Assistant. This rapidly emerging and increasingly hotly contested market has as its major selling point keeping mobile workers in touch, wherever they are, whatever they need.

Describing a Virtual Assistant is not easy, and the competing services do not share all of the functions to be discussed. However, a Virtual Assistant makes it easy for people to get in touch with you and for you to get the messages they have left for you. It acts like a helper, answering the phones, watching your faxes, and tracking your e-mail. With one phone number, people can communicate with you wherever you are. You also can make calls out and set up conference calls.

You let your Virtual Assistant keep track of your personal phone listings, and let it know where you will be and how best to get in touch with you. Then it lets you know when someone has been trying to reach you. When you call (by phone) or log in (by the Internet) to your Virtual Assistant, you have access to your voice mail, faxes, and e-mail.

There are a number of Virtual Assistants in the marketplace, including Webley (888-444-6400), Portico (800-PORTICO), and Wildfire (800-WILDFIRE) (Call the numbers given and listen to the demonstrations!) Each has a different personality—and we all know that each of us gets along with some personalities better than others. Webley and Portico have the strongest Internet orientation.

Many of the Virtual Assistant's functions can be duplicated with more pedestrian options. However, services like Webley offer value that is greater than the sum of its parts. Here are some of its major features and functions, along with some commentary on alternate choices.

1. Webley and Portico assign you a toll-free number, take your calls, route them as you wish, and take a message if you are unavailable. Webley receives faxes as well. Call forwarding can route calls to follow you. An answering machine or voice mail can receive calls. Some services are available to provide toll-free faxing. Virtual Assistants combine all these in one roof and can be administered using a toll-free call or by the Internet.

2. Virtual Assistants let you access your e-mail from a phone. Many Internet Web sites make it easy for you to get your e-mail wherever you can access the Internet (such as www.hotmail.com, which both lets you receive E-mail at username@hotmail.com and to register your other POP3 E-mail accounts for access through Hotmail). Other commercial services will do this task as well.

3. Virtual Assistants can maintain a contact list for you and can dial your contacts. A $5 black book or a $40 organizer can keep the numbers and an autodialer can hold your frequently dialed calls on that phone.

4. Webley lets you receive faxes at the same number as the voice number. A fax/voice switch can do that at your own site.

5. Unique to a Virtual Assistant, Webley lets you receive your calls from the Internet using RealPlayer and manage and save them. This can be useful if there is a local Internet access number but the toll-free number is unavailable and if you have one phone to surf and catch your calls.

6. Webley can notify you by pager or e-mail when you have a call, using caller ID to identify the caller. Few messaging systems can send you an e-mail, a helpful feature.

7. Virtual Assistants can use voice or touchpad input. Portico has a friendly female voice. Webley converses with you and your callers in a British accent. Webley's manner pleases some and really annoys others. As to the voice recognition—is that part a gimmick at this point? Many people prefer talking to punching in numbers.

8. Virtual Assistants will subtly interrupt a call to let you know another call is coming in, let you know who it is, and let you move between calls. This is somewhat like enhanced call waiting and caller ID—but it happens from any phone, not just one with a unit and the service. With Webley, you can tell it to take the call or take a message, not an option with call waiting.

9. Virtual Assistants can set up conference calls and send your voice messages to someone else via e-mail from any phone. Not easy to do otherwise.

10. Portico can track important news items and company information and lets you ask for corporate news on the fly. Portico can help the investor act more knowledgeably on stock tips.

11. Virtual Assistants costs around $19.95 per month, plus 15 cents per minute of phone usage. At 15 cents for calls through your Virtual Assistant, you could use a good calling card to check in your answering machine and place your own calls on the card—but you would miss out on the call waiting functionality. With Webley, wherever you have an Internet connection, you can pick up your phone calls for free, using RealPlayer.

From Here . . .

Chapter 4 discusses software needed to get started on The Internet.

Software for the Internet

This chapter describes the software you need to get started on the Internet. The following outline summarizes the contents of this chapter:

- *Web Browsers:* Web browsers are the tool for seeing the graphical web and the front-end of applications of the future.
- *File Management and Manipulation:* These tools help when using files on the Internet.
- *Design Tools:* Making your own Web page? A few products are standouts.
- *Utilities:* They don't create spreadsheets or keep your contacts, but they are necessary to keep equipment functioning properly.
- *Internet-integrated Products:* Which software products work best with the Web on a day-to-day basis? The section hits on a few.
- *Interview, John Patrick, IBM:* We conclude the chapter with the insights of someone leading the way for eBusiness: IBM's John Patrick, the Vice President-Internet Technology for IBM Corporation and Chairman, Global Internet Project.

WEB BROWSERS

The World Wide Web opened the Internet up to the masses, and the graphical Web browser is what opened up the Web to users. From Mosaic to its descendant Internet Explorer 5, the Web browser has emerged as one user interface people find easy to navigate. That has opened the door for the browser to become the front-end to everything from accounting software and electronic banking to SAP and ERP.

Web Browsers—And Then There Was One?

Internet Explorer 5.   Internet Explorer 5 (IE 5) was officially released in March 1999. Interestingly, two of the top architects of Mozilla (the Web browser formerly known Netscape Communicator) bailed out of the project at the end of March. Could Microsoft, which in 1995 dismissed the Internet, finally have brought about the end of Netscape as we know it?

IE 5 is acknowledged as a great Web browser. Why?

Speed: It is faster than previous versions of Internet Explorer. In our prior tests, it seemed like Web pages took forever to appear on screen. IE 5 is far more efficient, especially on larger Web pages.

Ease of Use: IE 5 is easier to use than its predecessors. For new users, Microsoft has added a "Go" button the user can press after entering the Uniform Resource Locator (URL)—in case they don't know they can press the Enter key after making the entry. If a Web page can't be rendered, better diagnostics help identify the problem and offer potential solutions. We experienced this screen all too often when moving around, especially to secured pages, and IE 5 did not properly diagnose the problem.

Before you even go on-line, IE 5 offers support for multiple connections. In the past, you had to hand-pick different connections through Dial-Up Networking. Now you can choose from your corporate connection, your home ISDN connection, and your road ISP connection from a drop-down menu in the Connect box. If only they let you put in an address book to make accessing your ISP in different cities more manageable.

IE 5 can do its best to fill in repeated entries in the Address bar, in forms, and in passwords. When you start to type the URL into the address bar, IE 5 automatically displays a drop-down box with previous entries. Because of IE 5's integration with Windows, if you type a partial path from your local or network disks, IE 5 will display directories and files. This functionality is important, as IE 5 can be used to open any Office 2000 document without having to know which application created the document—if you have Office 2000 loaded.

The built-in Search, History and Favorites lists now can temporarily share the screen with your browser, a carryover from IE 4 but with added power.

Search lets you easily find sites on the Internet, e-mail addresses, maps, and newsgroup contents and switch between the search engines you select and prioritize (See Exhibit 4.1.). Like Netscape, you can now do searches directly from the Address bar. History makes it easy to find out where you have been (See Exhibit 4.2.). You can review your sites by date, by site name, or by the number of times you have visited.

Favorites also has been improved, and the obtrusive channels from IE 4 have been moved into Favorites, making them more useful and less annoying. (See Exhibit 4.3.)

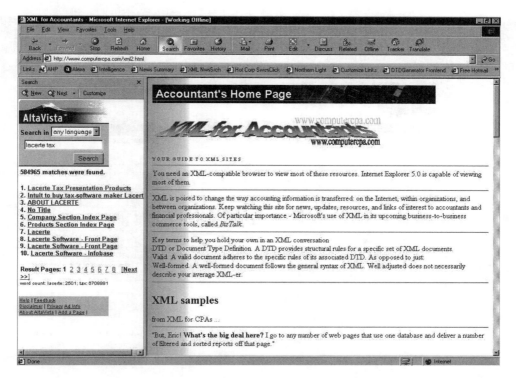

Exhibit 4.1 "Search" lets you find sites easily on the Internet.

Modularity and customization: More than ever before, you can download and install a minimal installation of IE 5 and then add other features later. A number of modules, called Web Accessories, from Microsoft and third parties add tremendous power and flexibility to IE 5. Some of these are already incorporated into third-party versions of the browser, such as the Alta Vista branded version. These add-ins include:

Microsoft's IE 5 Power Tweaks is designed to save keystrokes for those who want to go on or off-line quickly, copy URLs easily to the clipboard, or change the security ranking of different sites.

Microsoft's Web Accessories is an option that anyone who uses the Internet on a regular basis should add to IE 5, especially Web developers or trainers. For trainers, the accessories include right-click access to zoom in and out on images, highlight text on screen, and break out of frames. For developers, a right-click can bring up a new screen with the pages' links nicely summarized or a quick list of images with size and download times. A number of addi-

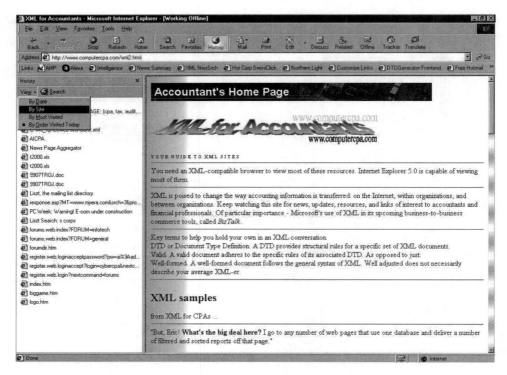

Exhibit 4.2   "History" makes it easy to find out where you've been.

tional search tools and the ability to quickly turn images on and off complete the collection.

Microsoft Web Developer Accessories also are useful for those interested in Web page design. They offer right-click access to view the Document Object Module (DOM) properties of a Web page and the ability to highlight a section of a Web page and view the source of that section alone (View Partial Source).

AltaVista Power Tools bring AltaVista's standard additional functions and its unique ability to translate between English and French, German, Italian, Portuguese, and Spanish as close as a right-click. Other options let you find similar sites using the Alexa utility, get Bloomberg stock quotes and business news, and customize the appearance of your browser.

Take the Web with You: IE 5 has a number of ways of saving Web pages to view later. The Save As function has been supercharged, letting you save the Web page, graphics, layout and all, in any encoding. If you choose to save the HTML only, you can do that as well.

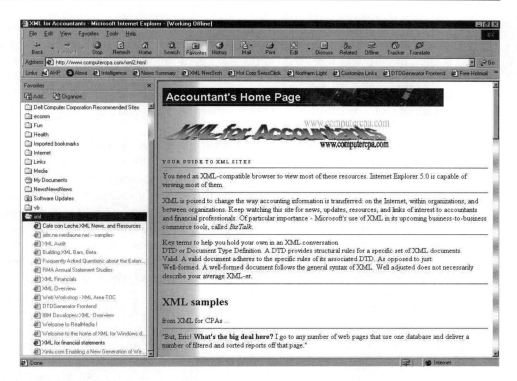

Exhibit 4.3 "Favorites" also has been improved.

In addition to saving a single page, you can pack up a site and take it with you. When you add a page to Favorites, you can choose to make it available off-line. You can then synchronize your off-line version to the on-line version on a schedule, on demand, or when your system is idle.

What Does IE 5 Lack?   You can have both Internet Explorer 5 and Netscape on the same machine—or even multiple versions of Netscape. One of Netscape's main claims to fame right now is the AOL/Netscape Instant Messenger feature, which makes it easy to tell when friends, family, or coworkers are on the Internet. But this latest version of IE 5 has a lot going for it . . . and Netscape may be nearing its end, as we know it.

Netscape 5.0 . . . Next Generation Technology . . . Gecko . . . Raptor . . . That's All, Folks?   Just before America Online purchased Netscape, and in response to Microsoft's ever-increasing share of the Web browser marketplace, Netscape made its source code available to developers and established

Mozilla.org. Netscape Communications and open source developers celebrated their first anniversary on March 31, 1999. Mozilla. org manages open source developers working on the next generation of Netscape's browser and communication software. Since the code was first published on the Internet, thousands of individuals and organizations have downloaded it and made hundreds of contributions to the software. Is it enough? Not according to some key players who ought to know.

Alternatively known as Gecko or Raptor, and formerly known as Next Generation Technology or NGT, the next-generation layout engine and core of Netscape 5.0 is fast and small enough to fit on a single floppy disk (instead of filling a CD). Sources estimate that the entire Netscape Communicator 5.0 suite (with browser, HTML editor, e-mail, and news) could be as small as 5 MB. Gecko has the potential of being the Web browser of choice for handheld computers, telephones, fax machines, and Internet television. It is available for Windows, Mac, and Linux and should be transportable to any other platform. You can download a copy of Gecko at (http://developer.netscape.com) if you dare.

Anyone brave enough to download the software should be warned that it is pre-beta, pre-alpha, and may not even work. It is not for the faint of heart, but it doesn't immediately crash your computer and erase your hard drive either.

Our early tests of Gecko show its roughness. (See Exhibit 4.4.) You need to start a DOS application named APPRUNNER.EXE to start up Gecko. Seeing browser operations being chronicled in the DOS windows of APPRUNNER while Gecko runs can be unsettling. Many of the bells and whistles do not work yet. However, it is small and fast, as advertised.

With the next-generation project taking so long, Netscape has had to spend its time upgrading and augmenting its present suite of Internet tools. Communicator 4.6 includes a built-in version of AOL Instant Messenger, a real-time chat client. With Instant Messenger, an implementation of the popular AOL-owned ICQ (I Seek You), as many as 23 people can participate in a chat simultaneously. The new Net client also includes "Quotes Anywhere," which gives users quick access to stock prices through the company's portal site, Netcenter's finance channel. The upgrade for Communicator is available free at http://home.netscape.com/download. IDT Corp.'s Net2Phone service will be an included feature in a to-be-released version of Netscape's Internet software suite, Communicator. Personal computer users will be able to make long-distance Net-based telephone calls, with IDT paying Netscape an up-front fee along with a share of revenues.

Is Gecko too much, too late? Has the opening of the Netscape source code to developers brought in a synergy that exceeds the results of Netscape devel-

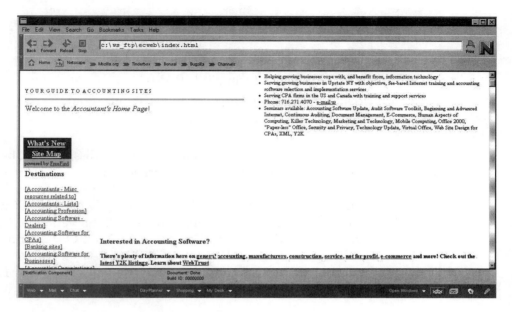

Exhibit 4.4 Early tests of Gecko show how rough it is.

opers alone? No, according to the former head to Mozilla, a man credited with the development of the first UNIX version of Mosaic, the precursor to Netscape, Jamie Zawinski. Zawinski recently quit the Mozilla project in frustration, blaming not Microsoft but Netscape's lack of innovation for the last few years and the corporate culture.

Opera. The Web browser market has been dominated since 1996 by the two biggest browser developers, Netscape and Microsoft. Between them, they account for at least 90% of the browser market. Who can compete when they give away great software for free?

Bucking this trend, Opera is gaining an increasingly strong foothold in the market—not necessarily to compete with Microsoft or Netscape, but to offer a sound and solid alternative to millions of Internet users.

Opera can be downloaded from the Internet at <http://www.operasoftware.com/download.html>. The size of the download file is about 1.3 MB, making the process very quick and painless. Installation is a breeze and takes less than a minute. The download is for a 30-day free trial. After that, you can purchase it for $35 (U.S.).

The core qualities that set Opera apart are:

- The speed at which the program starts and retrieves information from the World Wide Web
- The size of the program (installation and executable)
- The resource requirements (using little RAM)
- The user-friendliness (easy navigation and customization)
- An impressive useful-features-to-size ratio

Opera offers features for people with different types of disabilities. It became the first Web Browser catering for this special target market.

Opera does lag behind the major browsers for their features but offers an advanced, fully functional browser that runs happily on a 386SX with 6 MB (2 MB) of memory. Opera is available in 16- and 32-bit versions. The 16-bit version runs on Windows 3.1x, Windows NT3.51, OS/2, and Unix WABI. The 32-bit version runs on Windows 95, Windows 98, and Windows NT 4.0; with Virtual PC it also runs extremely well and fast on MacOS. Unique to Opera:

- Multiple windows: Opera retrieves multiple documents and images at the same time. The documents are loaded faster and you need not wait for a single document. You can just browse in another window.
- Window toggling: Done via the 1 and 2 keys on the keyboard or via the normal Ctrl-Tab combination.
- Full keyboard interface: For navigation on the Internet for those with "mouse sickness" and for an efficient execution of commands.
- Scaling/zooming: From 20 percent to 1,000 percent at the touch of a key.
- Load page in background: This feature allows the loading of a Web page as a new window in the background without "destroying" (overlapping) the currently active window. This is extremely useful when browsing search engine results and loading multiple documents from the search engine results page. Performance increases are in the region of 8 to 10 times, saving significantly on on-line time and costs.
- On-line graphics toggling: The graphics of each window can be toggled in real time without having to change Preferences. Options are On/Off/Show only loaded images.
- Document/User Settings toggle: How often these days do users come across one of these nasty pages with inverted layouts (white print on a black background)? We all know how dreadful they are to read, but only Opera allows these pages to be displayed exactly the way the user would like with just one click. A real lifesaver, and on top of that available per

individual window. The same applies to tables and various cascading style sheet settings.

- Add all documents to hotlist: The advanced and highly sophisticated "docked" hotlist allows all currently opened documents to be added as bookmarks with two clicks or keystrokes. Similarly, users load all book-marked documents in a subfolder. Drag and drop into new or open windows is a standard feature.

- Save Windows settings: This allows users to start right where they finished off the previous session. All window positions, history entries and document settings are saved.

FILE MANAGEMENT AND MANIPULATION

Web browsers sometimes need a little help to play, display, or run, files found on the Internet.

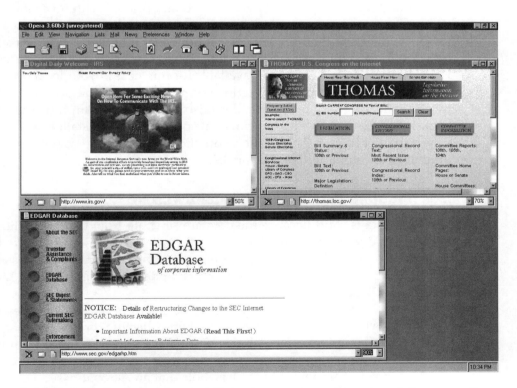

Exhibit 4.5 Opera receives multiple documents and images at the same time. Used with permission from Opera.

HTML Does Not Display Content Consistently; Enter Acrobat

Hypertext Markup Language (HTML) serves as the basic set of instructions to make Web pages look like Web pages. HTML includes instructions for collecting and acting on data entry from visitors to the Web site. There are a number of problems with HTML as a forms-based data collection tool: inconsistent display and the separation of the data from the form are two of them. HTML displays data inconsistently across browsers. For example, Microsoft's Internet Explorer and Netscape's Communicator Web browsers do not display Web pages exactly alike. For most the most part, the small differences are insignificant. However, if you are attempting to print a tax form from the IRS (http://www.irs.gov), you must print it within precise specifications.

Whether you are attempting to get a tax form from the IRS, Year 2000 guidance from the AICPA (http://www.aicpa.org), or articles from the *CPA Journal* (http://www.nysscpa.org) or the *CA Journal* (http://www.cica.ca), you will be faced with PDF (portable document format) documents, also known as Adobe Acrobat files. Adobe Acrobat was designed so publications like tax returns and manuscripts can be distributed and printed with no change from the original—without requiring the end user to own the same word processor and have the same fonts loaded. (See Exhibit 4.6.) Whether you are on a Mac, a PC, or Unix, you can create sharable documents with the Adobe Acrobat Publisher or Adobe Acrobat 4.0 (available for purchase at your local computer store or on-line at <http://www.adobe.com>.) and read and print PDF documents with the free Acrobat Reader (also available at <http://www.adobe.com>). The Acrobat Reader can run on its own or can be installed as a plug-in to your Web browser. Then, when you click on a PDF file, it will appear in your browser window. (See Exhibit 4.7.)

HTML Does Not Store Data Securely; Enter UWI.com

HTML also falls short because the data are separate from the form. The data are not saved with the form; data cannot be entered, verified, and saved off-line; the context of the form is lost after submitting the data. Adobe has tried to overcome these hurdles with a recent free update to Adobe Acrobat 3.0 and the Acrobat Reader.

You may never have to worry about filling a form out in triplicate again. The World Wide Web is emerging as a tool for collecting input from users and tying that information into databases. But what about when "the form is the thing"?

Almost every accountant who has looked at an Acrobat-based Form 1040 has begged for the ability to enter data directly onto it. However, until recently doing so was not efficient. Adobe has now announced the Adobe

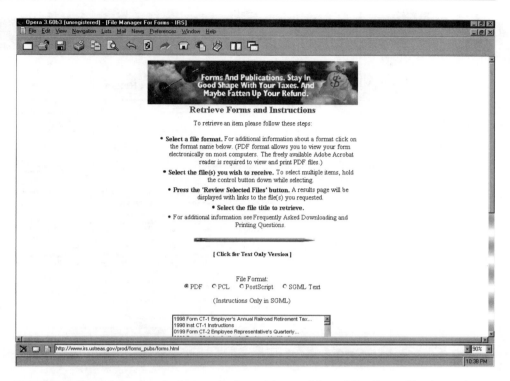

Exhibit 4.6 Adobe Acrobat was designed to enable publications like tax returns to be distributed and printed with no change to the original. Used with permission from Opera.

Acrobat Forms Plug-in Update. With Adobe Acrobat Forms, you can save forms to be completed, printed, or submitted later. In addition, JavaScript can be incorporated to verify data, perform formatting, and make calculations as the form is filled in. This "client-side" processing means errors can be detected while filling out the form, not later. The Acrobat Forms Plug-In Update can also act as an interface to database systems.

Hot on Adobe's heels is UWI.Com (http://www.uwi.com), which made news in a pilot project for the Internal Revenue Service. *Federal Computer Week* reported that the IRS has selected VeriSign, UWI.Com, and Intuit, Inc., to supply technology for a pilot program on presenting and signing tax returns. This program will test the use of digital signatures on tax returns that are filed electronically.

Like Adobe's forms the forms created with UWI.Com's software can be saved and completed off-line with the InternetForms Viewer and created with the InternetForms Designer. UWI.Com's products also boast the capability to

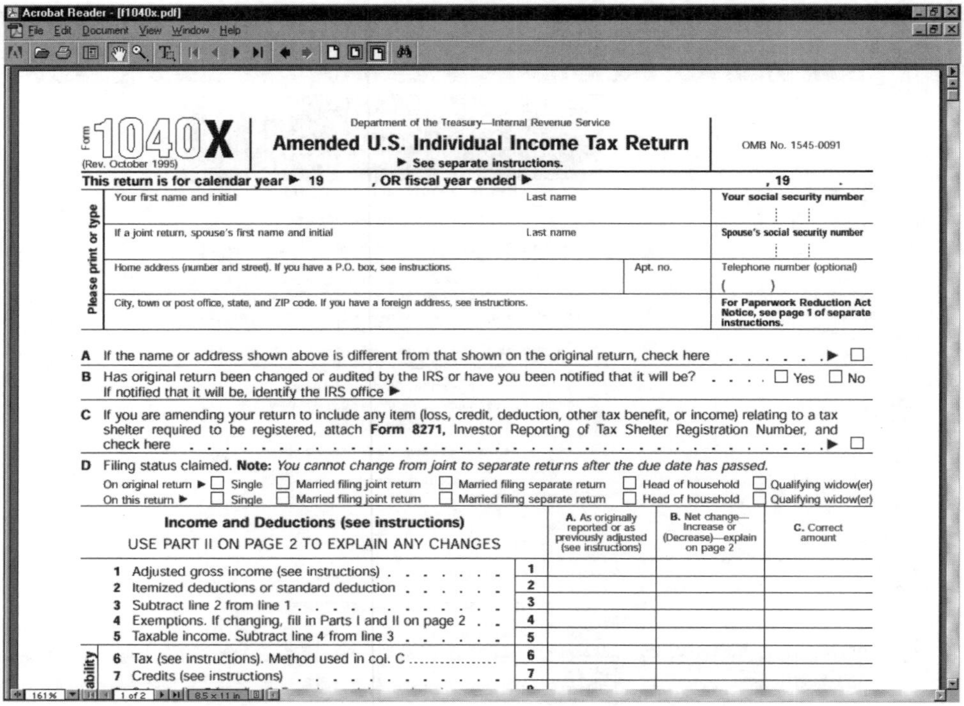

Exhibit 4.7   When you click PDF file, it will appear in you browser window. Adobe and Acrobat are trademarks of Adobe Systems Incorporated. Used with permission from Adobe Systems Incorporated.

store a digital signature with the form to make the records tamperproof. Finally, UWI.Com has incorporated the XML (eXtensible Markup Language) protocol, to better incorporate their product into the workflow systems of the future.

Preparing Files for Transfer and Storage

Many of the files you will find on the Internet have been changed, for ease of storage and transfer. The files are often compressed (altered so that the original can be reconstructed, but temporarily placed in a smaller, nonusable form). Files that are frequently used together are archived (in this sense, multiple files are altered so that the originals can be reconstructed, but the many interrelated files are stored in one larger file).

The advantages of compression and archiving are reduced space on the server, reduced time to transfer the files from computer to computer, and reduced steps to acquire the necessary interrelated files.

How can you take the hot air out of computer files so that transferring them through the Internet is more efficient? How can you keep a large number of related files together for safekeeping? The idea of archiving files to reduce their size for transfer or keeping multiple files together as one that has been dominated in the DOS/PC marketplace by the "ZIP" format. As DOS backup is no longer the standard, ZIP can make backing up and restoring files that are too large for one floppy disk more simple.

Compression and archiving programs are dependent on the hardware platform, such as DOS, Unix or Apple Macintosh (Mac). Most commercial programs today use these techniques for reducing the number of diskettes you must handle when loading their software. These include the PKZIP format from PKWare (which also has a self-extracting version that requires no additional software to re-create the original files) and Unix with its built-in Z or tar. PkWare's website is <http://www.pkware.com>. Pacific Gold Coast Corp.'s offers TurboZip: <http://www.pgcc.com>.

Utilities for the compression and decompression of files come in many forms. Some work on demand and others in real time. Some simply do the compression and decompression, while other permit easy inventory, viewing, and using zip files.

The Fun Stuff—Sights and Sounds

The Internet is a huge warehouse for multimedia, and the World Wide Web is the showroom. Recent developments for the WWW include an explosion of CD-quality music with files called MPGs, expanding on the real-time sound tools like RealPlayer (http://www.real.com) used for listening to radio broadcasts, speeches, and television programs. (See Exhibit 4.8.) However, many popular sites are dedicated to movie, television, and other sound effects (use all these within the bounds of appropriate copyright law, please), clip art and photographs, and video footage. These offer files for fun, instruction, and business use (multimedia presentations).

Many of the Web browsers, such as Netscape Communicator or Microsoft's Internet Explorer, have built-in tools to work with these multimedia files or have bundled popular tools with their browsers. If you click on an icon representing a sound with Netscape, a program will start to play that sound for you. However, those using older browsers or working with these files external to the browser will need extra help.

Sounds. Sound has been an integral part of the Mac since its inception. Windows took years to catch up. Most computers now come with the hardware necessary for enjoying sounds.

The primary sound files on the Internet are MPG, WAV files, the Windows format, and AU (audio) files, the popular Sun Unix standard. Playing these

Exhibit 4.8   Tools like RealPlayer are used for listening to radio broadcasts, speeches, and television. All rights reserved. RealNetworks, RealAudio, RealVideo, RealGuide, RealJukebox, and RealPlayer are trademarks or registered trademarks of RealNetworks, Inc.

files duplicates the original, like a tape recording of the sound. These files vary in size, depending on the fidelity desired when recording and length.

MPG files offer CD-quality sound and are shaking up the broadcast industry. RealJukeBox lets you control your CD and MPG files for easy listening on your computer. (See Exhibit 4.9.)

MIDI files (MID) are special instructions for your hardware and can drive external keyboards and other MIDI-compatible instruments. Unlike the WAV and AU files, MIDI can produce very different results on different computers, like the difference between a Philharmonic Orchestra and a bluegrass quartet playing from the same sheet music. Because MIDI only describes what to play and does not contain the sounds themselves, these files can be much smaller than the others. The Windows Media Player lets you play MIDI files as well as most of Microsoft's the other multimedia formats Microsoft has embraced. (See Exhibit 4.10.)

Exhibit 4.9   RealJukeBox lets you control your CD and MPG files for easy listening on your computer. Copyright © 1995-2000 RealNetworks, Inc.

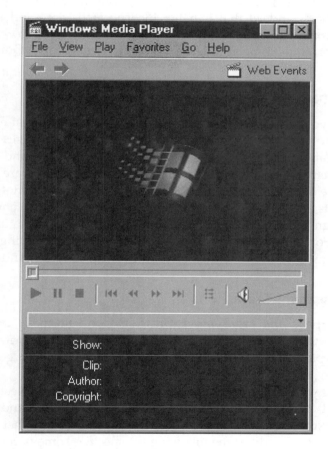

Exhibit 4.10   Windows Media Player lets you play MIDI files as well as most of Microsoft's other embraced multimedia formats.

Lights! Camera!   One of the most eye-catching aspects of multimedia is the use of full-motion video on the computer. Being able to bring up video footage at will lets you bring in experts and evidence when you need them, better illustrates the use of products for sales and training, and generally makes presentations more appealing.

Sound files can get very large depending on the quality of audio recorded; video files incorporate sound files and video, with a choice of resolutions. Even a low-resolution video will be megabytes large.

Microsoft Video for Windows (AVI) and Apple Quick Time (MOV or QT) each have its own video file format. The video format is being used for more than playing standard movies or television: Apple's Quick Time VR lets the user manipulate the video to "walk around" the movie and pick up and turn around items in the video. MPEG (Motion Pictures Expert Group) video is another standard that is being incorporated more and more into hardware vendor's equipment. Microsoft is found at <http://www.microsoft.com>; <http://quicktime.apple.com> is where you will find Quick Time.

DESIGN TOOLS

Everyone can have his or her own home page. Almost every Internet access account has room for a page. You can get free Web pages at Geocities (owned by Yahoo!). Many sites now have automatic tools and templates to create attractive Web pages. Numerous Web design tools are available for every range of expertise. But just as desktop publishing did not make CPAs graphic artists and Turbo Tax did not turn the general populace into tax experts, Web design software does not guarantee an attractive or useful site.

For those who do not design Web pages for a living, the Microsoft Web design tools are more than adequate for the tasks at hand.

Web Development Tools

Frontpage and Frontpage Express.   I don't normally begin individual sections with an apology, but here comes one. My favorite Web design tool is Notepad. This is sad, because Notepad is not even a good ASCII editor, let alone an HTML editor.

If you are like me, you often resort to Microsoft's lowest technology Notepad (Start | Programs | Accessories | Notepad) to do fast and furious, HTML editing. Notepad has major weaknesses as an ASCII editor that affects its capabilities as an HTML editor; the following list specifies some of the most important features that an HTML gearhead needs to do work. However, Notepad starts up quickly, doesn't get in your way, and doesn't make changes on its own.

Minimum Expectations of a Tool for Directly Editing HTML

- Search and replace
- (File | Open) remembers last few files you opened
- (File | Open) lets you open more than one file at a time
- (File | Save) lets you save files with an .htm or .html extension

FrontPage and Frontpage Express are Web design tools from Microsoft that are relatively inexpensive and able to do most of the tasks a CPA would require. FrontPage is better for managing large Web sites, offering numerous tools, like the *Parabolic View* (yes, they know it has nothing to do with a parabola), to maintain multiple-page Web sites. Both FrontPage and Front-Page Express let you add special programming functionality to a site—if your Web host supports that functionality. (Look for sites supporting FrontPage extensions). (See Exhibits 4.11 and 4.12.)

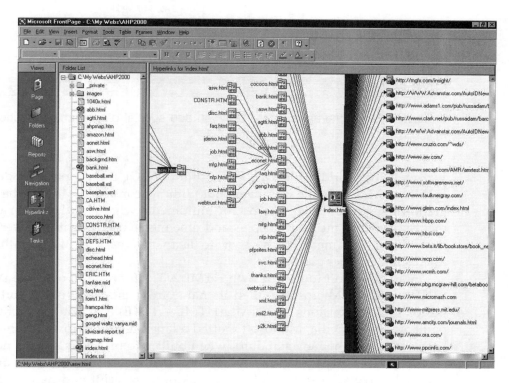

Exhibit 4.11   FrontPage offers the parabolic view to maintain multiple-page Web sites.

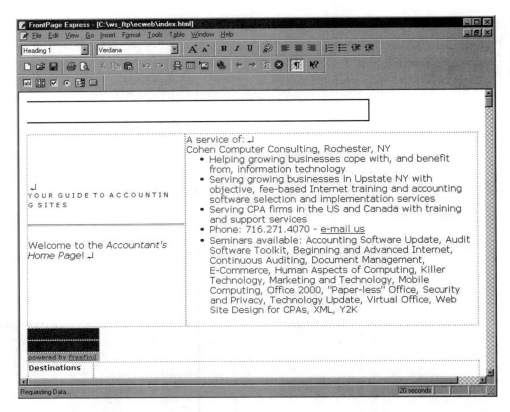

Exhibit 4.12 FrontPage Express lets you add special programming functionality to your site.

VizAct. The World Wide Web Consortium (W3C), the people who declare HTML or XML as standards, came out with Synchronized Multimedia Integration Language—SMIL—to do for multimedia what HTML did for documents: provide a means to display and time media elements in a player window. SMIL was meant to be easy to learn and easy to work with. But Microsoft has other plans.

First, Microsoft touted its own HTML + TIME proposal over the W3C's SMIL standard. Microsoft pulled its name from the SMIL effort and suggested Time Extensions for HTML (HTML + TIME). With the help of Compaq and Macromedia, Microsoft crafted a language interwoven in the Web browser itself. The new standard, when built into browsers, means no one will have to download plug-ins like Shockwave or Flash. There are no external players—just a lot of scary-looking JavaScript and new HTML + TIME tags.

Microsoft has kept a low profile with HTML + TIME. All those antitrust proceedings and other product plans have kept its efforts in a Web multimedia language all but invisible. But that has changed recently.

Microsoft's Vizact 2000 is a time-line–based Web output tool for use within the Office 2000 family of products. In the old days, we called it multimedia. Now you can set up documents running on the Internet or intranet that swirl and twirl and open and close and highlight and hide elements— on your timetable and without needing to learn sophisticated tools. Oh, yeah—you need Internet Explorer 5 to see the pages as they are meant to be seen.

Microsoft calls Vizact "the first document activation application." Using simple controls, users can control when elements such as text, pictures, audio, and video appear and disappear, their movement over time, and how they react to a reader's mouse. For example, Vizact 2000 users can add interactive bullets to easily transform a lengthy, two-page list of products and descriptions into an activated page that is half as long. Click on the interactive bullet, and the underlying text expands. Similarly, the text can expand and contract on a time schedule, leading the reader through an automatic presentation.

Vizact also helps users impress their readers with predesigned effects and wizards. Graphics can be made to shrink, grow, or pulsate; text can fade in and out using special effects or be highlighted with sparkles, bubbles, or smoke; graphics can be sent along a path over time.

Vizact may serve as the tool that turbocharges Office 2000 documents or brings PowerPoint-like scripting to the Web without needing to learn programming or scripting. The planned integration with Word and Excel means that CPAs will be able to create presentations using a mix of traditional tools and power presentation tools designed specifically for nonprogrammers. For accountants wanting to deliver information in new and exciting ways, Vizact may be the solution.

Your Word Processor or Browser.   Most word processors and Web browsers have limited Web design tools built in. Microsoft Word, for example, is both a poor browser and a middling Web design tool. (See Exhibits 4.13 and 4.14.)

Other Ways to Add Content

Sometimes the best ways to add functionality to your site is to let someone else do the work. Due to restrictions on the Internet Service Provider we chose for our Web host (our selection process: (1) Are they cheap? (2) Is it easy to get there?) we were missing some functionality we consider basic from a Web host. In particular, we needed a search engine.

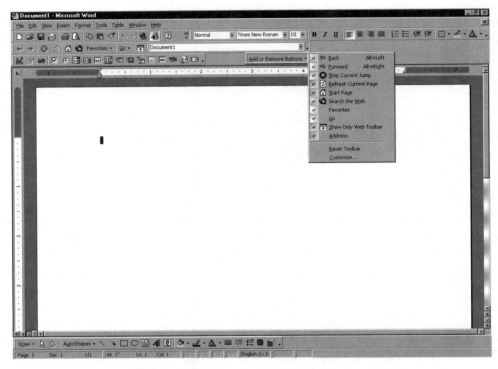

Exhibit 4.13   Microsoft Word has limited browser capabilities.

Then we happened on FreeFind (http://www.freefind.com/control.html). FreeFind offers tools to make search engines, site maps, and site update listings painless. In addition, they offer reports of what people are looking for on your site.

It starts off at the Freefind control center. From here you can integrate the search process more closely with your site by choosing your own look and feel, including your own background and logo. You can request that their spider (the program that reads your pages and indexes your content) visit your site, you can change your password, and more.

Reports for your FreeFind account let you see your daily search activity levels, the most common queries used on your site, and your most recent queries.

You can ask the Web spider to update your site index on demand. If you make changes to your site contents, you can ask the spider to reindex your site instead of waiting for a scheduled reindex.

You can customize the look of your query and search results pages. You can choose from a variety of backgrounds and search logos, or you can use

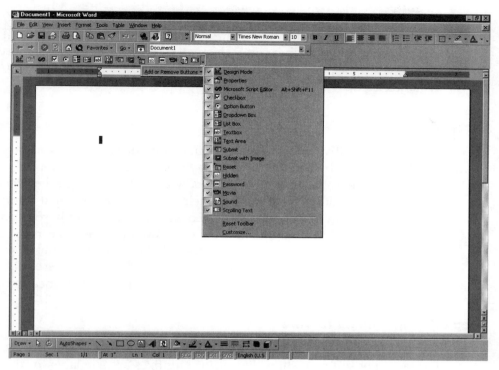

Exhibit 4.14   Microsoft Word is also limited as a Web design tool.

your own logo and background to integrate the search process seamlessly into your site.

FreeFind automatically generates three types of site maps for your site. You can choose to turn maps on or off and to customize your site map.

UTILITIES

Antivirus

Viruses are self-propagating programs that are loaded on your computer and run without your knowledge or desire, sometimes with little effect and sometimes causing great damage to your computer and making your life miserable. These programs can be copied off a floppy disk, downloaded off the Internet, received as e-mail, or ferried through a rogue process. The latest iterations of viruses take advantage of the Internet using ActiveX, Java, Microsoft Office macros, or VBA and or can come as an attachment to e-mail.

Solutions include Dr. Solomon's Anti-Virus Deluxe (http://www. drsolomon.com), CA InoculanAntiVirus (http://www.cai.com), IBM Anti-virus (http://www.av.ibm.com), Network Associates McAfee VirusScan (http://www.mcafee.com), and Symantec Norton AntiVirus (http://www. symantec.com).

Encryption

If you have sensitive information on your computer, and others can gain access to it in person or by a network, you may want to make that information inaccessible to others. Security (covered in Chapter 8) including a hardlock lock, passwords, and other methods may help. Encryption runs that information through a Captain Midnight Secret Decoder Ring, so that only someone with that ring can access and understand the data. You may wish to encrypt e-mails you are sending to others for "their eyes only" reception, or make your own disk useless for anyone but you. Solutions include Computer Associates CryptIT (http://www.cal.com) and McAfee PGP Disk (http://www.mcafee.com).

Keeping Programs Up to Date

These days you will not hear "We will ship no software before its time." Instead, new software ships and major bug fixes are available for download long before all the bugs are worked out. It is important to get the most up-to-date versions on a regular basis. Once again, utilities can come to the rescue. They can keep an inventory of your software and develop a schedule to download updates from the Internet. Some solutions include McAfee Oil Change (http://www.mcafee.com) and Norton Live Update (http://www. symantec.com).

Remote Access, Remote Control

Need to provide support to a user from afar or use the resources on your office computer from the road? Remote control products let you do everything but change the paper and insert a disk. Your screen mirrors the office computer, your keyboard runs its keyboard, and you can direct the printing wherever you want. Telecommuters will find Symantec's pcTelecommute of particular interest with its call management and synchronization capabilities. These let you provide support of a network or the Internet. Solutions include Traveling Software Laplink (http://www.travellingsoftware.com), Symantec pcTelecommute, and Symantec PC Anywhere32 (http://www. symantec.com).

INTERNET-INTEGRATED PRODUCTS

The Network is the computer, or so says SGI. Microsoft has had to agree to an extent. It now says the Internet is the computer and the browser is the front-end. As shown in Figure 1.1, Goldmine Software now incorporates the Web in its daily functions. Microsoft Excel can extract data from Web sites and include them in spreadsheets automatically. Even Quicken and Quickbooks rely on the Internet for bug fixes, support, banking, and payroll and investment purposes. (See Exhibit 4.15.)

With Office 2000, the intranet is the network. Users can collaborate on-line (Tools | Online Collaboration), work with files on the Net as if they were on their local computer, and save and retrieve word processing documents, spreadsheets, and presentation as HTML documents, which can then be retrieved back into the application with little or no loss of formatting or functionality.

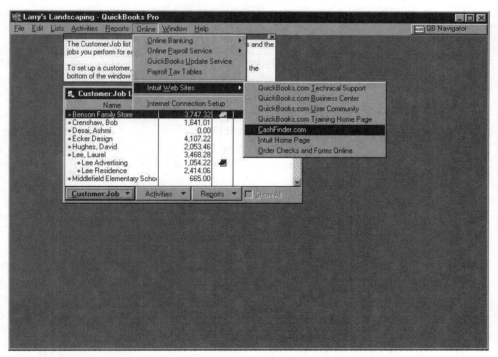

Exhibit 4.15 Even QuickBooks relies on the Internet for bug fixes, support, banking, payroll, and investment purposes. Used with permission from Intuit.

Microsoft's competitor to Quicken, Microsoft Money, has gone out of its way to integrate Money with the Internet. Here are just a few of its Internet functions.

Internal Browser: Access and browse the Internet from within Money. Just click an Internet link in Money, and Money will display the Web page, making a connection to the Internet if required.

Web Financial Services: You can download bank records and stock quotes from your financial institution's Web site and update your records electronically so your Money file always matches your bank. If your financial institution (bank, brokerage house, and credit card provider) supports it, you can even pay your bills on the Web site and download that payment information into Money.

Direct Statements: Electronically update your bank and credit card records, transfer funds between accounts, check your account balances, and order new checks from participating banks. You also can download on-line statements (electronic lists of the transactions that have cleared your financial institution). You can use these lists to update your account records electronically so that the information in your Money file is up-to-date with the account information at your financial institution.)

Direct Bill Payment: Pay bills electronically through your computer. This works with any checking account in the U.S. Direct Bill Payment (a direct banking service that allows you to pay bills electronically, which can be used with any checking account in the United States). After you set up direct bill payment at your financial institution, you can have money electronically debited from your account and your financial institution will send that money to your designated payee. It is offered as a part of Direct Financial Services in Money.

On-line Quotes: Here you can electronically update the prices of your stocks and mutual funds.

Electronic Bills: Have your bills delivered to you electronically through a secure, private Web site where you can view and pay them at your convenience. Associate your e-bills (bills you receive and pay over the Internet; same as electronic bills) with the recurring bills you set up in Money, to help you manage more of your finances from one location.

Financial Information on the Internet: Have Money notify you when new articles about subjects you're interested in appear on the Internet. Just click the links that appear on your Financial Home Page.

Microsoft Investor (Financial Suite only): This site lets you connect to Microsoft's Investor Web site for the latest investment and financial market information.

Decision Center: With links to articles on the Web (for Financial Suite users only), this is your personalized guide to the basics of good financial management and planning. By combining expert guidance, easy-to-use tools, and your own Money data, Decision Center helps you make smarter financial decisions.

Microsoft Money Home Page: Connect to the Money Web site for information on Money and personal finance, a forum for getting your questions answered, updated product information, and more.

INTERVIEW: JOHN PATRICK, IBM

Interview with John Patrick, Vice President of Internet Technology, IBM Corporation, and chairman, Global Internet Project. Contact him at patrick@us.ibm.com or http://www.ibm.com/patrick or www.gip.org. John gave a keynote address at the 1999 AICPA Technology Conference. Some of his comments are added to his interview questions with his permission.

How did you first get involved in the Internet for your own use?

I have been a PC hobbyist since 1977 when I got one of the first Radio Shack TRS-80s. I was also an early user of home banking services, CompuServe, Prodigy, and other on-line services. I first used the Internet as a way to exchange e-mail between IBM and various people on MCI Mail using IBM's Internet gateway, which had been built by IBM Research. I used the gopher and then later the web.

How did you/your firm begin offering Internet-oriented services to your "customers"?

In 1988 IBM won a bid to build the NSFNet, the first backbone of the Internet. We partnered with MCI and the Merit System of Michigan. Our first broadbased offering was in 1994, when we launched the IBM Global Network Internet Connection service.

What is your impression of CPAs and their Internet use?

I believe CPAs have been quick to see the potential of the Internet for communicating and sharing information. Creative accounting services on the Internet will likely be developed by them.

How about their clients?

There will be millions of e-businesses on the Internet. They will range from multibillion-dollar companies to companies of one person. They will all be global.

What makes your/your firm's Internet offerings unique?

What is unique about IBM is our ability to put all the pieces together: the hardware, the software, the consulting, the systems integration, education, financing, and actual operations. We do any or all of these key elements and make it all work for the customer.

What is your vision for accountants' use of the Internet?

I believe that accounting services will emerge which enable clients to "click here for an audit of your books." The appropriate data will be encrypted and transferred via the Internet to a service where it will be examined.

What is your vision for your own institution/firm?

Our vision includes millions of e-businesses reaching billions of customers around the world.

Do you think the Internet has had a profound effect on accounting and accounting practice?

Yes, because of the radical improvement in communications and collaboration.

Do you think the Internet has had a profound effect on corporate accounting and finance?

Ditto.

Most of the action is in business-to-business. You don't read about it as much [as business-to-consumer] but that's where the action is. It's much, much bigger than business-to-consumer. Everyone has their own numbers, but I think its maybe 10 to 1. E-Bay may have done $24 billion in sales, but I know a little company that brokers loans—it did $250 billion of loans last year.

What about the effect on Accounting Education (continuing and preparatory)?

Widespread availability of resources makes continuing education via the Internet a given.

The Internet offers 7×24 learning. We are all short of skills, whether large or small. IBM's LearningSpace technology is being used at a number of universities. They are out of [physical] space [to grow]—except on the Net. Wharton, Harvard, Penn—they have no space to build, except on the Net. These schools will be offering 25 percent more courses each year. Soon they'll have a million students instead of 400,000. People who learn this way expect other things this way.

What about globally? What effect has the Internet had on global accounting (International Accounting Standards)?

Development of standards will accelerate because of the communications and collaboration capabilities of the Internet.

What should accountants be doing to keep up and prepare for the future?

Be on the Internet regularly and learn what is going on.

What do you see as the greatest challenges still to be faced?

There are many more opportunities than challenges. Aggressive self-regulation is a key thing for us all to focus on so that restrictive or expensive regulations are not developed.

Do you have favorite Internet resources and software?

[IBM] www.ibm.com [of course].

Anything else you would like to add?

If you build it, they will come.

From Here . . .

Chapter 5 discusses marketing tips for the Internet.

Marketing Tips for Accountants: Establishing a Marketing Presence

This chapter provides advice to accountants on how to use the Internet to market their services. Techniques and technologies used by accountants and other businesses and sites of particular interest to accountants who wish to make their products and services known are highlighted. In addition, we discuss the costs of doing Internet marketing and forecast what CPAs stand to lose if they do not establish a marketing presence on the Internet.

The following outline summarizes the contents of this chapter:

- *Introduction to Internet Marketing:* This section is an introduction to marketing and the accounting profession, for many years a contradiction in terms.

- *Marketing Process:* This sections explores the marketing process. Marketing is more than paying for an advertisement. It requires planning and forethought to make the most from your investment.

- *Marketing Sites:* This section explores sites dedicated to marketing for (and to) the accounting profession. Your firm is listed on the Internet right now, whether you know it or not.

- *Other Aspects of an Internet Presence:* This section describes some steps for moving toward Internet marketing.

INTRODUCTION TO INTERNET MARKETING

At first glance, Internet advertising may seem unsuitable for a traditional CPA practice. After all, advertising, in general, is relatively new to the profession. Twenty-five years ago, advertising was not permitted at all. Human interaction was paramount. Clients were gained through referrals and friendships with the partners. Country club memberships and involvement in civic organizations brought practitioner and prospective client together. Firm brochures, yellow pages advertising, speaking engagements, and newsletters were pushing the envelope of marketing propriety. Staff members bridled at the thought of becoming junior Ed McMahons.

Society (and CPA firms) has changed. Traditional write-up and personal tax work is evolving and decreasing, as accounting software and tax preparation packages proliferate. With electronic filing, families are electronically communicating directly with the Internal Revenue Service. To compensate for the loss of traditional services, personal financial planning and consulting divisions have become more popular; non-CPAs often staff these offices. Advertising is not only permitted but widespread: Big 6 firms take out advertisements on television and in the *Wall Street Journal.* CPAs use direct mail services and conduct "cold call" campaigns.

Cold calling is a painful experience, and the stuff of aluminum siding salespeople and penny stockbrokers. Cold calling does not necessarily promote the image of the CPA as having much integrity, objectivity and independence. How else can accountants take an aggressive yet dignified push into marketing? The Internet can both provide a channel for aggressive marketing and permit the crafting and maintenance of the image the CPA firm desires.

The Internet has been used successfully by businesses as diverse as Federal Express, florists, and funeral homes to market their businesses. A number of Internet tools are available to gain exposure in the marketplace.

Web sites act as electronic storefronts, and you can offer electronic subscriptions to newsletters aimed at your clients or prospects using *mailing lists. Advertising space* on popular Web sites is a growing but unproven opportunity to target market. *Junk e-mail* (unsolicited e-mail sent to electronic versions of direct mailing lists) and *spamming newsgroups* (sending messages inconsistent to the purpose of the group to many news groups) also lets you target your audience, but with some ill feeling on the recipient's side. Answering questions and offering viewpoints in ongoing conversations in those same *newsgroups* lets you establish your expertise in a forum where you may be able to identify potential clients.

The Small Business Administration offers many resources to help in starting, financing, and expanding a business (http://www.sba.gov). (See Exhibit 5.1.) Any company hoping to expand needs a marketing plan. As part of a complete marketing plan, the Internet permits both targeted marketing and broad exposure to markets and people at the same time. The two effective words are *marketing* and *plan.*

MARKETING PROCESS

Introduction

The first word to be considered is *marketing*. The life of a professional is a life of marketing. Someone who can generate clients has an excellent opportunity

Exhibit 5.1 The Small Business Administration offers many resources to help in starting, financing, and expanding a business.

for advancement within a firm. CPA firms often provide an incentive (a percentage of fee income) to employees who bring in new clients; they also have clauses to compensate for lost revenues if the employee takes clients with them when they leave the firm.

Whom do business owners or individuals want to speak to when it comes to their business or personal finance? Someone they can know who has exhibited expertise in tax and accounting. Someone they can trust. This selection may be determined by asking others what professional they use or by knowing a professional from their mutual community involvement.

In many cases, however, personal contact is not as important as geographical coverage, expertise, or being at the right place at the right time. Internet marketing can help establish a firm's capabilities and communicate those capabilities to a broad audience. An Internet presence, similar to a Web site, is available seven days a week, 24 hours a day, is accessible around the world, and makes being in the right place at the right time easier.

Planning

The next word is *planning.* Planning for an Internet presence is more than declaring that the firm needs a home page on the Web. In the next sections, we discuss the questions to ask before setting up shop on the Web as well as how to go about establishing an Internet presence.

Those questions are:

- To whom are you trying to communicate? (your audience)
- What do they think about you now? (getting feedback)
- What do you want them to think about you? (your desired image)
- What can you communicate to them so they think about you in the desired way? (your messages)
- Where is your audience, and how will you get the message to them? (proper communications channels)

To Whom Are You Trying to Communicate? (Your Audience). A CPA firm needs to communicate to many groups of people to be successful. From a marketing standpoint, this includes prospective and current clients, prospective and current employees, and referral sources.

Clients: They receive services and are supposed to pay fees that sustain the firm.

How many prospective clients will you find on the Internet? As the Internet grows in popularity, more individuals and businesses will be researching firms on the Web. Currently a highly technical segment of the marketplace does a portion of buying and most research through the Internet; a Web presence may be the only way to reach this marketing segment. Other CPA firms getting involved in Internet marketing will become aware of your products and services, so they will become aware of your peer review and specialist services.

A firm's current client base is also a fertile ground for marketing. No matter how many meetings clients have had with the partner or how often services are discussed in a client newsletter, clients still are unaware of the breadth of services a firm can offer. The Web is an unobtrusive way to keep your capabilities before your client base.

Whom do you want as clients? Is your focus your town, county, or region? The Internet can be used to attract people moving into your area or to contact clients around the world. Are you willing to travel? Can you effectively serve clients in other areas of the country or world? The Internet breaks down the barriers of geography, for better of worse.

Employees: They are the official marketing arms of the firm. Like clients, employees often do not understand the breadth of services a firm offers. In smaller firms, where employees act more as generalists, they may be unaware of special consulting services. In larger firms, a junior staffer may spend all of his or her time preparing expatriate tax returns or researching Ohio sales tax, railroad rolling stock, or geothermal brine. A Web site can be effective in giving employees marketing tools by teaching them how to use a Web site to communicate client services.

Prospective employees also can be reached through the Internet. New graduates, taught to prepare for interviews through research techniques including Web searches, and experienced staff in other areas of the country can find your site, find out about your firm's personality and people, and communicate their desires to you.

Referral Sources: These are the goldmine of the CPA practice. At one of my former firms, we were told, "If you have the choice of befriending an engineer within a company or a stockbroker, and it's all the same to you . . . befriend the stockbroker." Referrals are one of the greatest sources of new clients in practice, and Internet marketing opens additional lines of communication. Other professionals involved in Internet marketing also can become excellent cross-referral sources.

You may want to communicate with others through your Internet presence, including your own vendors and regulators.

What Do They Think about You Now? (Getting Feedback). Once you have determined with whom you want to communicate, you need to determine your present audience's perception of your firm. Getting feedback from your audience is important at all stages of the marketing plan. Your firm knows the image it is trying to create; your audience can tell you how successful you have been in the past in portraying that image and help you determine what steps you need to take to communicate your vision more clearly.

A survey of current members of your target audience can help you find out:

- *What do people think about your firm?* Are you friendly, approachable, state-of-the-art? Do you serve particular industries or have internal expertise that makes you different than your competitors?

- *What do they consider the attributes of an ideal firm? What is their picture of the ideal firm?* Do they want the lowest cost, quickest turnaround, generalists, or specialists? Do they want a firm with a great deal of experience in their industry or one that does not work with their competitors?

- *What services do they think you offer?* Here is where you find out how well your message has gotten out in the past.

- *What services are they looking for that you may provide but they do not know about?* Not only does this help you to better communicate your services, but it offers immediate opportunities to fulfill their needs in response to the survey.

- *Do they wish they could contact you more easily?* Would e-mail or other automated methods of delivering questions or requests for information be perceived as a valuable service?

- *Do they wish you contacted them more frequently?* A professional's time is the inventory and stock-in-trade. Many clients are discouraged that the only contact their CPA has with them is at tax or audit time.

- *What information do they wish they could obtain more easily from your firm?* If one client has an interest in a topic, others may as well. Tax filing schedules, tax changes, and business tips can be sent in an automated manner.

- *Are they using the Internet or on-line services? What are their e-mail addresses?* Until your Internet presence is established, you will need to collect this information by mail or phone. Your clients may appreciate the opportunity to give you feedback. In addition, it is an opportunity to communicate your new Internet knowledge and efforts.

Once your Web presence is established, it will be easier to get feedback from your audience using your Web site or e-mail. Make sure that your phone numbers, fax numbers, and e-mail addresses are all published, and design your Web site so that e-mail is directed automatically to the person most appropriate to the topic. Survey forms can be added to the site, which provides both automatic replies, easier data input into a database, and structure to otherwise free-form e-mail responses.

Feedback can be painful, and needs to be taken in the spirit to which it is given. However, you can position your firm properly only if you deal with preexisting perceptions and move to strengthen or change them.

What Do You Want Them to Think about You? (Your Desired Image). CPA firms have always tried to portray an image. CPAs do not want to be known by their green eyeshades or as bean counters, and work very hard to dispel that image. Gray suits, white shirts and burgundy ties, oak and glass, knowledge, working relationships in the banking community, expert on taxes, accounting system specialists—CPAs work in many ways to seek to set themselves apart from their nonprofessional competition.

A firm's image is a function of its founders, its partners, its locale, and the clients it hopes to attract. The firm's mission statement drives the image, problems in the profession degrade it, and it is communicated by the way the phone is answered, documents are typed, and employees behave.

In order to maintain an image, most firms establish standard policies and procedures so that everything that comes out of a firm properly represents the firm. The Internet has brought informality inconsistent with these policies and an expectation that requests for information will be met with an immediate response, even when it is prudent to spend time developing a proper answer. The Internet is just a tool; it can be used to continue to craft an image, while a firm takes care not to fall into an improper and haphazard habit.

The Internet is of special benefit to smaller firms. More than a third of the membership of the AICPA are members of small firms, and many of them are in sole proprietorships. A one-person firm is not going to put a two-page spread in the *Wall Street Journal* or buy a Super Bowl ad (at least, not without venture capital). The costs of creating the advertisements and airtime are prohibitive.

On the Internet and the Web a small firm can have as impressive a presence as a multinational. As they say, "On the Net, no one knows you use a Mac."

Everything that you do must be put through the filter of your image. Does it enhance your image? Does it contradict it? What is the effect of injecting humor into your site—will your audience appreciate a funny accountant? What about associating your firm with businesses or organizations that may be distasteful to your audience?

What Can You Communicate to Them So They Think That Way? (Your Messages). Now that you know your intended audience, have feedback, and have determined the image you hope to convey, you can develop the message you plan to express. You will bring together words, images, and graphics into one vehicle that delivers your message.

Message Expressed. You will be describing your firm explicitly with information on your partners and staff, the services you offer, and the types of clients you work with. *Prospective clients*, including individuals and businesses, need to be aware of the benefits of working with your firm: your experience, knowledge, track record, or your competitive fee structure. *Present clients* need to be aware of additional services they can trust in you for. *Referral sources* should be able to find out what type of clients you work with and what services you can offer. *Employees* should be able to find out about the firm's services as well as their place in the firm.

Message Implied. Along with any message expressed with words, the layout, graphics, and sophistication of your site speaks volumes about the company. They speak to the commitment your firm has to the Internet, to its Internet site, to the kind of output a potential client can expect to see from your firm.

Where Is Your Audience, and How Will You Get the Message to Them? (Proper Communications Channels).   Now that you know your intended audience and have determined what you want to tell them, you need the way to get the message to them. The Internet can be used as both a passive and active tool for finding clients and communicating to your audience. The Web is the most obvious place to set up shop.

How difficult is it to get a Web site? Today the question should be rephrased to: How difficult is it to get a Web site that does what you want? Many places offer free listings, free Web sites, and even free storefronts. But secure Web sites without advertising (what—you thought there wasn't any catch?) that you can access using the domain name of your choice are a bit harder to come by. Finding the right combination of price, support, and performance can be a challenge.

Yahoo! Geocities lets you roll your own Web page for free. Geocities was a powerful force—so Yahoo! bought it. An annoying advertising message pops up over your page—but you save the bucks and know that Yahoo! will work to keep the performance up. Many people set up these sites despite the fact they could have a non–advertising-driven site (or in the case of AOL, five Web sites) as part of their subscription to an on-line service provider. On these sites you still could not have your own domain name—you were listed at a name like <http://members.aol.com/cybercpa>—but it was nowhere as tacky.

For around $10 a month, you begin to get the whole shebang: no advertising and your own domain name (such as www.computercpa.com). In fact, for just a little more, you could have as many individual Web sites as you might like. Then there are other options, including support for NT's FrontPage Extensions, a digital certificate, and a shopping cart. The cost: whatever the market will bear.

Marketing on the Web

The Web represents the fastest-growing way of communicating your message to the masses, a computerized version of a firm brochure, client newsletter, and marketing director, all rolled into one.

A Web page is both simple and sophisticated at the same time. An eight-year-old can create one in minutes, and a firm can spend months developing one. At the minimum, a Web page takes a Web host and HTML-encoded files. A number of other considerations go into developing the Web site and making it known.

Consider Your Web Host.   Your Web pages live on a *Web host.* It may be disk space on CompuServe, America Online, or your Internet Service Provider. It can be on your own computer, if you are on the Internet. Different hosts offer services and benefits that may be important to you.

If someone wants to visit your Web site, he or she can become disappointed if it is not available, is too busy to access, or is too slow. It is not especially difficult to become an Internet Service Provider; newspapers are filled with stories of teens who run Internet servers from their bedrooms (and soon become billionaires). Your Web host may go out of business without notice, taking your site out of business (temporarily, at least, and without notice). Their investment in computer hardware and fast telecommunications lines may limit the number of people accessing their system, and the bandwidth available may make access to your site unbearably slow.

Some firms will charge a series of fees for initial setup on their system, the initial design of your pages, or software to design or upload your pages. A local Internet Service Provider with whom the author was working demanded that all its customers use its graphic designer for Web design or find another Web host, reportedly to ensure a highly attractive site that people would want to return to. In addition, there may be additional charges for design changes to your page, upload charges to make changes, and traffic to your site.

Will Your Host Let You Register a Domain Name?   When people access your Web page, they type in your Uniform Resource Locator. The URL for the author's page is <http://www.computerpa.com>. It used to be <http://www.servtech.com/re/acct.html>. The URL indicates the service provider (in this case, Service Tech of Rochester, New York, now owned by Verio), a subdirectory, and an HTML file name. However, it offers little indication of the author's firm affiliation. Larger companies have registered a domain name that better represents the company. In general, you can find a Web page for a company by using the URL <http://www.companyname.com>, where the company's name, such as Kodak, Xerox, or Sony, replaces "companyname".

A personalized domain name is not necessary for an Internet presence, of course. Having your own domain conveys more status, a more corporate image. It is easier to type, in most cases, than an URL like the author's. However, once your URL is in a client's hot list or bookmark, or registered with a search engine, the actual URL becomes less important.

Registering a domain name normally requires a special relationship with the Internet Service Provider. The Web page hosting service included with most on-line service providers does not include the ability to get a domain name. Because of the need to dedicate an IP address to the domain name, the ISPs may charge $30 per month or more for domain name services, along with the cost of registering the name in the first place ($70) and an annual renewal fee ($35) after two years. The Internet Service Provider also may charge an additional fee for the domain name, or limit the names you can choose.

There are two alternatives to this normal relationship.

First, URL forwarding services will let you establish a domain name that will be attached to their system; they then redirect all traffic between your visitors and your actual Web site, even if it is listed under another organization's domain name. For less than $50 per year, you can have a domain name that uses the free Web site included with your AOL or ISP account. This is the method used by top-rated free home page site Homestead (http://www.homestead.com). Yes, you can build a home page for free and easy at that site; check out a site put together in 10 minutes at <http://www.homestead.com/addfast/index.html>. And for a small fee, URL forwarding can be added, so an address www.yourcompany.com will go to the Homestead site.

Second, Dynamic IP services let you have a dial-up connection, where the IP number assigned to your computer changes each time, and "sign-in" to a central routing service. That routing service then controls traffic between those that send data to your domain and your computer, despite the changing IP. Dynamic IP is more expensive than URL forwarding, but for less than $200 per year from organizations like DynIP (http://www.dynip.com) you can have an Internet name using your own top-level domain name (e.g., yourhostname.yourdomain.com), unlimited aliases for your machine (like www.yourdomain.com, ftp.yourdomain.com), and maintain your own Web host on connections that might not otherwise support it (such as Cable, dial-up, and other nondedicated connections.

A domain name is helpful for receiving e-mail and presents a more professional image on business cards and stationery than using a service provider's name. In addition, a domain name is portable; you can file for a "change of address" if you move from one provider to another.

Domain names are currently obtained through Network Solutions, aka the InterNIC (http://www.networksolutions.com). However a change has been in the air, for years.

The Internet Corporation for Assigned Names and Numbers (ICANN) (http://www.icann.org) is the new nonprofit corporation that was formed to take over responsibility for the IP address space allocation, protocol parameter assignment, domain name system management, and root server system management functions now performed under U.S. Government contract by a number of other entities.

In April 1999 ICANN selected five new registrars to test a system allowing competition among mutiple registrars for the .com, .net, and .org top-level domains (TLDs). One of these is the Internet Council of Registrars (CORE; http://www.corenic.org), which plans to administer new names, including .firm, .shop, .web, .arts, .rec, .info, and .nom.

The initial five testbed participants were selected based on technical, operational, and financial criteria, plus their additional abilities to provide enhanced technical and engineering support to interface with Network Solutions, Inc. (NSI) during the test phase. After completion of the test NSI will provide registry service access to all registrars receiving accreditation through ICANN.

Does the Host Help with Promotion of Your Site?   With the number of Web hosts and Web sites increasing so rapidly, setting up a Web site with no promotion is like doing no advertising, filing for a sales tax certificate, and then wondering why you do not have customers breaking down your door. Some questions to ask your Web provide follow.

Will the Host Submit your Site to Web Search Agents?   Although we will discuss how to submit your Web site's address to the Internet search tools, your host may be willing to do this for you.

Will the Host Advertise Its Site Address to Get People to See Its/Your Site?   Many Web sites have begun large advertising campaigns on television and in the press.

Will the Host Have Promotions to Get People to Its/Your Site?   Would you be interested in 1 million frequent flyer miles? A new IBM laptop? Internet advertisements for contests and other giveaways often lead the enticed surfer to Web sites for advertising purposes.

Will the Host Have a Series of Highlights of Its Users' Sites?   Half the fun of shopping in a store is what you see on the way to your intended purchase. Many of us have taken out library books we never considered that we ran in to on the way to the book we needed. Many hosts have a rotating series of highlighted sites featured on their main page, to offer additional exposure when visitors come to visit other sites.

Miscellaneous Services.   Additional services that are not found with basic Web services include database links and forms, automation tools (CGI scripts, Perl scripts, Java, and Visual Basic), and electronic commerce capabilities (such as electronic cash services, secure orders, and credit card authorization). As the author found out, sometimes basic Web services do not provide vital services such as counters and site search tools.

Design Your Site

Now that you know your message and have a place to host your Web site, it is time to pull together the text files, graphics, and other files you will use for your Web page. A firm brochure may be a good place to start.

Designing a Web page is very similar to developing a newsletter or brochure, as in standard desktop publishing. Although many tools let people design their Web sites on the fly, rough sketches, like a storyboard, laid out on paper are an excellent way to begin.

Each page is a trade-off. A single page filled with text and many graphics will load slowly but is more likely to be indexed by the search engines and will be more easily searchable by users. Small pages that fill one screen (and no more) will load quickly but be more difficult to navigate and maintain.

Separate pages also let you define multiple entry points; you can publicize and index each page separately. If you specialize in not-for-profits and manufacturing, you can have the search engines link directly to your separate nonprofit and manufacturing pages, both of which lead back to your own main page.

Web pages contain a few basic elements.

Text.   Most Web sites present information about their firm using simple text. They should include information about your firm, its services, employment opportunities, and affiliations with other groups. Many firms include resumes of their partners and staff, information about seminars and newsletters, and tax advice. Text-only Web pages are made from the simplest type of word-processed files: ASCII text. If you create a document with a standard word processor, you should save the document as ASCII text, not in standard Word-Perfect or Word format. If you have a newer word processor, it may have a built-in capability to take your text, add enhancements like fonts, bold, and underline, and then convert that document directly to HTML, which Web browsers translate into enhancements on your screen. HTML codes also can define the background and text colors that visitors to your site will see. Anyone who used Wordstar or has developed an ACCPAC Plus financial statement will be familiar with the concept of adding codes to their files for enhancement purposes.

If you already have the text for your corporate brochure in a word processing format, your Web document is well on its way. You will just need to add the HTML coding to your present text. Otherwise, you can begin to develop the text in text editors such as DOS's EDIT or Windows' Notepad, standard word processors such as WordPerfect or Word, or in special HTML editors such as Softquad's HoTMetaL Pro or Microsoft's FrontPage. These HTML editors include additional capabilities, such as predefined templates, the capability of organizing multiple-page Web sites, and artwork libraries.

Most Office Suite products incorporate Web design tools. Corel WordPerfect Suite, Lotus SmartSuite, and Office 2000 all have powerful Web design capabilities. Microsoft Publisher makes a tremendous design tool with the brains to match.

For older versions of Office, Microsoft makes available, at no charge, tools that let you take Word documents, Excel spreadsheets, PowerPoint presentations, and Access databases and turn them into HTML-coded documents that can be added to your Web page. These Internet Assistants for Office (before Office 95) are available at Microsoft's web site (http://www.microsoft.com).

Photographs and Illustrations. Photographs are not quite as easy to get into your Web page. Unless you are working with a digital camera, you will need to have your photographs scanned into a computer-readable format. Many printers and business/copy centers can help you with this; often colleges and universities also offer this ability.

Graphics, like illustrations and logos, are often created on computers, and may already be in machine-readable format. If not, you will need to have them scanned as well. However, even if you have machine-readable graphics, you may have to take an additional step or two.

First, most Web browsers can work with graphics in two formats: GIF or JPEG. If your graphic is in a standard Windows format like a bitmap file (BMP) or is a WordPerfect graphic, you will need to convert it. Popular graphics programs such as CorelDraw can perform this translation, and many shareware packages are available as well.

In addition to the basic format problem, graphics files can be very large. A typical scanned color image can be over 1 megabyte. On the Internet, however, any graphic over 100 KB takes more than a minute to download at normal modem speeds and will discourage users from viewing your site. That 1 MB image will take 10 minutes or more. Software that can compress images to a manageable size will let you use more graphics and make your site more interesting and visually stimulating.

Other Graphics. In addition to text, photographs, and illustrations, you may want to include other graphic elements, such as separator bars, embellishments, or bullets (graphic markers next to items that are parts of a list or menu choices). Some designers use them only for show; others add coding to make these graphics part of the selection process. The most sophisticated sites use little traditional text at all; the only text is part of large graphics called Image Maps, where the designer painstakingly measures out areas on the images to make each area act as a link. Animated graphics are eye-catching and can be accomplished a number of different ways. One of the simplest is using a special kind of GIF file.

Links. Links can serve many different functions. Some move you to another area on the same page or to another page that is subsidiary to your main page.

You may link to another company or organization's pages. A link may be used to download files, send music or video, or start up the visitor's e-mail system to send you an e-mail message.

Multimedia.   Many sites incorporate sound and video, both static and real time, in their Web sites. You could provide a tour of your office, excerpts from a speech, a welcome from the managing partner, or news for your clients, staff, or prospects. Real-time multimedia requires special software on your Web server. Making available audio files (WAV, AU, RA), video files (AVI, MOV, QT), and presentations using presentation graphics tools is as easy as a link to another site. More advanced Web sites even offer a live link to a receptionist through an IRC or Internet phone connection.

Remember that copyright laws should be considered as you add graphics and multimedia to your site. Obtain the appropriate permissions for artwork and other copyrighted items.

Forms.   If you would like to collect information about your visitor, you may want to define a form. Forms usually require a more sophisticated Web host than a simple on-line service account provides. A *form* has fill-in-the-blank areas where you can request your visitor's name, address, phone, and interests. These usually require special scripts. Ask if your service provider can help you with scripting. Once a form is filled out by a browser and submitted, the script creates a file that can be incorporated into a local database or turned into e-mail messages. These e-mail messages can be reviewed manually, or used by automated tools to collect registrations, requests for information, submissions to discussion groups, or respond to surveys.

Other Features.   There is an ongoing battle of the browsers, a fight for supremacy between Netscape Communicator and Microsoft's Internet Explorer. Microsoft in particular pushes the window of what HTML can do, exceeding the industry standard with new features. XML, Java and Visual Basic, VRML (Virtual Reality Markup Language) and other automation tools make for eye-catching sites that stand apart from their static text competition. However, these features often are visible only on the latest version of one company's browser, more likely Microsoft's. This means that your site may be partially invisible or cause errors in other browsers.

You probably know some people who are still using the computer they bought in 1990 or 1987. (If it wasn't for the Year 2000 problem, they would be permanent features!) With a technology as young as the Web, change must come more quickly. The world quickly leaves behind those still using Lynx, a text-based Web browser popular on dial-up UNIX shell accounts, or Internet Explorer 3. Some estimates gave an Lynx 80% usage share in 1994, down to 20 percent at the end of 1995. Graphics show up only as "[IMAGE]" in Lynx; clicking on an image map is out of the question. However, some other capabilities, such as Cascading Style Sheets and XML, are not included in more recent browsers. Be thoughtful of users of older browsers; either have multiple versions of your pages if you must use the latest and greatest, or cater to the lowest common denominator to get your point across.

Page Design

As quick as CPAs are to joke that a tax package does not make the average person a tax expert, we are slow to accept the fact that not many of us are graphic designers. It is easy to create a Web page, but how cheap do you want your firm to look?

A common complaint about many Web pages is that engineers have designed them; why haven't we been using engineers for all of our marketing efforts to date? "Way cool technology" may be fun for the technologically apt but it is not the main purpose of a Web page: Attracting your target audience is the goal.

Once your content has been considered, it is time to put everything together. There are many opinions as to who should do this development.

Do It Yourself. Many firms choose to develop their own Web pages. This serves to develop Web expertise among their staff. If done wrong, it can create a really ugly Web page. In fact, some firms choose to use the home page that America Online creates automatically, which will create a page that is completely inappropriate for a professional office. Most HTML design packages include wizards to help lead you through the design steps, and templates, which are carefully designed pages waiting for your customization.

A careful review of other accounting offices' Web pages is an excellent place to start. The CPA Microcomputer Report site (http://www.cpamicrocomputer-report.com) has regular and blunt reviews of many CPA offices' Web sites.

Use Outside Help. Other firms seek help from the outside in developing their sites. These firms believe that developing your own site is a waste of your hourly billing rate even if you have the expertise and that most small shops do not have the desire or ability to come up to speed. The ideal site will be developed with the help of experts in many disciplines.

Media Experts. Advertising and marketing experts can help hone the message and the presentation according to what makes people tick. An organization that specializes in marketing for CPAs, Mostad and Christensen (http://www.mostad.com), offers prepackaged Web pages.

Programmers.   Programmers can develop the coding to collect information and make a site exciting to visit.

Internet Experts.   Internet experts know the ins and outs of how to maximize the performance of a Web page. They can tell you how to set up the page's title to get interest or how to put in codes to increase the likelihood of your site being chosen from a Web index.

College Students.   Local college students bring expertise and resources to the development of a site at very reasonable rates. A co-op student who helps you with your site today may be an ideal staff person tomorrow.

Give Them a Means of Communicating Back to You.   An important part of a marketing-oriented Web page is a means of collecting information about qualified people who visit your site. The simplest way is to encourage your visitors to send you e-mail, using a special link that brings up their e-mail software with your e-mail address automatically included. A *guest book* lets the users tell more about who they are and what their interests may be.

People on the Internet love something for free; if you planned to put a newsletter up on your site, it can be more efficient to ask visitors to subscribe on-line. Then you will have their name and e-mail for later follow up.

Give People the Incentive to Come Back to Your Site.   Just like the major cola companies keep their company in front of the consumer, your marketing will be more effective with multiple exposures. That means you will want to give the visitors the incentive to return to your site on an ongoing basis. This can be accomplished by regularly changing the content of your pages, including news, tips, and reprints of articles or speeches. An update service, like the URL-Minder   (http://www.netmind.com/URL-minder/URL-minder.html) can be used to send e-mail to anyone interested when your site changes.

Consider the Possibilities of Accepting Advertising.   To offset the costs of maintaining a Web site, many firms accept advertising. The obvious advantage is the revenue stream. The disadvantages include a potential loss of the appearance of objectivity and an increased responsibility to make sure the site is maintained professionally.

Announcing Your Pages

With your site developed and loaded up on your host, it is time to let everyone know about it. Make sure to announce it in your traditional newsletters and advertising. Make sure your URL is added to your business cards and stationery. A helpful site for learning about marketing your Web site is (yet another) Microsoft-owned venture: Link Exchange (http://www.linkexchange.com) from MSN. Amid the sales pitches, you will find helpful resources to help you select a Web host, find tools for building your site, open a store, buy banner ads, keep in touch with the mailing list, Listbot (see "Mailing Lists" below), promote your site, check your site for proper form and search engine position, and much more.

How can you get your needle in the haystack to stand out?

Register Your Site. The search engines can all use a little help in finding out about your site. You can go to each search engine to let it know about your site, or you can use a site submission service that helps in getting your site introduced to a number of services at once. The best-known site is Submit-It! (http://www.submit-it.com).

Get Publicity for Your Site. Your site must be listed where your target audience will see it.

Get Linked. Many firms and organizations are providing free inclusion in their listings of CPAs and financial organizations. Bowling Green State University claims that its listing of CPA firms is the largest on the Web (http://www.cpafirms.com), with 4,000 firms listed. It even has a graveyard listing of sites that once were but are no more.

Cross Link. Indeed, one of the best ways to get your site known is to develop relationships with your clients and other organizations and offer a cross-link: They will provide a link to your site on their Web site, and you will return the favor.

How good is a Web site? An upcoming trend with search engines is not just to rate a search by how closely a site meets the search criteria but also by the strength of that site's presence on the Internet. One measure of the power of a Web site is by determining how many other Web sites link to that site.

Search engines are excellent tools for measuring this statistic. For example, to find out how well connected a site is using Alta Vista (http://www.av.com), you can type the following into the search engine: <link:domain.com-url:domain.com>. This search will give you a listing of the sites that link to the domain.com that does not include any internal references from within domain.com itself.

Be Announced. A number of publications, including *Accounting Technology, Accounting Today,* the *Journal of Accountancy,* and the *CPA Software News* are looking for Web sites to announce and provide exposure for.

Do Something Wild at Your Link.   Half the fun of the Internet is the way news spreads. If you do something really wild at your Web site, the news gets around. Offer awards for the top 5 percent CPA/CA Web sites, have a give-away or contest, or sponsor an unusual event—anything to get people talking about your site.

MARKETING SITES

Having your Web site available through another site can be perceived as an implicit recommendation on your part or theirs. Many organizations limit their affiliation with other organizations for that reason. For example, the author requested permission from L.L. Bean to show its Web site during semi-nars and include it in this book but was not given permission. As you consider your firm's image, it is important to consider where your name comes up.

Some places where you can have a link or a site include the following.

Malls

Designed after the model of a mall or strip of storefronts, a number of organi-zations have developed electronic malls. Malls can be a draw to people look-ing for services and products, and can lead them to your firm and its Web site. Malls can be regional, national, or international in nature. More important malls are aimed at special interest groups and minorities. Malls have not proven to be successful unless there is a common bond that brings people to the Web site and motivates them to use someone connected with the site.

Clearinghouses

A growing number of organizations aimed at marketing for accountants pro-vide special listings of CPAs. These clearinghouses offer limited listings for any CPA listed in the Yellow Pages; more sophisticated pages are available for a fee. Others list only members who have paid a fee for inclusion.

AccountingNet

Not associated with the Anet education consortium, AccountingNet (http://www.accountingnet.com) is a very aggressive marketing site. AccountingNet offers listings to CPA firms; every firm has a free listing, searchable by state, city, name, and specialty. More advanced listings and links back to another Web site are also available.

In addition, AccountingNet links to a number of state societies and provides editorial content of interest to accountants.

CPA Directory

The CPA Directory (http://www.ineedacpa.com) is a California-based directory service of CPAs. Other directories include CPA Links (http://www.CPA-Links.com), CPA Select (http://www.cpaselect.com), and CPA Firms (http://www.cpafirms.com).

Professional Societies

Many professional societies are providing links from their Web sites. For example, the Utah Association of CPAs provides an on-line search tool for recommending member firms: http://www.uacpa.org/choose.html.

Software Vendors

Many software vendors provide links to practitioners and consultants using or reselling their software. Do you consult in QuickBooks or another accounting software product? Your listing may appear, or your name may be returned when a visitor asks for support in their area.

OTHER ASPECTS OF AN INTERNET PRESENCE

The Web is not the only way to establish an Internet presence or to use the Internet as a marketing vehicle.

E-mail: Basic but Powerful

Most accountants are familiar with e-mail. With e-mail, a single message can be sent to 1 or 100 recipients at no incremental cost in most cases. E-mail software lets the sender type in an e-mail address or choose addresses from an address book. Most address books let you establish groups, which let you assign multiple recipients to a single group. Then when it is time to send out a mailing you can select one entry, for example "Newsletter", instead of selecting individual names over and over. E-mail is a familiar and easy to use tool. However, E-mail has some limits.

If you are sending the same information to a static list of recipients, e-mail will serve you well. However, once you need more capabilities, e-mail begins to groan under the weight. If the list of recipients changes frequently or if the recipients' needs differ, basic e-mail is too basic a tool. One step up from basic e-mail is a contact management tool like Goldmine from Goldmine Software (http://www.goldminesw.com).

Internet-Integrated Contact Management: Customization and Flexibility

Relationship marketing is the latest business buzzword. Major marketing relations firms (http://www.1to1.com) are now promoting the consultative relationship accountants traditionally have held with their clients—except doing it better. In these relationships, CPAs know what is going on with their clients, because clients are friends and neighbors, and we are familiar with their lives. With judicial use of contact management software, we can have that type of relationship with more of our clients. Yet few firms have embraced such software. Internet-integrated contact management software like Goldmine lets you select your recipients based on demographic information and filters. For example, if you want to send a notice of a seminar to everyone in a certain SIC code, you can set up a filter for that purpose on the fly. In addition, Goldmine lets you merge in information from the contact management system so each recipient can receive a customized e-mail from a single master.

Goldmine also has the ability to establish campaigns, a series of events that can be triggered and changed by events. Once you have sent out an initial e-mail, you can follow up with additional e-mail, phone calls, or other actions. Should the client or prospect respond, the campaign can automatically react to change the series of events that should follow.

These campaigns, called Automated Processes in Goldmine, are designed to help us remember that one "touch," or impression, is not always enough to move our clients or prospects to action, any more than Coke or Pepsi needs to advertise only once to keep market share.

Therefore, contact management software is an enabler. It lets us

- Communicate information to our clients on a scheduled basis or according to a pre determined "campaign"—as series of steps to orchestrate our relationship.
- Keep track of important information about our clients and schedule follow-up at appropriate times.
- Date- and time-stamp notes to document discussions with our clients. In this manner, the primary client contact can leave information for others to use when client communication is necessary and the primary contact is not available.

- Maintain contact more easily with our clients, getting and capturing any changes or vital information on a regular basis. This makes the relationship with our tax clients more than just a year-end event.

- Attach certain "profile" listings to our clients' records. This helps the firm send targeted information to the client or better identify clients who may require attention when changes to tax laws apply.

Popular contact management software includes ACT! (http://www.symantec.com), Goldmine (http://www.goldminesw.com), and Telemagic (http://www.telemagic.com). New versions of these products designed specifically for the CPA are in the works. An interesting client database system from Canada is BalaBoss (http://www.balaboss.com). While it does not keep contact history, it is preconfigured to store more of the common information in the accountant's office, such as where files are located and important filing dates.

Although contact management software offers more flexibility in selecting recipients and customizing the message being sent out, the communications from these products is still largely one-way. It requires more administration than many tasks require, while not permitting the sense of community that experts advise to capture and keep an audience. For this purpose, mailing lists are a traditional and useful tool.

Mailing Lists: Empowers Your Audience

One of the best ways to keep "touching" your clients and prospects is to stay in regular contact with them by developing a community in which they can contribute. While you can work with your Internet Service Provider and Web Developer to design a community for you, a number of advertising-supported services can provide these functions for you for free.

One such free service is ONElist (http://www.onelist.com) from ONElist Inc. It offers sophisticated mailing list management, surveys, group calendars, and many other features, all with an easy-to-manage front-end. ONElist's service hosts over 130,000 lists, with members exchanging more than 13 million e-mail messages each day. ONElist also offers a private, list-specific area where members can exchange documents, such as photos, recipes, articles, and business documents. ONElist Calendar allows users to easily post meetings and events that are of interest to each ONElist community. The ONElist calendar also allows owners to send e-mail notification to members reminding them of upcoming community events. For example, a CPA firm offering tax seminars can utilize the ONElist Calendar to alert members to upcoming tax conferences, important filing dates, and future discussion forums, while a ONElist small business user can use the calendar to schedule appointments for clients or alert them about upcoming product specials or sales. ONElist User Survey Tool enables list moderators to quickly and easily issue questionnaires to their community members.

EGroups (http://www.egroups.com) is probably Onelist's primary competitor.

Options available in mailing lists:

- **Moderated** mailing lists require the list owner to approve all e-mails before they are sent to the list.

- **Restricted** mailing lists require the list owner to approve all subscription requests to the list.

- **Announcement** mailing lists do not allow anyone except the list owner to send e-mails to the list. If any subscribers try to send e-mail to the list, the e-mails are ignored. These types of lists are good for keeping people up to date with changes with a Web site or company.

- **Archives** are previous list messages, stored on your Web site. For sensitive topics, this can be very important. You may choose to keep no archives, private archives (which are viewable only by subscribers), or public archives (which are viewable by anyone).

- **Digests** let you receive all mailings for a period of time as one e-mail rather than as individual messages.

- **Profiles** of your subscribers can be made available to subscribers of your list through a software list management feature.

- **Banned** users are those whom the list owner wishes to remove from participation in the list.

Mailing list software for your own computer is available as well. The most popular products have been Listproc (http://www.cren.net/listproc/index.html), Majordomo (http://www.cis.ohio-state.edu/~barr/major-domo-faq.html) and Listserv (http://www.lsoft.com).

Seminars

Some cynics say the only people making money on the Internet are people who sell Internet services to others. Your clients are looking for guidance in whether they should get involved on the Internet, its benefits and areas to be cautious about. You can develop seminars about the Internet, announce them on the Internet, and even conduct them through the Internet. Your content can be presented immediately using tools like International Relay Chat (IRC) or in a delayed fashion through uploaded text or audio or video files. Major corporations like Digital Equipment Corp., Microsoft, and Asymetrix Corp. use the latest multimedia tools like RealPlayer (http://www.real.com) to present real-time audio and video presentations.

Forum and Group Interaction

You can get mileage from participation on other on-line areas. E-mail, mailing lists, and newsgroups all can supplement your Web presence.

Ask or answer questions in newsgroups and on mailing lists, being very careful that your message includes your sig (electronic business card).

Look for newsgroup submissions you can respond to, followed with the opportunity "For more information, call our office. . ."

Set up an "E-mail responder" that will provide literature fulfillment with a simple e-mail message as the catalyst.

For a small monthly fee, mail servers let you deliver newsletters to hundreds or thousands of subscribers.

You could, but should not procure lists of e-mail addresses and send junk e-mail. (The author deplores this practice.)

Making the Databases

Sometimes you just need to know the right people. The Small Business Administration has an extensive marketing network, called PRO-Net (See Exhibit 5.2.). Wind up the right databases and take advantage of the right connections, and who knows what will happen next?

Final Thoughts

Internet marketing is just one part of an effective marketing plan. In the United States, recent estimates place home ownership of computers at over 40 percent, and many of those use on-line services. That leaves a large portion of U.S. homes with no Internet access. A large segment of the market does not use the Internet at all. In addition, the accounting profession's reputation for trust has been hard-earned. We help our clients based on much that we find out about them indirectly and through intuition and experience.

An Internet presence can help recapture the market that is happy with feeding information into an anonymous, nonthinking tax package and submitting data to the IRS while providing exposure for the person-to-person services accountants are known for.

An Internet exposure also can provide support and a point of communication for clients gained by conventional means. In other words, combined with other marketing tools, it can supplement a coordinated effort.

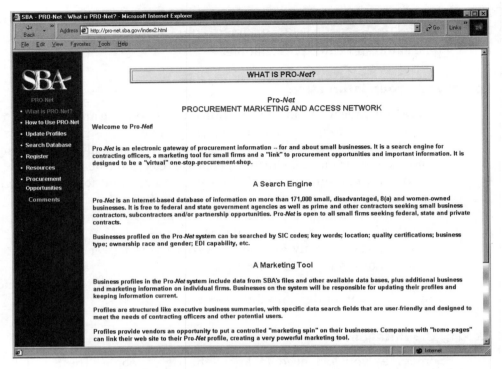

Exhibit 5.2 The Small Business Administration has an extensive marketing network called PRO-Net.

From Here . . .

Chapter 6 covers research on the Internet, highlighting tools for the accountant and auditor.

Research and Search Tools

This chapter covers how to find things on the Internet. It discusses the search tools and techniques you need to find what you want efficiently and as painlessly as possible. The following outline summarizes the contents of this chapter.

- *Introduction to research on the Internet:* You may be amazed by the resources available on the Internet. What is there? Can you trust it? This section helps you find out.

- *Web searches:* This section covers finding what you need on the Web. The Web's popularity means that the latest and greatest is found on it and nowhere else.

- *Non–Web-oriented searches:* Certain resources are not available through the Web. This section discusses traditional search tools for the older Internet services.

- *Places to research and search:* This section lists some sites that let you search through databases, do periodical searches, and find out how to run your office more efficiently.

- *New and unusual tools:* This section discusses software-based search tools that can help you in your task.

- *Putting it all together:* A Web search is one step in taking advantage of the resources of the Internet. This section provides a few ideas to be more thorough.

INTRODUCTION

It Tells You Everything You Need to Know about Anything

The following is an excerpt from the *Hitchhiker's Guide to the Galaxy* by Douglas Adams (1980).

> Ford handed the book to Arthur.
> "What is it?" asked Arthur.
> "The *Hitchhiker's Guide to the Galaxy*. It's a sort of electronic book. It tells you everything you need to know about anything. That's its job."
> Arthur turned it over nervously in his hands.

"I like the cover," he said. "Don't Panic. It's the first helpful or intelligible thing any-
body's said to me all day."

"I'll show you how it works," said Ford. He snatched it from Arthur who was still
holding it as if it was a two-week-dead lark and pulled it out of its cover.

"You press this button here you see and the screen lights up giving you the index."

A screen, about three inches by four, lit up and characters began to flicker across
the surface.

"You want to know about Vogons, so I enter that name so." His fingers tapped
some more keys. "And there we are."

The words *Vogon Constructor Fleets* flared in green across the screen.

Ford pressed a large red button at the bottom of the screen and words began to
undulate across it.

What You Want Is There; Watch Where You Step

Douglas Adams, in his popular book *Hitchhiker's Guide to the Galaxy*, spoke
about an electronic book where, by typing a few words into an index, you
could find out all you need to know on any topic. It let you bring up any one
of a million pages at a moment's notice. It contained contributions from
countless numbers of travelers and researchers. However, the editing was
uneven, reflecting what seemed to the editors to be a good idea at the time. It
omitted many things and much that was included was apocryphal or at least
wildly inaccurate. Searching for information on the planet Earth brought up
only the one word description, "harmless."

Welcome to the Internet 2000.

You can get an answer to almost any question from the Internet—if you
know where to look. You can find out about any topic. If what you want is not
there already, the inhabitants of the Internet will get it for you. Of course, you
need the wherewithal to discern whether any answer you get is valuable.
GIGO (garbage in, garbage out) quickly comes to play in electronic research.
The source must be weighed carefully.

Many resources are as valid electronically as they were in traditional form.
If you trust the objectivity of a major publisher, you will appreciate when its
Web site makes the last three years of its technology publications available for
full-text searches through the Web. Would you question the advice in "Jim-
Bob's Tax and Pit Bar-B-Que Quarterly," mailed weekly except for hunting season? Then you have what it takes to recognize that even the most professional-
looking sources of information on the Internet provided by unknown people
and organizations have no promise of reliability whatsoever. Just because you
can search through three years of USENET postings does not mean that the
messages you find are any more or less authoritative than the writing you will
find on a bathroom wall in a high school or thruway rest stop.

With an attitude of caution, you can head into the waters prepared. What are
you looking for, background information on a new client or industry? Advice on

purchasing new equipment? Exposure drafts or tax publications? The Web offers many tools for finding out about anything you may want to know.

What Is There and How to Find It

Search engines are the card catalogs of the Internet. Well, more than that. They offer compelling information on their own. Some use robots that index every word of the Web pages they scan and newsgroup (USENET) submissions, providing an abundance of resources for you. Other organizations have developed hierarchical indexes, where someone has categorized the Web sites listed, and may let you find pages that contain the information you need or point you to other resources. Where the resources you need are contained within one organization, most Web sites offer internal search engines to let you find specific information about that company or organization.

Traditional research tools for accountants have not all found their way to the Internet for free—yet. Most of the authoritative accounting literature, such as accounting standards, is not available. However, many companies and organizations that have provided the research tools in more traditional on-line or CD-ROM format have found their content made available by the government for free through the Internet or otherwise have provided new content on the Internet. Some provide search services for a fee, such as Lexis-Nexis (http://www.nexis-lexis.com), while others make information available for free which formerly was a chargeable service.

The Web brings a new depth of resource available, with tools to make getting at the enormous volume of governmental and commercial resources. You can find 10 K and 10 Qs at EDGAR, tax information at the IRS, census information at the Census Bureau, and software specifics at the pages of Microsoft, Lotus, and other vendors.

If you would like to know more about something, you will be able to find out more than you ever cared to know about that topic by searching the Internet. The Internet community has made an enormous amount of information available, most of it at no charge. The trick is how to go about finding it. Here is where to begin.

WEB SEARCHES

Millions of Pages: Where to Begin?

The Web is where it is at. Businesses are developing their presence on the Web, with sales and marketing, technical support, and employment opportunities. People are putting up information about their hobbies and families. Kids are maintaining their own sites. Almost everyone with access to the

Internet has the capability of having his or her own Web page at no additional cost.

With millions of pages available, finding those that are relevant can be like finding the proverbial needle in a haystack. How can anyone find what might be helpful on the Internet, and especially the Web?

Tools of particular help are starting points, indexes, hierarchical categorizers, metasearch tools, and vertical specific listings. To get the latest news on search engines, visit the *Search Engine Report,* a monthly newsletter that covers developments with search engines and changes to the Search Engine Watch Web site (http://searchenginewatch.com).

Starting Points

Few things are so lonely as a blank computer screen. Where do you begin? What do you type? The major on-line services, such as CompuServe and America Online, present you with a menu of options when you log on to their systems. The Internet, however, is not centrally run; it is up to you to know what to do when you log on. Fortunately, there is a plethora of portals to get you going.

Most of the major search engines offer news, search tools, and jumping-off points to make your surf easy.

Indexes

A number of organizations have set up tools to let you search through the full text of Web sites or USENET newsgroups. By typing in a few key words, you can find Web sites that use those words or phrases that have been indexed by that particular service. The sites that offer these search services differ slightly in the tools you can use in placing the searches and differ greatly in their speed and in how extensive and complete they are.

Most of these sites operate for the advertising revenue they draw. Some display a rotating series of advertisements. Others display ads based on your search term. If you type <flowers> you will get an ad from a florist. Type <map> or <travel> and you might get an ad from a travel agency or airline. Type <job> or <career> and you may be presented with a personnel service or an opportunity to go directly to a job-oriented Web site.

Alta Vista (http://www.altavista.com) or (http://www.av.com)

Alta Vista is a personal favorite, and offers foreign-language search and translation, natural-language questions (thanks to AskJeeves, below), and a wide range of power searching commands. Alta Vista opened in December 1995 to showcase Digital's equipment. It was owned by Digital and then by

Compaq (which purchased Digital in 1998), and now is owned by CMGI group, which also owns Lycos and HotBot.

Ask Jeeves (http://www.askjeeves.com) or (http://www.aj.com)

Ask Jeeves is a human-savvy search service that aims to direct you to the exact page that answers your question based on an inventory of 10 million or so stock questions. It is also a metasearch tool and provides matching Web pages from various search engines. The service went into beta in mid-April 1997 and opened fully on June 1, 1997. It's the search engine even a managing partner can love.

AOL NetFind (http://www.aol.com/netfind)

AOL NetFind is Excite in sheep's clothing. AOL NetFind launched in March 1997.

Deja (http://www.deja.com/)

Deja was the first organization to make searches through USENET widely available as a free service. Deja's services includes special tools to refine news-group searches as well as many other tools to build community.

Direct Hit (http://www.directhit.com)

Direct Hit is a popularity engine, offering sites in its search results that turn up as the sites users pick from previous searches.

Excite (http://www.excite.com)

Excite is another personal favorite, more as a portal than as a search engine. It offers one of the best news search services available: Excite NewsTracker. Excite was launched in late 1995. It grew quickly in prominence and consumed two of its competitors, Magellan in July 1996 and WebCrawler in November 1996.

Go (http://www.go.com)

A match of technology and Mickey, Go is a portal site produced by Infos-eek and Disney. It is another portal cum search engine.

Google (http://www.google.com)

Google is growing in stature as a search engine that finds good links. It makes heavy use of link popularity as a primary way to rank Web sites. How will you fare on Google? Remember the search engine trick—search for your site in place of mine using "link:www.computercpa.com -url:www.computer-cpa.com" and see how many people link to you.

GoTo (http://www.goto.com)

GoTo is not entirely objective in its positioning of search results because it sells its listings. Companies can pay money to be placed higher in the search results, which GoTo feels improves relevancy. Huh? GoTo launched in 1997 and incorporated the former University of Colorado–based World Wide Web Worm. In February 1998 it shifted to its current pay-for-placement model and soon after replaced the WWW Worm with Inktomi for its nonpaid listings.

HotBot (http://www.hotbot.com)

HotBot is a funky search engine. Its GenX exterior masks its power, which is borrowed from Direct Hit service and Inktomi. HotBot launched in May 1996 as Wired Digital's entry (hence the GenX appearance) into the search engine market. Lycos purchased Wired Digital in October 1998 and continues to run HotBot as a separate search service. CMGI buys Lycos and Alta Vista and there you go.

Infoseek (http://www.infoseek.com)

Infoseek is rightfully one of the more popular search services on the Web. It routinely brings up many fewer listings than Alta Vista, but of similar or better quality. Infoseek launched in early 1995.

Lycos (http://www.lycos.com)

Lycos has some great tools to look up people, maps, graphics—and it is a search engine too. Lycos started out as a search engine but shifted to a directory model similar to Yahoo! using listings from the Open Directory project, with secondary results from sending its spiders onto the Web. Lycos is one of the oldest search services, starting in 1994 at Carnegie Mellon University.

MSN (Microsoft) (http://www.msn.com)

Microsoft's MSN service features both directory listings and search engine results from various services. Not a direct first stop for heavy research.

Netscape (http://www.netscape.com)

Netscape Search also offers links to numerous search engines. Netscape's NetCenter has benefited from the tie to America Online and offers many tools for the searcher.

Northern Light (http://www.northernlight.com/ or http://www.nlsearch.com)

Northern Light offers searches through literature, including accounting publication published by Faulkner and Gray. It features a large index, along with the ability to cluster documents by topic. Searching through the document databases is free, but there is a charge of up to $4 to view them. There is no charge to view documents on the public Web—only for those within the special collection. Northern Light opened in August 1997.

ReMarQ (http://www.remarq.com)
Like Deja, ReMarQ makes its mark through easy access to reading and posting to the USENET.

Snap (http://www.snap.com)
Snap is human-compiled directory of Web sites, supplemented by search results from Inktomi. Like LookSmart, it aims to challenge Yahoo! as the champion of categorizing the web. Snap launched in late 1997 and is backed by Cnet and NBC.

Hierarchical Categorizers

A hierarchical categorizer does not look at the content of a site to let you know it is relevant to you. Instead, you select areas that generally cover your topic and then choose topics through layer after layer that more specifically describe your interest. The advantage of a hierarchical categorizer is that someone has taken the time to consider what category or categories a site should be listed under. With full-text search, words that mean drastically different things in different contexts (such as <heavy metal>) can bring up sites that are completely wrong for the search. Yahoo! is considered one of the best categorizers; other sites also offer this capability.

Along with sites that are indexed by their owners, some of the search services offer a rating or reviewing service, which is supposed to be some assurance that the site is somewhat reliable.

About (http://www.about.com)
About has a myriad of "experts" who collect their favorite links on just "About" any topic imaginable.

LookSmart (http://www.looksmart.com)
LookSmart is like Yahoo!, not a true index but a human-compiled directory of the Web. In addition to being a stand-alone service, LookSmart provides directory results to Alta Vista and many other partners. Alta Vista provides LookSmart with search results when a search fails to find a match from among LookSmart's reviews. LookSmart launched in October 1996.

Yahoo! (http://www.yahoo.com)

Ask a CPA what search engine he or she uses, and you will probably hear Yahoo! is the Web's most popular search service and has a well-deserved reputation for helping people find information easily. Then you tell them it is not a search engine, it is a hierarchical categorizer. It does not send computer robots on the Web to collect data. Instead of searching a huge index of terms found in the Web sites, it searches through its own internal organization and hierarchy.

The secret to Yahoo's success is human beings. It is the largest human-compiled guide to the Web, employing 80 or more editors in an effort to categorize it. Yahoo! has at least 1 million sites listed and supplements its results with those from Inktomi. If a search fails to find a match within Yahoo! listings, matches from Inktomi are displayed. Inktomi matches also appear after all Yahoo! matches have first been shown. Yahoo! is the oldest major Web site directory, having launched in late 1994.

Metasearch Tools

Metasearch tools are the like the librarian, whom you ask to look things up in the card catalog because it is too hard to do yourself. Metasearch engines take your request and pass them along to multiple search engines on your behalf.

Popular metasearch tools include:

Dogpile: http://www.dogpile.com
Inference Find: http://www.infind.com
Internet Sleuth: http://www.isleuth.com
SavvySearch: http://www.savvysearch.com

Vertical Specific Listings

If you know where you are going, you will find sites devoted to listing the best sites for a particular interest or profession. A number of organizations have set out to list the best business and accounting-oriented sites. Some sites of special interest include the AuditNet Resource List (http://www.auditnet.org), the IOMA Business Page (http://www.ioma.com), and the author's own Accountant's Home Page (http://www.computercpa.com). These sites list thousands of resources specifically aimed at business and finance professionals.

Which to Use?

• When you research from general to specific, use a hierarchical categorizer. For example, if you are searching for Job sites for employment information, choosing "Jobs" on Yahoo!'s main page should be more efficient than searching for the word "jobs" in AltaVista.

- To move from very specific to general, use an indexer. If you are looking for sites that mention the Entry Point Service, but are not sure where to look, an Indexer is preferred over Yahoo!

- To submit to many search engines at the same time, use a Metasearch. If you would like to gain many perspectives on an issue, such as Area 51, a Metasearch tool will search places you may not normally visit, offering new perspectives.

- Use a natural language tool for beginners. When you are unsure how to begin a search, a natural language tool will let you ask your question in a way more familiar to you.

Searching Techniques

Today's Web-based search tools try to provide a common interface for finding many things, including files, information, and people. The basic search techniques are similar to those used on older on-line services and CD-ROM research products.

How do you perform a search in the search engines? Most of the techniques are standard from search tool to search tool. You type a few words into a box and hit a button to begin the search. After a few seconds, you are presented with a list of Web sites that include or match your search term. However, the results the search services return can be so complete that typing in a phrase like <AICPA> will not just bring up the AICPA's Web site, but the home pages of all CPA's who have indicated that they are members, the listings of every tape from conference copy that came from an AICPA conference, and the archives of every news item where an AICPA spokesperson was present.

For example, let us assume you have a client in the metal stamping industry and want to find out about competitors and the industry. If you ask about "metal," you will have to look at far more information than you are interested in. You will be presented with tens of thousands of results (called "hits"), and they will be unfocused. Unfortunately, computers are not very good at concepts and will obediently find every place a word exists. You cannot tell the computer, "I mean the shiny hard substance, not musical style." You will have to filter through "heavy metal" and other irrelevant topics.

Computers are very literal. Type a word and they will find it. Most of the time you are trying to pick and enter a few words that you think may appear on a page in which you are interested but will not appear on a page you are not interested in. This makes searching an art rather than a science. Certain words are very specific to accounting, such as "debit," which appears in debit cards and few other nonaccounting situations. "Credit," on the other hand, appears in movies, television, and many other contexts.

More words are better than fewer words in a search, unless the topic you are researching has some very unusual words. "Hypothermia" will likely bring more relevant results than "Accounting." The more words you associate with your topic, the more focused your selections. If you find one or two relevant choices, often you will find cross-references from those Web pages to other relevant resources. You also may be able to tell the search engine that you want another Web site similar to the one it has listed, if the results listed say something like "See also: Similar Pages", as with InfoSeek.

To help researchers, search engines let you use Boolean logic. Each engines has a way of signifying include (the word should be there), exclude (the word should not be there), AND (both words must be there), OR (if either word is there), and "as a phrase" (the words together and in that order). For example, if you need information on taxes in the country of India, you may be better off purposefully excluding words, by saying "India Not America."

You have a number of choices when you type in multiple words. Most search engines assume you are looking for Internet resources that include *any* of the words. Prefixing the search term with a "+" (plus sign) means that the search word *must* appear in the resulting pages.

If you type terms in lower case, the search engines will do a case-insensitive search, looking for both upper- and lower-case results. Using a capital letter in the search will force only upper-case entries to match.

Phrases are identified by surrounding words that belong together with quote marks. Otherwise, the words of the phrase can be anywhere in the document. A search for <Eric Cohen> will bring up text with Erics and Cohens, but not necessarily "Eric Cohen." Searching for Monty Hall will bring up entries about "three card monty" and the "Hall of Justice," but <"Monty Hall"> will bring up only the game show host.

The more sophisticated search engines also let you define how close search phrases should appear to each other: in the same sentence, within five words, next to each other. Typing <accounting software> may bring up any document that says both words or either word; <"accounting software">, with the quotation marks joining the two words together, would only bring up documents where the two words were adjacent to each other and in the order <accounting> first and <software> second; <accounting/5W software> may bring up any document where the terms are close to each other, such as either <accounting software> or <software for accounting>.

One approach to searching is "from specific to the general." It is easier to find 10 excellent matches and then spread out to other sites from the links provided in those 10 sites than to sift through 993,000 weak matches. To get very specific, it is sometimes helpful to think of a phrase that a document might contain. If you think the phrase "how to handle section 165" or "diagram of a 10Base-T network" is what you are looking for, try typing the phrase surrounded by quotes in AltaVista, the sophisticated indexer of Web documents. It will be far easier than typing "165" or "10Base-T" and dealing with the results.

The other approach is starting off with the general and moving to the specific. Starting off with Yahoo! the Web's hierarchical categorizer, and moving from the general to the specific also may lead you to what you are looking for, especially if you do not quite know what that is (you are familiarizing yourself with something new) or the topic is very popular and will be well documented by many Web sites.

Searching in Brief

Type a few words into a search engine. Step back; you are bound to get tens of thousands of matches. How can you make this task more efficient?

This cheat sheet works in many cases. To become proficient at searching, it is good to learn the site's advanced language or to master the advanced forms of one or two sites

1. Find a word (Debit)
2. Type it (debit)

Boolean "Or" (either derivative or option)
Type both words (derivative option)
Word must be on page (Debit)
Use + (+debit)
Phrase must be on page (rock and roll)
Surround with quotes ("rock and roll")
Word not on page (references to heavy metal, but not the music kind)
Use – (+ "heavy metal" – "rock and roll")

Other Web Search Tools

Not all of the search tools on the Web are for searching the Web. Some helpful search sites are designed to help users find people and businesses.

Personal Information. Your firm receives a notice from the IRS, and you must find where a former client or employee has moved. Where can you turn to? With no central authority in charge of e-mail addresses, a number of companies have developed indexers that search Internet newsgroups for names and e-mail addresses and make the database available to others.

For traditional postal addresses, companies have turned to a number of resources, including taking commercially available databases and putting them on-line. When I wrote the first edition, my favorite personal search engine (http://www.wyp.net) announced it was going off-line after receiving a letter from the company whose address database it had used as the core of its site. The site was quite an exception, as it provided a dashboard not only for finding addresses and zip codes, but its developer also linked the entries to the mapping databases found on the Internet <http://www.lycos.com> has the link to the service that will provide a map with an "X" marking the address provided), to searches that will find the selected person's contributions to the USENET, and other demographic tools.

Of course, with the growth of personal home pages, you may just find pictures, maps, and the life story on anyone you want by typing the name into a standard search tool.

Addresses and Phone.   If you are interested in tracking down the address and phone number of people, two sites to try are Switchboard (http://www.switchboard.com) and Four11 (http://www.four11.com).

E-mail.   If you hope to find someone's e-mail address, some services to try include Bigfoot (http://www.bigfoot.com), Internet Address Finder (IAF) (http://www.iaf.net), and Who Where? (http://www.whowhere.com). Some of these sites go beyond e-mail, to also provide mailing addresses, personal home pages, and company pages.

Mapping Information.   Lycos (http://www.lycos.com) will not only find a person's address but present it on a map with an "X" marking the spot. Its Road Map feature is a great productivity tool (and a little scary).

Company Information
Looking for a Business.   There are active, passive, and Yellow Pages listings of businesses on the Internet.

Active sites are those where the company has purposefully made its presence known by providing its own Web, ftp, or gopher site. Active sites are a company's marketing vehicles. They can be found by using the search engines, or a whois client, or by typing the company's name or nickname between "http://www." and ".com" and seeing what comes up. Active sites are also sometimes part of malls, or storefronts.

Passive sites include friends and enemies who have set up resources about a company. Users of Computer Associate's ACCPAC Plus accounting software can find out more about ACCPAC from either Computer Associates itself (http://www.cai.com) or at the ACCPAC Online site (http://accpac. com). Microsoft haters can find solace at a site directed against Microsoft by visiting an anti-Microsoft site (http://www.micro$oft.com). Passive sites normally will be found in the search engines, and are sometimes referenced from the corporate pages.

Listing services that have incorporated database of Yellow Pages listings into their search engines. The search engines provide many tools for searching through their listings. Most include simple name or category searches, as is possible with paper-based directories. After that the options may include searches by zip code, phone number, or street name, or even the capability to click on a map and have it return all of the businesses there, further refined by business type.

Yellow Pages directories include the AT&T Toll Free directory (http://www. dir800.att.net), BigYellow (http://www.bigyellow.com), GTE Superpages (http://www.superpages.com), and LookupUSA (www.LookupUSA.com).

WHAT'S NEW AND WHAT'S LIKE NEW?

How can you find what you need on the Internet? What are the latest tools, sites, and concerns? In this section we cover search tools and strategies you can use to find what you need on the Net.

What's New?

The Internet is an important tool to provide better client service by keeping up on changes in tax law and the business environment that can affect them. Hundreds of Internet sites provide resources, updates, and other tools to help. However, there are also tools that work while the practitioner is otherwise occupied. These "agents" are culling information from the Internet that meets predetermined search criteria.

What's in the News: Tools like the Newstracker at <http://www.excite. com> search through the news reports found at thousands of newspaper and other on-line news sources to bring you the latest in the issues that face your firm and its clients. Click on "Newstracker" and set up as many news research agents as you want. Then you can go to your Newstracker whenever you want and have Excite present what it hopes are relevant news articles for you. Newstracker even suggests other terms that may be helpful in further modifying your searches for relevant articles.

Newstracker makes you come to it. If you are interested in what's in the newsgroups, the results can be e-mailed to you. The newsgroups are the great discussion groups of the Internet, where "the entire realm of human knowledge passes every four days." The free Web site (http://Reference.com) lets you set up agents that filter through the gigabytes of daily newsgroup postings and bring you relevant discussions. You don't have to go to Reference. com to pick up your results—they are sent to your e-mail on a cycle you define. TracerLock, at <http://www.peacefire.org/tracerlock>, has similar functions and may be more reliable.

What Do People Think about the News?   Deja (http://www.deja.com) offers you searches through newsgroups, as well as Deja Ratings, instantaneous access to unbiased peer ratings, and comments on a vast array of products, services, and other stuff. Deja Tracker allow you to follow "threads" or conversations within discussion forums and continue searching without even turning on your computer. You can use Deja Tracker to tag a conversation, and it will send you e-mail notification when there are new messages. It also has e-mail discussion forums, mailing lists for each and every discussion forum in their archive. This enables you to subscribe to and participate in any discussion forum on Deja.com via daily individual e-mails, daily summaries, or full-text-version digests.

How Do You Find New Web Pages?   Check out The Informant (http://informant.dartmouth.edu), your personal bot on the Web. It looks for new and changed Web sites that match the terms you seek.

New Search Tools

Search engines help you identify Web sites, newsgroups, news reports, and publications that meet your requirements. Search engines used to be hard to work with. This has changed as searching has become such an important part of using the Web.

In the latest versions of Netscape and Microsoft Web browsers, if you type "FIND" followed by search terms where you would normally type the Web address, you can find relevant sites without going to a search engine.

Netscape has also added two other search features. First, if you type a company's name where the Web address goes, Netscape will do its best to find the company's Web page, even if the company's name is not the same as its Web address (the "key word" feature). Second, one of the most important new features in Netscape 4.5 and above is the "What's Related" button. Once you have found a Web site that has helpful resources, press "What's Related." A list of other sites that offer similar resources will be appear.

Alexa (http://www.alexa.com), the source of "What's Related" and an add-in to Internet Explorer, is a two-edged sword, letting you know about other sites while tracking where you go. When you find a site of interest to you, Alexa will show related sites. It also offers background information on the site you are visiting (such as the owner, how fresh the content is) and offers ratings and comments. Netscape 4.5 and later offer a "What's Related" button that offers similar capabilities.

Hot Search Engine Features.   Search engines have grown far beyond their original purpose—to offer a guide to where you can find things on the Internet. Like the browser battles, competition among the major search engines has moved from sheer speed and comprehensive coverage to tools to make finding resources easier.

Some Hot Features Offered on Some Search Engines

- *Results Clustering:* You type in your search term and find the first page of results dominated by one site. On the next page, the same site appears. With results clustering, even if one site has multiple pages that match the search terms, that site shows up only once. This gives you access to more sites, reducing the domination of search results by one or two sites. (This feature is available on Infoseek, HotBot, Lycos, and GoTo.)

- *Family Filters:* A wide variety of materials on the Internet are not designed for family consumption. If you use the Content Advisor feature built into Internet Explorer, you will not be able to receive any results from some search engines, which block their listings completely to the Advisor due to uncontrollable content. Now the search engines can provide their own filtering, which offers families some protection from sites that may be considered objectionable.

- *Foreign Language–Limited Searches and Language Translation:* Perhaps you are a fan of the television series *JAG*. Try typing that into your Web browser. Can I just see the English-language sites? With language-limited searches, you won't have to worry about scientific terms bringing up Norwegian and Danish pages. If a page comes up in Spanish, French, German, or Portuguese, don't fear—some search engines can translate the page for you—while you wait. (This feature is available on Alta Vista.)

- *Highlighting Search Terms in Returned Pages:* Why did that search engine bring me to this page? I have no idea what it thought matched my terms! When the search engine highlights the search terms, you can see what makes the page relevant or irrelevant to you.

- *Related Searches:* These offer help with results from searches similar to the one you submitted. (This feature is available on Alta Vista, Excite, HotBot, Infoseek, and GoTo.)
- *Find Similar:* This offers sites similar to the one you pick. (This feature is available on Excite, Infoseek, and Lycos.)
- *Limit by Date Range:* This makes it easy to find really new (or really old) sites. (This feature is available on Alta Vista, HotBot, MSN Search, Northern Light, Snap, and Yahoo!)
- *Search Within:* This helps you winnow down huge numbers of results by searching only through the current results. (This feature is available on Infoseek and Lycos.)

NON–WEB-ORIENTED SEARCHES

The Internet, as we have said, is more than the Web. The Web has been the collecting point of information for only a few of the 20 years of the Internet's official existence. Much governmental, educational, and nonprofit information is available in its prior form, which may include files to be downloaded (ftp), menus to be sorted through (gopher), or specially indexed text (WAIS).

An Internet Service Provider

How do you find an Internet Service Provider? Try the list of Internet Service Providers at <http://www.thelist.com>.

Domain Names

One of the next databases that a company needs access to when it makes a formal presence on the Internet is the listing of domain names. It is important to know what names are available for your company. The InterNIC (http://www.networksolutions.com) is responsible for these names, and its site can be searched for entries. Shareware tools like Win Whois can access the InterNIC registration from your Web-linked PC.

E-mail

With e-mail, you have two primary components: the address of the person to whom you want to send mail and the content of the mail.

Mail Addresses.　Although there is no official organization responsible for maintaining and making available listings of e-mail addresses (and the revolving door of people using American Online on a trial basis would make that a difficult task), a number of organizations make search engines for e-mail information available.

Although a number of non-Web address books are available through gopher and telnet, the Web sites mentioned above are far superior in capability and ease of use.

Mail Contents. The contents of e-mail messages are not supposed to be stored and archived on a publicly available server. That means that there are no public tools for searching through mail on historical basis.

Over time, people are on the Internet, they will begin to accumulate e-mail that they need to refer to at a future date. The list of mail items includes instructions for getting off mailing lists, discussion items that may be of use in the future, and tasks to follow up on.

Because the mail is on your own computer, you have a number of tools for finding mail that discusses a particular topic.

For example, most mail software provides folders in which to file messages. With folders set up for each type of message, you can reread those of value more quickly. Other software adds search tools to look through the messages in those folders.

In addition, most new word processors and document processing software provides an indexing tool that lets you index your e-mail and include it in the system's index database. Then you can search through the messages very quickly. The text database tools, such as AskSam from AskSam Systems (http://www.asksam.com), provide excellent tools for storing, categorizing, and accessing archived mail information.

Mailing Lists

Mail lists are an offshoot of electronic mail, where messages are sent directly to subscribers' e-mail. Some of these groups convey very sensitive information, and their managers encourage participation with no outside access to the discussions. Others convey information that is time-sensitive and not useful afterward. However, many mail lists keep archives of their correspondence and make them available through their Web sites. For example, a number of the ANet mailing lists are archived and available for review; this combines the immediacy of a mail list with the more liberal access and search capabilities of a newsgroup. ANETDEV-L: On-Line Services archives the historical contributions and responses to the mail list from the ANet regarding on-line services. They can be searched directly and are included in the indexes of the major search engines.

To find a mail list, try Liszt (http://www.liszt.com).

Newsgroups

Newsgroups convey an enormous amount of information, good and bad. Most Windows-based newsgroup software provides basic abilities to read and respond to submissions but pale in comparison to UNIX-based newsgroup software that lets you look for particular authors, topics, or words in the text.

More powerful software for reading newsgroups enables the user to search through contributions to the 35,000 newsgroups that Internet service providers make available. However, there are three limitations to searching through the newsgroups.

1. Most popular desktop applications do not have the powerful search capabilities of the UNIX newsreaders.
2. Many ISPs do not carry all of the newsgroups you may be interested in.
3. ISPs limit the amount of newsgroups entries that they will maintain on their systems to two weeks or less, due to the sheer volume of entries.

A number of tools are available to make up for these limitations.

SIFT.   Reference.com has taken over the responsibilities of the newsgroup agent SIFT (http://www.reference.com) from Standford University (http://sift.stanford.edu). With SIFT, you can set up a series of search requests, and SIFT acts as a clipping service, automatically e-mailing you a summary of all newsgroups submissions matching your request. SIFT has been having difficulties recently, so TracerLock (http://www.peacefire.org/tracerlock) may be a better choice for now.

Search Engines.   As explained previously, the Web search tools often double as newsgroup search agents. In particular, the multipurpose sites AltaVista (http://www.altavista.wcom), Excite (http://www.excite.com), and InfoSeek (http://www.infoseek.com) and the dedicated newsgroup tool Deja (http://www.deja.com) let you find information in the newsgroups on request.

FTP

With the enormous library of programs, FAQs, and other files distributed around the Internet, a number of tools were developed to let users find which computers those files are stored on. These services maintain indexes of the files on computers that permit anonymous logins and make finding and retrieving those sites easier.

As files are incorporated into Web sites, they will be available on searches with the Web search engines. Until that time the older tools may be the only way to find the files you need.

Archie.   Archie is the primary tools for finding ftp files by their title. The Rutgers Archie Gateway (http://archie.rutgers.edu) is a Web-based tool for getting at Archie.

WAIS.   WAIS (Wide Area Information Servers; http://www.wais.com) was an attempt to make searching available not only through the file names but through the contents of the files, including multimedia and program files. With efforts such as the Gutenberg Project, which is attempting to make every great piece of literature available through the Internet, this approach made sense but was difficult to use. A WAIS engine is available at the WAIS site and at <http://sunsite.unc.edu/cgi-bin/fwais.pl>.

IRC Channels and Servers

Internet Relay Chat channels come and go. While some of them have been around a long time, others are set up for a few minutes and then disappear. Most IRC software has tools to make using the LIST command easier—a command that lets you find active channels with a particular number of participants and where the name of the channel contains a search string. The shareware program mIRC32 lets you filter through the groups to find appropriate channels (while reducing the clutter of those you would prefer not to see).

Gopher

Gopher is the tool to browse through the older and separate Gopherspace of the Internet. To find information in the series of menus that makes up Gopherspace, you can turn to Veronica and Jughead.

Veronica.   Veronica (Very Easy Rodent-Oriented Net-Wide Index to Computerized Archives) is a search tool that searches through the menus in Gopherspace and delivers a gopher menu with the results. Because gopher menus deliver not only gopher results but also ftp, telnet, USENET archives, and Web sites, you will find many helpful results on a good search. Veronica can be accessed through gopher clients, such as WSGopher, or through Web browsers.

Using Veronica is usually as simple as choosing a menu item. After you type a search term into an input box, your gopher client will return the matches in another gopher menu.

If the gopher site your gopher client uses as a starting point does not include a menu item leading to Veronica, you can always point your gopher client to the Mother Gopher, (http://Gopher.micro.umn.edu), if she's still kicking.

Jughead. Jughead (Jonzy's Universal Gopher Hierarchy Excavation And Display) makes up in depth what it lacks in breadth. Instead of seeking to capture every menu item of every gopher site, Jughead permits more in-depth searching through particular sites. The home of Jughead is <http://gopher.utah.edu>.

News

News engines go through news sources on the Internet to bring you results. Some places to find out what's going on:

NewsBot: http://www.newsbot.com

NewsHub: http://www.newshub.com

News Index: http://www.newsindex.com

NewsTracker: http://nt.excite.com

NewsTrawler: http://www.newstrawler.com

Northern Light's Current News: http://www.northernlight.com/news.html

PLACES TO RESEARCH AND SEARCH

The information on the Internet can be sliced and diced to find out much about any topic. Some sites provide resources of their own worthy of special mention.

Educational Sites

When you hear the word "research," you may think about sites that promote research themselves. Colleges and universities have a strong presence on the Internet. You will find many accounting departments that link to other accounting departments and resources and publish their student and staff research on-line.

Accounting Net (ANet). Looking to hook into an international resource of accounting and auditing information? The ANet is a cooperative venture of individuals and organizations, primarily academic, around the world that seeks to provide a networked, electronic forum for the exchange of information and the discussion of issues in the broad accounting and auditing disciplines. It is one of a group of three primary sites and a number of smaller sites that make up the International Accounting Network. The other major sites are Rutgers University's Rutgers Accounting Web (RAW) and the Summa Project from the University of Exeter in the United Kingdom.

The Accounting Net, not to be confused with a more commercial entity with the same name, is centered in Australia at Charles Sturt University. From ANet, you can find out about accounting organizations and journals around the world, launch off to other accounting-related Internet services, and participate in discussion groups pertaining to accounting in many areas, including auditing, accounting, ethics, financial accounting, governmental and nonprofit accounting, taxation, and teaching and learning. By joining these mailing lists, you can have all of the discussions e-mailed to you on a regular basis. The ANet is found at <http://wwwc.su.edu.au/ANetHomePage.html>.

The sites on the ANet link to each other and include a cross-site search engine. The research tools at the sites are appropriate for members of the American Accounting Association and other educational and governmental sponsors and participants. A brief tour of the Rutgers' RAW site (http://www.rutgers.edu/Accounting/anet/research/index.html) includes, among other tools, a bibliography database, with tools to search by search terms or by topics. The topics include:

    accounting ethics

    accounting history

    accounting information systems

    accounting research

    accounting theory

    auditing

    company accounting

    cost accounting

    financial accounting

    international accounting

    small business accounting

In addition to the bibliography, you will find internal listings of journals, societies, and organizations, software, Internet resources, and accountant e-mail listings.

Accounting Research Network Homepage. Academic journals have long been a vehicle for making the research of aspiring academicians known. However, geography and mailing costs have limited the speed and ability to spread the word around. Enter the Accounting Research Network (http://www.ssep.com/ssep/arn.html), publishers of the *Journal of Accounting Abstracts.* From this site you can subscribe to mailing lists offering accounting, economic, labor, and other abstracts.

Professional Sites

Professional societies are also deeply involved in research. The AICPA (http://www.aicpa.org) will be providing even better links for research from its made-over Web pages when they unveil their newly designed Web site, scheduled for late 1999.

Governmental Sites

The government is a great source for research information, and a number of its sites are providing for free what used to be an expensive on-line offering from commercial vendors.

EDGAR. The Securities and Exchange Commission has made available its on-line database of filing information, called EDGAR (http://www.sec.gov/edgarhp.htm). The database can be searched by keyword to bring up filings like 10-Q, 8-K and proxies.

The EDGAR project began at New York University's Stern School of Business with a main goal of "enabl[ing] wide dissemination and support for all levels of user access to the corporate filings submitted to the Securities and Exchange Commission." EDGAR was sponsored by the National Science Foundation and undertaken in conjunction with the Internet Multicasting Service. Fierce demand has kept it alive for now, although it may be dropped.

Thomas. When you are doing tax planning, it is interesting to see what Congress is thinking. Their Thomas site (http://thomas.loc.gov), named after Thomas Jefferson, lets you browse or search through all pending and passed legislation to find out if a potential law will make your tax planning useless.

The U.S. Congress, through its library, has set up THOMAS: Legislative Information on the Internet. This treasure trove of legislative information provides full text of legislation of House and Senate bills for the 106th Congress, full text of the *Congressional Record,* How Our Laws Are Made, the Resolution Adopting the Rules of the House of Representatives for the 106th Congress, the House of Representative's gophers and constituent e-mail, the Senate gopher, the C-SPAN gopher, and links to the Library of Congress World Wide Web and gopher (which, along with the Library of Congress on-line, has links to numerous other federal, state, and foreign on-line sites). A simple search in the full text of legislation on the floor for the fighting 106th brought over 100 bills that contained the word "tax." They included everything from a balanced budget bill, to an attempt to outlaw retroactive taxes, to special bills that were obviously favors to constituents.

Technology Publications

When you or a client is about to purchase new software or consider new technologies, how would you like to quickly get a summary of every article written about that topic?

CMP (http://techweb.cmp.com), IDG (http://www.idg.com), InfoWorld (http://www.infoworld.com), PCWORLD (http:/www.pcworld.com), and ZDNet (http://www.zdnet.com) are Web sites from leading technology publishers who permit full-text searches through their families of periodicals.

Commercial Sites

Yes, for access to commercial sites you will have to shell out a few bucks, but you can do your research anywhere, anytime, from any computer attached to the Internet. The Internet is fast becoming a major research vehicle for tax professionals. Internet tax libraries are taking their place among, and in some cases replacing, books, CD-ROMs, newsletters, and news services.

Top Tax Research Services

CCH INCORPORATED
4025 West Peterson Avenue
Chicago, IL 60646-6085
(800) TELL CCH
http://www.cch.com
Service: CCH Tax News Direct and CCH Internet Tax Research Network
URL: http://tax.cch.com

RIA Checkpoint
Research Institute of America
90 Fifth Avenue
New York, NY 10011
(212) 645-4800
http://www.riatax.com

Service: Checkpoint
URL: http://www.checkpoint.riag.com

TAX ANALYSTS
6830 North Fairfax Drive
Arlington, VA 22213
(800) 955-3444
http://www.tax.org
Service: TaxBase
URL: http://taxbase.tax.org

Thompson Publishing Group®
1725 K Street NW
Suite 700
Washington, DC 20006
(202) 872-4000
Service: TaxLibrary.com
URL: http://www.taxlibrary.com

NEW AND UNUSUAL TOOLS

Software to Help in Your Work

When it is time to get more power, sometimes you will need to find additional
software to supplement your searches.

Copernic 99.   Copernic 99 is an intelligent agent that carries out your net
searches by simultaneously consulting the most important search engines of
the Internet. (See Exhibit 6.1.) These are grouped under categories, such as
The Web, Newsgroups, and E-mail Addresses. It features a history of your
searches, making sure that the precious information found on the Internet is
always organized and handy. Copernic 99 is free from <http://www.coper-
nic.com> and offers only three categories. The commercial version Copernic
99 Plus, on the other hand, includes 21 categories, giving you access to some
125 search engines and specific directories. Additional categories in Copernic
99 Plus are: Buy Books, Business & Finance, Games, Health, Kids, Life,
Movies, Music, Newspapers, Newswire, Recipes, Sciences, Software Download, Sport News, Tech News, Tech Reviews, Top News, and Travel.
Copernic 99 offers:

• A search wizard eases search creation.

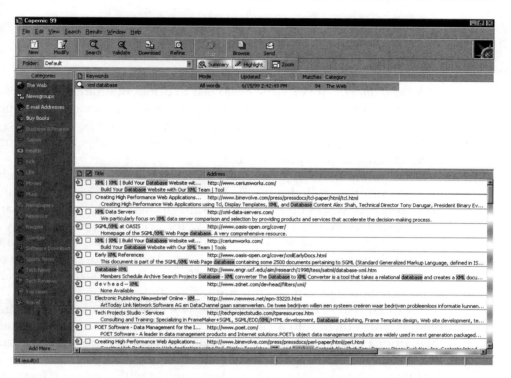

Exhibit 6.1 Copernic 99 carries out your Net searches by simultaneously consulting the most important search engines. Used with permission from Copernic Technologies, Inc.

- Found documents are scored and displayed according to their relevancy.
- Keywords are highlighted in results.
- Duplicate matches are removed automatically.
- Invalid and unreachable document links may be eliminated.
- Matching documents may be downloaded for off-line browsing.
- Searches may be refined from downloaded documents by using logical operators (AND, OR, EXCEPT).
- Search reports may be generated in Web page format for easy browsing, filtering, and sorting of documents.
- Searches may be updated, grouped into folders, and so on.
- Search reports may be exported or e-mailed in various file types.
- Full Internet Explorer 4.0 (or later) integration exists: An ergonomically designed Result Explorer window can be used to browse, filter, and sort found documents more easily and faster; the default Internet Explorer

search window can be replaced by Copernic (4.x versions only); Copernic can be launched from the Quick Launch toolbar.

Web Printsmart.   If you have ever need to print out multiple pages of a Web site, you know that it takes a long time, you may miss some link or subpage, and it doesn't print well. Pages spit out with a few words, tables cross pages without the header being repeated, and the basic layout is designed for a 640 × 480 screen and not a printed page.

One solution is HP's Web Printsmart (http://www.hp.com/peripherals2/webprintsmart/index.html). The good news is that it is free; the bad news is it only works on Hewlett-Packard printers. HP Web PrintSmart software optimizes Web content specifically for printing. It automatically eliminates orphans and widows—those pesky words that take up an entire line. It avoids splitting tables. (If a split is necessary, it adds headers to the top of both pages.) And it lets you select templates, font styles, and sizes so you can have a consistent presentation to your printed Web sites.

With HP Web PrintSmart software, you identify the sites and pages and then organize them into a single document. It is simple to select a site and then, from a tree diagram, pick the pages and subpages you wish to print. HP Web PrintSmart software can save your selections as a PrintSmart document for future use and print it as a single document with consistent formatting. A handy preview feature lets you select which pages you want to print. And HP Web PrintSmart software will automatically add a Table of Contents and Index of Links to the file.

HP Web PrintSmart works with Windows 95 and Windows NT 4.0 and with Netscape Navigator 3.0 and above and Microsoft Internet Explorer 3.0 and above. (HP Web PrintSmart shares its cache and cookies with Internet Explorer.) It adds a tool bar to your browser to let you print directly form the current page on the browser or use that page as a starting point for working within HP Web PrintSmart.

HP Web PrintSmart is a bargain both for its price and its use of only 5 MB of incremental hard disk space. If you regularly print Web pages to an HP printer and want more control and a much easier time of printing multiple pages at a time, download a copy today.

PUTTING IT ALL TOGETHER

An exhaustive search for information on a topic will include Internet and traditional resources. Having sophisticated research tools available does not make anyone a research expert. Local libraries and librarians can be excellent resources for help in finding information and additional resources to follow up with.

If you hope to find out all you can on a topic, here are some of the steps to follow.

Search through Historical Information in USENET

The newsgroups are an excellent source of information and a means of finding helpful resources on the topic you are interested in. Using the search engines (DejaNews, AltaVista), you can find what groups include discussions on your topic and identify people who might know about it. By perusing the archives of their discussion, you may find your answer. You will find e-mail addresses of people who may be willing to help out as well as their Web sites, or Web sites they may recommend visiting.

If you send an e-mail to participants, the worst they can do is ignore you, say they will not help you, or respond cruelly. On the other hand, you may find a leading expert in the field who will be pleased to help out.

The Web sites of participants and those they mention may reflect their interests, which would most likely include the topics they are spending their time discussing on the newsgroups.

Find People to Ask

The Internet helps bring people together to share. From the latest chat communities (Excite Voice Chat) to old-line BBS replacements, people with similar interests or looking for help have a place to go on the Net.

However, most practitioners think of the Web as one-way communications—this despite numerous arenas for sharing on the Internet. These arenas include:

- Accounting-oriented discussion areas: <http://www.computercpa.com/disc.html> lists many of them
- Innovations like Third Voice, which let you add opinion to a Web site that other Third Voice users can read
- Instant Messaging, Excite Chat, ICQ, IRC, and other real-time chatting communities
- Newsgroups
- Mailing lists that build community

Internet users are one of the most forgotten elements of the Internet. An idea can catch fire on the Internet. Isolation can turn into belonging—for bad or for good. When discussions are open to the public, they can be drawn off course intentionally or led off course by those who enjoy the sound of their own voice, misunderstand the purpose of a gathering place, or bring their own agenda and needs. When you're sitting in a room of 45 people, you understand your relevance. When you can't see the other participants, you may demand to stand out at others' expense.

Post a Question in a newsgroup

Once you have identified some newsgroups where your topic is appropriate, you can post general messages to others. Most inhabitants of the Internet feel that helping others is part of their purpose in being on-line. By placing a question in a newsgroup, you call upon a crack research team that can multiply your efforts.

You should be cautious, of course, that anything posted is maintained and searchable by others. You need to be as clear as possible while protecting any sensitive information that could be used against you, your firm, or your client in the future.

Ask Someone on IRC or in a Topic-Specific Real-Time Chat Room

Internal Relay Chat areas may have some ongoing discussions with people who could possibly give you some guidance on your topic. Most of the time these free-ranging discussions will be completely off topic, but sometimes you will find people willing and capable of giving guidance in your area, especially if it is technology related.

If IRC has any advantage, it is that you will get immediate feedback on any question you ask.

Do Not Forget Gopherspace

Organizations that have been using the Internet for many years have resources on their old gopher systems that may never be transferred to the Web. A Veronica search through Gopherspace may reveal resources that could be helpful.

Use Search Engines to Find a Relevant Web Site

While you are taking advantage of the kindness of the population of the newsgroups, some answers you want may be already waiting for you on the Web. Using search engines, you can find some sites that seem to be near topic or companies and organizations that might be related to the topic, and see if they have any pertinent information.

Most of the time you must rely on how well sites are organized to find the information you need. A number of sites have begun adding search engines that let you search through their contents or site maps to better navigate their pages.

The nature of the Web is that related organizations and sites link to each other. By taking a ride through hypertext links, you may find yourself on another site that has the exact information you are looking for.

You also can contact a Web site's owners, if they solicit comments and questions, for guidance on where to look for more information.

Set Up a Web Site to Elicit Comment on the Topic

If you do not find any Web sites that cover your topic, it may be an excellent time to set up one yourself. By leaving your e-mail address or using more sophisticated forms capabilities, you can elicit responses and gather information on a topic. Then you can make it available to others, giving back to the community as you have taken.

Virtual Offices like Visto Briefcase (http://www.visto.com) and OneList (http://www.onelist.com) let you establish user-friendly areas for discussion, file sharing, and sharing calendars of events and project schedules.

Examine Web Sites: Reading between the Lines

As you do research on a company, its vendors, and its customers, their Web sites may not explicitly state their financial position but may speak volumes by what they look like and what they include. Here are 10 points to consider.

1. Does the company have its own domain name?
2. Is the site professionally done?
3. Is it kept up to date?
4. How well does the site present its products and services?
5. How easy does the site make it to buy from the company?
6. Are press releases included at the site, and what do the press releases say?
7. Are job openings listed and what positions are being advertising for?
8. What are the capabilities of the company's personnel?
9. What type of communications are offered to keep visitors current on company offerings?
10. What feedback is solicited from visitors?

Strategies for Successful Research

When the need for information is critical, a strategic search will extend beyond the best-phrased Boolean search. Your firm may develop its own set of procedures to make sure a research job is thorough; here is one possible course of action.

Step 1: Identify the Experts.   The first step in doing research is determining who the experts are in the area you are investigating, finding out what they say, and seeking direction. After all, they probably have gained assistance from others on the Internet in their work, and they may provide some tips in finding appropriate resources or even share the results of their own research.

You can find experts by finding out who has demonstrated knowledge in the area. Judicious use of the search engines will lead you to:

- Web pages they have created or contributed to, or which promote their work
- Discussions in the newsgroups, mailing lists, or private discussion areas in which they have been active
- Conferences or publications in which they speak or write

A brief e-mail expressing your request for direction is the next step. Offering to pay for services works even better. Of course, in the steps you have just taken, often you will find more Internet resources with links to other sites that may be helpful to you.

Step 2: Find the Pioneers.   Once you have enlisted the help of the official experts, it is time to find fellow strugglers. When it comes to research questions, often we are not the first to ask a question. Who has asked similar questions before you?

If you can find your question being posted, you may find an answer (which, of course, you need to take with a grain of salt). What did they find out?

If you find no replies, you can contact the original poster, asking if they have received an answer. If so, having been helped by others, they may be more willing to share with you. If not, you can work together to get an answer.

If you find a reply, you now have two resources—the original poster and the person who offered the answer.

To do this step effectively, you need to find all the places where questions of this nature could be posted. That means not only the public discussion areas of the Internet but also private discussion groups, such as the CICA forums, and corporate knowledge bases, such as the excellent help offered by Microsoft (http://www.microsoft.com).

Step 3: Commit Yourself to Master a Search Engine (or Two). Do independent searching as well. To do this effectively, you will want to master the advanced search features of a few search engines.

A search engine like Yahoo! (http://www.yahoo.com) is designed to help you see the depth of resources available on a topic. You start with a basic idea, and it helps you drill down to more specific resources. Because all of Yahoo's sites are entered by humans, the depth of available sites and freshness of content are not competitive with a search engine like Alta Vista (http://www.altavista.com), which actually captures the text on Web pages.

Once you have mastered Alta Vista's advanced search tools and query language, you can be very specific about what you want to find on a page. By typing in very precise search criteria, and even date ranges that can help limit the content to what is truly relevant, you will find one or two Web sites that are absolutely to the point—and that will lead you off to other resources of value. This is a better strategy than going through the results of 30,000 listings that may or may not be to pertinent. So be as specific as you can with your queries; only broaden your query later. Don't forget to use a thesaurus when you are doing searches.

Step 4: Take What You Find with a Grain of Salt. As you go about your research on the Internet, always conduct a reality check. The newspapers are filled with tales of postings placed in the newsgroups that defame a company and spread falsehoods for unscrupulous purposes. While it is almost true that the entire realm of human knowledge passes through the news groups every four days, it is also true that the average person uses less than 10 percent of their brain, and with these people, that seems entirely evident.

When resources are free on the Internet, there is no contractual agreement between you and the knowledge provider. No fee means no freshness or accuracy guarantee. It will be up to you to judge the source. Just as we have to judge paper research sources—which news source is more authoritative in your mind, *Kiplinger's* or *Billy Bob's Tackle and Tax News?*—you can question any source, including the governmental sites, on timeliness, accuracy, and objectivity.

With this knowledge and the hot sites listed throughout this book, you are ready to hit the research trail. Safe surfing!

From Here . . .

Chapter 7 discusses conducting business on the Internet.

Electronic Commerce

This chapter discusses issues relating to conducting business on the Internet. Business use of the Internet has exploded over the last five years. The opportunities are difficult to ignore. The problems for accountants, especially dealing with accounting standards (SAS 80, electronic evidence, and SAS 55 and 78, internal control), sales tax, and security are yet to be fully determined. This chapter discusses the successes, issues, and players in the on-line world of business. The following outline summarizes the contents of this chapter:

- Introduction to electronic commerce
- Underlying technologies
- Ordering on the Web
- Issues paving the way for electronic commerce
- Establishing standards for commerce
- Where does the CPA fit in?
- Interview with Great Plains

INTRODUCTION TO ELECTRONIC COMMERCE

To be successful in electronic commerce, first you need a gimmick. Let's find a way to help people get out of jury duty on-line. Then money, lots of it; that means venture capital. Advertising—perhaps you can get CBS to offer lots of free air space in exchange for some ownership (http://cbs.marketwatch.com). Then a recognizable spokesperson. Captain Kirk is busy, but for this . . .

The World Wide Web has exploded on the scene, and buying on the Internet has exploded in popularity. A CommerceNet/Nielsen Media Research poll showed that the number of Internet users in North America reached 92 million in April 1999—and 55 million of them shop on-line. One-half of North Americans on the Net, and a quarter of them shopping. Other polls show that, as of May 1999, over 10 million investors have on-line accounts.

Five years ago, accounting information on the Internet was extremely limited. Now Web sites spring up like dandelions. Books, roving seminars, and newspaper advertisements scream out that $$$Millions$$$ can be made on the Internet. Visions of hordes of customers placing orders directly into their computer 24 hours a day dance like sugar plums in business owners' heads. If not customers, at least venture capitalists and investors putting $$$Billions$$$ into companies with no earnings to show excite the mind.

The Internet is a business opportunity that is difficult to ignore. For merchants, it is an opportunity to make products and services available to a new global marketplace at a fraction of the cost of traditional advertising. Although a small software firm can hardly compete with Microsoft with a new spreadsheet or word processor sold through distribution, brilliant Internet software can make (and has made) a college student an instant millionaire. Teenagers have taken snow-shoveling money and started firms providing Internet access. Web software has flown off the shelves of bookstores, and subscriptions to on-line services like America Online and Internet service providers like Erols (http://www.erols.com) have grown dramatically with promises of easy Internet access.

In response, large computer, financial, and communications companies have had to change their corporate direction and marketing thrust, acknowledging the momentum of the Web. Important new announcements come out daily. IBM and Microsoft have continued their own major assaults on the marketplace, successfully taking back momentum from upstart companies like Netscape. Banks, credit card companies, communication companies, and software companies are picking partners carefully to make sure they, jointly or singly, are part of electronic commerce into the next millennium.

Picking a business partner carefully—establishing trust—is what leads to long-term business relationships. Establishing trust is what most companies are working on to make Internet commerce grow. Commerce started with an agreement based on a handshake. Soon every agreement had to be signed in triplicate and approved by an attorney. With electronic commerce, some people fear that things have regressed and become so informal that even a handshake is more of an assurance that business will be conducted properly.

As business moves to the Web, accountants need to be aware of the direction of electronic commerce, its parallels to traditional commerce, and accounting, auditing, and systems issues that need to be addressed.

ELECTRONIC STOREFRONTS

The transition to Internet commerce in America has not been an easy one, although it has been flamboyant. Mom-and Pop stores have largely given way to understaffed but competitive discount and superstores. Catalog sales permit shopping at home by phone and make it easy to compare prices even before picking up the phone, without having to leave the comfort of home. Stores that do business on the Web combine some of the most competitive features of these businesses. A comparison of traditional and virtual shopping is found in Exhibit 7.1.

Electronic storefronts, Web sites marketing a company's products and services, offer 24-hour-a-day exposure for a company around the world. These storefronts both stand alone, visible through the various indexing systems a potential buyer may use, and are part of electronic malls or special interest group pages.

Malls are designed by the Web provider to highlight its clients geographically and by product or specialty for additional visibility. Malls often offer additional services, such as search tools to find products or services among their participating vendors; fax on demand, so that brochures can be faxed to the user instead of making the user download and print out large files; and electronic ordering capability.

	Virtual Shopping	Traditional Shopping
Hours	"Open" 24 hours	Often limited
Distance	Global, but in our living room	Limited to travel distance and time
Product availability	Cannot touch product	Can touch and examine product
Comparison shopping	Can visit many stores in an hour or use a shopping bot	Travel time limits stores you can visit
Delivery time	Need to wait for delivery for tangible products; instant delivery of software, information	Can take a physical product with you
Product selection	Often large	Selection limited to in-store
Payment	Limited to credit card, digital	Cash, credit, check
Service	Impersonal	Possibility of personalized service
Discounts	Often discounted	Sometimes discounted
Ease of approach	Computer knowledge	Driving/walking knowledge
General availability	Internet access	Almost anyone can shop at a store

Exhibit 7.1 Comparison of Virtual and Traditional Shopping

Portals have been more successful than malls at offering space on Web sites with high traffic and then directing potential buyers to storefronts. Portal sites are Web sites that are designed to make you come by and come often, offering information, most often customized for the visitor's particular needs, such as news, sports, investment portfolios, television, mail, and other communications. Lotus has entered into an agreement with Lycos to develop a Lotus Notes portal giving access to the popular corporate groupware product. Enterprise resource planning (ERP) developers also have seen the vision of portals—to the extent that they are working with companies that would prefer, or will mandate, that their employees get their news and information from the inside, from a customized portal.

The Web has emerged as a popular user interface for ERP systems. As more and more people become familiar with the Web and Web browsers, such as Internet Explorer and Netscape, they come already trained in the basics of using corporate systems. Consider: How many people will state they feel comfortable with the basic use of an IBM AS/400, and how many will line up to say they can run Netscape?

ERP portals from vendors SAP AG (EnjoySAP or MySAP.com), Oracle Corp., PeopleSoft Inc (MyWorld), J.D. Edwards (ActiveERA), Lawson Software (SEAPort), Siebel (Sales.com), and Baan Co. now offer systems that let employees, and soon customers, to the database.

Shopping bots are personal buyers, searching through storefronts to allow easy comparison shopping for potential purchasers. Shopping comparison tools can do a good job at highlighting the different strategies of selling on the Internet. Some firms charge as much or more than their traditional stores; others (such as <http://www.buy.com>) sell for less than dealer cost—sometimes significantly less than dealer cost. One of the most popular shopping bots is MySimon (http://www.mysimon.com).

MySimon allows on-line shoppers to comparison shop more than 1,300 merchants. As an independent company, MySimon is able to offer consumers unbiased information on how and where to buy all types of products online. Unlike other shopping services, merchants do not have to pay to be included in MySimon's searches. Currently, real-time pricing information is available on products in more than 170 categories from over 1,300 on-line merchants. In addition, the company's PocketShopper™ application now allows users of 3Com's Palm VII and other portable units to access the MySimon shopping service wirelessly.

Other shopping bots include <http://www.bottomdollar.com> and <http://www.pricescan.com>.

We have sped up everything else using e-mail, why not invoicing? Right now companies like Intuit (http://www.intuit.com) are quietly setting up the full pipeline of all of your money going through their hands. They are quietly developing electronic bill payment, funds transfer, and document and banking interfaces. These will be delivered through integration of financial applications to Internet or value added services-based solutions.

GENERAL ADVERTISING

Currently many companies use their storefront as a digital billboard, a lead-generation device, hoping to develop a mailing list to send out more traditional, paper-based catalogs or to provide fax-on-demand response to requests for information. A Web site can include text describing the background of a company, photographs of the owners and employees, listings of products and services, a graphic with a map of the company's location, and financial information for potential investors. New products and services can be highlighted immediately, without the lapse of printing and mailing time. Many companies post help-wanted listings and financial statements along with marketing information.

ACCOUNTANTS

CPAs are also on the Web, individually and as groups. This topic is covered in more detail in Chapter 5.

Are you not ready to do taxes over the Internet? Don't wait too long. An informal poll of 300 CPA/tax preparers showed that few had e-filed in 1999. Why? The Internet may be the death of a large portion of the average practitioner's work—and in the not in the too-distant future.

Some states are promoting Internet filing of tax returns. Visitors to the Arkansas Department of Finance and Administration Web site (http://www.state.ar.us/dfa), the Maryland state comptroller's Web site (http://www.marylandtaxes.com), or the Minnesota Department of Revenue Web site (http://www.taxes.state.mn.us) may be surprised to learn that their states promote such filings. The IRS is also heavily pushing eFile—so much so that it bought banner ads on AltaVista.

Why are states and the IRS pushing electronic filing?

- eFile removes the risk of loss or mishandling inherent with paper returns.
- eFile reduce errors in data entry. According to some estimates, the error rate for paper returns is 18 percent, while it is less than 1 percent for electronic returns.

- eFile gives you a guaranteed acknowledgment of IRS acceptance of your return.
- eFile offers a fast review of your tax return to make sure that you are paying what you should be paying based on the given information.
- eFile refunds may come in eight days or less. Some states (like Maryland) predict a 48-hour turnaround via direct deposit.
- With eFile, you don't have to send in payment until April 15, later in some states. That way the IRS can check your return over for accuracy and let you know if you owe an different amount from what you calculated.

Some states, such as Oklahoma (http://www.oktax.state.ok.us/oktax/clickon.html), are offering free eFiling for both federal and state returns. Many services offer free preparation and filing for those in the military and low-income taxpayers. In many cases eFiling is relatively inexpensive, on the order of $9.95 to $14.95 for both federal and state, including preparation—cheaper than certified mail costs alone.

Some time in the not-too-distant future (2002), eFiling will be mandatory for anyone using a PC to tax returns. Obviously someone thinks that the ability to use a printer and the skills required to use a modem are not drastically different (a point with which I do not agree).

To make eFile a success, seemingly all that was needed was someone to go after the IRS and the states. That someone was Secure Tax.com, recently purchased by Intuit. SecureTax has established working relationships with 36 states. At least four—Oklahoma, Minnesota, Michigan, and Arkansas—highlight the option on their own Web site. Secure Tax.com is aggressively attacking the marketplace, taking out banner ads on Yahoo! and plans to market through Microsoft's site. SecureTax.com's primary competitors:

> http://www.irs.ustreas.gov/prod/elec_svs/partners.html (Intuit)
>
> http://www.webturbotax.com (Thomson Investors Network)
>
> http://www.onetax.com/OneTaxWelcome.asp

AUCTIONS

eBay is an Internet auction. It is the world's largest classified ads, a virtual flea market, a conduit of hope of getting a great deal or dreams of selling with heavy bidding. eBay brings together buyer and seller and takes a fee for each listing as well as part of the proceeds. It is up to buyer and seller to coordinate payment and shipment. The site is easily searched, and listings can include description, pictures, and diagrams. eBay will let potential buyers list their highest bid in secret and then automatically bid higher and higher incrementally as a proxy— your bidding agent working against someone else's bidding agent, ensuring the seller will make at least as much as the second highest bidder's maximum bid. eBay will even send you an e-mail if you are losing a bid or win an auction. The bidders let eBay do the work without needing to be logged on.

The huge success of eBay runs contrary to the polls, which say people are afraid to use their credit card on the Internet, because of the hassle of the $50 limit and the phone calls. Yet people are checking out the 2 million products on eBay and sending certified checks to the seller—on faith. People are concerned about buying from established businesses on the Internet but are buying products from individuals, businesses—anyone—when they have the incentive. And what incentive! Want a deal on computer equipment? You will find some great deals on-line. In fact, some products can only be purchased on-line. New companies are selling their products at auction as a first step— like a movie going directly to video instead of starting out at the theaters. Their plan? Get their name known.

Want a bargain on something you need—or really want? Keep an eye out, and place your bids often. Maybe you are the only person who has bid on that battery for that two-year-old laptop.

Want a 1963 Corvair? A Corgi James Bond car like the one you owned 30 years ago? Baseball cards or Beanie Babies? They are there—and your bid may be the winning one if no one else bids higher in the next 36 hours!

An analysis of eBay's success makes an excellent study for planning your own e-commerce future.

- eBay makes it easy to buy—even raising bids for products automatically and paging you if your attention is required.
- eBay gives you reason to come back often—to see what great bargains are available.
- eBay builds community, offering opportunities to offer feedback on vendors to build trust in their offerings or warn others away.
- eBay offers an incredible variety of products that may be a bargain—perhaps at any price.

AUTOMOBILES

J. D. Powers and Associates (http://www.jdpower.com) reports that new car dealers were having good success selling through the Internet. Imagine never seeing a car salesperson again. Services like Autobytel.com (http://www.autobytel.com) Inc. and Microsoft's Carpoint.com (http://www.carpoint.com) are proving to be more effective tools for buyers than individual dealer Web sites. Over 72 percent of dealers are satisfied with their on-line buying services, and nearly all dealers responding to the survey indicated they expect their on-line sales to grow significantly in the next year. Customer satisfaction, however, is still lagging.

Used car sales are humming along as well. America Online has entered into an exclusive relationship with AutoConnect.com, which claims to be the largest used car site on the Web. AutoConnect says 31,000 dealers across the nation make available their listings to the company, totaling more than 750,000 used trucks and cars. Visitors to AOL.com will also be able to list their cars for sale free of charge.

BANKS

Visiting your bank on the Web is a natural extension to the automatic teller machines that have found their ways into supermarkets and downtown alleys. While cash will not come out the bottom of your monitor, banks hope to let you check your balances, transfer funds, and pay bills electronically. In addition, they can advertise new accounts, loans, credit cards, and other services. Investment services in particular are considered fertile ground for promotion. Insurance (life, health, automobile) applications are also a natural extension to the Web.

Banking on the Internet is a great way to do business. You can pay bills in your jammies, start an IRA, or establish a checking account that you can access from anywhere. Nothing can go wrong . . . go wrong . . . go wrong. At least the FDIC's Web site (http://www.fdic.gov) is here to help. (See Exhibit 7.2.)

Banking on the Internet started pretty slowly. Most traditional banks were hesitant to establish an on-line presence for security reasons, among others. Security First Network Bank (http://www.sfnb.com) was the first bank to appear only on the Internet; at the time, it had no other presence—and it was FDIC insured. Soon other banks began to realize the marketing and cost benefits of the Net. Cost estimates showed that a banking transaction on the Internet cost the bank a fraction of the cost of teller, ATM, and even proprietary system transactions.

Research from Gomez Advisors, Inc., rated the top banking sites in mid-1999. Their bankers' scorecard listed the five following sites as the best:

1. Security First Network Bank: http://www.sfnb.com
2. Wells Fargo: http://wellsfargo.com

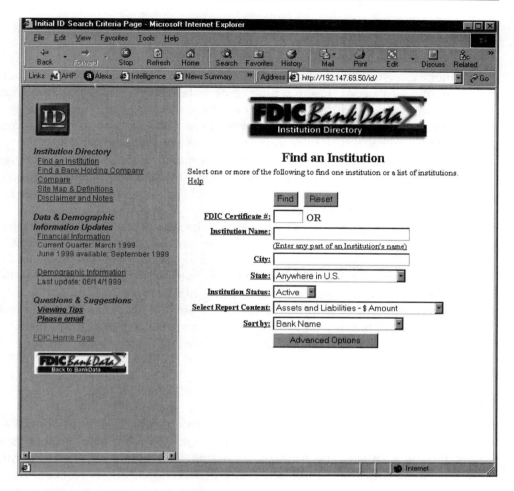

Exhibit 7.2   FDIC's Institution Directory.

3.   Citibank: http://www.citibank.com
4.   Salem Five Cents Savings Bank: http://www.salemfive.com
5.   Bank of America: http://www.bankamerica.com

As of that time, 39 out of the 100 largest consumer banks offered Internet bill payment, up from 17 one year earlier. In addition, banks are making it ever easier for customers to use the Internet to take care of their banking needs: 82 percent either pre-enroll customers for Internet banking or give customers on-line enrollment forms. Around 62 percent give up-to-the-minute information on ATM transactions through the Internet, although only 7 percent are prepared to give customers real-time approval on credit applications.

Many people use an ATM at a shopping mall to get quick cash. This did not escape the notice of a scam artist, who rolled his own ATM into a shopping mall. Many people inserted their cards, entered their passwords, and were disappointed to find the machine "out of cash." Or so they thought. In fact, the ATM machine was there with one purpose—to collect people's cash card and PIN numbers, which the enterprising scam artist could use elsewhere.

According to the FDIC, a small number of banks are misrepresenting themselves on the Internet. If you see the First Bank of Eric, how do you know whether it is safe to put your funds there? (Who cares if you get a free toaster, Beanie Baby, or trip to Bermuda?)

The U.S. government has created a site where you can check to determine if an institution has a legitimate charter and is a member of the FDIC. Visit <http://www.fdic.gov/consumer/suspicious> to find out. (See Exhibit 7.3.) Of course, Internet banks are not the only ones with a history of difficulties. At <http://www.fdic.gov/databank/index.html>, you will find a number of publications containing statistics on FDIC-insured commercial banks and savings institutions as well as analyses of financial, economic, and industry trends as they relate to banking. Is your bank solvent (for now)? Find out here.

BOOKS

The success of Amazon.com (http://www.amazon.com) in selling books online had a chilling effect on traditional booksellers—so much so that their first year was called "the Amazonian Basin" for traditional sales. The value of Amazon.com's stock exceeded that of traditional books resellers Barnes & Noble (http://www.bn.com) and Borders (http://www.borders.com) combined. Now books, tapes, games—they are all on sale on the Internet. Although you don't have the immediacy of walking away with a treasure to read or gift that day, you will be able to find a specific book at a reduced price (although you need to watch those shipping charges!) far more easily on-line than on a trip around town.

COMPUTER SALES AND SUPPORT

For companies in computer-related fields that have in the past offered computer bulletin board services (BBSs), the robust Internet capabilities permit not only the dissemination of sales literature but also provide a means to distribute software—patches, fixes, updates, and demonstration versions—with

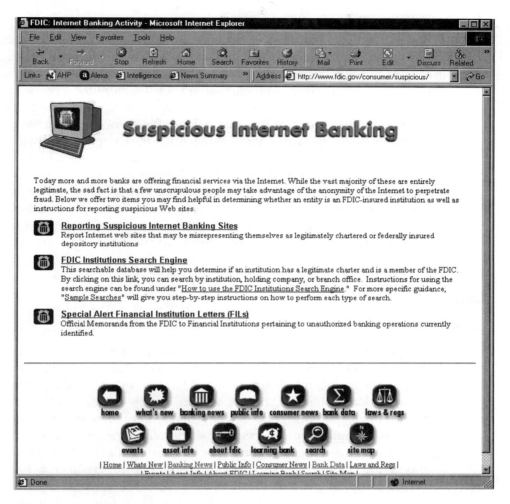

Exhibit 7.3 Suspicious Internet Banking site.

no media or postage costs. Where in the past a company like Computer Associates distributed the first version of a new software product for only a postage charge (to build market share), now it can flood the market at the cost of a phone call. Most software for the Internet, for example, is available in pre-release form from the Internet, encouraging widespread testing and feedback.

It is a rare computer vendor that has yet to get on the Web. A call to a BBS is a long-distance call for most users, and often the phone lines are busy with other users leaving messages or downloading software fixes. Visiting and downloading software from a BBS can be inconvenient and expensive. Internet access offers more concurrent users for the price of the Internet connection.

The Internet also provides superior tools to those available for a BBS for organizing text files and allowing searches through written group discussions on topics. Support questions can be taken, answered, and made available to others in easy-to-access databases called *Knowledgebases* and frequently answered questions (FAQs) categorized and highlighted. Dell Computer Corporation, for example, uses the AskJeeves natural language interface to make searching through its technical support files easy. Microsoft's Knowledgebase has a wealth of information on almost any situation regarding the company's software.

Many people are already comfortable with using catalogs and superstores to buy computers and electronics. Thus buying computer-related products through the Internet is not a major change. The Web as a place of business lets the potential buyer visit many stores, look for the best price, and buy name-brand merchandise quickly and easily. Dell Computer Corporation is one of the leaders in this arena, selling in excess of $10 million per day on the Internet.

CREDIT

Loans

Getting lenders to compete for loans: that's the premise behind Lending Tree, an Internet venture that encourages consumers to browse its site for the best deals on mortgages, auto loans, credit cards, and more. LendingTree doesn't underwrite loans. Instead, it prequalifies borrowers for lenders. For consumers, it offers a unique chance to have lenders compete for their business.

The loan origination process can be shortened for lenders, and they can draw potential customers from a larger geographical area. For borrowers, it's a time-saving convenience and also can result in lower credit costs because of increased competition among lenders for a customer's business.

To get started, you go to their home page (http://www.lendingtree.com) and click Start Looking for a Loan. Choose the loan type you want and complete the on-line qualification form, which takes about 15 minutes. Within two business days, each lender will post its decision about your loan request on the Web site. When each lender posts its decision, Lending Tree will notify you via e-mail that a response has been received. If your qualification form was sent to four lenders, you will receive separate four e-mails. To find out the responses, go back to Lending Tree's home page and click Check Your Loan Status.

Consumers who visit LendingTree in search of a credit card fill out one simple Qualification Form, a 10-minute process. The form is immediately sent to up to four lenders in the LendingTree Network whose credit criteria match the consumers' information. Within seconds, consumers receive e-mails notifying them to return to the site to view lenders' responses. Consumers can choose the credit card offer that is best for them and accept the offer on the LendingTree site. The lender is immediately notified and, if the consumer qualifies, a card is issued.

LendingTree, Inc., founded in 1996, is the only place—on- or off-line—where a network of lenders compete for consumers' business. Loan types include mortgage, home equity, personal, auto, and credit cards.

Some of the other players in the loan arena are E-Loan (http://www. eloan.com), GetSmart (http://www.getsmart.com), Microsoft'sHomeAdvisor (http://www.homeadvisor.com), and iOwn (http://www.iOwn.com).

Credit Cards

The delivery of financial services over the Web has a promising future. As credit card use on the Internet continues to grow in popularity, the creation of new credit cards and customer service by no-name back-office providers who sell their services to the brand owners seems natural.

Enter NextCard, an on-line credit card issuer. NextCard is using the Internet to build an entirely new independent credit card brand in America, a task not seen since the Discover card. The company's Web site (http://www. nextcard.com), offers a vision of what credit cards over the Web ought to look like in future.

- Customers can get a color image of their choice on the card, which they can upload on the Web.
- Customers can check a year's account history on-line and can download the data into financial packages like Intuit's Quicken and Microsoft's Money.
- They get insurance against fraudulent misuse of the card on-line.
- They also get a partnership with eWallet that allows NextCard holders to buy at a number of leading merchants using only one click instead of filling in an on-line form to open an account with each merchant separately.
- Approval is provided in 30 seconds. But don't think they give out cards to everybody. NextCard has received more than 1,700,000 on-line applications for credit cards yet has issued fewer than 70,000 cards.

INVESTMENTS

Investments on the Internet are going crazy. Day traders take advantage of low transaction fees and lightning-quick access to news and quotes to spend their days making (and losing) large amounts of money on small stock movements. Investment-crazy employees are trying to look busy while diligently culturing their portfolios.

On-line brokers like E-Trade (http://www.etrade.com) have broken down the walls to investors, with low trading fees and easy access—once the account is opened. TheStreet (http://www.thestreet.com) is one of the hottest investment sites of the year.

In mid-1999, Dataquest estimated that 15 million U.S adults are involved in on-line investing activities but only 8 percent of on-line investors are performing activities on-line more than 30 times per month. There are 4.5 million people actually buying and selling on-line. Forrester Research believes that figure will escalate to 10 million by 2003. Traffic measurement company Media Metrix agrees with these figures, noting that 8 million people did their investing from the office, up from 6 million in December. The time those users spent visiting the top 10 financial sites from work rose to an average of 64 minutes.

The top financial sites at work were Yahoo Financial, reaching 2.2 million users; Quicken Financial, 2.008 million; AOL Personal Finance, 1.72 million; MSN's MoneyCentral, 1.157 million; and CBS.MarketWatch.com, 891,000. Credit Suisse First Boston estimates that almost 16 percent of all stock trades now take place in cyberspace.

How have traditional brokers responded? Merrill Lynch announced plans to introduce a new account that will allow customers unlimited trading in most equities, mutual funds, and bonds for a minimum annual fee of $1,500. The brokerage also said it will offer on-line trading for $29.95 per transaction, matching commissions from Charles Schwab, starting in December 1999. The move is an indication that traditional brokers are throwing in the towel.

So how long does it take to place an order? That's what the folks at the Keynote Web Trading Interest can tell you. (Check out the indices at <http://www.keynote.com/measures/brokers>.) The Keynote Web Broker Trading Index shows the average response time in seconds and the success rate for creating a standard stock-order transaction on 15 selected brokerage Web sites.

Gomez Advisors, Inc., offers ratings on Internet brokers at their Web site. In mid-1999 it rated the top 20 firms as follows on a scale of 0 (low) to 10 (high):

1. E*TRADE 7.52
2. NDB 7.35
3. Schwab 7.31
4. DLJdirect 7.19
5. Discover Brokerage 7.04
6. AB Watley 6.87
7. Datek 6.77
8. SURETRADE 6.66

9.   Quick & Reilly 6.49

10.   Fidelity 6.47

11.   My Discount Broker 6.34

12.   Bidwell 6.30

13.   Firstrade 6.27

14.   Waterhouse 6.20

15.   Banc One 6.14

16.   RJ Forbes 6.03

17.   WallStreet Electronica 6.01

18.   Scottrade 5.92

19.   Wang 5.89

20.   Mr. Stock 5.88

POSTAGE

The United States Postal Service (USPS) (http://www.usps.gov) has its job cut out for it. Since being restructured as a semi–quasi-public company, it has had to fend off attacks on at least four major fronts.

Freight services such as Federal Express (http://www.fedex.com) and United Parcel Service (http://www.ups.com) have taken a bite out of the USPS. Both have made an art out of making real-time or near–real-time delivery status available as well as scheduling pickup and printing pickup-ready documents. The freight companies have worked long and hard to have their delivery records count as authoritative a date as a USPS postmark.

E-mail has become a major tool in communications. The USPS has said that e-mail is lacking in security and is offering its own channel for the secure transfer of e-mail. (See Exhibit 7.4.)

Fax machines offer instant delivery of documents. Services like eFax (http://www.efax.com), PeopleFax (http://www.peoplefax.com), and Swiss-Click (http://www.hotcorp.com/swissclick) offer free transfer of printed documents via e-mail. In 1995 the USPS brought forth the Information Based Indicia (IBI), a digitally printed postage meter stamp. This was designed to stop the illegal printing of counterfeit postage meter stamps by copiers and laser printers. In 1999 older postage equipment was replaced with more secure electronic and digital meters. A new 2-D bar code configuration plus readable copy as a printed IBI is the next step for an electronically composed digital meter stamp. (See Exhibit 7.5.) Competitors include E-Stamp Corpora-

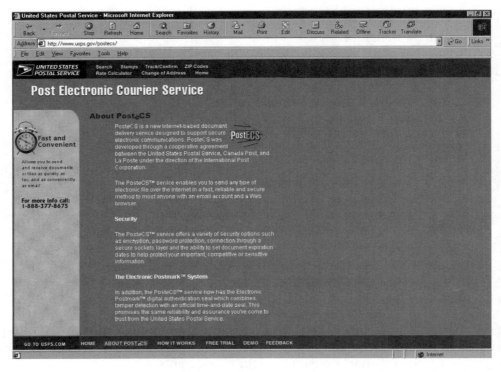

Exhibit 7.4 The USPS is offering its own channel for the secure transfer of e-mail.

tion (http://www.estamp.com), which was the first company to begin beta testing in this arena, Neopost (http://www.neopost.com), Pitney Bowes (http://www.pitneybowes.com) and Stamps.com (http://www.stamps.com). E-Stamp charges 5 to 10 percent on top of postage costs but can save significant time and money. With electronic postage, you don't have to buy or lease postage equipment, worry about specialized ink, or make trips to the post office to buy postage. Postal authorities exempt E-Stamp packages from the security measures required for packages over one pound, as the E-stamp identifies the sender.

TRAVEL

Making travel arrangements on the Web is a natural extension of the travel services that have become popular on various on-line services. However, more than just schedules and pricing, the Web can deliver in-depth information about travel sites. Almost all of the major airlines and hotel chains are on-

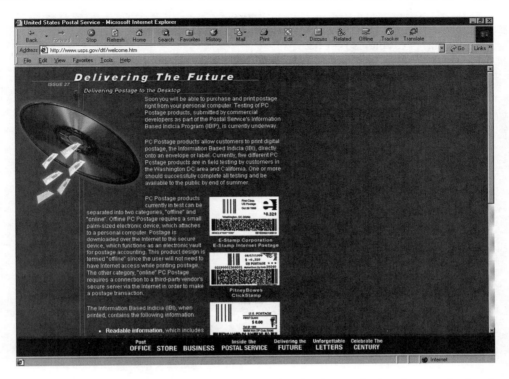

Exhibit 7.5 A new 2-D bar code configuration is the next step for an electronically composed digital meter stamp.

line, offering information about their properties. Hot services like Priceline (http://www.priceline.com) offer vastly discounted travel arrangements at a price you offer to them—and who hasn't heard Captain Kirk (William Shatner) touting how Priceline is "going to be big—really big"?

Here are the top 24 firms, as rated by Gomez Advisors:

1. Preview Travel 7.55
2. Internet Travel Network 6.88
3. Travelocity 6.57
4. Trip.com 6.54
5. 1Travel.com 6.52
6. BizTravel 6.50
7. Expedia 6.42
8. Travel Network 6.40

9. Uniglobe Travel Online 6.36
10. Traveler's Net 6.26
11. Airlines of the Web 6.17
12. Yahoo Travel 6.08
13. Atevo 6.04
14. TravelResDirect 6.01
15. UAL.COM 5.95
16. TravelScape 5.53
17. Travel Base 5.20
18. Travel Now 4.83
19. Flifo 4.56
20. BananaTravel.com 4.54
21. Bon Vivant 4.45
22. LeisurePlanet.com 4.21
23. Internet Travel Services 4.15
24. Global Online Travel 3.99

PROCUREMENT

Commerce is not only done between businesses and consumers (the *business-to-consumer* model) and between different businesses (*business-to-business*, or *B2B*). The rich Internet tools and communications capabilities have made *intranets,* the use of Internet technology to share information within a company, popular.

Microsoft has attempted to lead the way in the electronic back office with the Web-integrated Microsoft Office 2000, Windows NT with Internet Information Server, and Microsoft Exchange Server.

Analysts thought Lotus Notes, a tool designed to facilitate communication between groups, would become obsolete as the Internet grew in popularity. Lotus managed to extend Notes functionality to the Web with the introduction of Domino.

Novell has been working to make its GroupWise product a powerful competitor on the Internet.

Electronic procurement offers business the promise of saving money. Preapproved items can be bought by authorized employees instantly instead of being lumped in with manual requisitions and purchase order forms that may take days to approve and submit. The same shopping carts that allow 24-

hour-a-day, 7-day-a-week shopping for consumers can reduce the costs of preparing and buying goods within the environment of a business approval process. People can order what they can while parallel processing of orders speeds up the approval process.

E-procurement reduces the number of touches on a request while promoting policy control. It lets an organization group together like purchases for better pricing and easier receiving and routing of goods. By making buying easy, e-procurement reduces maverick purchasing—people working around the system, using the inefficiencies of the current system, and buying from unauthorized or favored sources, at nonnegotiated prices, and with kickbacks and other possibilities. By moving maverick buying into the system, the company gets better overall recording of the corporate needs and superior management reporting.

Vendors include PeopleSoft/Commerce One. SAP and Oracle have e-procurement options and J.D. Edwards has arranged a procurement deal with Ariba. WebMethods of Fairfax, Virginia, has a B2B product that is making waves, using XML technology.

UNDERLYING TECHNOLOGIES

The extent to which a company can duplicate the traditional storefront on the Web depends on management commitment. While most companies are putting up some advertising literature and soliciting e-mail responses, others are making their entire catalogs available and soliciting orders. The technologies to accomplish these two tasks are developing quickly.

Tying Databases into the Web

If a company plans to conduct business on the Web without restrictions, it will need to make its entire product line available for review. Although this can be done by redesigning the HTML of the Web pages manually to include new products, change prices, and update information where necessary, doing so can be impractical for large databases. If the strength of the Internet is the ability to broadcast timely information worldwide at a minimum cost, tools to tie the corporate database into the Web are necessary.

The developers of most major industrial databases offer tools for linking their databases to the Internet. Whether your corporate standard is Microsoft's SQL Server (http://www.microsoft.com), IBM's DB2 (http://www.ibm.com), Oracle (http://www.oracle.com), Sybase (http://www.sybase.com), or Informix (http://www.informix.com), developer's tools are available to permit controlled external access to the database through the Web.

If your corporate data is in one of the popular database formats, you can automate the link between your data and your Web server in a number of ways.

- *ODBC:* A number of companies are offering products to make databases available to the Web. Microsoft's Internet Information Server works with Windows NT to permit ODBC (Open DataBase Connectivity) access of databases. ODBC lets any application access data from any ODBC-compliant database. Crystal Reports, one of the most popular report writers for the Microsoft Windows platform, can now be used to create HTML on demand for the many databases it can access.
- *Programming extensions:* The Java programming language form SGI and Active Server Pages from Microsoft also promise the ability to extract information from databases automatically.
- *XML:* The emerging XML technology provides a new hub for the easy transformation and transfer of data files in industry-standard formats.

Internet access to a database has advantages internal to a company as well. Many companies have PC-compatible, Macintosh, UNIX, and proprietary computers throughout their facilities. Using Internet standards, all of these disparate computing platforms can access a company's data.

ORDERING ON THE WEB

After making all of a company's products available for review on the Web, the next step is the process of taking orders on the Web.

Software for Orders on the Web

As discussed in the first edition of this book, only a few hardy and foolish companies had created accounting software that integrated with the Internet. SBT Accounting Systems, Inc. (http://www.sbt.com) was the first major accounting software vendor to develop a link between their accounting software and Web software for collecting orders. Their commerce site, Business1 (http://www.business1.com—don't type that wrong or you will get a naughty site), offered a showcase of Web-ready merchants. Now it is a shell of its former self. Big Business (http://www.bigbusiness.com) offered an inexpensive solution including a Web server. Unfortunately, it was in business, out of business, and now back in business. What of its affordable Internet order solution? Even Peachtree had gotten into the act, with a relationship with EDI provider Harbinger to offer on-line sales mixed with integration to inventory and order entry. Everyone else promised a solution RSN— "real soon now"—and most are still making that promise.

Accounting software developers have had to face many challenges over the last few years. Internet integration has taken a backseat to Y2K, 32-bit processing, and Microsoft SQL Server. At the same time, as a rule companies have not been bringing in fast communications lines and setting up their own servers. They have been getting fast enough connections to offer e-mail and Web surfing for their employees but have not seen the benefit of opening their main network to the world. Security risks, administrative overload, and lack of perceived benefit have reduced the demand for accounting-integrated Internet order systems.

The lure of a 24-hour-a-day, 7-day-a-week sales office and the success of companies like Dell, Amazon.com and Priceline are strong incentives to consider e-commerce. However, without integration between Internet systems and day-to-day systems, orders get lost, returns and refunds are a problem, customers are not served efficiently, and double work is necessary. If the accounting is not integrated with the orders, there are big problems.

The number of available solutions is growing. One is moving the accounting out to the Internet along with the order entry. Accounting Solutions Providers (ASPs) take the entire accounting system and outsource it. This keeps hardware costs and software acquisition costs to a minimum, capitalizes on familiarity with Web browsers to make training easier, and keeps the software and data upgrade and safe—if conducted with a reliable hosting service.

For example, Great Plains Software (http://www.gps.com) has entered into an arrangement with IBM to provide outsourced and reliable access to their software in an outsourced environment. Great Plains promises a much lower initial investment to start out or upgrade than buying equipment and software and regular monthly payments for the service. It handles equipment repair, data preservation and recovery, and ongoing administration. Other companies are beginning to offer equivalent services for solutions that would otherwise be cost prohibitive but can be affordable in a shared environment.

For larger companies, on-site servers that integrate a commerce/merchant server with the backroom accounting are relatively simple. Most major vendors of higher-end products, such as SAP, Baan, J.D. Edwards, and Lawson, have developed Internet integration. For smaller, growing companies, setting up servers on-site is possible with a limited number of vendors: AccountMate (http://www.accountmate.com) offers Visual AccountMate Internet Order; Great Plains has a large selection of Internet-enabled products; Sage Software (http://www.sota.com) has released "Internet.access" e-commerce modules.

The year 2000 will see the rollout of Microsoft's next-generation electronic commerce products. Most major accounting software developers have pledged support for its commerce technology. Until that time, most accounting software vendors promising e-commerce solutions are using a temporary solution provided by a third-party developer or product reseller. This means that adopting one of those solutions is a short-term investment. Otherwise, integration of accounting to e-commerce tends to be a custom-programming job—the beginning of a difficult and potentially expensive path.

Competitors for Microsoft Commerce Server are few and floundering. Chief among the contenders in the "inexpensive but capable" marketplace is a product called iCat, now owned by Intel (http://www.intel.com). iCat Commerce Online, an entry-level e-commerce solution, is used by thousands of businesses nationwide.

ACCOUNTING SOLUTIONS

AccountMate

Visual AccountMate Internet Order (http://www.accountmate.com) provides customers with a convenient way to place orders over the Internet by means of a secure connectivity program separate from a typical Internet browser. Customers place orders at their convenience and create a sales order that passes from the Internet server into the database associated with the AccountMate Sales Order module. Customers also can create sales quotes without submitting an order, thereby saving the vendor customer service labor.

Advanced Software

Advanced Software claims its U.A. E-Commerce is the only true end-to-end e-commerce solution. It offers automated functions (wizards) to help you:

- Create, define, and manage catalogs using your inventory items and materials
- Create customized storefronts or catalogs
- Set rules for automatically filtering out frivolous or unusual orders or freely send orders to a queue for manual review before processing
- Connect to leading ISPs through connectivity wizards
- Publish your site directly from the e-commerce module and immediately go live
- Have transactions automatically integrate with your U.A. Corporate Accounting system to generate invoices, process credit card payments,

post the transaction to your accounting ledgers, generate order fulfillment tickets, and e-mail a confirmation to the customer

Great Plains Software

Great Plains Software (http://www.gps.com) offers numerous electronic commerce solutions.

e.Commerce is a consumer-to-business order processing system, linking eEnterprise to Microsoft Commerce Server. It provides high-volume order processing for companies that want an electronic storefront on the Internet. It leverages the features of Microsoft Commerce Server to allow customers to order products over the World Wide Web. e.Commerce allows eEnterprise customers to expand their business into a global organization, using the World Wide Web to offer their products and services to customers around the world.

e.Order combines the global reach of the Internet with the power of your accounting system to dramatically improve the way you do business. When you implement e.Order through the World Wide Web, you'll enable your established customers to enter orders securely right into the eEnterprise Sales Order Processing system. In addition, those customers can check on the status of their orders, any time day or night. e.Order is ideal for businesses that employ remote salespeople. Using e.Order, sales executives across the country and around the world can enter orders directly into your sales order system, at their convenience and without making you duplicate order entry efforts.

Other solutions include e.View for online reporting, e.Requisition for online entry of purchase requisitions through the Web, e.Employee for payroll and human resource information and complete hosting services provided by IBM.

Sage Software

Sage Software, Inc. (http://www.sota.com) offers "internet.access," a MAS 90® e-commerce module that dynamically links data from a Web site with Sage's MAS 90 accounting software. This module allows MAS 90 user companies to conduct business with clients over the Internet and includes the abilities to perform account inquiries and order entry functions in a secure Web-based environment. MAS 90 user companies will be able to grant their clients the ability to safely log on to and place orders on their Web site, which will directly feed information into MAS 90. The initial capabilities of internet.access consist of a core internet.access system module and two applets called "internet.inquiry" and "internet.order". The customer inquiry applet allows for account and order inquiry capabilities, and internet.order is a shopping cart applet that can provide order entry functionality. Planned future inter-net.access enhancements include additional applets addressing further capa-bilities, such as field sales, HR self-service, and vendor purchasing.

The release of the MAS 90 internet.access module represents Sage's sec-ond phase in taking MAS 90 to the Internet. Sage's MAS 90 Client/Server for Windows NT offers companies with multisite offices the ability to run MAS 90 between offices using virtual private networking with a local dial-up connec-tion to an ISP.

STOREFRONTS IN A BOX

iCat

iCat has led the way in the field of e-commerce. It was the first to offer an off-the-shelf, turnkey, e-commerce solution, the first to provide cross-platform e-commerce software, and the first to develop a partner channel composed of trained professionals in each and every aspect of Web store development, cre-ation, and hosting.

iCat has an online store where it manages your wares for a reasonable price—but it is not going as far as Yahoo! has in opening the door to integra-tion. Yahoo!Store permits file uploads and downloads, such as sales results into Excel.

Yahoo!Store

When growing fast is more important than becoming profitable, you need to get a reliable Web host to support you. If you want to grow from nothing to something—FAST!—Yahoo! has an offer for you. Its Yahoo!Site service is a very fast and easy way to begin to develop a Web presence. The service, found at <http://site.yahoo.com>, offers the reliability of Yahoo!, your own domain name, and Web and wizard-based site development software that literally gets a handsome and functional site up in five minutes from anywhere with a Web browser. The cost is $29.95 per month, consistent with mail order–quality hosts and well below many local hosting services. There is no startup fee, no time commitment, and no charge for registering domain names. The monthly fee also includes e-mail forwarding to an existing e-mail address (or to a @yahoo.com address you can get free).

The Yahoo!Site service is free for 10 days. You can test the site builder soft-ware and the response time to see how it compares with comparable services.

We tested the Quick Setup. In less than five minutes, we had developed a five-page Web site, complete with a site search engine and response page. The pages the site builder developed were very handsome and comparable to those developed by the better low-end HTML development tools. For someone with no HTML experience, the site created would act as a brochure with e-mail response. However, some knowledge of HTML was helpful to develop links to other resources.

Bigstep.com

Are you afraid of the commitment behind making the big step into e-commerce? Maybe you can start small—and free. At press time, Bigstep.com opened, offering free e-business sites. Will they be around when you read this? Perhaps the next $$Billion$$ IPO?

Features to Look for in a Storefront
Wizard-driven site builder

Catalog browsing and search engine

Quantity breaks and preferred pricing

Stock availability

Credit card or payment terms supported

Shopping cart review and edit

Anonymous shopping supported

E-mail confirmation of orders

Self-serve order status checking

Software download capability

Secured transactions through SSL

High Web-browser compatibility

Storefront templates

Navigation

Search engine

Sales and specials

User customization

Shopping advisors

Configurators and sales add-ons (Do you want French fries with that?)

Registration

Shipping

Sales tax

Catalog

Shopping cart

Payment and credit card clearing

Integration with Accounts Receivable, Order Entry, Inventory Management, General Ledger, Customer Support/Help Desk, e-mail

ISSUES PAVING THE WAY FOR ELECTRONIC COMMERCE

Electronic commerce and Internet commerce, in particular, have come under fire. Unscrupulous people have broken into supposedly secure systems and taken lists of credit card holders, posting them publicly. Traffic on the Internet often slows down so that efficient use becomes impossible. Popular commerce sites like auction house eBay (http://www.ebay.com) or stockbroker Charles Schwab (http://www.schwab.com) fail without warning.

The complaints of the lack of security are not all justified, especially where Internet commerce is compared to traditional commerce. While sending information on the Internet has been likened to sending confidential information on the back of a post card, current Net security makes the secured transfer of a credit card number far safer than using that same card at a restaurant or gas station. When you give your credit card to a waiter or tell it to an operator on a toll-free phone line, anything can happen to it. Reports from the credit card providers indicate that the incidence of credit card abuse over the Internet is markedly lower than on traditional business channels. The danger is more for the merchant than for the consumer. As of this writing, not a single credit card sent while encryption was in place using SSL had been intercepted and misused. One could justifiably argue that the biggest problem with doing business on the Internet is not security, but marketing.

What issues affect Internet commerce, and who is involved in bringing electronic commerce into the mainstream? Some of the most important areas have to do with standards, security, payment methods, and the effect of electronic commerce on the audit.

Standards

In a normal business transaction, there is a standard for business: the monetary unit of the country in which you do business. In the United States, a dollar represents a standard for exchange. Although doing business for barter has grown informally, and there are barter groups that track barter accounts between participants, using currency takes the guesswork out of the value of what is being transferred.

In the United States, customers assume that they can walk through a store to find something they would like to buy and then approach a cash register to purchase what they want. If there is no obvious register, they find a salesperson to finish the transaction or get the information they need. Payment is normally made by cash, check, or credit/debit card. A customer service desk is available for complaints or questions in larger stores.

In electronic commerce today, customers are just learning what to expect. There are few standards in place for navigating an Internet store. A Web site is not a supermarket, and familiar sites like cash registers or customer service desks are few. Every site is designed differently. Unfamiliarity is a major roadblock to getting the general public to change the way it does business.

Without standards, automating the flow of business is nearly impossible, as each type of business must be handled on a case-by-case basis. While this is not as important for an individual, it makes transacting business more difficult for businesses. One exception to this lack of current standards is business that is being transacted using *Electronic Data Interchange* (EDI).

Electronic Data Interchange.   EDI has been a viable method of the computer-to-computer transfer of business information for over a decade. National and international standards organizations, such as the Data Interchange Standards Association Inc. of Alexandria, Virginia (http://www-edi.itsi.disa.mil), are involved in the definition and refinement of the way information is transferred. With EDI, trading partners enter into official agreements with each other. (The parties know in advance who they will work with.) EDI data must conform to a series of standard file formats. Because the data are in a format that is largely the same worldwide, many companies have developed EDI integration to accounting software, which is suitable for working with a number of different partners.

Traditionally, the data are sent electronically to the computer systems of an independent third party, a *value added network* (VAN), to a computer mailbox set up specifically for that trading partner. The trading partners send and receive batches of information representing purchase orders, stock requests, shipping notification, invoices, and other standard business transactions. The VANs are companies like IBM or General Electric: large companies with massive computer departments with the resources and expertise to guarantee the privacy and integrity of the data. Although the transmission costs through these third-party VAN services might seem high, the costs of sending and receiving EDI is often a fraction of the costs of manually preparing the paper equivalents of each type of business transaction. It is transacted at greater speeds, entered with much lower chance of error due to misunderstandings or mistyping, and not limited by time and language constraints, easing doing business internationally.

You can find more resources about electronic commerce and EDI at <http://www.fedworld.gov/edicals/locator.html>. (See Exhibit 7.6.)

Moving EDI to the Internet.   Moving EDI from a VAN to the Internet offers greater speed and convenience and cuts the costs of transmission greatly. However, the services offered by the VAN, including privacy and integrity, must be compensated for. Harbinger (http://www.harbinger.com) is a leading provider of EDI solutions for the Internet.

The promise of XML has led users of EDI to consider how XML can be used to make EDI even more accessible to trading partners large and small.

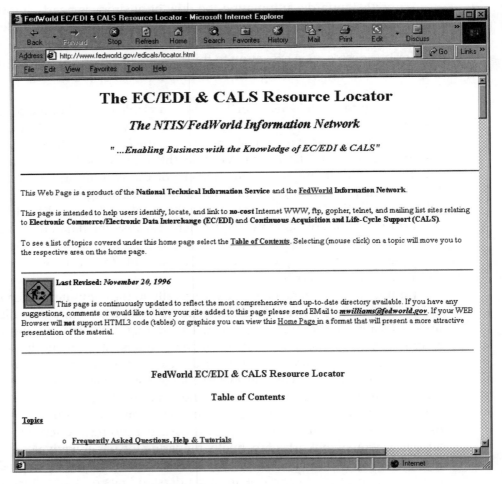

Exhibit 7.6   EC/EDI and CALS Resource Locator.

Moving away from EDI.   EDI has a well-established and continuously evolving series of standards that has been successful in the business marketplace. However, it falls short in being immediately applicable to the entire realm of commerce as projected for the Internet. It is not appropriate for noncommercial, nonrepetitive business. EDI software can be complicated to use and expensive. Even though EDI can't be applied to every kind of business transaction, a series of standards needs to be developed.

Establishing Standards for Commerce.   Many companies have tried to establish new standards for doing business on the Internet. However, none has had the level of trust or power in the industry to establish that standard. One group of businesses and organizations has banded together to establish the standards of commerce: CommerceNet. CommerceNet (http://www.commerce. net), headquartered in Menlo Park, is a consortium of over 500 companies and organizations whose charter is to accelerate the use of the Internet for electronic commerce applications. Consortium members include leading companies in the electronics, computer, financial services, and information service industries, and other companies and organizations committed to electronic commerce. Information about CommerceNet can be obtained by visiting CommerceNet's Internet site.

CommerceNet's Web site addresses issues related to doing business on the Internet. Its participants work on projects that test and showcase the new capabilities related to Internet-based electronic commerce. CommerceNet offers a tutorial illustrating some areas of interest to merchants: presenting catalogs of items for sale, providing on-line ordering, providing payment by check, and controlling information through the Internet.

Other Issues Standing in the Way

Electronic Issues.   With an industry based on something as immature as the Web, certain other technology issues come into play. Most Web sites conspicuously post that "This site is best viewed using Netscape 4.x (or Internet Explorer 5.x) or above. Click here to download it." For the 10 percent of Web users using text-based browsers like Lynx or older graphical browsers, many of the Web's multimedia and commerce aspects are hidden; the pages are set up to display their contents graphically—the sales information in tables, and order taking in forms—which these older browsers do not handle well, if at all. Even surfers using 1998 or earlier versions of Internet Explorer or Netscape may be missing some of the essential features.

The battles of the browsers may mean that doing business will continue to have its roadblocks in the short run. The leapfrog of new functionality found only in some versions of Web browsers, technologies useful only when using fast connections, or processor-specific sites that require a Pentium III may limit site acceptance.

Nonelectronic Issues.   Along with systems-related issues, a number of other issues make Internet commerce interesting, including those pertaining to customs and international business, taxation, laws and regulations, custom and language. Although most of these fall outside the scope of this book, a proper audit trail for governmental and financial purposes is covered later in this chapter.

Security and Privacy

Once people and companies determine that they can do business with each other, they must overcome one of the best-publicized weaknesses of the Internet: security, or the lack of it. The very nature of the Internet has the information from a business transaction being transferred from the originating computer through a number of other computers before ending up at its destination.

In addition, the need for privacy within the United States and that demanded by our international trading partners, such as the European Economic Community, has filled the newspapers with fears of U.S. governmental intervention for consumer protection and control of the Internet. (See Exhibit 7.7.)

See Chapter 8 for a full discussion of this topic.

Payment Methods

With methods to communicate between buyer and sender in place, and assurance that the commerce is secure, appropriate methods of payments must be set up. Between businesses, these may be based on predetermined and approved house accounts. However, in the marketplace, not all business is repeat business on account. Credit cards and new methods of commerce come into play. Organizations like the JEPI (Joint Electronic Payment Initiative) have been created—and disbanded—to try to get the electronic commerce leaders to link the electronic payment systems with a universal payment platform.

Internet Payments.   Digital cash has faced a rocky road on the Internet. Lack of acceptance, too many players with no standard, and the success of using traditional credit cards has stymied those trying to make the use of digital cash widespread. Think back to the 1996 Olympics. If you watched much television, you were subjected to a barrage of commercials touting the convenience of stored value cards. As I recall, a pilot flying in the Out-

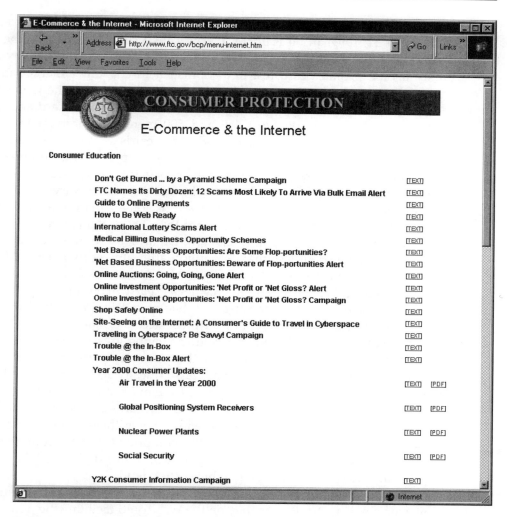

Exhibit 7.7 Federal Trade Commission E-Commerce and the Internet site.

back of Australia lands by a soda machine, only to find himself short of cash. Not to worry—he pulls out his smart card and his thirst is a thing of the past. Smart cards were not propelled into everyday life in the United States at the 1996 Olympics, despite popular acceptance in Europe and Asia. Consumers did not want to put money into cards not accepted by the merchants, and merchants did not want to invest in the equipment necessary to take the cards without customer demand. Now three major trials of smart cards have come to an end, and Americans seem no closer to wanting to use them than before.

Visa's 15-month smart card pilot project in New York City came to an end December 31, 1999, and it is either a technical success (according to the company) or a failure (according to the critics). The Manhattan project was the first major U.S. smart card test in a sophisticated consumer market and the first step toward a cashless economy. In the pilot project on the Upper West Side, Visa and Citibank issued Visa cash cards, while MasterCard and Chase issued Mondex cards. Between 450 and 600 merchants participated in the pilot, and according to Visa, users loaded the cards 53,000 times, averaging $38 each time, and merchants used the cards to deposit $813,000 into banks. Lukewarm consumer response may be the reason for the relatively low participation and acceptance. According to a Britain Associates survey, more than half of those polled felt that transactions took longer than with cash. Users didn't perceive the speed and convenience to be better than cash.

In a highly publicized trial in Guelph, Ontario, by Mondex Canada, consumers will have spent less than $2 million after almost two years. Mondex Canada had trumpeted its plan to move Mondex across Canada within the first year. Now it has written off the results as "early experiments."

It is reported that Burger King also has ended its initial trial of stored value cards, but there are no reports as to its success or failure.

Smart cards as stored value cards are receiving great acceptance in many other parts of the world. They are the "Jerry Lewis" of payment methods—highly valued in France and somewhat less critically acclaimed in the United States. They are being used for everything from mass transit to paying migrant workers. In the United States, the safety of credit cards and easy availability of banks and ATM machines still seem to win out over the options. As electronic wallets and smart card devices built into computers become commonplace, perhaps digital currency may make a comeback. While digital cash has been a flop so far, a new arrival is hoping to break that trend.

Most participants in the first round of digital cash are now casualties. However, small amounts of money on the Web could facilitate the purchase of information. That's why companies like the *Wall Street Journal* and governmental organizations like the U.S. Department of Commerce are signing on with Qpass (http://www.qpass.com). The *Wall Street Journal* has been one of the few to have a successful subscription-based site. However, the cost of a year's subscription to the Interactive Edition may turn investors off. Why not offer a one-day pass? Financially, submitting credit card payments for small amounts is not cost effective. Enter the *Wall Street Journal* on a "day pass" for $1.95 as part of its adoption of micropayment technology developed by Seattle-based Qpass. At this writing, Qpass said three other publishers have signed up to use its newly developed system to deliver research reports and data on a per-item or time-sensitive basis: mutual fund research publisher

Morningstar Inc., Internet trade magazine *The Industry Standard,* and the U.S. Department of Commerce. If you visit the Department of Commerce at <http://www.stat-usa.gov/Newstand>, you will be able to purchase only the reports and releases you need to make important business, career, and personal decisions. Its Newstand was designed to offer their most popular items on an individual basis.

All you have to do is register for membership with Qpass, which is free. When you find a Newstand article you want to purchase from the list, click on the link, then follow the instructions to become a Qpass member. If you are already a Qpass member, just click on the link and enter your Qpass user name and password.

How did Qpass pick up such lofty clients in its first month of service? The time was right for making information available easily and cheaply.

Until Qpass or another product takes a commanding lead, banks, credit card companies, and other financial service firms will try to keep their part of the payment marketshare. While credit cards rule e-commerce, certified checks rule the auction sites, and intellectuals tout the promise of digital bearer settlement as the future of commerce, checks are still to be highly promoted as a viable e-commerce payment method. Banks have a lot invested in keeping checks going. The *American Banking Journal* recently quoted a McKinsey and BAI/PSI study showing that in 1995, before all this Internet stuff really broke out, 40 percent of bank operating profits came from noncredit card payments through fees, float, and spread. Banks obviously have a strong interest in building on the current paper-check system rather than bypassing it. With so little digital transaction history, the digital cash industry has not had an opportunity to develop much in the way of protection, whereas electronic checks would be covered by existing check laws. To learn more about the emerging world of electronic checks, check out <http://www.echeck.org>.

CheckFree Holdings Corp. also believes Internet payments is the place to be. It has announced a link with a large Internet portal (the *Wall Street Journal* says it's Yahoo!) to become your ATM machine on the Internet. Although CheckFree works with many banks, it does present the bills for many major companies, including IBM, and processes 70 percent of all electronic consumer payments. CheckFree has the unenviable job of convincing you and me to let it access our checking accounts at will.

For more information on the world of Internet payments, you may wish to visit the Internet Information Payments Collaborative at <http://www.iipc.net>.

From Customer to Vendor. Because of the fear of credit card manipulation or misuse, consumers have different levels of trust in giving out their credit card numbers. This leads to three possible scenarios.

In the most conservative situation, when an order is placed, some companies call the customer on the phone or request a fax with the credit card number. This limits the chance that the credit card number will be intercepted during transmission but leaves the chance that the number will be misused at the vendor, as in a traditional transaction. In addition, the cost of a voice or fax call may exceed the profit available from a sale.

The boldest purchasers are not concerned about misuse, knowing that the credit card companies limit purchaser's liability to $50 in case of misuse. Many people feel comfortable entering their credit card number in a nonsecure transfer, knowing that their exposure is possible but limited.

Users who plan on conducting business regularly on the Web make sure they use Netscape or another secured browser. These systems provide encryption for secured data transfer, although many people are concerned that any security algorithm can be breached.

A means of providing a secure way to store credit cards on your computer is the digital wallet. A wallet can hold card numbers and authorization in an encrypted storage file.

SET, ECML and Digital Wallet   Credit cards have remained the way to do business in the United States. Keeping the credit card number safe from misuse by the vendor or capture from the vendor's site was the major thrust behind the *Secure Electronic Transactions* (SET) effort. SET would make using a credit card on the Internet much safer than using a card in a traditional store; the credit card number would be shared only by the banking institutions, and the vendor would never see it. Yet after more than three years, the consortium that manages and promotes the SET standard announced a series of initiatives designed to kick-start market acceptance. Among them: the formation of a Business Advisors Group made up of leading financial institutions and payment companies that plan to work together to market SET aggressively. SET got a lot of important players around the table to talk. Now the seats around that table have been warmed up again.

To further enhance the on-line commerce for consumers and merchants, almost every major player in hardware, software, and financial services has come together with a new, potentially groundbreaking standard for storing credit information on your computer. It reads like a dream list. Name the most important folks on the credit card front: MasterCard, Visa, and American Express. How about hardware vendors? IBM, Compaq, SGI (Sun Microsystems). Can't go anywhere without Microsoft. Add CyberCash, SETCo, and a few others not well known to us but well known to the other parties, and you have a powerhouse of a consortium.

Think it is hard enough to get all these folks in one room? How about getting them to agree enough to collaborate on a universal format for wallets and merchant Web sites? The format, known as Electronic Commerce Modeling Language, uses a set of uniform field names that streamlines the process by which merchants collect electronic data for shipping, billing, and payment. What is that process?

If you have bought goods on the Internet, you know that one of the most dreaded points in the purchasing process is when you have to fill out the personal information and credit card information. A February 1999 report from Jupiter Communications on digital wallets found that 27 percent of on-line buyers abandon orders before checkout due to the hassle of filling out forms.

Each store seems to do it differently, and there is no spell checking or validation and often no going back. Merchants have their own set of forms, their own data format, and there is so much to type. It isn't like this at the corner store (unless you visit Radio Shack, where you get asked personal information even when you buy a 99 cent battery or clip).

Internet Explorer and upcoming versions of Netscape Navigator have a built-in digital wallet that can ease this situation. While digital wallets normally reside on the consumer's PC, server-based wallets will allow buyers to keep that data stored on their bank's server. This makes buying from computers other than your own possible.

A digital wallet is an application or service that assists consumers in conducting on-line transactions by allowing them to store billing, shipping, and payment information and to use this information to complete a merchant's checkout page automatically. Enter the data once, and use it again and again. This greatly simplifies the checkout process and reduces the need for a consumer to complete a merchant's form manually every time. In fact, SET requires a digital wallet for its use.

But lack of standards has hampered acceptance of digital wallets. Many people also fear putting their credit card information into their computer, especially with news that Microsoft collected information about its users without telling them. Here is Achilles' heel number one: Will people be afraid of privacy issues, even if they have the illusion of control over their wallet?

ECML provides a simple set of guidelines (the current specifications are found at <http://www.ecml.org/spec.htm>) for Web merchants that will enable digital wallets from multiple vendors to automate the exchange of information between users and merchants. It is a simple agreement on interoperability that can extend beyond the Web to many other areas.

ECML has been designed as an open standard that can be used by anyone and does not require any licensing or usage fees. ECML will be submitted to the Internet Engineering Task Force (IETF) and the World Wide Web consortium (W3C) P3P committee and ultimately will be handed over to an international standards body. Here is Achilles' heel number two: Can a committee of such strong personal interests and conflicting desires make this work quickly and effectively?

ECML does not replace the security of SSL (Secure Socket Leyes), the communications of SET (Secure Electronic Transaction), the tagging of OBI (Open Buying on the Internet), XML (the eXtensible Markup Language), or IOTP (Internet Open Trading Protocol) or the technology of smart cards.

There is widespread market appeal for the ECML format among on-line retailers who are looking for a way to close the gap between an abandoned shopping cart and a completed transaction. A Jupiter survey found that "76 percent of merchants surveyed indicated they are willing to participate in a multi-site wallet enterprise," because "multi-site wallets offer reduced acquisition costs that far outweigh the risk to merchants of losing an existing customer."

From Vendor to Bank.   The vendor now has the responsibility of getting the credit card validated and getting its money. This transfer can be as open to attack as the original purchase.

Once a credit card number has been received from a customer, the vendor can verify the card manually, as if the transaction was received on paper or on the phone. The transactions can be run through clearing systems separately. If the order system includes clearing services, credit cards are verified automatically as part of the service.

The greatest losses in using credit cards has not been to the consumer but to the vendors and the banks.

Affect of E-Commerce on the Audit

E-commerce affects almost every aspect of business. As accountants are involved in so many aspects of business, it is no surprise that the accounting issues are legion:

- Electronic evidence
- Internal controls
- Risk and legal liability
- Jurisdiction
- Out-of-state and country sales considerations
- Tariffs and taxes
- Foreign currency and banking relationships
- Electronic data interchange and its successors

- Banks with cash management solutions that prepare electronic files that automatically do the cash receipts into accounting systems
- On-line procurement and bill presentation
- Investing and business valuations

Real-time information may require continuous auditing (or at least a lot more frequent auditing) done efficiently and cost effectively. The need for tools (IDEA (http://www.cica.com), ACL (http://www.acl.com)) to sift through electronic information is stronger than ever. Is the profession ready? Do most CPA firms continue to audit around the black box with little risk of discovery? Will clients be enticed by another CPA firm that offers personalized information securely on-line?

Clients are installing e-commerce systems and looking for help. What can you provide? XML is transforming the way data are transferred within an organization, between partners, and making financial research more efficient. Do you understand it?

International boundaries are coming down and the IAC is making new pronouncements affecting international accounting.

EDI, EFT, and other "large-company" issues are moving down to smaller companies. Even emerging firms are targets for Web-based ERP systems.

Your clients are installing NT. Seeing business owners compare the benefits of T-1 lines with IDSN is fascinating, if not scary.

Every company that hopes to have a CPA firm audit its books needs to know that engaging in new methods of electronic commerce may have unseen circumstances: a vastly increased audit fee and confused auditors, perhaps making an audit impossible. Financial management in audited firms should discuss plans to embrace Internet commerce with their CPAs.

The CPA profession has two large tasks related to auditing the electronic commerce business. The profession needs to develop standards for carrying out audits of these systems and communicate its needs to its clients. In addition, we need the appropriate tools to examine these systems, efficiently and in preparation for the evolution of the communication of financial information.

Audit Standards. At the time of this writing, the American Institute of Certified Public Accountants was just issuing a new guide for auditors in the area of EDI, more than 10 years after EDI won general acceptance as a means of commerce. It's called "Audit Implications of EDI" (No. 021060CLA1) and is available from AICPA Order Department, CLA1, P.O. Box 2209, Jersey City, NJ 07303-2209; (800) 862-4272, dept 1, Operator CLA1. The profession needs to begin to develop audit standards for electronic commerce, including Internet commerce, immediately.

Automated Tools. As a financial pipeline is established and data flows from original transactions to financial statements, a new means of verifying and testing financial data must be established. The profession will need to embrace new computerized tools that tie directly into the pipeline and review the data flowing through. Electronic agents for audits will become an important part of the CPA's automated toolkit to filter through a company's data, retain confidence in the systems, and report on the financial statements.

INTERVIEW: GREAT PLAINS

How did the organization first get involved in the Internet for its own use?

Great Plains first developed a Web site (http://www.greatplains.com) to market its products and services to prospects and customers. We also used our Web site to educate visitors about our company and about our heritage. We also developed an intranet to help educate our team members on our products, programs, services, learning and development opportunities, corporate events and news.

How did it begin offering Internet-oriented services to its customers?

Initially we offered our reselling channel sales, service, and marketing support via an electronic service called PlainsOnline. That evolved into what is known today as PartnerSource—a complete knowledge center via the Web with sales and marketing tools, discussion threads, demo downloads, technical support, and more. CustomerSource was also launched at this time to provide our Dynamics platform customers information on upcoming products releases, access to technical support knowledge databases used by Great Plains own support staff, product demos and downloads, on-line training courses, and on-line users' group sessions.

What is your impression of CPAs and their Internet use?

We believe CPAs look for strategic technologies, like the Internet, that benefit their own organizations as well as the clients they support. More and more firms are posting Web sites and beginning to really harness the power the Internet provides in marketing their services and supporting their clients. The Internet can bring greater levels of efficiency and performance in client services, allowing CPAs to save time and increase profitability.

How about their clients?

The Internet, through its technology, levels the playing field, allowing small businesses to enter markets that before they would not have entered, now competing with much larger organizations—and often beating them. This new economy fueled by the Internet will continue to spark entrepreneurs into business. Their clients are also using the Internet for worldwide marketing, allowing them to extend their reach of markets and customers they serve.

What makes your Internet offerings unique?

The Internet has transformed a marketing medium into a place for businesses to expand into new and global markets, sell their products, service their customers, and extend information to their own staffs, essentially creating on-line communities connecting their various constituencies together. Great Plains' Internet or electronic business solutions lend themselves to this idea of an on-line community by providing a number of different types of applications, including electronic commerce, self-service, and business intelligence applications. The key to successful electronic business is seamlessly integrating the internet solutions with existing backbone (or back-office) business management systems. This seamless integration reduces costs and increases accuracy, thereby increasing satisfaction and providing a higher RIO.

What is your vision for accountants' use of the Internet?

A connected environment where the accountant has a secure, direct view into clients' systems to be able to proactively provide consulting to their clients. The accountants can help assure the integrity and reliability of their clients' systems.

What is your vision for your own firm's use of the Internet?

Great Plains will continue to build an on-line community, connecting customers, vendors, CPAs, and employees together over the Internet. On-line support will continue to grow, as will on-line purchasing and an environment of individualized service.

Do you think the Internet has had a profound effect on accounting and accounting practice?

Clearly anything that affects organizations and how they do business will have an affect on their accountants over time. As the Internet becomes even more pervasive and more businesses look to integrate their electronic store-fronts with front- and back-office components, accountants will be used to assure the integrity of the data among the systems. Accountants will be conducting real-time auditing, correlating and analyzing data from many sources, and managing financial data.

How will the Internet affect education (continuing and preparatory)?

The Internet is dramatically changing both preparatory and continuing education. Great Plains added electronic training opportunities to its Great Plains University education program in 1997. Today we offer more than 100 courses on-line. In addition, we offer weekly "interact" sessions with highly trained staff on a variety of topics from year-end closing, to marketing techniques (to our partners), to sessions on e-business itself. Great Plains also sponsors an Education Alliance Network where colleges and universities can use Dynamics in their accounting and IT curriculums—enabling students to access the software and thus complete lessons via the Internet.

What about globally? What effect has the Internet had on global accounting (International Accounting Standards)?

The Internet brings new awareness to the disparity between the standards of different countries. As customers shop globally over the Internet, the cultural differences in business practices, accounting standards, and things like shipping rules are clearly affected and brought to the forefront.

What should accountants be doing to keep up and prepare for the future?

Attend local and national accounting and technology conferences to better understand new and strategic Internet technologies and the benefits they provide to clients. Get on-line both for their own firm's visibility as well as to learn about the vendors, products, and trends in the marketplace. CPAs need to become wired to their clients and their clients' other service providers, such as banks. Look for ways to extend their firms into an on-line community with their clients.

What do you see as the greatest challenges still to be faced?

Continuing to educate businesses and CPAs alike on the benefits and possibilities provided by the Internet. Putting the infrastructure in place to truly reach a totally on-line environment where customers, vendors, CPAs, and other business consultants are interconnected, sharing information, yet maintaining security and accounting integrity. The accounting professional's IT skills and competencies will have to broaden and deepen.

Do you have favorite Internet resources and software?

Great Plains Dynamics.Commerce [grin], Excite, Internet Explorer, Netscape, art.com, barnesandnoble.com, toysmart.com, accountingsoftwarenews.com, accountingnet.com, hotmail.com (to use for anonymous e-mail for shopping).

Sites that provide downloads for software updates such as virus scanning products, application plug-ins, media players, etc. These would be number one.

Sites that provide personalized, one-to-one marketing services such as blue-mountain.com, 1800flowers.com, marthastewart.com, ibmnet.com, etc.

Microsoft.com—lots of great stuff here.

AICPA.org and ITA.

From Here . . .

Commerce is exploding—but so are issues relating to security and privacy. These topics are covered in Chapter 8.

Security and Privacy

This chapter helps you better understand security risks dealing with viruses and other system stoppers, learn about privacy issues, know how to protect your firm and clients, understand the major threats on the Net, see accountants' opportunities and responsibilities, find tools and techniques to combat hackers and recover from attack, and uncover resources to find out more. The following outline summarizes the contents of this chapter.

- *Security* This section covers how to offer access to those who need it while dealing with uninvited visitors or abusive users.
- *Privacy* This section describes the problems of the perceived total lack of privacy on the Internet and some important issues for any business.
- *Assurance* Building trust will make e-commerce grow. This section describes trust and assurance issues and other opportunities.

SECURITY

Internet break-ins. Employee revenge. Human error. In today's age of reliance on networked, integrated business systems, companies can suffer heavy losses and disruption of service when America Online goes down or a virus attacks. When small companies embrace the same technologies as larger companies, they face many of the same security risks. Here we compare and contrast small and large business security risks and approaches.

The Internet has hooked together the world. Computer systems that were once insular, facing attack only from within (such as the accidental introduction of a virus by an employee loading games on their PC), are now facing attack from the outside. As more business is transacted over these public pipelines and the population becomes more technology savvy, the security challenges increase.

Security. A word that brings thoughts of comfort, perhaps, but actually a series of trade-offs that protect what you have. Security has a cost, and sometimes the cost can exceed the benefits. Security means vastly different things to a small business than to a large one. Although they face similar challenges, they have different exposure. Their risks and approaches to security can be totally different.

Introduction

Security has become a huge issue, especially as companies have opened the doors to their system using Internet technologies. Intranets and extranets are great for letting people in but not so good at keeping them out. E-commerce is taking off, requiring more open doors. ISO 9000 documentation efforts mean that there is full documentation of every business process on-line, available for industrial espionage. Mobile workers are looking for connections to the office network, and downsizing brings former employees with time on their hands and grudges.

The basic issues in security are covered by the acronym PAAIN: privacy, authentication and authorization, integrity, and nonrepudiation. The following issues must be dealt with:

- *Let the right folks in.* Great security that keeps people from doing their work is not so good. Security has to let the right people do the work they are supposed to do.

- *Keep the wrong ones out.* Good security will do a lot to keep people from accidentally or purposely seeing things they should not see and changing things they should not change.

- *Keep the right folks from doing the wrong things.* Even people who should have access to a system should have their access limited to the tasks they need to do, not for punishment but for their own protection.

- *Ensure timely delivery and receipt.* Make sure information goes where it needs to when it needs to. Information loses its value if it is not sent and received when it needs to be. Business relationships can be strained. A late EDI message, for example, can turn into a six-figure fine when working with a Big 3 automaker.

- *Maintain integrity.* Information should not be changed without authorization. In some cases, loss of integrity may have little effect, as in a letter of invitation to a seminar. In other cases, the effect could be catastrophic, such as in the medical, pharmaceutical, or aerospace world.

- *Promote privacy.* Make sure only those eyes that should see information do to reduce the risk of stolen information and embarrassment.

- *Demand authentication.* Help make sure that people represent themselves as themselves and not as others.

- *Require authorization.* Make sure that people have the power and right to do what they are asking to do.

- *Provide nonrepudiation.* Do not let someone deny that he or she has done something.

Threats

The downside of your security measures being breached can be costly. If data have been altered, you may act on misinformation. If information has been forged, you may expend resources that should not have been expended. Fraudulent actions may occur without notice. Legal problems may ensue if the company is drawn into difficulties. Business interruptions may slow down or stop the business of the firm.

External attacks come from people not affiliated with the organization; internal attacks come from people who have some right to be part of the system.

People from the outside may pretend they are someone on the inside or someone attractive to the organization by masquerading as someone else. People on the inside may disclose information that should not be disclosed. Workers may work at lower efficiency than they should as they surf the Web, post their resumes and scan the job sites, or do day trading or run a business on the side. Their activities may open your firm to legal liability, such as displaying or sharing offensive content in the office.

Either group may alter data, bringing a loss of informational integrity. For any numbers of reasons, these people may try to slow down or stop the information flow, which is called denial of service. Getting something for free (also known as theft and misuse of resources) is also an attractive possibility for many people. Staying ahead of someone who really wants to get in to your system is a difficult task.

Most operating systems have back doors that are well documented on the Internet. Web browsers have flaws that compromise the workstation running them. A visit to a Web site like <http://www.ntbugtraq.com> or <http://www.eeye.com> shows how almost every week a major flaw with Microsoft's Windows NT is published for all to see. Even if you had your hardware and communications lines completely protected, some smooth-talking con artist can trick a new staff person or support staff to give up their login name and password—or impersonate a cleaning person to find that information on some manager's computer monitor, attached with a yellow sticky note. If the price is high enough, those involved in industrial espionage are not beyond bribery, collusion, Dumpster diving, extortion, and other methods of coercion.

Java, Active X, and Cookies. The relatively new programming languages of the Internet, SGI's JAVA and Microsoft's ActiveX, may make Web sites dance, but they also open the door for mischief. Java is more thought out for security but has still been stretched to let people have more access to computers than they should. ActiveX is far less secure, and a rogue ActiveX applet can do anything to your computer.

One of computer users' main fears is that personal information stored on a computer might be taken or changed. In particular, people are afraid someone will affect their cookies. (Cookies are bits of information stored on your computer to make up for some of the limitations of Web browsers compared with traditional programming languages.) If your bank or an on-line store saves your account on credit card number in your cookies and someone takes your cookie file, the thief may have more information about you than you would like.

Documentation of Their Work.   If Microsoft, the CIA, the Justice Department, Wal-Mart, NASA, and the United States Air Force cannot protect themselves, how can we? Clever but misguided people regularly deface important Web sites. While it may bring a smile to your face to find some cracker (someone whose sole aim is to break into secure systems) has changed the Web site dedicated to finding extraterrestrial life (SETI) and replaced the home page with a picture of former television star ALF (Alien Life Form), we would not want people doing that to our sites.

Links to Sites Showcasing Altered Web Pages
http://www.skeeve.net/cia

http://ourworld.compuserve.com/homepages/bgeiger/sies/html#hacked

http://www.2600.com/hacked_pages

Viruses.   Viruses are self-replicating programs (or ones that use the Microsoft Visual Basic or macrolanguage) that grow like weeds. They may have only a small effect, or they can be destructive.

Virus writers are getting cleverer. They now work harder to fool you into falling into their trap than ever. You get e-mail from a friend. A bit brief and cryptic, but since your friend seems to be in a rush, he's sending you an electronic greeting card, or some documents you are expecting, or—well it could be anything. Surprise! The Trojan horse delivers its payload and it's party time!

Melissa was bad enough. The Melissa "virus," once activated, would send itself along to the first 20 entries on your e-mail address book. Melissa's successors hide themselves in even more clever ways. Its most recent child—Worm.ExploreZip—responds back to e-mail, so you have even more reason to believe the e-mail you received and its associated attachments are legitimate.

Have we reached the point where each e-mail must be limited to a simple message with a link to a known Web site? Have you started throwing away attachments from folks you don't really know?

Web Sites to Learn More about Viruses

http://www.drsolomon.com/home/home.cfm

http://www.nai.com/products/antivirus

http://www.symantec.com/nav/index.html

Hoaxes. The lack of a virus can almost be as big a problem as its presence. Most of us have received e-mail warning us that there is a virulent e-mail with the title "Pen Pal Greetings" or "Join the Club". We are encouraged to send an e-mail to everyone we know warning them about this horrible virus—and to tell them to tell everyone they know.

The problem is, these e-mail bombs are *hoaxes*—they do not exist. The only self-replicating portion of these documents is that unsuspecting users blindly obey and messages go on and on, replicated by unwary readers. Likewise, *urban legends* are stories that aren't true that also populate the Internet. A boy wants postcards or e-mails. Walt Disney and Microsoft want to give you a free trip. The post office wants to levy a 5-cent tax on each and every e-mail. In the old days, when a stamp and an envelope cost something, we would think long and hard before passing along a rumor. Now that it is as easy as "forward to everyone in my address book," untruths grow.

Different Approaches to Data Access

A primary difference between small and large businesses is how far ownership is from the data entry function.

Small companies are based on trust. They thrive on informality and flexibility. Instituting procedures, checklists, audit trails, and other security-oriented protections are seen as unnecessary and a troublesome burden, especially when the owner's spouse does the basic data entry.

In a small business environment, separation of duties is a problem, as the person in charge of the security is often a systems administrator or programmer, who may leave under less than optimal circumstances. This leaves the business open to that individual's whim; sometimes the system is unusable simply because no one else knows the administrative passwords. Re-creating a system in the case of problems usually requires finding software that is long lost, reloading tapes that have not been well kept, or starting from scratch. Small companies are seldom motivated to put proper planning into security.

They know they need passwords, but improperly planned passwords limit people from doing their jobs or force sharing of passwords, losing any effectiveness.

Large companies, on the other hand, have multiple lines of communication and management far from the data entry function. A department of people is dedicated to developing and enforcing procedure. Evidence of procedures being followed, audit trails for accountability and closed back doors to data are vital. Where a back door to the database lets a small company make changes quickly and efficiently, it is a huge problem in a large company.

Different Levels of Experience with Computer Security Issues.   In the past, many small businesses all but ignored their internal systems. The checkbook and inventory counts were all that was needed to re-create their business results. Now they must come up to speed on these issues. Larger companies needed strong systems in place for their accounting or ISO 9000 audits, and are accustomed to showing their adherence to proper accounting by showing planning, rules, and adherence to those rules. Recent accounting pronouncements and standards changes have tightened the requirements for internal control and evidence in an electronic age.

Different Resources to Turn To.   Small companies have to rely on the kindness of strangers and their trusted advisors (CPA firms, hardware, and network support) for guidance. Large companies have internal staff trained in security issues and can look to organizations like Information Systems Audit and Control Association or the Institute of Internal Auditors (http://www.theiia.org) for guidance on the Web (http://www.isaca.org).

Points to Ponder
- Where does your business fit on the spectrum?
- What will happen to your business if you can't go on-line, your e-mail stops, your server crashes, or your system administrator leaves?
- Where are your areas of potential loss, and what is the cost of security compared with the potential loss?
- Are your business systems flexible and open, or highly closed off and controlled? Can people get the information they need to do their work and respond in a timely way to information requests, or does the need to ensure privacy and security outweigh the benefits of easy access to the data?
- Do you have adequate backup? A disaster recovery plan? Do you have written procedures and policies? Have you considered the legal dangers of your firm's name being involved with postings to the Internet?

- Do you promote the proper use of passwords? Scan all incoming disks for viruses? Ensure you have the proper number of licenses for software?
- How quickly can you replicate your present systems in case of disaster?
- Are you sure?

Fraud on the Internet

The Dark Underbelly of the Internet.   There is a dark side to the Internet. eFraud is on the rise. According to Internet Fraud Watch (http://www. fraud.oralifw.htm), the consumer watchdog agency, complaints about fraud on-line jumped sixfold in the United States between 1997 and 1998.

On-line auctions lead the list of complaint topics being heard by Washington, DC-based, nonprofit National Consumers League (NCL; http://www. natlconsumersleague.org), which operates Internet Fraud Watch. Almost 70 percent of the complaints fielded by the group in 1998 involved auctions, up from 26 percent the year before. General merchandise sales, computer products, Internet services, work-at-home business opportunities and franchises, multilevel marketing and pyramid schemes, credit card offers, advance-fee loans, and employment offers round out the fraud top 10.

The majority of fraudulent payments—a whopping 93 percent—were made "off-line" by check or money order sent to the company. The NCL advises strongly that if you buy something over the Net, don't pay by cash; use a credit card so you can dispute the charges if there is a problem.

Often this is not possible on popular sites like eBay, where many on-line auction sales are made by individuals who are not equipped to take credit card payments. IFW recommends that buyers use escrow services, which take payment from buyers and pass the money along to the sellers only after verification that the goods or services were satisfactory. There is an additional charge for escrow services, so until burned once, most buyers probably will take a chance.

The National Consumers League, founded in 1899, is America's pioneer consumer organization. Its three-pronged approach of research, education, and advocacy has made it an effective representative and source of information for consumers and workers. NCL is a private, membership organization dedicated to representing consumers on issues of concern. Internet Fraud Watch (http://www.fraud.org) should be a regular stop for anyone involved in e-business.

Bad People.   Someone always seems to want to spoil it for the rest of us. Some people realize the chances of being caught for electronic harassment and theft are smaller, the potential reward is far greater, and the chance of being hurt or killed is drastically reduced, compared with doing things the "old-fashioned way." Others are drawn in by the community on the Internet where they meet seemingly normal human beings with jobs, family, a great deal of smarts, curiosity, and possibly an agenda to pursue.

Someone with a grudge can send mail bombs to make your individual mail service suffer. Crackers (sometimes called hackers, although traditional hackers were just early computer superenthusiasts) delight in breaking into high-profile Web sites like the CIA, Air Force, and Justice Department, and replacing their contents with lunacy and drivel.

It is relatively simple to cause havoc. Reports circulate regularly about ways to bring down computers attached to the Internet with 10 mouse-clicks. Sometimes hacker sites advertise their pages as instructional resources to learn how to protect your own systems, but, hey, let's get real. It is a blast to see how easily you can bring down a major organization's computer by typing a simple phrase into your Web browser. How did we get so far out on the ledge, and what can we do to protect our businesses from computer attack?

The average person is at risk and is not trained in how to deal with the war at hand. Most users are defenseless, driving down the highway at 65 mph with a doughnut in one hand and a newspaper in the other. When nothing goes wrong, all is well. But hit a pothole, and you lose control. To make matters worse, many of the highest-profile security risks are not risks at all but merely hoaxes. Our offices get warnings about "Pen Pal Greetings" or "Join the Club" from many well-meaning readers. But these are not real threats, just clever hoaxes that cause novices to send misleading e-mails to everyone they know. Most users do not have a firm grasp of what is a problem but think they know otherwise.

This is bound to change. Internet Service Providers will learn how to adapt to one attack and soon face another. Soon we will set up the rules of the electronic superhighway just as we set up conventional warnings. Instead of "Don't talk to strangers," we will say "Don't give out your password or credit card number to strangers." Instead of "Exercise defensive driving," we will say "Exercise defensive surfing."

What will Internet-age parents teach their young disciples to protect them from hazards? Here's a few hints:

- Scan everything you download from the Internet with a virus scanner before you use it.
- Help your employees to not make innocent mistakes.
- Guard your systems from the less-than-innocent.

- Don't reply positively to spam. You only encourage it.

- Take nothing at face value—just because it looks like Microsoft, don't assume it is Microsoft.

- If it sounds too good to be true, it probably is.

- Don't put all your eggs in one basket; have an alternative if/when your Web or mail server lets you down.

Access: Necessary for Growth, But . . .

Imagine computer terminals everywhere. Some are sitting in a dark side street downtown. Some are in swanky stores, financial institutions, and corporate offices. Some are in children's playrooms, and others are run by organized crime. You hope to use this system to buy and sell things. The opportunity to get your message out is very high. But the possibility that people will attempt to abuse the system is also very high.

The Internet enables a business the opportunity to automate and personalize its relationships with its customers. As more businesses are automated, the browsing and buying patterns of customers can be better monitored. Tools to better integrate current software with the Internet are promised, with Microsoft announcing a systems developers' kit (SDK) to Internet-enable Microsoft's products. The bad news is that the opportunity for automated theft increases as well.

There is no way to make access to the Internet available only to fully bonded, high-credit-rating individuals. In the past, the high entry cost of a computer and modem may have deterred some people from getting involved in the Internet. The industry is now looking at $300 computers with free, full Web access. In the past, using the Internet was considered obscure, but recent software makes it much easier to use. In the past, getting connected to the Internet was limited to expensive agreements with companies in major cities; now ISPs let people connect to the Internet for as little as $15 a month for unlimited use, at least in the United States. Access is becoming easier in Canada as well. However, Mexico and most other countries do not have the same penetration into the home.

How often have you picked up your telephone and found the call not valuable? Children and adults playing pranks, multiple calls placed for annoyance or harassment, wrong numbers from people not paying attention when they dial, automated sales calls—a large number of calls occur with no value to the recipient. With greater access to the Internet, these same things will happen to a business site set up on the Web. Where a phone call from "Mr. Fox from the Zoo" is an annoyance, 100 or 1,000 orders entered programmatically into your automated order entry system in the same time frame can be crippling.

With inexpensive, unlimited access, security becomes more of a problem than ever. Access brings up three distinct areas where problems can occur in a business transaction: problems relating to the buyer, to the information in transfer, and to the vendor. Additional access results in the temporary slowing down of communications on the Internet as well.

Problems Relating to a Buyer

Authentication. One of the first issues in security is that people can misrepresent themselves over the Internet. Mail messages can easily be sent with other people's e-mail addresses as identifiers or through anonymous servers that hide the original sender's identity. How does the merchant know the buyer is authentic?

Without computers, authentication is done by calling the buyer's phone number and faxing or mailing a follow-up to make sure that the information given was correct. These verification methods can continue with electronic commerce, but the costs of the sale must warrant the expense.

With computers, security begins with the login name and password. Most computer systems assign rights based on a name and password combination. Years of attempts to get users to choose passwords that can not be easily chosen, to change their password regularly, and to not give the password to others have proven this is not a secure method of identification. Call-back systems have the host computer call the user back at a predefined phone number. This has limited usefulness in general commerce.

Certification. Some companies are setting out to assign license plates for the information superhighway. These certification authorities are proposing a number of means of identifying and certifying a person's identity.

PGP is a grass-roots group has attempted to begin certification with a technology known as PGP (Pretty Good Privacy). Senders encrypt their messages so that they are unreadable without a translation table provided by the use of public and private keys. PGP's proponents hope to encourage everyone to begin to use the system. Acceptance of PGP is limited: Using PGP requires many additional steps necessary, and many people believe that only criminals need to use encryption for everyday use, so using PGP is only hiding illegal activity.

Hardware Solutions. In addition to what you know (passwords) and software solutions, hardware devices are coming into favor as security devices.

The SecurID card, from Security Dynamics Technologies, Inc., of Cambridge, Massachusetts (800-SECURID), is a credit card–size device used for personal identification. SecurID uses a random number generator to create a unique access code every minute. A host computer maintains a catalog that lists the user, the device serial number, and the "seed" used to create the random number. When users log on to a system, they must provide all three pieces of information: login name, password, and the number appearing on the secure ID card at that moment. The host can then prove that it is the unit assigned to that particular user and can approve or deny entry.

Nonrepudiation. In traditional commerce, a contract is sealed with a signature, which proves that the contract was agreed to. In electronic commerce, there is also a need to prove that the transaction took place with the buyer's agreement. This is called nonrepudiability.

Until recently electronic signatures were worthless. A faxed signed contract was not binding in court. However, recently electronic signatures have become more binding in certain circumstances. An effect to develop a uniform standard is in process to deal with differences between each state's laws.

Problems Relating to Information in Transfer

Working over a public network offers price advantages and accessibility. However, problems exist much like doing business on the phone. On the phone, especially on cellular phones, there is a fear of being overheard. Phone connections can be filled with static, making the message difficult to understand. At peak times, you may not be able to get a call through because "all circuits are busy." Most businesses have received faxes meant for other organizations accidentally, sometimes to great embarrassment. Of all these problems, the one receiving the most attention is confidentiality.

Confidentiality. Few people conduct their business affairs in public places. Competitors and others can misuse the information. The pricing given to one customer may be different from that given to another. There are many reasons that privacy must be maintained. How can two business entities communicate without eavesdropping or the alteration of their message?

In the past, much electronic commerce was conducted over a third-party service that guaranteed privacy or through direct computer-to-computer connections. In these cases, someone would have to tap into private communications networks to get the information they needed.

On the Internet, information travels from computer to computer. Anyone who breaks into a computer that your message passed through on the way to the proper location can read your message. Others may see what they are sending over the Internet. For this reason, making the message unreadable at these sites, using encryption methods, becomes important.

Problems Relating to the Vendor

Merchants face two problems in establishing themselves on the Web. First, they must get people to trust them to buy from them. Second, they need to protect their internal systems from outside attacks.

Merchant Trust.   On the Internet, people from around the world can set up business. In traditional advertising, a large advertisement in the Yellow Pages conveys stability, even if it misrepresents a dishonest company. That company must be able to pay for the large advertisement. On the Internet, a formidable presence is inexpensive, and the trade laws of one country may not apply to a business site from another country. How does the buyer know the merchant is authentic?

The rule of "buyer beware" does not stop because a company is on the Internet. Doing business with well-established companies is still important. The same certification process that works to identify the buyer also identifies that sellers are who they say they are. In addition, as electronic malls spring up, some have begun to offer a guarantee that their participating merchants are trustworthy.

Protection from Attack.   How do merchants protect their systems from attack? Along with standard tools to identify and authorize system users, companies are putting in place firewalls, hardware and software that shields the internal network from the Internet to protect their internal systems from outside attack.

Firewalls.   A firewall is used to shield the business's network from the Internet. All incoming Internet traffic is actually addressed to the firewall, which is designed to allow only e-mail into the business network environment. Traffic through the firewall is subjected to a special proxy process that verifies the source and destination of each information packet. The proxy then changes the packet's IP address to deliver it to the appropriate site within the network. In this way, all inside addresses are protected from outside access, and the structure of the business's internal network is invisible to outside observers.

How Do You Deal with Security Threats?

Know Your Hackers and Employees.   There are numerous tools to monitor employees' work on the computer as well as to identify unauthorized access and act on it. A listing of hacker sites is included at the end of this chapter if you wish to see what they know and what they do.

Evaluation.   Determine your weaknesses and evaluate the risks.

Take an inventory of your equipment, communications lines, and protection.

Evaluate the risks of various kinds of attacks and the costs of preparing for those attacks.

Determine the cost/value of data. What is lost if confidential information is made available to the public, if nonreproducible information should disappear, or if data are changed without your knowledge?

Preparation.   Prepare for the attack.

Help educate and prepare your people. Limit the information they can access to protect them and ensure others do not masquerade as them to gain access or throw investigations off track.

Prepare your computers by limiting access.

Prepare your organization through education and policies.

Consider testing your preparation by hiring outside experts, sometimes known as Tiger Teams, to try to infiltrate your system.

Access Control.   Access controls help keep out those who should not have access. Access is given based on what you know, what you have, and who you are.

Passwords are what you know, and should be kept secret.

Hardware/software tools that work with computers, such as tokens or smart cards, are what you have that others don't.

Finally, biometrics is who you are; systems that can scan and analyze your eyes, face, voice, fingerprints and palm prints, and other body measurements are projected to replace passwords in the not too distant future.

Disaster Recovery and Control.   Be ready for the worst. Make sure you have backup of your data, your software, your equipment, and even your facilities.

Have a plan for how to deal with an incident when it occurs. Some Web sites that can help you in this process:

ASSIT (DoD): www.assist.mil

CERT: www.cert.org

CIAC: ciac.llml.gov

FedCIRC: fedcirc.llnl.gov

FIRST: www.first.org

NASIR: www-nasirc.nasa.gov

PRIVACY

Problem with Privacy: You Have None

All people who use the Internet need to be made constantly aware that anything they reveal about themselves, their family, or their business can be used against them for legal, marketing, or perhaps more malicious purposes. Some of that disclosure we bring upon ourselves. Some of it comes from new databases being set up on the Internet.

There is a saying: Big Brother no longer works for the government. He works for direct marketing.

Of course, even off the Internet, personal data are available from many sources with nothing more than a Social Security number, mother's maiden name, date, or place of birth, all collected by various direct marketing concerns in the process of giving you a free subscription to a controlled publication journal or magazine. However, nationwide databases bring a new ease to finding out almost anything you want to know about someone.

Every time you go to Usenet newsgroups and make a posting, you reveal something about yourself. Using a tool like Deja (http://www.deja.com), it is easy to find and review all the postings one person makes. If you are in the personnel department, you could potentially find resumes your present staff is posting, or learn about some unusual hobbies prospective employees might have. What information about your employees is listed on your Web site? If you knew that it was being examined for malicious purposes, would you change what is there? Many people have their listings in the phone book obscured, but their life is completely exposed on their Web profile for their firm's Web site.

Sometimes the disclosure is forced upon us. In December 1998, the Virginia State Police Department set up a Web site listing the names and addresses of convicted sex crimes offenders. They expected 5,000 visits; however, the *Washington Post* reported that in its first 12 hours alone, the site was visited 45,000 times. The Virginia State Police Department joins the ranks of many other governmental agencies in making available information that privacy advocates would want left private. Other agencies make available personal data such as motor vehicle and real estate records. Colleges routinely publish the Social Security numbers of their students, and Securities and Exchange Commission filings with similar information about corporate officers are also easily and freely made available.

Your Life on the Net

What can I find out about you on the Internet? I can go to any number of people searchers and get your address and phone number. Start off at the caller-id stage, and I can crisscross to this information. I can print a map and directions to your home, the names of your immediate neighbors, and nearby businesses. Depending on where you live, motor vehicle records, real estate records, and other public records may let me in on more information about you and your family.

Do you or your firm have a Web site? Even if your phone listing is limited to your first initial and no address, your personal page or your staff listing at your company's site may give away far too much information, from the name of family members to hobbies and background. Stolen identities are not a rare occurrence. One CPA I met indicated that the cleaning crew for his firm was accessing the firm's tax software to get clients' Social Security numbers, bank accounts, and other private information. Then they applied for credit cards. What will your family, business associates, governmental representatives, bank, phone and other personnel be willing to reveal on the phone to someone who can provide all the right information about you?

Can I get access to your computer? I can see where you have visited by looking at your History list. I also can see what you looked at by examining the contents of your Web browser's *cache,* which stores almost every piece of text and every graphic that you have viewed from the Internet. Some flaws with Web browsers have even made it easy to review information normally protected by a password—if it was stored in your History and cache.

Problem with Privacy: They Really Care in Europe

The European Commission set in place in October 1998 new rules about doing business with the European Union (EU). If proper privacy measures were not in place, e-commerce would have to cease. Since that time, European Commission and U.S. government officials have been edging toward an agreement on data privacy. With a goal of being ready by the end of 1999, talks have been continuing to help the EU recognize U.S. data privacy policy as respecting EU standards. If an agreement is not reached, transatlantic data flows could be blocked.

In 1993, a five-year plan was developed, stating that an EU directive on data privacy would take effect five years later. It took effect on October 25,

1998. The directive introduces high standards of data privacy to ensure the free flow of data throughout the 15 EU member states and gives individuals the right to review the personal data, correct it, and limit its use.

The transatlantic tension stems form the directive's provisions that require member states to block transmission of data to third countries, such as the United States, if their domestic legislation does not provide an adequate level of protection, as interpreted by experts from member states and the European Commission in a so-called Article 31 committee set up by the directive.

The good news is that only a few member states have implemented the directive (Belgium, Greece, Italy, Portugal, Sweden, the United Kingdom, and Finland), which has helped to defuse transatlantic friction. The European Commission is not blocking data flows to the United States because the government is working on rules that would allow U.S. companies to provide "adequate" privacy for EU citizens.

We are not alone. The EU is holding similar talks with all its major trading partners, including Switzerland, Japan, Australia, and New Zealand, but no agreements have yet been reached.

The U.S. government released a draft set of guidelines on April 19, 1999 posted at <http://www.ita.doc.gov/ecom>, that are designed to serve as a "safe harbor" for U.S. companies wanting to receive information about EU citizens.

However, not everyone is excited about the negotiation between the United States and the European Union. An international coalition of more than 60 consumer groups, meeting in Brussels, vowed to oppose the data privacy compromise now being debated by the United States and the European Union. The TransAtlantic Consumer Dialogue coalition, which includes such organizations as the Consumer Federation of America and the U.S. Consumers' Union, said that the U.S. Commerce Department's recent "safe harbor" proposal doesn't go far enough to protect Internet users' data privacy. They urged the United States and the EU to work together on an international convention on privacy to safeguard consumer privacy and bolster e-commerce.

Problem with Privacy: No One Cares?

With the growth of on-line investing comes the growth of on-line problems. SEC chairman Arthur Levitt said complaints regarding on-line investing had increased 330 percent between 1998 and 1999. Easy, cheap trading does not always lead to wise trading. According to Levitt, "I believe that investors need to remember the investment basics, and not allow the ease and speed with which they can trade to lull them either into a false sense of security or encourage them to trade too quickly or too often."

While many on-line investors show common sense, many don't. This was proved when more than 200 people committed to $10,000 to $50,000 investment packages promising a threefold return on their money—with no prospectus or proof that the company existed. Fortunately for them, it was an April Fool's hoax by the Australian Securities and Investments Commission (ASIC), which has been running a massive Internet investment hoax site, and would have netted $4 million.

Roughly 25 percent of the duped investors hailed from outside Australia, including the United States.

Offer Me a Free PC and I'll Follow You Anywhere: The motivation was the free use of a Compaq computer for two years. The offer was limited to the top 10,000 prospects willing to give away detailed demographic information about themselves and to endure advertising on the computer that displayed whether on the Internet or not. With eBay already showing that people are willing to do business with others by personal check, sight unseen, the Free-PC program showed that hundreds of thousands of people are willing to give up their privacy for the chance to use a computer.

More than 1 million people applied to try to get the computers being offered by entrepreneur Bill Gross's Free-PC.com. Free-PC.com expects to sift the applicants' demographic responses for as long as 90 days before deciding who will participate in its test to determine whether targeted advertising can pay off. It seems that when the carrot is large enough, the masses are willing to do almost anything. The Web site that will sell dollar bills for 95 cents in return for personal data must be on its way. Promise me frequent flyer miles or a 10-cent call for free, and I will give up my privacy, if it is easy to do so. The U.S. government has indicated that it will have to intervene if businesses that collect personal data do not illustrate their privacy policies. (See Exhibit 8.1.)

Solutions

Policies.   An important tool in the privacy area is to have corporate policies in place that spell out what is private information and what is public. Can you, the employer, get into trouble reading your employee's e-mail?

What's the problem?   Fact: Most companies treat personal computers more like toys than tools, which teaches their employees to do the same. Fact: Viruses are running rampant and now can span operating systems. Analysts believe most viruses are brought in on disks from home. Fact: Having your company's name on your employee's correspondence to the alt.home.bomb-making Internet newsgroup may not enhance your reputation in the commu-

Exhibit 8.1 Small Business Administration promotes privacy policies.

nity. Opinion: Every company needs to put a plan and a policy in place to deal with the problems these facts can lead to: misuse, mismanagement, system failure, and legal liability.

Internet use in business has grown very quickly. The number of companies with their own domain name and presence on the Internet has tripled since January 1996. As companies come on board, they find it valuable to offer Internet access to their employees, a powerful tool—in the right hands. However, any tool, improperly used, can damage the user or the surroundings, with dire results. Training and guidance in a tool's proper use are vital.

Benefits of an Appropriate Use Policy for Your Employees. One of the most obvious ways to offer guidance is through an official corporate Internet-use policy. A policy has at least three major purposes: (1) promoting the efficient use of a business asset and powerful tool; (2) protecting the firm from problems directly associated with the Internet; and (3) protecting the firm from problems indirectly caused by the Internet. The following information does not constitute legal truth but rather common sense; on business property, on business time, on business equipment and connections, the Internet is not a toy but a tool and its use, an extension of firm business.

To many, the Internet is fun. You can find out almost anything you want to know about anything. However, the goal of Internet use in most business environments should not be to explore the Net's far reaches but to maximize employee efficiency. That means that certain ground rules must be set to maximize the potential.

Protecting your firm from the direct affects of the Internet requires diligence. The Internet is a teacher of two great and wonderful things: patience and disappointment. With that comes the potential for data loss or damage, loss of efficiency, and viruses.

The unforeseen problems that must be dealt with are the possible repercussions of your employees being seen as acting on your behalf and the potential legal liability that brings. A corporate Internet policy that is enforced and modeled is proof that actions taken by those not following the clearly stated and well-promulgated policy were not made on the company's behalf.

Elements of an Employee Policy. What follows are some of the basic elements you should consider in developing your policy. While this list is incomplete, make sure to consider all of these elements. In sum, an Internet policy should be consistent with agreements, with law and Internet culture, and with the Golden Rule.

Consistent with Agreements. Few organizations plug into the Internet without the services of an intermediary. Your organization's agreement with that intermediary may include limitations and restrictions on your use. (A ban on conducting commercial business may be one of those limitations.) Your policy should contain provisions to make sure use is consistent with permitted use per your agreement with your access provider. Make sure that you know and publish the limits so your staff can abide by them.

Consistent with Law and Internet Culture. While it may seem ridiculous to have to state formally that your employees should not break the law, the Internet is a place of anarchy and freedom. Anything you may want is available there, including copyrighted and illegal materials. On the Internet, your employees are members of multiple societies, both legal and electronic, with laws and customs.

Your policy should guide your employees away from breaking the law; your firm should make some effort to keep your staff informed as to changing rules about copyright, freedom of speech, and other evolving issues on the Internet. The Net's global nature makes more than just U.S. trade and copyright laws important; the customs, laws, and rules of other nations can come into play.

In addition, the Internet has established its own set of rules, punishable by flaming and retribution. The current court rulings about America Online's efforts to stop junk e-mail point out the struggles of clashing culture and commercialism. Your policy should discuss rules of Internet etiquette (netiquette), anonymity, illegal misrepresentation, and flames.

Consistent with the Golden Rule. We are members of humanity. On the Internet as in real life, be a good citizen and a good visitor. Leave things cleaner and better when you leave than when you arrived. The Golden Rule comes into play on the Internet: Treat others in the manner you would like to be treated.

Example

General Principles. Internet services are provided by the firm to support open communications and exchange of information and the opportunity for collaborative work. The firm encourages the use of electronic communications by its employees. Although access to information and information technology is essential to the missions of our firm and its users, use of Internet services is a revocable privilege. Conformance with acceptable use, as expressed in this policy statement, is required. All employees are expected to maintain and enforce this policy.

At a minimum, users of Internet services provided by the firm are expected to:

- Make a reasonable effort to inform your employees of this acceptable use policy and acceptable and unacceptable uses on the Internet in general. The burden of responsibility is on the user to inquire as to acceptable and unacceptable uses prior to use. Compliance with applicable acceptable use restrictions is mandatory.
- Use firm-provided Internet services for firm-related activities and not for personal business.
- Respect the privacy of others.
- Respect the legal protection provided by copyright and license to programs and data.
- Respect the privileges of other users.

- Respect the integrity of computing systems connected to the Internet.
- Know and follow the generally accepted etiquette of the Internet. For example, use civil forms of communication and avoid being drawn into "flame wars."
- Avoid uses of the network that reflect poorly on the firm.
- Users should remember that existing and evolving rules, regulations, and guidelines on ethical behavior of CPAs and the appropriate use of firm resources apply to the use of electronic communications systems supplied by firm.

Specifically Acceptable Uses
- Communication and information exchange directly related to the mission, charter, or work tasks of the firm.
- Communication and exchange for professional development, to maintain currency of training or education, or to discuss issues related to the user's firm activities.
- Use in researching issues for clients.
- Use for advisory, standards, research, analysis, and professional society activities related to the user's firm work tasks and duties.
- Announcement of new state laws, procedures, policies, rules, services, programs, information, or activities.
- Any other governmental administrative communications not requiring a high level of security.
- Communications incidental to otherwise acceptable use, except for illegal or specifically unacceptable uses.

Specifically Unacceptable Uses
- Use of the Internet for any purposes that violate a U.S. or State of New York law.
- Use for any for-profit activities unless specific to the charter, mission, or duties of the firm.
- Use for purposes not directly related to the mission, charter, or work tasks of the firm during normal business hours.
- Use for private business, including commercial advertising.
- Use for access to and distribution of indecent or obscene material.
- Use for access to and distribution of computer games that have no bearing on the firm's mission. Some games that help teach, illustrate, training, or simulate firm-related issues may be acceptable.

- Use of firm-provided Internet services so as to interfere with or disrupt network users, services, or equipment.

- Intentionally seeking out information on, obtaining copies of, or modifying files and other data that is private, confidential, or not open to public inspection or release. No intentional copy is to be made of any software, electronic file, program or data using firm-provided Internet services without a prior, good faith determination that such copying is, in fact, permissible. Any efforts to obtain permission should be adequately documented.

- Intentionally seeking information on, obtaining copies of, or modifying files or data belonging to others without authorization of the file owner. Seeking passwords of others or the exchanging of passwords is specifically prohibited.

- Users intentionally representing themselves electronically as others, either on the firm's Internet or elsewhere on the Internet, unless explicitly authorized to do so by those other users. Users shall not circumvent established policies defining eligibility for access to information or systems.

- Intentionally developing programs designed to harass other users or infiltrate a computer or computing system and/or damage or alter the software components of same.

- Use for fund-raising or public relations activities not specifically related to firm activities.

Additional Guidelines

Computer Viruses on Downloaded Software: Any software obtained from outside the firm should be virus checked prior to use.

Passwords: Use passwords associated with a firm information system only on that system. When setting up an account at a different information system that will be accessed using the Internet, choose a password that is different from ones used on the firm information systems. Do not use the same password for both local and remote Internet-accessed systems. If the password used at the remote Internet-accessed site were to be compromised, the different password used locally would still be secure. Passwords should not be so obvious so that others could easily guess them, and passwords should be changed at least every 60 days.

- *E-mail:* E-mail is owned by the firm and can be reviewed or viewed by management without permission of the sender or receiver.

- *Logoff (Exiting):* Always make a reasonable attempt to complete the logoff or other termination procedure when finished using a remote Internet-accessed system or resource. This will help prevent potential breaches of security.

- *E-Mail Security:* Unencrypted electronic mail sent or received outside any department and on the Internet cannot be expected to be secure.

Large File Transfers and Internet Capacity: While routine electronic mail and file transfer activities won't impact other users much, large file transfers and intensive multimedia activities will impact the service levels of other users. Users contemplating file transfers over 10 megabytes per transfer or interactive video activities should, to be considerate of other users, schedule these activities early or late in the day or, better, after business hours.

Disclaimers. Users should avoid being drawn into discussions where disclaimers such as "This represents my personal opinion and not that of my firm" need to be used. When using Internet services provided by the firm, users need to remember that they are representing the firm.

Organizations

Who is looking out for your security and privacy? Lots of people with varied motivations. The following are some good resources. Many more are listed at the end of this chapter.

Internet Scambusters. Internet ScamBusters is a monthly (or so) publication that highlights the latest scams and problems on the Internet. To subscribe to Internet ScamBusters, send an e-mail to: scambusters@scambusters.org and write "subscribe" in the subject field.

EPIC. The EPIC Alert is a free biweekly publication of the Electronic Privacy Information Center. A Web-based form is available for subscribing or unsubscribing at <http://www.epic.org/alert/subscribe.html>. To subscribe using e-mail, send email to <epic-news@epic.org> and write "subscribe" in the subject field.

Back issues are available at <http://www.epic.org/alert>.

The Electronic Privacy Information Center (EPIC) is a public interest research center in Washington, D.C. It was established in 1994 to focus public attention on emerging privacy issues such as the Clipper Chip, the Digital Telephony proposal, national ID cards, medical record privacy, and the collection and sale of personal information. EPIC is sponsored by the Fund for Constitutional Government, a nonprofit organization established in 1974 to protect civil liberties and constitutional rights. EPIC also pursues Freedom of Information Act litigation and conducts policy research. For more information, e-mail: info@epic.org <http://www.epic.org> or write EPIC, 666 Pennsylvania Avenue, SE, Suite 301, Washington, DC 20003. (202) 544-9240 (tel), (202) 547-5482 (fax).

See also <http://www.fraud.org>.

Software

Software tools can help protect your privacy. In particular, you can protect your family and staff through safe browsers, search engines, safe places to surf using Internet Service Providers like Mayberry USA (http://www.mbusa.net, not to be confused with www.mbusa.com, the Mercedes Home Page) and using site-limiting tools. Internet Explorer has had a Content Advisor from version 3 on that can help limit information in. Other monitoring software that limits information from being given or improper graphics and files from being received include software products SitePatrol, CyberCop, NetNanny, and SurfWatch.

ASSURANCE

Assurance and the AICPA's Response: WebTrust

Privacy is a key factor in the growth of Internet commerce—and the general perception is that there is little privacy on the Internet. Too bad. Electronic commerce holds the promise of shopping without walls, competitive pricing, and the ultimate in convenience for Web users. Comparison buying is easy and impulse purchases can be made when the impulse strikes.

Internet stores, however, may be the lair of bandits—nameless, faceless hooligans hidden by the Web's immensity and lack of regulation. Anyone can open a store instantly for $10, bilk millions of consumers, and then disappear without a trace. How can the buyer beware? There are a number of assurance certification programs, including the accounting profession's Web Trust. We go beyond the "logo" to discuss the meaning of assurance certification programs and the problems that logos actually hide rather than disclose.

Ready, SET . . . Wait?   Most people fear giving out their credit card information over the Internet. However, there are few actual accounts of credit cards being misused on the Internet, and none when sent over secure connections.

Visa and MasterCard began an effort to provide assurance for credit card users who shop on the Internet. The resulting product, the *Secure Electronic Transaction* (SET) protocol, is safer than handing one to your local restaurant or gas station, but has been slow to catch on.

In like manner, many organizations have attempted to increase the comfort level of potential Web shoppers. The efforts vary widely in scope and often offer false assurance.

International Internet Sweep Day, an October 1997 review of Web sites by the Federal Trade Commission (FTC), the Australian Competition and Consumer Commission (ACCC), and 60 other organizations worldwide, found hundreds of sites selling merchandise that doesn't exist, promoting loan scams, offering pyramids schemes—all sites that scream for regulation. In addition, the FTC has been busy reviewing sites that collect visitor information to see how those sites handle privacy issues, especially as it pertains to children.

"The Internet's development as a commercial medium is transforming the global marketplace—carrying with it the potential to provide enormous benefits to consumers," said Jodie Bernstein, director of the FTC's Bureau of Consumer Protection. "In order to ensure its potential, however, consumers need to know the extent to which consumer protections that apply in the off-line world also apply to the Internet. The Commission's experience has been that formal policy guidance generally results in voluntary compliance by industry."

The U.S. government's call is for industry to self-regulate—or the government will take over. Those with an interest in limiting government involvement in regulating the on-line industry must act quickly to encourage groups skilled in auditing and technology to develop programs of self-regulation, critically analyze them, and promote them heavily.

There are a number of efforts to offer buyers of goods and services on the Internet confidence in the trustworthiness of the e-store—often at a much higher level than when purchasing at a traditional store. It is now the responsibility of the press to educate consumers on what each certification and logo really means, and how to know if that logo is real.

What Do You Want in Assurance?   What knowledge would make you confident before buying from an e-store? Some basics:

- Does the store really exist, and is it who it says it is?
- Are the products fairly represented?
- Will I be billed correctly? When will I receive the goods? Will I receive what I ordered?
- What if I need to return my purchase or there is a problem with the goods? How will conflicts be handled in cyberspace?
- Will the store or someone else improperly use the information I send during our business dealings, like my credit card number?

How can you gain this knowledge? Perhaps by vendors disclosing their site policies. How can you trust their disclosures? By knowing that a disinterested but reliable third party has attested to those facts, testing them and stating that they are true to the best of their knowledge. (Of course, as with traditional stores, trust also comes from referrals, word of mouth, and sense of community.)

Enter the Reliable Third Party: A number of organizations have represented themselves as reliable and disinterested third parties with programs merchants can subscribe to. Once merchants have subscribed and met some of the reliable third party's requirements, the merchant can display a logo from that organization on his or her Web pages. This leads to two major questions when you see a logo at a merchant site.

1. *Is the logo real?*

As most users of the Web know, it is simple to copy a graphic logo—or the entire contents—of a Web site and reuse it elsewhere. The appearance of a logo on a page does not prove that the merchant site has won the right to use that logo. The problem is real; the Web pages of the certification organizations indicate that some Web sites are indeed falsely using the logos.

Before placing your trust in a logo from any organization, you must learn how to determine if it is authentic. Unfortunately, this often involves examining the results of digital certificates and the status of secure connections, and requires other judgments beyond the scope of the average consumer. For now, verifying a logo is a multistep process. Click here, look there, check out the digital certificate—who wants to do all that? As the assurance standard(s) emerge, Web browsers probably will be designed to do the verification automatically and transparently to the end user.

2. *If the logo is real, what does it mean?*

A very real logo can offer very little assurance. The first organizations out of the block with certification programs are the Better Business Bureau (BBBOnline), International Computer Security Agency (TruSecure), TRUSTe (supported heavily by CommerceNet), and the American Institute of Certified Public Accountants/Canadian Institute of Chartered Accountants (WebTrust). A brief, if not subjective, review of these programs follows.

BBBOnline (http://www.bbbonline.com)

Facts: The certification shows that the organization exists, is a member of the Better Business Bureau, will agree to BBB standards, and has paid a fee. These sites must have satisfactory complaint handling records. Eastman Kodak Company is a founding sponsor.

Commentary: Privacy issues, security issues, most business policy issues, and independent verification are not really part of this program. My one personal experience dealing with a complaint with a traditional

BBB member, in person, was wholly unsatisfactory. You determine how that will translate in cyberspace.

TruSecure (http://www.icsa.org)

Facts: TruSecure offers security professionals the assurance that their security procedures and policies address the latest cyber attacks.

Commentary: This does not provide the primary assurance potential buyers need.

TRUSTe (http://www.truste.org)

Facts: TRUSTe subscribers must document their privacy policies, which TRUSTe periodically tests.

Commentary: Documentation does not mean quality, and the TRUSTe logo may give that impression. TRUSTe is like ISO 9000 certification: You document what you do, and do what you document. Neither guarantees quality or privacy. Read the written policy! It may state that they will take your credit card number and engrave it on pens to be given out at the next Democratic Convention.

WebTrust (http://www.webtrust.org)

Facts: WebTrust assurance includes three major areas:

1. Business Practices Disclosures: The entity discloses how it does business with its electronic commerce customers.

2. Transaction Integrity. The entity (Web site operator) maintains effective controls and practices to provide reasonable assurance that customer orders placed using electronic commerce are completed and billed as agreed.

3. Information Protection: The entity maintains effective controls and practices to provide reasonable assurance that private customer information obtained as a result of electronic commerce is protected from uses not related to the entity's business.

Commentary: Start with a group (CPAs and CAs) whose very profession came into being because of the market's desire for a group of people with integrity, objectivity, and independence to report on the representations of companies. CPAs have a long history as experts in business auditing. Add a program that encompasses privacy, business practices, and data integrity and answers most of the questions posed above. Charge the merchant a lot of money. See if the program can gain the acceptance in the marketplace it deserves.

Of all the current programs, only one really begins to answer the questions a buyer is really interested in: WebTrust. It is not perfect, and the rules of the game will change wildly over the years upcoming because the game itself is changing daily. WebTrust is not the end-all, but it does seem to be the most comprehensive starting point. In fact, WebTrust gives you more knowledge and a greater assurance about the company you are dealing with than buying at a traditional store.

Other better known certification organizations are trying to make a buck in this arena but offer little assurance. Make sure you know what a Web certification logo represents and that the logo is authentic before trusting it.

Assurance Seals—Marketing Success?   At the time of this writing, there were approximately 3,000 BBBOnline sites and 23 BBBOnline Privacy sites, 675 TRUSTe sites, and approximately 20 WebTrust sites.

Some of the WebTrust sites include:

Altus Mortgage Corporation
Altus Mortgage (http://www.altusmortgage.com) offers low-interest home mortgage loans directly to customers. Altus guarantees all its closing costs and rates.

The American Institute of Certified Public Accountants
The AICPA (http://www.aicpa.org) is the national professional organization of CPAs with more than 331,000 members in public practice, business and industry, government, and education. It issues criteria of control guidelines, publishes professional literature, develops continuing education programs, and represents the CPA profession nationally and internationally.

Arkansas Society of Certified Public Accountants
The Arkansas Society of Certified Public Accountants (http://www.arcpa.org) is an active professional organization of CPAs working together to improve the profession and serve the public interest. With over 80 years of service to the accounting profession, its mission is to act on behalf of members and provide support in enabling members to perform quality professional services while serving the public interest.

Bell Canada
Bell Direct (http://www.bell.ca) offers a suite of self-serve electronic commerce solutions for its customers.

Cameraworld of Oregon
Cameraworld of Oregan (http://www.cameraworld.com) sells photography, audio and video equipment online

Competitor Communications Inc.

Competitor Communications Incorporated (http://secure.competitor. net/rrstore) is a national Internet design, hosting, and consulting firm.

E-Trade Group, Inc.

E-Trade (http://www.etrade.com) is a leading branded provider of on-line investing services.

Flexlease V.O.F.

Flexlease.nl (http://www.flexlease.nl) is a carlease company that uses the internet as its single selling channel.

Florida Institute of CPAs

Florida CPA NetLink (http://secure.ficpa.org) provides current news and information about the profession, membership benefits and programs, and on-line member Web services.

Les Systemes Fortune 1000 Itee

Fortune 1000 Accounting System (http://www.fortune1000.ca) is an accounting software developer in Quebec.

Main Net, Inc.

Main Net, Inc., (http://www.main-net.com) is an Internet Service Provider.

MediaComm Marketing International

GalleriaCyberspace (http://www.galleriaCyberspace.com) facilitates transactions of high-quality art and products between the creators and the community at large.

National Tax Institute

National Tax Institute (http://www.nti-inc.com) is a provider of continuing professional education (CPE) to CPAs and other tax professionals.

The Ohio Society of CPAs

The Ohio Society (http://www.ohioscpa.com) is a professional association dedicated to the advancement of the accounting profession in Ohio. The Ohio Society has 20,500 members.

Resource Marketing, Inc.

Resource Marketing, Inc. (http://resource-marketing.com) is an Internet Service Provider, and marketing organization, and is a promoter of Web-Trust.

VERSUS Technologies, Inc.

E-TRADE Canada (http://www.canada.etrade.com) is a leading provider of on-line investing services.

Webcoach Internet Services

WebCoach.com is a leading full-service Internet presence provider for entrepreneurs, consultants, and business coaching. It solves business and personal Web needs at the best price and provides current SSL, FrontPage extensions, domain hosting and registration, Web development and design, RealAudio, video, and Majordomo mailing lists.

Zurich Financial Services Australia Limited
Zurich (http.//www.zurich.com.au) provides needs-based financial services products and services information.

Other Opportunities. WebTrust and other assurance services may be a future service and revenue source for CPAs. Other, more traditional, tasks also come from security and privacy problems. These include:

Disaster recovery plans

Handling security incidents

Policy development

Risk, cost/benefit analysis

System review

Important Web Sites. To be better equipped, you need to keep up with issues in security and privacy. Some of our favorite Web sites are listed as follows:

Security

IIA: (Institute of Internal Auditors)	www.theiia.org
ISACA: (The Information Systems Audit and Control Association)	www.isaca.org
CERT: (Computer Emergency Response Team/Coordination Center)	www.cert.org
International Computer Security Association:	www.icsa.org
Small Business Adminstration Online:	sbaonline.com

Hackers

www.fc.net:80/phrack

underground.org

www.2600.com

defcon.org

www.10pht.com

www.paranoia.com

Privacy

shell.idt.net/~pab

www.w3.org/Privacy.Overview.html

http://www.epic.org/privacy

www.cdt.org

www.eff.org

www.privacy.org/ipcwww.osu.edu/units/law/swire1/pspriv.htm

http://www.fulldisclosure.org/stalk.html (the Stalker's Home Page!)

From Here . . .

In Chapter 9 we discuss how the Internet can make your firm or business more productive.

Productivity Ideas for Professionals

This chapter illustrates how the Internet can be integrated into daily tasks to do things more efficiently, accurately, and precisely. It provides examples and descriptions of how other financial professionals have used electronic resources. The following outline summarizes the contents of this chapter:

- *Internet and productivity: An introduction:* Is the Internet a technology looking for a use or the answer to your business problems? This section is a reminder of what it takes to be successful and how the Internet fits in.
- *Sites of special interest for office productivity:* This section provides coverage of Internet resources to make your firm more productive.
- *Cross-reference of practical uses for Internet services:* I know I have e-mail and Web access—what exactly are they good for? Ways to take advantage of your software.

INTERNET AND PRODUCTIVITY: AN INTRODUCTION

The personal productivity tools on the Internet are amazing. You can spend all your time learning them, and never get anything done.

Excite

Take a trip to a typical Internet portal. My favorite is Excite (http://www.excite.com), although you could make as good a case for Yahoo! (http://www.yahoo.com) or many other sites. As I was finishing up the first draft of this second edition, some great new features were added to Excite, including:

- Voice chat, which lets groups verbally converse on the Internet without any special software or setup.

- Excite Voice Mail, where you are given a toll-free number where people can leave you voice messages and faxes, which you pick up at the Excite Web site.

- Excite Assistant, which offers a small window on your computer that lets you keep up with news, sports, stocks, weather, and all the e-mail, voice mail, and faxes that will come pouring in.

- Excite Planner, which offers personal calendars, address books, and to-do lists that can automatically synchronize with Microsoft Outlook and Palm personal digital assistants.

The Internet is crammed with tools to make individuals, groups, businesses—anyone—more productive, with "information at your fingertips."

Excite is not alone. Similar functionality can be found all over the Net. For example, uReach is a site set up to make you productive both with private information (individual) and information you wish to make public (set up areas for workgroups) with:

Address books and e-mail

Calendars

Multilevel file areas

Bookmarks

Voice, fax, and e-mail with a toll-free number to send and receive voice mail (45 free minutes monthly)

Free!

INTERNET, PRODUCTIVITY, AND ACCOUNTING: AN INTRODUCTION

It is not that long ago that accountants footed and cross-footed trial balances with a 10-key, posted general ledgers manually, and prepared tax returns by hand. Computerization has made all of those tasks more efficient. The Internet can be a tremendous tool for productivity, helping accountants and financial managers accomplish more tasks in the time allotted.

For the CPA firm, the goals of productivity and success may be "a steady and increasing volume of billable and collectible work that can be done efficiently and accurately." In the corporate office, the mission statement may be "to collect financial information and produce more meaningful and useful financial analysis on an efficient and timely basis."

The Internet is an important tool to meet these needs for three main reasons: (1) instant information, (2) targeted information, and (3) value-added information.

Instant Results

The Internet provides *instant* information. Through the Net, you can pull down news before it hits the newspapers, such as the *Wall Street Journal* (http://www.wsj.com). You can get fact sheets and accounting software demonstrations immediately, instead of waiting for a week, from vendors like Sage (http://www.sota.com). You can get antivirus software the minute a virus hits (http://www.mcafee.com). You can get tax forms from the IRS at 11:45 P.M. on April 15 (http://www.irs.gov) and from many states, along with reviewing their codes. You can do all this now, wherever you are.

There are three categories of information on the Internet: Some is historical and fixed, and presumably growing; another is dynamic and changing, and history is not important; and some users themselves place for others to see and respond to. The Internet lets you access this information immediately and provide feedback. Although some users use the Net only as a conduit (e-phone, e-support, e-commerce), others use the Net as a repository and a library.

The Internet can be a less expensive, if somewhat more aggravating, replacement for the telephone, proprietary on-line databases, and CD-ROMs. The Net's lack of reliability is offset by instant updates, low equipment needs, no need for availability (store and forward), and low-cost connections.

CD-ROM is great for the historic but not for the immediate. The primary advantage of CD-ROMs within a business had been the ability to maintain 700 MB of corporate information and make it available cheaply to all staff, without a phone connection. Larger hard drives, exceeding 20 gigabytes (GB) at press, make some of this less important. Copyright inclusion of some information on the premastered CD-ROMs as well as the cost of commercial CD-ROMs for staff make a central Web distribution site cost effective without the need for portable CD-ROM units. News can be updated immediately, with the Web's common user interface used to access it.

Second to immediacy comes familiarity/ease of use. Intranets became popular because of the price of the tools and the minimum of training needed to become accustomed to the system, due to familiarity with Web tools at home. Intranets use Internet tools (e-mail, newsgroups, mailing lists, Web pages) and technology within an organization as group-enabling tools. Firm procedures, firm and personal scheduling, and access to legacy databases are inexpensive and easy with Internet tools.

The Internet is being used to replace encyclopedias, phone books, and a stack of CD-ROMs. The Internet is good for someone in an office, great for people who must travel and need to have the resources wherever they are. Someone with an Internet connection can never have an excuse for not being prepared again. It is a speaker's dream, with background information on any topic or place. Need information on a hotel? You can get brochures, pictures, and register on-line immediately. Instant feedback is the key. Instant information, instant maps, instant demonstration copies of software, instant background papers, instant contact with support, Internet forms, Internet video, Internet presentations—a salesperson on your door whenever you want one. So productivity tool number 1 is immediacy.

Targeted Results

The Internet provides "targeted" information. You are not limited on the Internet to broadcast television and local radio. Instead, there are millions of resources, a stream of targeted news and discussions. You can develop any number of portal pages that automatically pull together just the information you want, such as the Microsoft Network (http://www.msn.com), My Yahoo! (http://www.yahoo.com), Netscape (http://www.netscape.com), and Excite (http://www.excite.com). Over 90,000 mailing lists and 35,000 newsgroups cater to particular needs. The Web serves as a publishing tool for the masses.

Value-added Network

The Internet is a broker, making the whole greater than the sum of its parts. It serves as a matchmaker, bringing together people from around the world with similar interests. It provides a tool for collecting the contributions of individuals and creating *knowledge bases,* databases of others' ideas, struggles, and solutions. Do you really think you are the first person to have a problem or a question? If someone has asked it before, it is out there. The Net provides a structured opportunity for people to help others, for altruism, pride, or because *they* have been helped by someone else. In particular, within a firm, the Internet provides a workgroup collaboration environment that rivals that of products like Lotus Notes.

The Internet is immediate, cost effective, convenient, and easy to learn. You will find a world of people developing new technology for free—nonproprietary technology for discussion, speech, sharing. The Internet is productive because there is a world of people who want to help others, share their knowledge. Unlike any other method, the Internet brings together people of similar interests or similar goals to share knowledge, discuss options, and drive toward goals. It acts as a broker through IRC, discussion groups, and Web sites. The search engines also lead people to places where they can contact others. The closest similar non–on-line method is to find some association or user group. The Internet, a virtual users' group—experts and "legends in their own mind"—makes answering uncharted questions easier.

Productivity and the Internet: An Oxymoron?

Some people believe that the terms "Internet" and "productivity" are oxymorons: they go together like "jumbo shrimp" or "Microsoft Works." However, implementing any new technology has its challenges, and the lure of the nonchargeable can be managed. The Internet can be a tremendous tool for productivity.

In many areas the Web is providing convenience and low cost—things that, as trade-offs, may not be suitable for a professional environment. If security and reliability are important, a proprietary connection to a database or software company may make sense. If up-to-date information is important, paying for that accuracy may be more important than the free ride on the IRS site. Many databases available on the Web are also available on CD-ROM (phone books, route mappers).

Computers raise problems where there were none before. Slow or poor connections make tasks difficult. An important e-mail message can disappear with the accidental touch of a button. Moving from one computer to another means the loss of hot lists, cookies, and other person-specific information. Being away from a phone line limits work to that captured on the computer by saving sites for off-line use. Without a paper backup, and with the proliferation of electronic files, things can go berserk. Are the benefits worth it? When you can't get your e-mail for a day or sell your goods on eBay for a few days if it goes down, how does that affect you?

What are the alternatives to using the Internet? Paying for outside research or letting the research go; continuing to require staff to come into the office (more travel expense, wear and tear on staff). What is the downside of this? What is lost? Human interaction? A sense of belonging? The nuances of management that require you to see, hear, and feel the other person, to know if something other than the ordinary is going on?

Often a sales department's hopes of using the Internet are somewhat reduced when they consider that sometimes a face-to-face meeting by cross-country air will close a deal when an e-mail won't. In addition, you need the right person to figure out that a trip through your competitors' Web sites may reveal a staff person with the best background for your new client. Do we become reliant on a service or a software package that may be obsolete tomorrow—do we plan for backups?

Is there a time where the work required to make you productive takes up too much time? Will the glut of e-mail—good communication that would not have taken place otherwise, combined with junk e-mail, fluff e-mail—make keeping up more of a problem than it is worth? The average employee now receives 100 e-mails a day. Will attempts to introduce integrated systems, with the benefits of reduced duplication of efforts and the reduced likelihood that information is incorrect in one area but correct elsewhere, bring suffering? Informal systems are supremely flexible, and finding predesigned systems that do exactly what your office/department does is unlikely.

Productivity Rules and Tools for Accountants.   There is an age-old formula for having a productive certified public accounting practice or accounting department. The challenge of applying that formula is having the discipline to assemble the ingredients, determine the proper portions, and let it cook long enough. Keeping your focus on the right ingredients, the critical success factors, will keep your firm on the road to success. Many certified public accounting firms and other small businesses are finding success by paying attention to these factors and using Internet resources to meet their goals.

The Changing Business Environment.   Small offices and home offices have gained great acceptance; an estimated 30 percent of the workforce is now in firms this size. This was predicted by Bill Gates, chair of Microsoft Corporation, in 1995—prior to the release of Windows 95, mind you.

According to Gates: "Small start-ups are at their highest mark in 14 years, and the number is climbing. [PC technology] has evened the competition in many respects by giving small companies the tools to match those of the big players. . . . Small business and home office use of computers is enabling that shift in the economy from large structures to lean and agile smaller businesses." What Gates did not see until a year later is that the Internet would even the competition even more.

Approximately 320,000 CPAs are members of the American Institute of Certified Public Accountants. Forty-one percent are in business and industry, and many belong to firms in the Big 6. There are between 40,000 and 50,000 small (that is, less than 20 employees) CPA firms in the United States; more than 80 percent of those are single-person firms.

The Internet can be a resource to accounting firms and departments both small and large. For the small firm, the Net's resources help augment those within the business. With larger firms, it can augment the firm's capabilities and also help to better take advantage of capabilities already available within the firm. Communications and resources are the best ways to cope with the accountant's greatest challenge: change.

The Accountant's Big Challenge: Change.   Everything you know is wrong. Well, not everything. However, tax laws and forms change. Audit standards change. The tools we work with change. When tax law changes, the experienced preparer and someone right out of school are, to some extent, on a level playing ground.

The challenges facing CPA firms and accountants are seemingly accelerating. Rules, tools and roles are changing. Client and employee relationships, increased competition, and information overload bring additional struggles. The CPA Vision Project says we are to be something so different from what we are now that audits and taxes should not be among our top tasks.

Our Rules and Tools

Were you in practice in 1980? Back then, few small companies had computers. CPA firms used service bureaus or processed tax returns and financial statements manually. CPAs were allowed to advertise for the first time. Just a few years ago, under federal pressure, CPAs in many states were allowed to accept commissions for the first time.

Many in the profession have cried, "Where is integrity, objectivity, and independence?" The role of the CPA, the non-CPA, and the Uniform Accountancy Act remain hot issues. Accounting firms, in particular the Big 6, regularly take out large advertisements in newspapers and on television. Ernst & Young (http://www.ey.com/us), in particular, is looking toward the Internet as a tool to go after the small CPA's traditional client base. With its on-line consulting business, Ernie (http://www.ernie.com), it has created an electronic consulting practice that can answer questions with a virtual accounting office—without a local presence.

Computer technology stands out as a change of major importance for accountants. In a 1995 survey of 4,000 AICPA members, 98 percent of respondents said they use a computer at work. In addition, 96 percent agreed that technology was becoming a necessity in order to do business. Also, 91 percent said "development of technologies to organize work and maximize efficiency and productivity" was very or somewhat important. However, the respondents did not feel that they had a great deal of knowledge or the time and resources to keep up with changing technology. By 1999 little had changed.

"The results show that while members realize information technology is important to their success, they still have a lot to learn about technology and need to do a better job utilizing it to maximize profitability," said Robert Wynne, chair of the Information Technology Executive Committee. "That's why the AICPA had cited getting members up to speed on information technology as one of its top strategic initiatives."

Acceptance of these new rules and tools divides firms. Often older partners are not comfortable with these changes, especially in the area of information technology. However, many CPAs realize the need for technology to do business.

Our Traditional Role

The most traditional role of the CPA, and one divides our profession from any other, is the attest function. No one else can put his or her signature on an audited or reviewed financial statement (although some states, such as Florida, seem to be trying to change that rule as well). However, other traditional roles, such as collecting a company's records and providing a summary of the results, have come under attack. Consulting service offerings are not keeping up with the needs of our small business clients.

The CPA firm's role as bookkeeper is rapidly decreasing. Clients do not see the value of having a CPA partner review the detail that goes into their monthly compilation. The proliferation of PCs and easy-to-use personal finance/accounting software as well as tax packages make in-house reporting easier for small businesses.

Business is doing business differently at the turn of the century—often electronically. Manual books and records have given way to bar-coded data input and executive information systems output. Businesses are using electronic data interchange (EDI) to send quotes, invoices, and payments—not with paper but with bits and bytes. Sales that earlier would have been done by phone or mail order are now being conducted on the Internet. CPAs have found themselves scrambling to keep up with the advice their clients need.

Many small businesses are competing in the global marketplace, bringing international issues to the forefront. In addition, many large companies now demand that their trading partners (often smaller businesses) implement EDI and bar coding. The Internet has brought the terms "electronic cash" and "electronic storefront" into the accounting language.

"Successful accountants have begun to move up the value chain in the services they provide to clients," says Matt Davis, formerly Microsoft's manager of accounting industry marketing. "Technology usurps lower-value functions because it makes tools for data input and routine transactions easier for the clients to use themselves. As they master new technologies, clients begin to expect more value from the dollars they spend for accountants.

"This move up the value chain is reflected in the decline of revenue from traditional accounting services—tax, auditing, and write-up—and the explosive growth of business consulting. According to a survey conducted by Accounting Today, four of the top 10 highest growth accounting firms in the U.S. in 1994 were consulting firms. And that number is growing, as accountants come to realize that they cannot serve clients by performing rudimentary bookkeeping and tax services. The future of the accounting industry is not in finding the numbers, but in correctly interpreting what the numbers mean, and helping clients define strategies for moving the company forward."

Many CPA firms are learning how to use products like Intuit's Quicken and Quickbooks to exchange information with their clients. It is not that they recommended these programs—but the popularity of these products has made accepting client data on disk a necessity. They are being led by the nose by their clients.

Our role in the marketplace is changing. At every corner, our efforts to keep a clean audit trail, with paper documentation and the separation of duties, is being thwarted. Electronic commerce, corporate downsizing, and the increased volume of detail being maintained in systems make life difficult.

Our Clients and Employees

Old rules of business are gone. Clients and employees are not automatically loyal: A competitive bid will quickly pull either away. The ease with which people file lawsuits has been a big factor in hurting the CPA's image, sapping financial resources and pulling professionals away from their work. The employee pool has changed as federal regulation and changing personal priorities have strained standard personnel practices. The change in education requirements for new CPAs are causing a large gap in the number of available CPA candidates.

Our Competition

Our competition has changed. Big 5 firms bring sophisticated presentations and impressive credentials to small business clients. Non-CPA ownership of CPA firms and other non-CPA big-name competition remains an active issue, on the front burner with the Uniform Accountancy Act.

Our Information Sources

We are in an era of information overload. The answers are all out there, but an avalanche of irrelevant facts, figures, and opinions has drowned them out. The tyranny of the urgent has drowned out the important. Whether it is a new FASB pronouncement, tax law changes, the latest business philosophy, or the latest technology tool, it is being discussed somewhere. You can hear about it on audio or videocassette, see it on your computer, or read it in a newsletter. The problem is knowing what to ask and where to look, and finding out how to get what you need when you need it. It is even harder to find out what you need to know when you do not know you need to know it.

Every CPA firm faces these issues. However, small firms lack the resources of larger firms to sift through the avalanche of information, to have specialists who can master new areas, or to invest in research and other overhead items. Large firms face the task of communicating changes to their branches, partners, and employees.

Change seems to be the only constant. How can accounting firms find success despite the challenges?

Productivity and business success. The first step in cooking is knowing what you want to make. Keeping sight of your personal and corporate goals is the only way to measure if you are finding business success.

AIMING TOWARD THE GOAL

Braving flooding and tornadoes in New Orleans, Louisiana, 35 managing partners of small and growing CPA firms from throughout the United States and Canada met for a workshop. These partners were members of INPACT (http://www.inpactam.org), a nonprofit association dedicated to enhancing the management, marketing, and profitability of its member firms. These partners meet regularly to share their problems and successes with other members and to figure out jointly how their firms can prosper. Because they are not direct local competitors, these CPAs are free to share their struggles and strategies.

INPACT polled the members present to determine what areas of their business they felt were critical to their success. If the firms ignored these areas, there would be consequences to pay; if they acted upon them, they would reap the rewards.

The critical success factors they documented are common to any CPA firm. They are what it takes to achieve "a steady (and increasing) flow of billable, collectible and profitable work that can be completed efficiently and accurately." Any deviation from this goal works against the success of the firm.

Accountants not in public practice have much in common with CPA firms. They have tasks to perform, people to manage and delegate tasks to, information to gather, and money to track. They have computers to run, assignments to complete, record keeping to maintain, stuff to buy, and places to go.

What differs are the lines of management decisions must go through, the levels of internal computer support and competence, the ways money is allocated for use, and the people from whom accounting information must be obtained and to whom it must be communicated.

MEETING THE MISSION

The five top critical success factors determined in the poll were:

1. Finding and keeping the right clients (CPA firms)
2. Hiring and keeping the best employees
3. Establishing and nurturing a base of business partners (CPA firms)
4. Keeping up with change
5. Working as efficiently and accurately as possible

Finding and Keeping Clients

The source of income for a CPA firm is its client base. A new client can provide an annuity, as much work is of a recurring nature, such as tax returns or financial statements; this can provide a guaranteed stream of funds for many years. Clients stay when they trust their CPA, believe they are receiving value for their fees and can get their needs met. On the other hand, loyalty can go out the door just as quickly. Loyalty is lost when clients feels as if their CPA has ignored them and used them, the services they received were generic and available anywhere else (lowest bid accepted), or their trust has been violated.

Satisfied clients can provide referrals (additional work outside the current client base). Satisfied clients mean the annuity will continue and perhaps increase, and they provide some of the most fertile ground for additional services. Many CPAs are amazed to find their clients do not know about all the services they can offer and would be interested in using those additional services if they knew about them.

Without clients, there is no income. The marketing costs to gain new clients far exceed those of keeping current clients happy. CPAs on first-time assignments ignore certain start-up costs because of the inefficiencies involved, such as setting up the write-up package for the first time; the CPA will never be able to recapture these costs after the former client leaves. Dissatisfied clients may lead to lawsuits, wasting time and money.

The right client base can spell instant success for a firm. With the wrong type of client, the rewards may not justify the costs and frustrations of doing business. How can you attract the right clients?

Using the Internet to Find Clients. Technology can make the smallest firm look as technologically advanced and sophisticated as the biggest firms. A Web site, an electronic newsletter, and participation in newsgroups can give your firm a strong presence on the Internet. We covered marketing on the Internet in Chapter 5.

Many firms feel their alumni are an excellent source of future business (whether directly or referrals). Use the Internet to keep in touch.

Keeping Clients. Do your clients know what you are doing on their behalf? What additional services you can provide for them? Small CPA firms are more successful than large ones in maintaining close ties with the small business owner, but often they could do more to communicate their value to their clients.

One tool that many firms find success with is to seek feedback using satisfaction surveys. A feedback form is not just a vessel for feedback. It can uncover dissatisfaction before a competing bid pulls your clients away, communicate available services your firm provides, and find out if your clients can use other services, which you can add to your mix. These forms can be set up on your Web site as a constant reminder of your desire to please your clients. Services like OneList (http://www.onelist.com) let you establish surveys and provide statistical recaps of the results, at no charge.

To get around the frustration of phone tag, some firms are promoting e-mail as a way for their clients to communicate with them 24 hours a day, confidentially, and in depth. The Internet provides a virtual meeting place for client contact.

The same newsletters and Web sites used as marketing vehicles can let you touch your client regularly. In addition, when you find a new mailing list, newsgroup, or Web site of interest, a quick e-mail (or paper mail) will let clients know you are thinking of them.

Hiring and Keeping the Best Employees

A CPA practice is a people-oriented business. A good staff is the result of a careful selection process and a large investment by the CPA firm in training and experience. Hiring bright, aggressive people whom you can turn into technicians, marketers, managers, and, eventually, partners (and pay for the retirement of the current management team) is vital to the continued operation of the firm. A team attitude (traditionally, CPA work is not 40 hours a week, especially during tax season) is necessary.

Good employees mean the partners and managers can keep their attention where it belongs: on running the business as a business.

Keeping the wrong employees or losing good employees results in low morale, personal infighting, loss of clients, potential for lawsuits, inefficiencies, and a questionable line of succession within the firm.

The phrase "CPA firms and employees" may conjure a picture of young, impressionable and naive staff, with partners taking advantage of them while the staff serves out their mandated apprenticeship with long hours and low pay. Once they have been there awhile, the partners begin to hold out the carrot of partnership to keep them in line. In this grueling crucible of long hours and extended carrots, stress and physical problems take their toll.

Hiring the best employees requires a best face forward. Without the reputation of a Big 6, small firms must work for respect. A prospective employee must find out about the partners' reputation, client base, office environment, and opportunities over the near and long term. Even these are not an infallible index for picking an employer. Will the employee gain portable skills and expertise that will help him or her wherever they go? Does the firm take care of its employees?

Finding Employees.   Prospective employees can be found graduating from business school, working for competitors, or in local businesses. Traditional methods of finding employees include college interviews, help wanted advertisements, recruitment from the competition, and recruiting firms services.

A growing method of finding employees is the on-line resumes found on the Internet and on-line data services. Prospective employees are learning to design their resumes with key words so they will be more likely to come up in an on-line search. Need a litigation support specialist? An expert in sales taxes? Type in a few key words and you will find a computer-friendly person looking for work.

Resumes and job postings are available at many different career and accounting-oriented resources. In particular, general career sites such as Career Mosaic (http://www.careermosaic.com) and accounting sites such as AccountingNet (http://www.accountingnet.com) are clearinghouses for resumes and job postings. The newsgroups, such as <biz.comp.accounting>, are used more often by agencies with job postings.

Once again, your firm's own Web site is an excellent place to post job offerings and paint the picture of your firm you would want a candidate to see.

Your competitor's Web site is another excellent place to look for personnel. Need an experienced senior with manufacturing experience? Check out competitors' personnel listings.

Before you hire, you may want to take advantage of one of the search engines that searches USENET (AltaVista, InfoSeek, Excite) for postings your prospective employee may have made. If you find their name in the alt.bombs.homemade section, you may want to consider again.

Keeping the Best Employees.   How do you keep employees? A basic rule of management is to let employees know what you expect of them and how well they are meeting your expectations, through recognition.

Along with letting employees know how well they are performing, management needs to consider and manage the additional expectations employees have. Some of these include the proper equipment to do their work, a growth path, and a vision of the greater goal.

Many Internet tools can help. These include e-mail, which reduces the frustration of not being able to meet with a manager or partner during office hours. Web sites can communicate firm goals and direction and list job postings and opportunities. Education through the Internet lets staff learn when they want to. Staff newsletters can keep them in good morale, on site or away from the office.

Promoting Partnerships

Until 15 years ago, the profession chose to prohibit any manner of advertising for its members. Over the years, referral sources, especially among other trusted professionals such as attorneys and doctors, were a primary source of gaining new clients. Also, because of the interrelationship between investment counselors (aka stockbrokers) and tax preparers, referral relationships sprang up between these two groups.

Traditionally, one of the most important relationships has been that of the CPA with bankers. Many small businesses enter into their first relationship with a CPA only when they are forced to. The client needs to acquire financing from a bank. The bank needs a financial statement. Bankers know which CPA's financial statements will provide the information they need and will steer clients toward those CPAs. Nothing makes a CPA look as good as being able to get financing for a client that the client was previously unable to obtain.

Today's strategic partners can span every industry, depending on the vertical and horizontal niche marketplaces the CPA serves. Bookkeeping, medical billing and payroll services, controllership and management consulting practices, hardware and systems shops—anyone who provides a complementary or overlapping business service who can develop a relationship of trust with the CPA can be a source of new work and lead to a more satisfied client base.

CPAs need to know many people: bankers, lawyers, and specialists in many fields. Developing a network of partners fills in for the many weaknesses that might otherwise cripple a small firm or eliminate it from consideration for a bid.

Business partners provide a referral base for new clients and grease the skids for the client in many areas (like getting that loan), making for satisfied clients. Business partners can assist the small firm by providing additional expertise for more efficient work.

Without business partners, getting new business is more difficult. Clients may leave to find a CPA with relationships that will help in acquiring loans, or to find one with the expertise they need to run their business.

The Internet can be used to find business partners. A bank, attorney, or doctor with a Web page has taken the same interest in technology as your office. Using search engines or perusing local business malls, you can find people you may wish to contact. Likewise, the image you portray on your Web page may bring the right type of referral source to you.

E-mail is a great tool for nurturing business partners. You can exchange referrals, pass along tips on dealing with clients, share the results of meetings; and you can send all this information between partners without wasting a lot of time on the phone. An electronic copy of your firm's newsletter is another tool to reach your referral source and give them ideas for referrals.

If your referral source has a Web site, cross-links (listing their site on yours and vice versa) provide an automatic lead-sharing mechanism.

Internet tools that create community help bind your clients to you. Virtual office tools help you build special places that meet your clients' felt needs.

Extranets let you offer clients access to customized news, historical accounting and tax information, and analysis of their business on-line that they can access from any Web browser.

A Knack for Knowledge

CPAs are supposed to interpret changing tax and business regulation on behalf of their clients. CPAs must keep up with constant change and make plans based on the likelihood of potential changes. In addition, business philosophy and mechanics are changing. Recent trends in managerial reporting (activity-based accounting), business philosophy (just in time, total quality control), and computer systems (electronic cash on the Internet) have caught the business world by storm. CPAs must come up to speed on these topics and stay there to support their clients. Wherever technology intersects the financial reporting system, CPAs can expect calls.

CPAs must keep up with change—and anyone who can be proactive will make a name for himself quickly, with whatever additional growth that brings. Niche market concentration is the effort of CPAs to recognize a changing need area and to differentiate themselves from competitors, large and small.

CPAs who cannot deal with change will find themselves out in the cold, unable to function competitively. Everything CPAs do is based on keeping up with change.

CPAs need the resources to educate their staff. Staff must know where to find information when it is needed, and know how to get at it, whether in tax areas, financial statement preparation, or technology. CPAs need the tools for the acquisition of this knowledge at the proper time, accurately, and at a reasonable cost.

Database Searches.   While on-line databases for research have been around for many years, the costs of searches and the need for special care in designing a query have been a limiting factor. Over the last few years, the dropping price of CD-ROM drives has brought computerized research within the means of most small firms.

On-line services are a resource for getting information in a hurry at any hour. The Internet offers access to thousands of Internet discussion groups. Topics include taxes, accounting, computers, and finance. Clipping services like *The Informer* will help make sure you are kept up to speed on topics of interest to you.

Continuing Professional Education. Continuing professional education (CPE) is now being delivered on the Internet. Older-style sites are simply delivering traditional computer-based training to your computer through a download from a Web site, rather than by disk. CPE is now being delivered in many other formats, including those that let you complete it on-line. A number of independent content providers are offering their services on the Internet.

Changing Regulations. Chapter 6 covered resources of particular importance to the accounting profession, such as links to the Internal Revenue Service (http://www.irs.gov) and Congress (http://thomas.loc.gov), the AICPA (http://www.aicpa.org), and state societies.

Many of the mainline service providers have started making their daily and weekly guides available for no charge at their Web sites. A tour of the Research Institute of America's site (http://www.riatax.com) will give you updates to the world of taxes while exposing you to their other commercial products.

Working Well

CPAs cannot make mistakes. They are embarrassing and potentially costly. If a lawsuit occurs, and if your firm has not properly documented everything and put it in its place, you could be facing a business-ending settlement. However, your staff must perform its work quickly, so your fees can be competitive.

Efficient operations mean fewer people can do more work, saving time and resources. Accuracy means the work is done correctly. It also means that all of the time on the work is tracked; that any extra work performed can be properly identified and billed; and that you can review the results to make changes for greater efficiency next time.

The potential of lost bids, lost work, reduced productivity, and lost lawsuits makes accuracy and efficiency an important area to seek to improve.

Efficiency. Efficiency almost always finds its way to the bottom line. CPA firms have found increased efficiency by automating processes, reducing the time spent on nonchargeable activities, and implementing standards and policies.

Automating Processes: Before audit workpaper software was available, many staff hours were wasted trying to balance manual trial balances. Then came spreadsheets like Microsoft Excel, tax software, and time and billing software. Much of the drudgery, inefficiency, and inaccuracies of the old 10-key has given way to these helpful software tools.

The pyramid structure of larger firms (lots of staff, a few managers, a smaller number of partners) is ideal for delegation. Where a staff person can perform a task more cost effectively than a partner, the firm can be more competitive in the bidding process. Many small firms do not have this opportunity to reduce costs and must find other ways to stay competitive.

Finding Better Ways to Collect and Communicate Information: The Internet provides superior tools for communicating information to management, stockholders, donors, investors (banks), and the government. The Web provides cross-platform tools to view and work with information like financial data. Organizations working with any of the major word processors or spreadsheets will find tools to take documents created in spreadsheets and word processors and convert them into HTML format or send them directly via e-mail. The information is probably better when received in written, electronic form in the first place (as opposed to taking down information on the phone, or via fax) as it can be duplicated exactly and more attractively in that format.

Reducing the Time Spent on Nonchargeable Activities: Three administrative tasks that consume time: staff time and billing, scheduling, and CPE administration.

Time and Billing Time and billing packages are the tool a CPA firm uses to capture staff time and expenditures, measure what it can bill, and calculate statistics for managing the firm. However, getting staff and partners to fill out their time and expense sheets is like pulling teeth. If a staff person is out at a client, getting to the office to submit the time sheet is an added burden.

"The most expensive time in a firm is the person to person time. Of course, there is a balance here, but we need to reduce person to person time, and reduce the water cooler syndrome," advises Matt Davis. The Internet is a tool for communicating and even submitting time sheets.

Software that makes it easy to capture statistics quickly, produce invoices while the service is fresh on the client's mind, and report on meaningful statistics, combined with tools to capture the necessary information, can make that process more bearable. Capturing the information automatically reduces the rush at the end of the day to answer "where did my time go?" When you time your work, those phone calls that seemed as if they only took five minutes often turn out to take 30 minutes or more.

Scheduling Another task that takes time is group scheduling. Scheduling would be easier if clients were always ready on time, engagements did not bog down, and conflicts never arose. However, that is not always the case.

Scheduling software lets you enter your staff and other resources, such as conference rooms and computer equipment. Then you can enter the demands on their time, such as jobs, vacations, meetings, and training. You can print out personal schedules and schedules for everyone on a common job or project. The system can assist in finding a time when different resources are available.

When every user on the Internet has access to other people's calendars, you no longer have to try to track down 10 people to try to find a suitable time to have a meeting. In addition, when the scheduling package can automatically create e-mail to communicate assignments and changes, staff can make appropriate plans more easily.

CPE   All of the major organizations offering continuing professional education materials have an on-line presence. The AICPA's calendar is on-line at its site; most state societies make their CPE catalogs available on-line as well, many of them at AccountingNet (http://www.accountingnet.com).

If you are going to continue to send staff out of office (and the partners want to go to Hilton Head because it is more conducive to learning), the airline, hotel, and travel information on the Internet is a tremendous resource. You can even track your frequent flyer miles on the Web.

STANDARDIZATION AND POLICIES

Establishing firm policies and setting standards for document generation can both be time and money savers.

Reinventing the wheel is a way to describe writing a client data availability letter, proposal or engagement letter, or projection from scratch. There are many sources for sample letters on disk that you can modify for your firm's use. Once you have modified the form, it can become the standard in your firm. Most modern word processors and spreadsheets, like Microsoft Word or Excel, let you save the document or spreadsheet as an HTML file. Then you can make the files available in native or HTML format from your Web site, so your staff always has the most recent version.

A series of checklists of the tasks that your staff should perform on different engagements also reduces planning work and helps ensure that standard procedures are followed. When you keep checklists in template form on your Web site, staff members can modify them easily for an individual client or engagement.

Standardization does more than make you and your staff more efficient: It can also protect you in the case of a lawsuit. The more you do to limit legal and other external costs, the better.

Systems Help

Of course, it is hard to be efficient when your systems are down. Every major hardware and software vendor is providing support through Olin services and the Internet.

Need to buy new equipment? Ask in the newsgroups about the reliability of products you are considering. Search through the computer magazines, such as at Ziff Davis (http://www.zdnet.com) for reviews. Order on-line from Buy.com (http://www.buy.com) not just at a discount but below cost.

Accuracy

Work done accurately should, by its nature, be work done more efficiently. Philip Crosby writes "Quality is Free." The costs of rework, the exposure to the costs of errors, and the good feeling that comes with a job well done are reasons that quality is its own reward. In a CPA practice, a job hastily done means that the reviewers must draw their attention away from the important and profitable to focus on the mechanics of the process.

Accuracy and proper judgment also may demand that you wear the hat of psychologist/fortune teller/gambler. Today's tax shelter becomes tomorrow's audit risk. A value-added tax or a national sales tax wipes out all of today's planning tips. The Internal Revenue Service has its position on tax matters, which may disagree with a ruling from a court in another jurisdiction; would it hold in yours? At the same time, the client may or may not want to offer information about her firm unless you specifically ask for it, and maybe not even then. When it comes to the gray issues, you have to know when to hold 'em and when to fold 'em.

Larger businesses are starting to put into place workflow systems that permit collaborative attention to projects. On a large level, these tools are being used to speed up the approval of loans or health insurance forms.

The Internet opens the door to increased workgroup collaboration. E-mail and other tools open the door to increased speed, with parallel processing of work papers. When tax or audit work is on the Net, review is not limited to the person in whose in-basket the staff person places the work papers. When the staff person is ready, he can send an e-mail message in the tax and audit managers' boxes, and they can attend to the work when they are ready.

Action Plan

How do you go about determining your technology direction? Follow a classic action plan.

Start with an analysis of your needs. Begin by encouraging communication within your firm or department. What are areas of frustration and opportunity? What new technologies or software have you heard about that you think may be worth looking into?

The selection process comes next. Meet with technology consultants, communicate with others you trust in similar operations, do your individual research, compare notes, and select some areas to further research and test.

Establish a pilot project next. Choose some of your more technological people as guinea pigs.

Implement what you selected. There comes a time when you actually roll it out.

The analysis and adjustment never end—continue to monitor your success. Then start all over again.

SITES OF SPECIAL INTEREST FOR OFFICE PRODUCTIVITY

As your firm uses the Internet, particular sites will make your work more productive. This section highlights some sites of general interest.

Business referral/Yellow Pages

If you need to find a store, a service, a restaurant, or a hotel (or want to find organizations in a certain industry for marketing purposes), the on-line Yellow Pages are a tremendous tool. One of these is Superpages (http://www.superpages.com), formerly BigBook.

The Yellow Pages listings all work in a similar manner. You type in a business name or a business type and a city or state. The site then returns a list of names with their addresses and phone numbers. Some, for a fee to the advertiser, will let the organization link its Web page to its listing.

Superpages is more than a traditional Yellow Pages listing. It lets its users vote for and review the businesses. That way you can get some input from others on whether the organization is worth your patronage. In addition, you can get a street-level map showing where the business is located.

Audit staff can use this tool to find where the business they are going to is located as well as hotels, restaurants, and entertainment in the area.

Superpages.com Yellow Pages provides business information for over 11 million businesses nationwide, including maps and driving directions. Yellow Pages search forms are located in the yellow sidebar on most pages. Superpages offers numerous ways you go about finding a business.

If you know the product or service you're looking for, try the Shopping Pages. This section provides links to hundreds of selected sites that allow you to purchase goods and service on-line. You also can find local retailers, classifieds, product reviews, and other relevant content.

From buying a home to planning a party, certain events can be complex. Idea Pages helps you shop for these occasions by providing helpful tips, links to on-line merchants, classifieds, product reviews, and other related content.

If you know where you want to shop, check out City Pages: local shopping guides with links to local Yellow Pages, city guides, classifieds, maps, driving directions, and places to shop locally.

Your favorite search engine/portal probably offers a similar service. Look for "Yellow Pages" to find features similar to Superpages.

Communications

Keeping in touch has never been easier—if you can cut through all the communications. Free services help you keep in touch in powerful new ways.

Chat with Folks On-line with No Special Software. Excite Chat (http://www.excite.com) lets you develop meeting rooms on the fly, with no need of special phone software, where groups can gather and literally speak to each other, using the multimedia features of their computers.

Receive Faxes by E-mail Wherever You Go. Want faxes on the road? Do you spend too much money at hotel business offices paying receipt charges to receive faxes? You could get that toll-free number we discussed earlier from Excite and check in on a regular basis. Or you can get eFax from <http://www.efax.com>. eFax offers a nifty way to receive faxes wherever you can get e-mail. It's particularly good for those who travel.

Here's how it works. When people want to send you a fax, they simply dial your unique (long distance for most of us) eFax number and press Send. Just like regular faxes, eFaxes can include text, graphics, or both.

Once sent, your fax is received at the eFax service center, is turned into a computer graphic, is compressed and protected with your personal password for security, and then is forwarded to your e-mail address.

In your e-mail, the fax comes as an attached file. You need a special viewer program, the eFax Microviewer, which comes to you as an e-mail when you first sign up, and which you can also download from the eFax Web site. (See Exhibit 9.1.) Before the fax opens, you'll see a bit of advertising. There are no ads on the fax itself.

The eFax Web site has lots of step-by-step instructions, so even the most inexperienced computer user can start using this service immediately.

You do have to sign up for the service, but it's free. The fax number is long distance, an inconvenience for those sending you faxes. And you can only

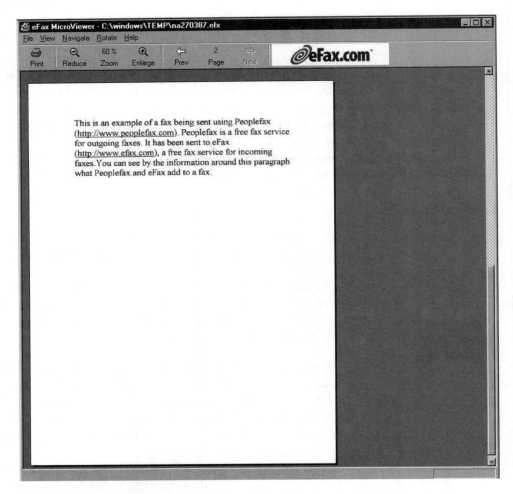

Exhibit 9.1 The eFax Microviewer. Used with permission from EFax.com.

receive faxes, not send them. But if you have a fax-modem on your computer for sending them but aren't in one place long enough to make that number available for receiving faxes, eFax can be a helpful tool.

A competitor with similar services is Callwave (http://www.callwave.com), which offers a similar services called FaxWave.

Send Faxes through Your Computer. Free faxing is not just for incoming faxes. You can send outgoing faxes as well. Just make sure that you know what the person on the receiving end must endure when receiving your fax!

If you are willing to subject the person to more advertising than message and are concerned with privacy, click over to SwissClick (http://www.hotcorp.com/swissclick). (See Exhibit 9.2.) The good news is that there is no registration required, so your privacy is somewhat maintained. The bad news is that no attachments are allowed, so you are limited to text massaging. But you can send faxes to the United States, the United Kingdom, and 13 other countries for free.

PeopleFax (http://www.peoplefax.com) has a registration process, but it is not too nosy. You can send attachments. The size of the e-mail you send is limited on a per-page basis, but you can store up extra page credits by visiting their advertisers. The Peoplefax free Internet service takes its toll more on the sender than the receiver. (See Exhibit 9.3.)

Receive E-mail by Phone.   Virtual assistants like Webley, Wildfire, and Portico are business savers at $20 per month plus usage charges. These offer a toll-free number for people to reach you, voice mail, and numerous other fea-

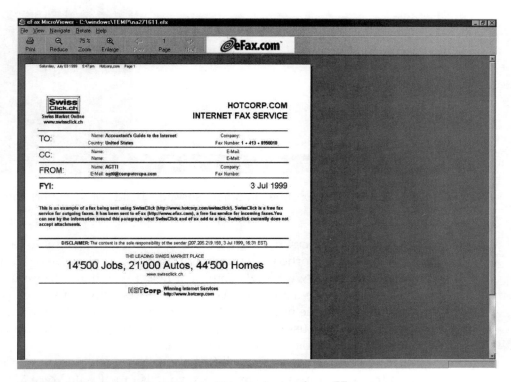

Exhibit 9.2   Swiss Click. Used with permission from EFax.com.

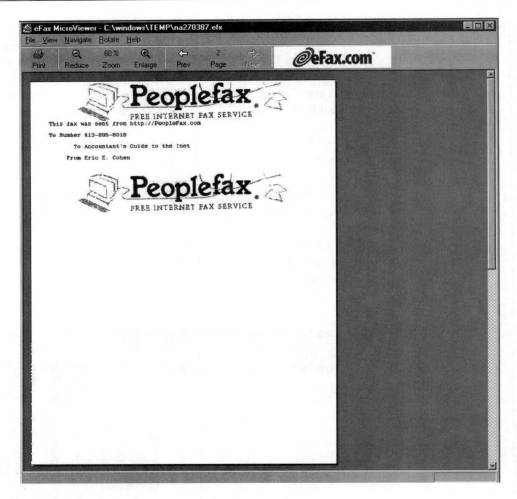

Exhibit 9.3 Peoplefax free Internet service. Used with permission from EFax.com.

tures as if you had a personal assistant tracking you down. But you can get a taste of the power of Portico in a number of new free services. Two examples:

My Talk (http://www.mytalk.com) is a new free e-mail service that lets you send and receive e-mail on the Web or on the telephone. To check your e-mail, you call a toll-free number and enter your personal code. My Talk then reads you your e-mail using text-to-speech synthesis. You can even reply, and MyTalk will attach a voice file to a return e-mail.

Excite Voice Mail gives you a toll-free number you can give to your associates. To retrieve your messages and faxes, you visit the Excite Voice Mail Web site and listen to your messages and view your faxes on-line.

Computer Support

Almost every business relies on its computers. What do you do to deal with problems? Fortunately, there is ample computer support on the Internet. Some examples:

Microsoft Corporation (http://www.microsoft.com) has worked diligently to conquer the Internet. Its site provides news about its products, marketing information, lots of free software that makes its products work better, and all of the information you care to know about its Internet products.

One of the best resources on Microsoft's site is found in its product support areas. Not only does it make all of its fixes available for free through the Internet, it provides tutorial information, lists of frequently asked information, and access to *knowledge bases,* Microsoft's collection of technical knowledge about all of its products. If you have a problem getting software to work, get error messages, or want to know how to do a task more easily in a product, the knowledgebases have sophisticated tools for searching and finding what you need.

Looking for information from a more neutral source? All major computer publishers have sites where you can get the latest news and browse through back issues of their families of publications for news and reviews. One of the most popular is ZDNet (http://www.zdnet.com). At the ZDNet site, you can get news, reviews, tutorials, and search through all of Ziff Davis's publications. A huge variety of shareware software is available that you can use for browsing the Web or increasing your productivity of your systems. Other great computer resources include TechWeb (http://www.techweb.com), CNet (http://www.cnet.com), and PC World (http://www.pcworld.com)

If you like to read, visit Macmillan Computer Publishing's Online Bookshelf (http://www.mcp.com). You can read the full text of many of their books on-line for free. In the Beta Book section Macmillan also highlights books being written so you can come up to speed on leading-edge technologies.

Maps

Superpages let you find businesses on the map. What about deliveries of tax returns to people's homes? One of the most helpful (and perhaps scariest) resource on the Internet are the street maps and directions available through most portal sites. One we like the best is the *Road Maps* available at Lycos (http://www.lycos.com). By typing in a street address, you will soon have a map show up on your screen. The map shows major streets, and an "X" marks where the address is on the map. If you need to see more major roads, you can click on the word OUT; if you need to see more of the names of cross streets nearby, you can click on IN. (You cannot yet click on "IN" enough to look in your own window . . . yet.) By typing in your starting location, you can receive a turn-by-turn set of directions to get to your final location.

Another favorite mapping site is MapQuest (http://www.mapquest.com).

News

News and the Internet. What is the worth of knowing something now instead of tomorrow? If you want news, there are many resources. Here are a few:

Quicken's Financial Network (http://www.quicken.com) is so good, it made it the main Quicken page. Microsoft Investor (http://investor.msn.com) is another resource to get stock quotes and business/industry news on demand. Although you pay for the *Wall Street Journal* (http://www.wsj.com), the Dow Jones site (http://www.dowjones.com) is free. In addition, many of the trading services offer powerful news resources to entice you to buy, such as E*Trade (http://www.etrade.com). Investors appreciate the wisdom of the Motley Fool (http://www.fool.com).

Want news more focused on the accounting profession? *Research Institute of America* (http://www.riatax.com) is one of many service providers supplying news updates at no cost to bring people to its site. Its home page lets you choose from the latest news in legislative and tax news; it hopes you will click on its products and services while you are there—or maybe look for a job with it.

Personal Information Management

Is the Daytimer passé? Does your Palm III need someone to talk to? You can now keep your personal schedule and to-do list on-line, accessible by Web browser from anywhere.

The number of offerings of free calendars and personal information managers (PIMs) on the Internet has exploded. This is partly because that which drives the Web—advertising—needs site owners to answer a big question: How do you get potential customers to see advertising or come back to a Web site repeatedly? The winning answer: content, content, and content. How do you give them compelling content? Let them build it themselves.

Appointment books serve many functions. They can act as the personal and private reminder of what you need to do and where you need to be. An appointment secretary may use an appointment book to schedule a doctor's time or to schedule the efficient use of a piece of equipment and a meeting room. A professor may post her office hours and let students reserve blocks of time. In a team environment, the schedule book is the primary communications vehicle used to get people together.

Let's put that schedule on-line. On-line calendaring appeals to any number of users. It appeals to deskbound managers or professionals, who can easily access their schedule at home or office. It appeals to teams that do not have a networkable scheduling program or that are in disparate locations. It appeals to anyone who wants to make parts of his or her calendar available to the public, such as a not-for-profit organization or club publicizing its events. It appeals to those who want to take advantage of on-line events schedules (such as sports, computer trade shows, or movies). And it appeals to those who don't want to deal with a PC-based scheduling product but want computer advantages.

Most online calendars can be used by themselves or be automatically integrated with computer-based personal information managers, such as Microsoft Outlook, and personal digital assistants, such as the Palm III or the Franklin Rex. With a few keystrokes, you can synchronize schedules on your pocket PC, your PC or network-based organizer, and your on-line calendar. (See Exhibit 9.4.)

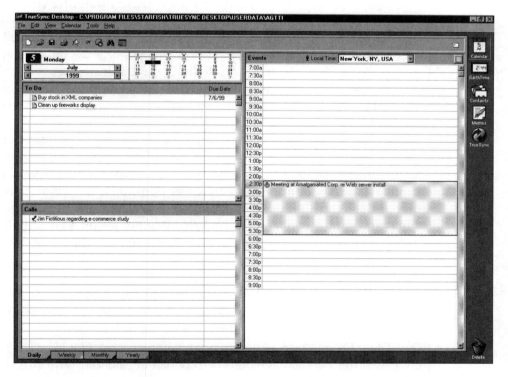

Exhibit 9.4 Desktop organizer that synchronizes with on-line calendar. Screen shot reprinted by permission from Stanfish Software, Inc.

On-line calendars let you stay in sync with others as well. They excel when there will be input from the Internet or output to the Web and e-mail. You may want to let a limited group of people, such as family or staff, make entries on your schedule, or you may want to open the door wide and let the public request your time. You may want to add appointments for seminars, trade shows, movies and television shows from Internet listings. On the flip side, you can send e-mail notices automatically to involved and interested parties when your schedule changes. You can instantly publish your own events for the public.

On-line calendars can serve many functions. They can be useful to those who sell their time. They can be marketing tools for events you are promoting. They can be the communications glue that keeps groups in touch with each other, even if they do not share a network computer system. For those who live by their e-mail, they can be a guide to important events and a reminder to get there. For those who do not have their own computer or do not want to deal with maintaining information manager software, they provide the necessary tools to organize your life without mastering your PC.

On-line calendars offer various features. Some offer integrated on-line contact and address lists, task and to-do lists, and other "virtual office" tools, such as shared file areas for keeping word processing documents, spreadsheets, photographs, and other documents. Some are designed specifically for groups, and some let you assign resources (like conference rooms and AV equipment) to meetings and tasks. Some have great synchronization tools and others don't.

Investigate the different calendaring services to select the ones that offer the combination of services you need for the different jobs you do. Some excel at small workgroups. Some shine for making information about your schedule available to the public. Others are great personal information managers. Check out their capabilities to integrate with your present PDA or personal information/contact management package. Want to set up a virtual office for a small group? Want to set up a shared calendar so people can track and request your time? Check out the options!

- Briefcase (http://www.briefcase.com): Visto's Briefcase lets you open your schedule up to others so they can request time with you. You can set up virtual offices to share files, photos, and group information.
- Day-Timer Digital (http://www.digital.daytimer.com): Not to be left behind, the DayTimer people have their own personal calendar with strong external events capabilities.
- Jump! (http://www.jump.com): Microsoft purchased Jump! and plans on turning it into an e-commerce powerhouse.

- ScheduleOnline (http://www.scheduleonline.com): Weak on synchronization, ScheduleOnline is great for workgroups, and tracks departments, groups, and outside guests, offers multiple access levels to administrate the system, and offers the best control for conflict tracking and controlling meeting invitation refusals.

- When.com (http://www.when.com): Has one of the best event tracking systems for personal and group calendars.

- Yahoo! Calendar (http://www.calendar.yahoo.com): Yahoo!'s synchronization is about the best out there. You can easily set up private and public calendars and make your public calendar easily available on the Web with a single hyperlink.

Other sites to visit include:

- AnyDay.com (http://www.anyday.com)
- appoint.net (http://www.appoint.net)
- JointPlanning.com (http://www.jointplanning.com)

Project Management

Open a Virtual Office.   Do you want to have a place where you can meet with clients and coworkers, share documents, schedule events, coordinate projects, and be more productive? Open a virtual office on the Internet. The Internet offers the functionality of groupware products (without the security and replication functionality) to help groups get work done. These are intranets for groups.

A fee-based service, HotOffice (http://www.hotoffice.com), offers greater sophistication, far less advertising, ease of use, and a greater chance for survival than the more entrepreneurial free sites. Of the free sites, Vista Briefcase (http://www.visto.com) is a wise choice. It lets you set up a number of self-standing areas, each of which has its own members, discussion areas, calendars, shared files, and e-mail notification services.

Coordinate Your Team and Projects.   Project management software tends to be too sophisticated at the basic tasks and weak on one vital task—keeping in touch with the participants. Enter iTeamWork (http://www.iteamwork.com/cgi-bin/login). iTeamWork is a free on-line team project management system that is easy to use and integrates an e-mail notification system.

Create a project, create a task for that project, and assign it to a person. That's all there is to it. iTeamWork's concept is to keep the management of tasks simple while providing a global view of project status. Backed by an e-mail notification system, everyone on a project is kept informed.

iTeamWork supports reassigning task to different people, changing a task's completion date, and converting tasks to full project status. It offers reporting and viewing capabilities and can send e-mails of projects you are interested in on a user-selectable schedule.

Services

When tax returns or other important documents need to be sent, many offices use the express services. When the package is not received, they offer a service to help you trace where the package went. Now you can access those services at no charge through the Internet.

Federal Express (http://www.fedex.com) has a very sophisticated site with information for those involved in logistics and shipping. It has saved itself a great deal of money (estimated at $2 to $4 per call) by letting customers do their own tracking. By entering the airbill number on the page, the user can review the history of the package and its shipment, down to the name of the person signing for it at delivery.

Federal Express has added shipping services to its site. Now its customers can initiate a shipment through the Internet, complete with bar coded documents printed and ready for pickup.

United Parcel Service (http://www.ups.com) also offers a similar service, letting its users schedule a pickup through the Internet.

Travel

Travel is one of the most popular areas on the Internet. Which is the best hotel in Cleveland? Which airline can get me there at a decent hour from Rochester? While travel agents still bring a great deal to the table, there are few resources to help the nervous traveler at 3 A.M. like the Internet.

Services like Travelocity (http://www.travelocity.com) and Microsoft's Expedia (http://www.expedia.com) help you find the best flights, keep up with changing prices, and keep up with flights in the air (or stuck on the ground!)

Many hotels are online. *Hilton Hotels* (http://www.hilton.com) lets you find hotels, learn about their services, and place a reservation online. *Marriott Hotels* (http://www.marriott.com) offers similar capabilities.

Check out flight schedules online. The major airlines all make their scheduling service available online. US Air's site (http://www.usair.com) has information about its services, frequent flyer program, and flights. After you type in your origination and destination cities and the date of travel, you will be presented with a list of available flights. What seat should you select to get an emergency exit or a bulkhead seat? The airplane seat diagrams are available at the touch of a button.

Since one of the things that makes sitting in coach class bearable is accumulating those frequent flyer miles, it is nice to keep track of them. Some hotels and airlines let you access their systems at their sites. Others rely on the Biztravel database (http://www.biztravel.com), where you can review your frequent flyer miles or hotel visits.

Weather

What will be the driving or flying weather? The U.S. Government's National Oceanic and Atmospheric Administration (U.S. Weather Service) (http://netcast.noaa.gov) has its computers ready to answer your every call. Its Netcast site offers detailed weather for any area in the United States and links to many other weather sources, including *USA Today* (http://www.usatoday.com).

Cross Reference of Practical Uses for Internet Services

You may have some software and want to know what you can do with it. In this section, we summarize some of the tasks you can do with different Internet services.

Mail
Interoffice communication

Intraoffice communication

Keep in touch with staff at client sites and away at training

Receive requests from clients, referral sources

Keep in touch with clients who prefer e-mail communication

Get support from software vendors

Coordinate with peers on committees, on boards of not-for-profits

Mailing lists
Offer electronic newsletters to clients

Offer breaking news to clients, staff, referral sources

Communicate with consultants, tax experts, and others in an ongoing roundtable discussion

Use clipping services for newsgroup searches

Keep up on support issues from software companies

Receive updates on what's new on the Internet

NetMeeting

Link together offices separated by long-distance lines

Communicate with staff, clients, investors in other geographic areas

Group training or meetings

Newsgroups

Request and receive support from computer areas

Get tax support from other states

Look for people in your area needing tax services

Discuss accounting software possibilities

Find out what's new on the Web

Research industry trends

See if you or your clients are being discussed

Web

Find people and companies

Research industries

Get support and software fixes

Keep up with the latest from the AICPA, state societies

Arrange travel

Check status of shipments with UPS, Federal Express

IRC and Instant Messaging

Receive real-time help

Set up conference discussions

RealPlayer

Develop your own radio programs

Keep up on accounting radio

Provide video from your office for others to download or hear in real time

Attend a virtual conference

Listen to newsmakers

Shockwave—Macromedia

Provide powerful presentations from your Web site

Attend virtual conferences

Intranets—HTML

Communicate internally

Post employment information

List job postings for firm and clients

Provide discussion groups

Provide files for easy download

Offer access to schedules, firm news

Provide real-time connection without phone calls

Commercial Application Integration

Goldmine

One address book for contact management, e-mail

Synchronize data across the Internet

Send and receive e-mail, tracking by client

Receive forms data, create client records, and inform people internally to follow-up

Do mail merge by filters and groups

Schedule resources

E-mail reminders to yourself and others

From Here . . .

Chapter 10 is our "Yellow Pages" of accounting-oriented Internet resources.

Accounting-Oriented Electronic Resources

This chapter provides a "Yellow Pages" of Internet resources of interest to financial professionals. It is a directory of resources on the Internet that will help readers find information, software, support, and people.

The following outline summarizes the contents of this chapter:

- Author's Pet Pages
- Accountants—CPE
- Accountants—Miscellaneous resources
- Accountants—Individuals and Listings of Listings
- Accounting—Profession
- Accounting Software—Dealers
- Accounting Software—Developers for CPAs
- Accounting Software—Developers of Commercial Products
- Accounting Organizations
- Accounting—Tax and Law
- Bar Code
- Publishers of Books and Magazines
- Business and Reference
- Computers
- Databases
- Diversions (After Tax Season)—Movies, Television, Entertainment
- EDI, ISO, Manufacturing, and Electronic Commerce
- Government Resources
- Internet—General
- Internet—Oddities
- Internet—Security
- Internet—Winsock and World Wide Web–Specific Resources
- Investments
- Law
- Mailing List Archives
- News and Magazine Search Tools
- On-line Services and National ISPs
- People and Business Listings (White and Yellow Pages)
- Software—Shareware
- Software—Commercial

INTRODUCTION

In a book this size, the URLs are as important as the content. This directory is only a highlight of the resources mentioned elsewhere in the book.

AUTHOR'S PET PAGES

The author provides an updated list of resources of interest at his home page. Other affiliated sites are listed in this section.

- Accountant's Home Page:
  (http://www.computercpa.com)   The author's home page, and host to the links mentioned in this section.
- John Wiley & Sons, Inc., Publishers:
  (http://www.wiley.com,   http://www.wiley.com/accounting)

Tax

U.S.: Internal Revenue Service (http://www.irs.gov)

Canada: Revenue Canada (http://www.revcan.ca)

US Law Online: Thomas (http://thomas.loc.gov)

Securities and Exchange

U.S.: Securities and Exchange Commission (http://www.sec.gov/edgarhp.htm)

Canada: System for Electronic Document Analysis and Retrieval for Canadian public companies (http://www.sedar.com)

Business Statistics

Canada: Industry Canada's Strategis (http://strategis.ic.gc.ca)

Other Governmental Resources

U.S.: Government Information (http://www.info.gov)

Canada: Federal Government Information Finder Technology (http://www.gc.ca)

Organizations and Societies

U.S.: American Institute of Certified Public Accountants (http://www.aicpa.org)

Canada: Canadian Institute of Chartered Accountants (http://www.cica.ca). The search engine found at (www.cica.ca/new/toolbar/e_srch.htm) lets you do full text searches through the site and through *CA* magazine.

Education
ANet (http://www.csu.edu.au/ANet)

Investments
Annual reports (http://www.annualreportservice.com)

Quicken and Quicken Canada (http://www.quicken.com,wwwquicken.ca)

Anything Else for Accountants
If you are looking for large listings of accounting-oriented sites, check out the following Canadian and U.S. resources:

US: Accountant's Home Page (http://www.computercpa.com)

Canada: Morochove's AccountNetGuide (http://www.morochove.com/netguide/)

International: http://www.best.com/~ftmexpat/html/taxsites/foreign.html

ACCOUNTANTS—CPE

On-line CPE Providers

AICPA:	http://www.aicpa.org
Accounting Net:	http://www.accountingnet.com
Bisk/Totaltape Publishing:	http://www.cpeasy.com
College for Financial Planning:	http://www.cpeinternet.com
Institute of Management Accountants:	http://www.rutgers.edu/Accounting/raw/ima
Learning Insights:	http://www.learninginsights.com
MicroMash Inc.:	http://www.micromash.com
National Tax Institute:	http://www.nti-inc.com
Practitioners Publishing:	http://www.ppcuniversity.com
Surgent & Associates:	http://www.surgent.com
WiseGuides:	http://www.wiseguides.com
Yipinet:	http://www.yipinet.com

ACCOUNTANTS—MISCELLANEOUS RESOURCES

Many other organizations and people attempt to keep up on resources of interest to accountants and financial professionals. You will find listings, large and small, of links to other resources at these sites.

AuditNet Resource List

(http://www.auditnet.org)　James Kaplan is an auditor, author, and lecturer, who with the Institute of Internal Auditors maintains a site of links to accounting resources that more than rivals the author's own site. You will find Web sites, mailing lists, e-mail addresses, and other resources listed, with an excellent explanation of what you will find at each site.

Accounting and Finance On-Line Resources

(http://www.bus.orst.edu/tools/other/acc_fin/acc_fin.htm)　Carol E. Brown, at the College of Business of Oregon State University, maintains a page of links to accounting and finance resources.

Accountants Thru Internet

(http://www.netaccountants.com)　If you have an interest in what affects accountancy in the United Kingdom, Accountants Thru Internet aims to provide information and links relevant to business activities for small and medium-size businesses. The Dyer Partnership Chartered Accountants from Guildford in southern England is the driving force behind the site. You will find filing schedules, news, business advice, links to Web sites for investing, and much more.

Accounting Software Seminar

(http://www.cpassoc.com)　CPAssociates Seminars, Inc. of Wauwatosa, Wisconsin, presents a traveling seminar series called Accounting Software Update, bringing accounting software developers and resellers to cities around the United States for demonstrations and lectures, while offering CPE credit to those attending.

CPA Online

(http://www.cpaonline.com)　Offers news headlines, feature articles, discussion groups, and more.

AccountNet Guide on the Web

(http://www.morochove.com/netguide)　Morchove's AccountNet Guide is a page of Internet resources for accountants prepared by Richard Morochove of Morochove & Associates Inc. of Toronto, Ontario, Canada. Morochove, a writer for *The Bottom Line,* a Canadian monthly for accounting and finance professionals, has assembled links for Canadian and U.S. accountants, and archives of his articles are available at the site. He lists accounting oriented mailing lists (Canadian) and Usenet newsgroups, and Web sites for accounting, government, investments, and software.

CTS Home Page

(http://www.ctsguides.com) CTS of Rockville, Maryland, is one of the most respected resources for independent reviews of accounting software. For information on their guides about buying accounting software and running a consulting practice, consult this site.

Franklyn Peterson's CPA Computer Report

(http://www.cpacomputerreport.com) The curmudgeon of accounting, Franklyn Peterson's *CPA Computer Report* is known for taking off the gloves and telling it like it is. Accounting software reviews, hardware, advice for CPA firms—you'll find it in the *CPA Computer Report.* The site lets you browse a recent issue, search through past issues for key words, view Web addresses mentioned in the newsletter, and get a CPA Joke of the Month.

Links to Other Appropriate Web Sites

(http://www.solomon.com/links.html) Solomon Software offers an extensive series of links to accounting and accounting software system-oriented Web sites and resources. Links are categorized by Solomon's strategic partners (such as Microsoft, Btrieve Technologies, and Novell), Solomon resellers and developers, accounting-related Web sites, Windows and Visual Basic-related Web sites, computer industry publications, Internet and Web-related sites, news sources, marketing resources, search engines, and a few just for fun.

Nerdworld Accounting Links

(http://www.nerdworld.com/nw1372.html) Nerd World Media is a *category tree* to help find and categorize Internet resources. You'll find many resources listed and automatically updated here. You can search entries as well as navigate the tree.

K2 Enterprises WWW Server

(http://www.k2e.com) K2 Enterprises offers an extensive list of Web sites for accountants, with a focus on Internet software and services. K2 Enterprises is a group of noted CPE seminar leaders and consultants, and has an on-line catalog of seminars.

ACCOUNTANTS—INDIVIDUALS AND LISTINGS OF LISTINGS

CPAs are marketing on the Web. This list includes the sites of a few practioners who have provided interesting links from their own Web sites and sites that offer lists of CPAs and accountants.

Accountants.org

(http://www.accountants.org)   The International Affiliation of Independent Accounting Firms is a nonprofit association headquartered in Miami, Florida. Members companies (IA affiliates) are listed. In addition, you can get advice on doing business internationally.

AccountingNet

(http://www.accountingnet.com)   AccountingNet is the one-stop shop for CPAs. It features articles, listings of accounting firms, job listings, Web resources, and commercial resources of interest to CPAs. Your firm has a listing there already, magically.

Berenson & Company, LLP

(http://www.berenson.com)   Berenson & Company LLP is a certified public accounting firm in New York City. Along with information about its firm, it offers useful business and tax links.

Cohen Greenstein & Company Home Page

(http://world.std.com/~harvey)   Cohen, Greenstein & Company (no relation to the author) of Boston, Massachusetts, is an excellent example of CPA marketing, and offers a series of tax and financial planning links on the Internet.

Coughlin & Gomola, CPAs Home Page

(http://www.ctcpas.com)   Coughlin & Gomola of Middletown, Connecticut, show off their products and services, and offer links to other pages by categories including government services, Connecticut information, finance, investing and other business services, Internet searches and indexes, computer companies, and some sites just for fun.

Ernst & Young LLP

(http://www.ey.com/home.asp)   One of the Big 5, their page has information related to industry practice, tax tips, and other information that could be of value to accountants.

Hacker Young Home Page

(http://www.hackeryoung.co.uk)   Hacker Young is a chartered accounting firm in the United Kingdom and worldwide. Its site includes useful links to other sites relating to investment, finance, and economics for the United Kingdom and the United States.

Hugo Schouten CPA Index

(http://www.ozemail.com.au/~dutch)   Hugo Schouten is an Australian accountant with an extensive and imaginative site. Hugo answers tax questions from his site and offers a series of interesting links. His hot list includes an international group of sites.

List of CPA Firms
(http://www.cpafirms.com)   Dave Albrecht wrote an extensive document about CPA firms on the World Wide Web as an assistant professor at Bowling Green State University. From the time he began his work, the number of CPA firms on the Net increased from 30 (July 1995), to over a 100 (in December 1995), to 4,100 in June 1999. His article, links, and listing of CPA firms can be found at this site.

OLAC Home Page
(http://www.olac.com)   The On Line Accountant, sponsored by Jack D. Burson, CPA, of Boulder, Colorado, offers a handsome switchboard to his service offerings and helpful Internet resources. Want to visit "Bill and Al's Page" (the U.S. Business Advisor)? You'll find a number of helpful tax and business links.

Referral Services
(http://www.uacpa.org)   The Utah State Society of CPAs has an interesting approach to getting prospective clients to its member firms. The society has a form you can fill out with your choice of firm size and experience areas, and it presents a series of firms that can meet that need. It also has listings of local and national firms with offices in Utah that have home pages.

Yurchyk & Davis, CPA's
(http://www.ydcpa.com)   Yurchyk & Davis CPA's, Inc., of Canfield, Ohio, have an interesting site. You will find links to accounting humor and One-Write Plus information. The site hosts the Peachtree and One-Write Plus Users Groups of Pennsylvania and Ohio.

ACCOUNTING—PROFESSION

Accounting—how to pass the exam, teach it, be recognized for it.

The Accounting Hall of Fame
(http://www.cob.ohio-state.edu/dept/acctmis/hof/hall.html)   The Accounting Hall of Fame was established at the Ohio State University in 1950 to honor accountants who have made or are making significant contributions to the advancement of accounting since the 20th century. Many leading American and foreign accountants have been elected to the Hall of Fame. You will find biographies and photographs or drawings of the Hall's members, which you can browse alphabetically or chronologically.

CPA Exam—Accounting Institute Seminars
(http://www.ais-cpa.com)   Accounting Institute Seminars provides CPA review courses. To serve its clientele, it has posted information about changes

to the exams, exam structure and dates, applying to take the exam (with addresses and phone numbers of the state boards of Accountancy, and answers to the last two exams.

Great Ideas for Teaching Accounting

www.swcollege.com/vircomm/gita/gita.html) Thomson Publishing is a $1 billion publisher from elementary to postgraduate education. As part of its commitment to education, Thomson's subsidiary, South-Western College Publishing, developed this site as an exchange for techniques in teaching introductory accounting. You will find ideas for anyone who speaks and teaches, including icebreakers, classroom management tips, and ideas specific to management or financial accounting.

Microsoft's Accounting Industry Page

(http://www.microsoft.com/industry/acc) Microsoft wants to get accountants on its side and provides information to help them and their business partners who would like exposure to the accounting profession. You'll find information on Microsoft-related products, features and articles, new and archived.

U.S. Army Training and Doctrine Command

(http://www.tradoc.monroe.army.mil/irac/index.html) The Office of Internal Review and Audit Compliance (IRAC) has a home page dedicated to its audits and the Internal Review Audit community. The page, which is for unclassified, nonsensitive, nonprivacy act use only, is brought to you by the United States Army Training and Doctrine Command (TRADOC), which is responsible for preparing the army to deal with joint, multinational, and interagency partners across its full range of operations. IRAC provides a full range of professional audit services to the command. You will find documents and links of interest to those in internal review as well as the status of its audits. It should be of special interest to anyone involved in Department of Defense work.

ACCOUNTING SOFTWARE—DEALERS

Looking for accounting software? These dealers may have information to help.

Excelco/Southware Home Page

(http://www.excelco.com/swinfo.html) Excelco of Arizona is a Southware reseller that offers an abundance of information on selecting and implementing accounting software at no charge from this site, including a vendor comparison of 120 packages, a downloadable questionnaire with 1,250 factors to consider, and more.

ACCOUNTING SOFTWARE—DEVELOPERS FOR CPA

Software resources from tax, research, and write-up software developers.

CaseWare's WWW Site

(http://www.caseware.com)   CaseWare is one of the most advanced audit workpaper and reporting packages available. You can find out more about CaseWare Working Papers for Windows and get support at this site.

CCH Incorporated Web Page

(http://www.cch.com, (http://www.prosystemfx.com)   What CPA office is complete without CCH's products? The Master Tax Guide (now in its 82nd edition for 1999!) is almost as important as lunch.

Computer Language Research, Inc.

(http://www.clr.com)   CLR is the home to many software packages in use in a CPA's office.

CPA Software

(http://www.cpasoftware.com)   As the developer of accounting and practice management software used by over 3,000 accounting, consulting, engineering, and legal firms, CPASoftware has customers spanning across the United States and Canada. Firms varying in size from small, sole practitioners to large multioffices, using single-user or network environments empower their practice daily with CPASoftware's suite of products.

Creative Solutions

(http://www.creativesolutions.com)   Since 1979 Creative Solutions has provided integrated tax, accounting, and practice management software designed exclusively for practicing accountants. Creative Solutions is the resting place of PDS Software, Microtique, and AICPA's ATB Software.

Intuit Proseries

(http://www.intuit.com/proseries)   Intuit, one of the leading providers of software for homes and small business, sells a tax preparation line for professionals. You can get (infrequent) tax law updates, get FAQs about the product, and get account information if you are using Intuit's Internet services, the Quicken Financial Network.

Lacerte

(http://www.lacerte.com)   Lacerte has been developing quality tax software for over 20 years. They offer a full complement of federal and state tax preparation software.

MicroVision

(http://www.microvision.com)   MicroVision is a leading developer of software tools and services for accounting professionals. It offers a complete line of cost-effective, easy-to-use, fully integrated software for tax preparation and planning, write-up, trial balance, payroll reporting, sales tax, fixed asset management, and personal financial planning.

SCS/Computer: (http://www.scs.com)
SCS/Compute develops Client Write Up software.

Tax and Accounting Software Corporation: (http://www.taascforce.com)
The CPA-based company was created to offer a fully integrated suite of software tools that would help accounting and tax professionals get far more done in less time. Today the corporation has grown to over 250 employees with a client base of thousands across the country.

Unilink Software, Inc.: (http://www.unilink-inc.com)
Unilink offers Practice Management, Client Write-Up, and General Business Accounting software. The site offers product information and support services.

ACCOUNTING SOFTWARE—DEVELOPERS OF COMMERCIAL PRODUCTS

Whether you are researching accounting software for a client or seeking support, the accounting software developers are coming on-line.

Low-end Software

AAtrix (Mac P&L, Peachtree for Mac):	http://www.aatrix.com
Business Maestro (budgeting):	http://www.planet-corp.com
DacEasy:	http://www.daceasy.com
Intuit, home of Quicken, QuickBooks:	http://www.intuit.com
MTX (Access-based accounting):	http://www.mtxi.com
M.Y.O.B. Accounting (USA):	http://www.bestware.com
New Views (Q.W.Page):	http://www.qwpage.com
Peachtree Software:	http://peachtree.com

Mid-range Software

AccountMate Software Corporation:	http://www.sourcemate.com
Adaytum Budgeting & Planning Software:	http://www.adaytum.com/ USAFrame.htm
Business Systems of America:	http://www.ordersplus.com
Business Vision:	http://www.businessvision.com
CHAMPION BUSINESS SYSTEMS, INC.:	http://www.champbiz. com

Cougar Mountain:	http://www.cougarmtn.com
MICA Accounting Software:	http://micasoft.com
Plus&Minus® Accounting Software:	http://www.talyon. com
SBT Corporation:	http://www.sbt.com
ACCPAC:	http://www.accpac.com
Computer Associates:	http://www.cai.com
CYMA Systems:	http://www.cyma-systems.com
Data Pro Accounting Software:	http://www.dpro.com
FACT Software International Pte Ltd.:	http://www.fact.com.sg
Flagship World Class Managerial Accounting:	http://www.flagsys.com
Flex Ware International LLC:	http://www.flexware.com
Great Plains Software:	http://www.gps.com
Macola Incorporated:	http://www.macola.com
MTX International:	http://www.mtxi.com
Navision:	http://www.navision-us.com
Open Systems:	http://www.osas.com
The Accounting Software Company (formerly known as Platinum):	http://www.platsoft.com
RealWorld Software:	http://www.realworldcorp.com
State of the Art:	http://www.sota.com
Solomon Software:	http://www.solomon.com
SOUTHWARE:	http://www.southware.com
UA Corporate Accounting:	http://www.advancedsoftware. com

High-end Software

BaanSeries:	http://www.baan.com
Computer Associates:	http://www.cai.com
CODA, Inc.:	http://www.coda.com
Comshare (budgeting):	http://www.comshare.com
Design Data Systems:	http://www.designdatasys.com
Dodge Group:	http://www.dodge.com
Dun & Bradstreet Software:	http://www.dbsoftware.com
EXACT INTERNATIONAL (NL):	http://www.exact.nl
FlexiInternational Software:	http://www.flexi.com
FourGen Software:	http://www.fourgen.com
Geac Computer Systems:	http://www.geac.com
Global Software:	http://www.glbsoft.com
Hyperion Software:	http://www.hysoft.com
JD Edwards:	http://www.jdedwards.com

Lifo Systems:	http://www.lifosystems.com
Mesonic:	http://www.mesonic.com/english/IndexE.htm
PeopleSoft:	http://www.peoplesoft.com
Ross Systems:	http://www.rossinc.com
SAP:	http://www.sap.com
SAP R/3:	http://www.sap-ag.de
SCALA International:	http://www.scala.se
Software2000:	http://www.s2k.com
Systems Union:	http://www.systemsunion.com
SQL Financials:	http://www.sqlfinancials.com

Miscellaneous

The Bottom Line:	http://www.butterworths.ca/tbl.htm
FRx Software:	http://www.frxsoft.com
Synchronics:	http://www.sync-link.com
Synex, makers of F9:	http://www.synex.com
TIMESLIPS Corporation:	http://www.timeslips.com
Yardi Systems:	http://www.yardi.com

ACCOUNTING ORGANIZATIONS

Professional associations from around the world.

American Institute of Certified Public Accountants
(http://www.aicpa.org)   The AICPA introduced the Web site in May 1996 and promised a complete makever for the end of 1999.

ANet
(http://www.csu.edu.au/ANetHomePage.html)   A cooperative venture of academic organizations around the world, the ANet seeks to provide a networked, electronic forum of the exchange of information in the broad accounting and auditing discipline. It includes a variety of electronic mail discussion groups and an on-line database of information. It is centered at Charles Sturt University in Australia. Together with the University of Exeter (United Kingdom), the Summa Project, and the Rutgers (New Jersey) Accounting Web (RAW), it is one of the three largest members of the International Accounting Network. (The Swedish School of Economics and Business Administration in Helsinki <http://www.nan.shh.fi> [also known as NAN—the Nordic Accounting Network] and the University of Hawaii <http://soa.cba.hawaii.edu/> are also part of the IAN.) At this site you will find listings of

the mailing lists, accounting organizations, resources for accounting software, courses, people and journals, and links to other sites.

AI/ES Section of AAA
(http://www.bus.orst.edu/faculty/brownc/aies/aieshome.htm)   The American Accounting Association is a largely academic organization of people interested in accounting education and research. This site is the home page of the Artificial Intelligence/ExpertSystems section of the AAA.

Cost Accounting Page/University of Oregon
(http://darkwing.uoregon.edu/ñfargher)   This page from the University of Oregon in Eugene offers notes and articles of interest to cost accountants and additional Web links.

Certified General Accountants' Association of Canada
(http://www.cga-canada.org)   The CGA is one of Canada's leading accounting bodies and a major force in international accounting education. You can review past issues of *CGA Magazine*, review the Canadian federal budget, and communicate with the provincial associations (i.e., state societies) through this site.

CICA/ICCA
English   (http://www.cica.ca/new);   French   (http://www.cica.ca/cica/f_cica.htm)   The Canadian Institute of Chartered Accountants site offers a view of *CA magazine* (classified ads and all!), exposure drafts, emerging issues abstracts, conference and course listings and more. It uses Adobe Acrobat for much of its literature.

Chartered Institute of Mgmt Accts—Ireland
(http://www.icai.ie)   The Home Page of the Charter Institute of Management Accountants in Ireland.

Chartered Institute of Mgmt Accts—UK
(http://www.cima.org.uk/cima)   The Chartered Institute of Management Accountants (CIMA) is the leading United Kingdom professional accountancy body for financial managers.

The Institute of Chartered Accountants of Ontario
(http://www.icao.on.ca)   Representing 30,000 chartered accountants and students, the Institute of Chartered Accountants of Ontario site is relatively new. However, it promises lists of upcoming events, information about the profession, lists of accountants who have passed their examinations, and other information of interest to members and students.

Rutgers Accounting Web
(http://www.rutgers.edu/Accounting/raw.html)   One of the three anchors in the International Accounting Network, RAW has a host of services and

links. It has a small AICPA -oriented page, large sections for the Institute of Management Accountants and the Institute of Internal Auditors, and numerous resources related to the Financial Accounting Standards Board (FASB).

State Societies

Alabama:	http://www.ascpa.org
Arizona	http://www.ascpa.com
Arkansas	http://www.arcpa.org
California	http://www.calcpa.org
Colorado	http://www.cocpa.org
Connecticut	http://www.cs-cpa.org
District of Columbia	http://www.gwscpa.org
Florida	http://www.ficpa.org
Georgia	http://www.gscpa.org
Idaho	http://www.idcpa.org
Illinois	http://www.icpas.org
Indiana	http://www.incpas.org
Iowa	http://www.iacpa.org
Kansas	http://www.kscpa.org
Kentucky	http://www.kycpa.org
Louisiana	http://www.lcpa.org
Maine	http://www.mecpa.org
Maryland	http://www.macpa.org
Massachusetts	http://www.mscpaonline.org
Michigan	http://www.michcpa.org
Mississippi	http://www.ms-cpa.org
Missouri	http://www.mocpa.org
Montana	http://www.mscpa.org
Nevada	http://www.nevadacpa.org
New Hampshire	http://www.nhscpa.org
New Jersey	http://www.njscpa.org
New Mexico	http://www.nmcpa.org
New York	http://www.nysscpa.org
North Carolina	http://www.ncacpa.org
North Dakota	http://www.ndscpa.org
Ohio	http://www.ohioscpa.com
Oklahoma	http://www.oscpa.com
Oregon	http://www.orcpa.org
Pennsylvania	http://www.picpa.org
Puerto Rico	http://www.prccpa.org
Rhode Island	http://www.riscpa.org
South Carolina	http://www.scacpa.org

Tennessee	http://www.tncpa.org
Texas	http://www.tscpa.org
Utah	http://www.uacpa.org
Virginia	http://www.vscpa.com
Washington	http://www.wscpa.org
Wyoming	http://www.wvscpa.org
Wisconsin	http://www.wicpa.org
Wyoming	http://www.wyocpa.org

ACCOUNTING—TAX AND LAW

These sites offer resources for tax professionals.

Barry Rubin's Links to States
(http://www.rubincpa.com)   Barry has come up with a wonderfully succinct list of where to get forms and search the statutes of the states.

Dr. Tax Home Page
(http://www.drtax.ca)   A developer of tax software for the Canadian market, the Dr. Tax page has a good hot list of Canadian governmental and professional resources.

For official IRS Forms and publications, you can go right to the horse's mouth.

IRS
(http://www.irs.gov)   The Internal Revenue Service is on-line, with a series of electronic resources. No more running out at the last minute to find a form—the IRS is open 24 hours a day, 7 days a week with its Digital Daily. Even when the government is closed, the IRS stands ready to serve.

RIAWeb
(http://www.riatax.com)   The Research Institute of America offers one of the nicest news sites for tax preparers available. Its site offers hot weekly news about Washington, D.C., federal, state, and local taxes, pension and benefits, estate planning, and international news. It also promotes its products, offers literature and software downloads, and advertises employment opportunities.

BAR CODE

Sites for consultants working with helping their clients investigate and implement bar coding and other auto-identification technology.

Bar Code/ADC Integrators

(http:mgfx.com/insight)   INSIGHT is an independent support group for users of bar code technology. A number of commercial sponsors in the bar coding and bar code personnel placement fields help sponsor the page and provide product information and job openings. You will find white papers and shareware, an interactive conference area, and more.

Automatic I.D. News

(http://www.autoidnews.com)   One of the most popular trade magazines in the AutoID arena is Automatic I.D. News. This site offers much of the content of the magazine on-line.

PUBLISHERS OF BOOKS AND MAGAZINES

These sites are the homes for book and magazine publishers, and offer news, shareware, and other resources.

Addison Wesley Longman

(http://www.aw.com)   Addison Wesley Longman, home of Addison-Wesley Publishing Company.

Bisk Publishing

(http://www.bisk.com)   Bisk Publishing offers CPA review and CPE materials. The former Totaltape Publishing offers downloadable demonstrations of its computer courseware.

Business Journals

(http://www.amcity.com)   The American City Business Journal publishes business journals in 28 cities in the United States.

Faulkner & Gray

(http://www.faulknergray.com)   Faulkner & Gray offer many publications in the areas of credit card, banking, mortgage, healthcare, accounting, and business strategy. The Accounting Products group has familiar titles like *The Practical Accountant, Accounting Today,* and *Accounting Technology.*

Gleim Publications, Inc.

(http://www.gleim.com/index.html)   Gleim offers knowledge transfer systems (books and software) to help people learn about accounting and aviation.

Harcourt Brace Professional Publishing

(http://hbpp.com)   Harcourt Brace offers many research and advisory resources. Its Web site offers imaginative services like a CPA's *Weekly News Update* service and the top-five Web site designation for accounting-oriented sites.

John Wiley & Sons, Inc., Publishers

(http://www.wiley.com, http://www.wiley.com/Accounting, http://www.wiley.com/cpa)   Modesty prevents us from discussing the excellent, practical, in-depth and helpful services provided by this company.

Macmillan Information Superlibrary

(http://www.mcp.com)   One of the leading publishers of books related to computing and the Internet, the Information Superlibrary offers links, shareware, business search engines, and other resources about the Internet. Read their books on-line.

MIT Press

(http://www-mitpress.mit.edu)   MIT Press is a publisher of computer, educational, and professional books.

Practitioner's Publishing Company

(http://www.ppcinfo.com)   Next to CCH's Master Tax Guide, the PPC family of products is a mainstay of practice. PPC markets its products here, along with an extensive hot list of accounting sites and a Five Minute Update of accounting, auditing, taxation, and disclosure topics.

Prentice Hall

(http://www.prenhall.com/index.html)   Prentice Hall is a leading text and reference publisher. You will find on-line catalogs and shareware to supplement its books. It has search engine to find what you want from the catalog.

Warren Gorham & Lamont

(http://www.wgl.com/acct/acct.html)   Warren Gorham & Lamont is a leading publisher of books and magazines for the accounting profession.

West Publishing

(http://www.westpub.com)   West Publishing is a leading publisher of legal and education materials. And you can find a lawyer.

Online Accounting Publications

Accountancy:	http://www.accountancymag.co.uk
Accounting Professionals Products News:	http://www.cpanews.com
Business Finance Magazine:	http://www.businessfinancemag.com
CA Magazine:	http://www.cica.ca/cica/camagazine.nsf/eCurrent/toc
CFO Magazine:	http://www.cfonet.com
Coopers and Lybrand Tax:	http://www.colybrand.com/tax/tnn/taxpub.html

CPA Journal:	http://www.cpajournal.com
CPA Software News:	http://www.cpasoftwarenews.com
Journal of Accountancy:	http://www.aicpa.org
Management Accounting:	http://www.mamag.com
Tax Practitioners Journal:	http://www.natptax.com
The Accountant's Ledger:	http://www.accountantsledger.com
The Electronic Accountant:	http://www.electronicaccountant.com

BUSINESS AND REFERENCE

This is the reference section of our listings, with business sites and the Institute of Management and Administration (IOMA), one of the most encompassing lists of business management sites.

The Business Traveler Online
(http://www.biztravel.com)   This is the site for biztravel.com, an on-line magazine about business travel. You will find links to travel-related sites and information about traveling to the United States, Canada, United Kingdom, Germany, Japan, and Mexico.

Looking to hire, or be hired? Here are three of the many job marketplaces.
Career Mosaic
(http://www.careermosaic.com)

Career Mart
(http://www.careermart.com)

Intellimatch
(http://www.intellimatch.com)

Dun & Bradstreet
(http://www.dbisna.com)   Dun & Bradstreet lets you search through its business database of U.S.-based businesses and provides on-line access to its *Business Background* reports for $20 per report. In addition, it offers news and business management tips at no cost.

Federal Express
(http://www.fedex.com)   Federal Express has won praise for its web-based package tracker and marketing page. You can download software to print bar coded shipping documents on your laser printer and manage shipping history information, review white papers on how to use logistics as a competitive weapon, or find out where your package is, on-line. For people with e-

mail access only, you can e-mail <track@fedex.com> with "airbill pkgnumber" (substitute the package tracking number for pkgnumber), for up to 20 airbills at a time.

IOMA Business Page

(http://www.ioma.com)   The Institute of Management & Administration (IOMA) page is a marketing center for IOMA's newsletters directed at business, accounting, and other industries. The IOMA guide to business resources is an exhaustive guide to business-related Web sites.

LEXIS-NEXIS

(http://www.lexis-nexis.com)   Accountants have used Lexis/Nexis to do research for some time. Lexis now offers information on the Web, most of it for a nominal fee. In the Small Business area, you can ask a business expert questions on any topic or review pertinent newsgroups at no charge. Want an article on a special topic? You can find previews and then purchase the article on a major credit card, securely, on the Web. In the iMMEDIATE! [*sic*] Answers section, you can get articles on a number of topics, also for a small fee. Lexis-Nexis is a division of Reed Elsevier, Inc.

United Parcel Service

(http://www.ups.com)   It started back in 1907, but UPS was never like this before. You can download tracking software, find out how much shipping a package will cost, track a delivery, and even request pickup by filling out a form on UPS's Web site.

United States Postal Service

(http://www.usps.gov)   Not to be completely outdone, the United States Postal Service has a Web site. It is a philatelist's dream, with pictures of stamps since 1994 on-line as well as zip code and city lookup, rate schedules, and forms and publications.

U.S. Patent and Trademark Office

(http://www.uspto.gov)   Have an idea for a new product? How about a transistor radio embedded in a pair of glasses? Good news. None found. How about a pointing device for a computer? Forty-five patents and counting. You'll find tools for finding and ordering patents and trademark information at this site.

WebWeather

(http://www.princeton.edu/Webweather/ww.html) The University of Michigan provides this site offering weather forecasts throughout the United States and lists cross links of interest in the area requested.

Other Interesting Business Sites.

Employment

Accounting

Accounting.Com:	http://www.accounting.com
AccountingNet:	http://www.accountingnet.com
Accounting and finance jobs for the United Kingdom:	http://www.gaapweb.com
CICA (jobs in Canada):	http://www.cica.ca/camagazine/e_index.htm
Gibson Martin (agency):	http://www.careergoals.com
Robert Half:	http://www.roberthalf.com
Accountant's Bulletin Board:	http://www.computercpa.com/abb.html
KPMG Careers:	http://www.kpmgcareers.com
Tax-Jobs.Com:	http://www.tax-jobs.com

Job hunting resources—General

Monster Board!:	http://www.monster.com
Career Mosaic:	http://www.careermosaic.com/cm
Heart (Career.com):	http://www.career.com:8500
CareerBuilder (used extensively by KPMG):	http://www.careerbuilder.com
Career Magazine:	http://plaza.xor.com:80/careermag
Online Career Center:	http://www.occ.com
QuestMatch:	http://www.questmatch.com
Wall Street Journal Career Site:	http://careers.wsj.com
World Wide Web Employment Service:	http://www.harbornet.com/biz/office/alpha.html
Yahoo!—Business and Economy: Employment: Jobs:	http://www.yahoo.com/yahoo/Business/Employment/Jobs

COMPUTERS

You will find sales support and investment information at the sites of the hardware manufacturers.

Compaq information

(http://www.compaq.com) Compaq is the top-selling computer hardware manufacturer. You can find product information, press releases since 1994, download software support files, review technical manuals, and more.

Dell information

(http://www.dell.com)   Dell is one of the most popular mail order and retail-oriented hardware manufacturers and is proud to point out that it is used by 5 of the Big 5. You can find out about its products and services, check out the status of your order, and get technical support from the site. Dell takes a very corporate angle to its site.

Gateway information

(http://www.gateway.com)   Gateway is a popular mail order computer manufacturer. You will find a product configurator to pick out the features you want and find out how much it costs, shareware, technical literature, and more.

International Business Machines (IBM)

(http://www.ibm.com, (http://www.software.ibm.com)   IBM is a major player in hardware, software, and the Internet. It has a multitude of Web sites for different aspects of the business.

Micron

(http://www.micron.com)   Micron is another mail order computer company, offering sales and support on the Web.

DATABASES

Database administrators and developers will find numerous resources online.

Pervasive, makers of Btrieve

(http://www.pervasive.com) Btrieve is the database used by most accounting software companies aimed at small to medium-size businesses. Pervasive's page offers marketing information about Btrieve, Tango, its other products, conferences, and employment opportunities.

DBMS Magazine

(http://www.dbmsmag.com)   DBMS is a magazine devoted to database technology. Anyone interested in report writers, data access tools, and electronic commerce (tying databases to the Internet) will find helpful information here.

MSACCESS Section

(http://coyote.csusm.edu/cwis/winworld/msaccess.html)   California State University, San Marcos, has a large shareware archive with an excellent section on Microsoft Access, a popular tool used by accountants.

Tony's Main Microsoft Access Page

(http://www.agt.net/public/ttoews/accsmstr.htm)   More resources for user of Microsoft Access.

EDI, ISO, MANUFACTURING, AND ELECTRONIC COMMERCE

If your business involves electronic data intercharge or ISO 9000, or you need help keeping up with electronic commerce and manufacturing philosophies, these sites can help.

APICS
(http://www.apics.org)   The American Production and Inventory Control Society (APICS) is the primary professional organization for inventory management professionals.

CommerceNet
(http://www.commerce.net)   CommerceNet is a nonprofit consortium of businesses and organizations with interests in electronic commerce. Its members are involved in developing an "industrial-strength" infrastructure for electronic commerce, trying to determine what the return on investment is in e-commerce, and setting up pilot projects for EDI on the Internet, catalogs, small business connectivity, and other aspects of electronic business. The electronic commerce jumpstation is an excellent starting point for learning about authentication, EDI resources, payment methods, security, and other issues of interest in tomorrow's business.

Cybercash
(http://www.cybercash.com)   One of the leading companies involved in the Secure Internet Payment System (electronic cash) field. Cybercash's relationships with organizations like America Online, Checkfree, CompuServe, and Netscape mean a strong short-term future. Cybercash involves an electronic wallet (currently on Windows PCs), merchant software, and communications with Cybercash itself.

Department of Defense Electronic Data Interchange Standards
(http://www.itsi.disa.mil/edi/edi-main.html)   The Department of Defense maintains this site with information on being a business partner with the government and the EDI standards in use.

Edupage: News items on IT
(http://www.educom.edu)   Edupage is a Washington, D.C.-based consortium of colleges and universities seeking to transform education through the use of information technology. The Edupage offers daily IT news items on the Web or by mailing list.

IBM Software Manufacturing Solutions Home Page
(http://ps.boulder.ibm.com)   IBM's page aimed at manufacturing systems.

Welcome to ISO Online
(http://www.iso.ch/welcome.html)   The home page of the International Organization for Standards (ISO).

ISO 14000 InfoCenter

(http://www.iso14000.com)   ISO 14000 deals with environmental reporting, the next great reporting requirements. Brought to you by the Environmental Industry Web site, published by Extended Marketing, Inc., a digital marketing consulting firm.

ISO 9000 Forum

(http://www.iso.ch/9000e/forum.html)   The International Standards Organization's information on ISO 9000.

Verifone

(http://www.verifone.com)   Best known for its credit card swipe devices found in retail stores, banks, and many other sites (5 million around the world), Verifone brings knowledge of transaction automation to the Internet by relationships with Cybercash and other electronic payment providers.

GOVERNMENT RESOURCES

The U.S. Government offers tremendous resources online.

Fedmart Home Page

(http://www.fedmart.com/)   Advanced Engineering and Research Associates (AERA), Inc., is a large training, engineering and logistics supply company with offices across the United States, dealing largely with the U.S. Navy and NASA. It has compiled a page of links for the government and with links to government sites.

FedWorld Information Network

(http://www.fedworld.gov)   The National Technical Information Service (NTIS) set up the Fedworld Information Network to provide a one-stop location for the public to find, order, and have delivered to them U.S. government information. Over 130 sites can be accessed.

FinanceNet WWW Home Page

(http://www.financenet.gov)   The mission of FinanceNet is to innovate and optimize the way governments manage and account for taxpayer resources. It is staffed by volunteers and associated with Vice President Gore's office. FinanceNet offers its Web site, listservers, electronic document libraries (gopher), Usenet discussion forums, and real-time conferences and meetings. Want to buy a Jeep for $50? You'll find government asset sales posted here.

FSTC Home Page

(http://www.fstc.org)   Financial Services Technology Consortium is a consortium of financial services providers, national laboratories, universities and government agencies working on interbank technical projects. Electronic commerce and fraud prevention and control are important topics.

IGNet—Inspector General's Office

(http://www.sbaonline.sba.gov/ignet/ig.html)   The IG Community consists of the Office of the Inspector General, who conducts inspections and investigations in more than 60 federal agencies as well as their peers in state and local governments, education, and the private sector. You'll find audit information, mailing lists, and a virtual library of links to related sites.

The National Performance Review

(http://sunsite.unc.edu/npr/nptoc.html)   The Clinton administration's mission to make government work better and cost less.

The New York State Assembly

(http://assembly.state.ny.us);   (gopher://assembly.state.ny.us)   Everything you want to know about the New York State Assembly, desperately in need of a good search engine. You can get e-mail addresses, biographies and pictures of your assembly members, and even tour the State Capitol. In addition, there is access (through telnet) to the current proceedings.

Occupational Safety and Health Administration Home Page

(http://www.osha.gov)   The U.S. Department of Labor maintains the OSHA Home Page. It offers expert system software, publications, standards and regulations, and links to safety and health related links.

The Small Business Administration

(http://www.sbaonline.sba.gov)   The U.S. Small Business Administration (SBA) offers assistance to small and growing businesses. Founded by Congress in 1953, the SBA's mission is to be the champion of the entrepreneur. The SBA site was designed to offer financing, training, and advocacy for small firms. There is also a shareware library with over 500 programs to help start, finance, or expand a business, including contact management and accounting software for many vertical industries.

U.S. House of Representatives Home Page

(http://www.house.gov)   Home to the U.S. code and links to other legal resources, public access to legislative information and the legislators.

The House of Representatives—Internet Law Library—
Computers and the law

(http://www.pls.com:8001/his/95.htm)   Another home to the U.S. code and an excellent collection of links to resources to let you know about the law and how it relates to computer use.

Securities and Exchange Commission

(http://www.sec.gov)

Edgar

(http://www.sec.gov/edgarhp.html)   Another excellent tool for anyone who can benefit from on-line SEC filings, such as 10-Ks and 10-Qs.

THOMAS: Legislative Information on the Internet

(http://thomas.loc.gov)   If you can benefit from keeping track of or searching through the floor action, debate, or hearings of the fighting 103rd and 104th Congresses, this gem of a site will make your day. A tremendous resource for planning.

U.S. Business Advisor

(http://www.business.gov)   Another excellent set of resources for business from our president and vice president.

The White House

(http://www.whitehouse.gov)   Tour the White House and find links to other governmental resources.

INTERNET—GENERAL

Search engines, Internet organizations and other resources are offered here.

All 4 One Search Machine; Results of four Web search engines side by side:

(http://easypage.com/all4one)   A multiple search engine search tool.

Archie Gateway

(http://www.4windsor.ca/archie.html)   Archie software lets you find files at ftp sites. From a command prompt, Archie can be difficult to work with. From this site, you can enter your search parameters into the form and let it do the work.

Backstage Internet: The Hard Part

(http://www.bluesky.net/rcn/backstage.html)   How to be a deliverer of Internet services.

BOBAWORLD Searchers

(http://gagme.wwa.com/~boba/search.html)   Lots of search engines all in one place.

Business@Web—Virtual Internet Conference

(http://www.busweb.com)   Keeping up on the Internet without ever leaving home.

Deja

(http://www.deja.com)   Specializing in searching USENET newsgroups. Your ISP probably keeps a week or two at most of historical postings. Deja keeps it as long as its hard drives hold out, and buys more hard drives if necessary.

HotBot

(http://www.hotbot.com)   A highly publicized search engine.

InfoSeek search engine

(http://www.infoseek.com)   The author's favorite Internet search engine.

inquiry.com—Home Page

(http://www.inquiry.com)   Information for programmers about software, development, and emerging technology.

Internet Audit Bureau

(http://www.internet-audit.com)   An independent verifier of visits to Web sites.

Internet Mail Consortium

(http://www.imc.org)   For the latest news relating to e-mail standards, check out this site.

Internet Society Home Page

(http://www.isoc.org/indextxt.html)   The Internet Society is one of the few accepted authorities in the coordination of global cooperation and coordination for the Internet and its internetworking technologies and applications. From here you can find the names of all the organizations who think they are in charge.

iWorld Information Desk

(http://www.iworld.com)   Internet news and views from one of the primary publishers and trade show sponsors specializing on the Internet.

Juno (free e-mail!)

(http://www.juno.com)   Juno offers free e-mail. Every message will have advertising stuck on it, and you do not have all the functionality of the more sophisticated e-mail programs, but it is free.

Lycos

(http://www.lycos.com)   Provides seaches, home pages, and much more.

Netscape Netcenter

(http://www.netscape.com)   A must-see page for all Internet users. Has the latest news from the envelope-pushing Web masters and links to resources of all kinds. The place the Web comes together.

SavvySearch

(http://www.savvysearch.com)   Sends your search request through multiple search engines simultaneously. Offers searches through search engines for the Web, people, news, software, images, and other types of information.

SIFT/InReference

(http://www.reference.com)   Stanford University provided a great service called SIFT (Stanford Information Filters Tool). It filtered through USENET listings looking for articles that met your requirements automatically and sent them daily to your e-mail address at no charge. Stanford transferred the SIFT service to a commercial concern, InReference, and it has not been the same since.

WAIS Search: Multiple Sources

(http://sunsite.unc.edu/cgi-bin/fwais.pl)   Web-based WAIS search tool.

The URL-minder: Your Own Personal Web Robot!

(http://www.netmind.com/URL-minder/URL-minder.html)   Some Web pages change on a daily basis and warrant a regular look-see. Others, such as the author's, have great resources but merit a new look when there is a change. With the URL-minder, you can get e-mail when a page of interest changes.

WAIS Inc.

(http://www.wais.com)   If you are interested in WAIS searching, this is the home of WAIS.

Yahoo!

(http://www.yahoo.com)   Yahoo provides a topical and key word search of the Internet and much, much more!

INTERNET—ODDITIES

The Internet is filled with Virtual worlds—and cameras pointing at real ones—this item of curiosity is purely Internet.

Interesting Devices on the Net

(http://www.pitt.edu/~sbrst4/html.camtitle)   A little odd, perhaps, but you can find cameras pointed at the most unusual things at this site.

INTERNET—SECURITY

The number-one fear of most people is the lack of privacy and security on the Internet, especially when it comes to doing business.

Additional Security Information

(http://www.iss.net/iss/addsec.html)   Internet Security Systems, Inc. provides a page of security links.

BBN Planet Crop

(http://www.bbn.com)   Discussions on security and other important issues to business are mixed with the information about BBN Planet.

CERT
(http://www.cert.org)   The focal point for security concerns of Internet users.

National Security Institute, Security Resource Net
(http://nsi.org/textonly.html)   A robust collection of information about security, Internet and otherwise.

RSA Data Security, Inc.'s Home Page
(http://www.rsa.com)   RSA's encryption is included in most commercial security standards. The RSA site is a good source of security, privacy, and encryption information.

INTERNET—WINSOCK AND WORLD WIDE WEB–SPECIFIC RESOURCES

Want to learn how to make a Web page? Here are tutorials, background information, and the future of the Web

A Beginner's Guide to HTML
(http://ctrhp3.unican.es/HTMLprogramming/primer.html)   Why buy a book? A complete tutorial about designing Web pages.

Doctor HTML
(http://imagiware.com/RxHTML.cgi)   Think when you create a Web page the job is over? Doctor HTML will let you know how good a job you did, checking it for proper coding, live links, and other tests.

The PostMaster—Announce Your URL Everywhere!
(http://www.netcreations.com/postmaster)   How do you get people to see your Web page? Do not be a needle in a haystack! Use the PostMaster to get your URL into search engines, 350 Web directories, media outlets, and what's new and what's cool lists—for $500. A free service gets you into 25 Web sites and search engines.

Real
(http://www.real.com)   Interested in listening to your favorite radio station when you are 1,000 miles from home? Real is the home to one of the most widespread streaming audio servers and players. With RealPlayer, you can listen to the radio on your computer. There is a large amount of RealAudio materials, from ABC news, PBS, the major computer publications, major radio stations, churches, and more.

W3C (World Wide Web Consortium)
(http://www.w3.org/pub/WWW)   No listing of Web sites would be complete without the home page of home pages—the World Wide Web Consor-

tium's own page. You will find the background of the Web, its direction of, software for it, and how to get involved with Web developers.

INVESTMENTS

As traditional brokers have found out, there are tremendous resources for investors online.

The American Stock Exchange—The Smarter Place to Be
(http://www.amex.com)   The first stock market on the Web, AMEX offers market updates, news, company backgrounds, and even videos of life on the floor.

Hoover's Online
(http://www.hoovers.com) Get quotes, market reports, and review Hoover's Online and DBC Online. Some services have a charge, some don't.

NASDAQ Exchange Information
(http://www.nasdaq.com) Keep up with the activity and companies of NASDAQ listed companies on the official NASDAQ site.

New York Stock Exchange
(http://www.nyse.com)   Keep up with the activity and companies of NYSE-listed companies on the official NYSE site.

Quarterly earnings reports
(http://web.usatoday.com/money/mds4.htm) *USA Today* offers some excellent resources; among them is this listing of the quarterly earning reports of some 200 public companies and links to other pages of corporate information.

R.R. Donnelley & Sons Financial Homepage
(http://www.rrdfin.com)   Donnelley Financial offers links and marketing information.

Welcome to TermFinance
(http://Finance.Wat.ch/TermFinance)   A four-language introduction to derivative instruments.

LAW

Want to be a legal scholar? You'll find many additional legal resources here.

Law—Topics in Law—Search our Legal Resources
(http://www.usalaw.com/topics.html)   Links to legal resources.

MAILING LIST ARCHIVES

Mailing lists aren't always available on the Web, but you can find some archives with backlists of discussions of the business use of the Internet.

ANETDEV-L: On-Line Services archives
(http://www.rutgers.edu/Accounting/anet/lists/anetdev-l) A popular discussion group on accounting and on-line services; you can review the archive of previous discussions.

DIVERSIONS (AFTER TAX SEASON)—MOVIES, TELEVISION, ENTERTAINMENT

We can't work all the time. On-line you'll see where television networks strut their stuff along with sports, *Star Trek,* and Dilbert.

ABC Television Home Page
(http://www.abctelevision.com) Follow your favorite ABC television productions and get a head start on the new season at the ABC home page.

Ad Age—**Facts and Features—50 Best Commercials**
(http://www.adage.com/Features/Commercials) A veritable marketing course, covering the best commercials of all time.

CBS Television Home Page
(http://www.cbs.com) Follow your favorite CBS television productions and get a head start on the new season at the CBS home page. Top draw—the David Letterman top 10 lists.

The Dilbert Zone
(http://www.unitedmedia.com/comics/dilbert) The popular cartoon that hits business management (an oxymoron?) head on, you can follow the comic strip "Dilbert," even if it is not available in your area.

ESPN
(http://espn.go.com) Home to sports.

Welcome to Fox
(http://foxnetwork.com) Follow your favorite Fox television productions and get a head start on the new season at the Fox home page.

NBC Television Home Page
(http://www.nbc.com) Follow your favorite NBC television productions and get a head start on the new season at the NBC home page. Top draw— previews of shows for the next few weeks.

NEWS AND MAGAZINE SEARCH TOOLS

Find out what has been written about that mail order company before you place your order!

Computer Article Database from CMP

(http://www.techweb.com)   If you want to find current articles on computer and computer-industry topics, you can search through this rich database of articles from one of the premier technology publishers.

New York Times Computer News Daily

(http://nytsyn.com)   The *New York Times* has a number of sites offering free and for-fee news.

c l net online front door

(http://www.cnet.com)   A source for computer news with practical implications. A computer magazine on the Web.

CNN Web

(http://www.cnn.com)   Up-to-the-minute news from CNN at your fingertips.

DBMS Magazine

(http://www.dbmsmag.com)

Internet Systems

(http://www.internetsystems.com)   Anyone responsible for database development, reporting, or tying corporate databases to the Internet will benefit from the resources at these sites.

IDG

(http://www.idg.com)

Welcome to InfoWorld

(http://www.infoworld.com)

Welcome to PC World Online

(http://www.pcworld.com)   IDG is a major publisher in the computer industry. This site offers resources from computer publications *InfoWorld, PC World, @Computerworld,* and more. *InfoWorld* is one of the most respected printed weekly computer publications. Searching through the publications is an excellent way to research software, hardware, and companies.

Mobile Office on the Web

(http://www.mobileoffice.com)   For users of laptops, notebook computers, personal digital assistants, and cellular phones, this site offers advice and links to other sites of interest.

The Wall Street Journal Interactive Edition

(http://www.wsj.com)   Dow Jones, which has a proprietary database for investors, is now trying to figure out how to put the venerable *Wall Street Journal* on-line in bits and pieces, some for free, some for their subscribers, and others for a fee.

PC Magazine Online

(http://www.pcmag.com)

PC Week

(http://www.pcweek.com)

Welcome to ZD net

(http://www.zdnet.com) Ziff Davis offers a broad range of computer-related publications. This site offers a wide variety of news, software, advice, full-text searches through its publications. *PC Magazine* is known for its authoritative reviews of accounting software.

Philadelphia Online

(http://www.phillynews.com) Making a trip to the City of Brotherly Love? Catch up on what's happening by reading the *Enquirer* and the *Daily News* on-line—even the funnies.

Welcome to U.S.News Online

(http://www.USNews.com) Read the weekly newsmagazine, link to the sponsors' Web sites, catch breaking news before it is published, and provide feedback to the editors.

ON-LINE SERVICES AND NATIONAL ISPS

Most of the on-line service providers prefer to talk to you on-line—that's a bit like reporting power outages on television. Find out what's up at your ISP or find a new one.

America Online

(http://www.aol.com)

CompuServe

(http://www.compuserve.com)

The two remaining online services—both owned by America Online.

ISPs That Folks Like and Dislike . . . and Why

(http://www.access.digex.net/~mcgatney/isprate.html) A clearinghouse for praise and complaints on the ISPs.

AT&T WorldNet

(http://www.att.com/worldnet/)

Mindspring

(http://www.mindspring.com)

PSINet

(http://www.psi.net) News, links, support, and the opportunity to pull down their latest software or subscribe to their business or individual services.

PEOPLE AND BUSINESS LISTINGS (WHITE AND YELLOW PAGES)

One of the most useful and scariest areas of the Internet. You can find people and companies and know more about them than they may care for you to know.

555-1212.com
(http://www.555-1212.com)   A business listing service that acts like a telephone book.

AT&T's Searchable 800 Directory
(http://att.net/dir800/), (http://www.tollfree.att.net)   Find a company's 800 or 888 number quickly on the Internet (if their number is AT&T's).

BigYellow (NYNEX Interactive Yellow Pages)
(http://www.bigyellow.com)   Find companies by name, type of business and location. Sixteen million businesses listed. Incredible.

BigBook Directory Search
(http://www.bigbook.com)   A business Yellow Pages, with street-level locations (maps) of 11 million businesses. You have a home page on BigBook, which you can modify at no cost, if you are currently listed in a Yellow Pages phone book.

Bigfoot Home Page
(http://www.bigfoot.com)   E-mail white pages.

Four11
(http://www.four11.com)   Six and a half million residential listings on-line.

Internet Address Finder
(http://www.iaf.net)   E-mail white pages.

Searchable the World Yellow Pages Network
(http://wyp.net/Search.html)   Every U.S. and Canadian residential and commercial listing, with maps and free home pages. Going to visit someone? Get a map, lists of restaurants nearby, and more. The ultimate research tool.

Switchboard: Find a Person
(http://www.switchboard.com)   Ninety million residences and 10 million businesses. Complete.

WhoWhere?
(http://whowhere.com)   A comprehensive site for finding people and companies on the Internet and traditional phone and addresses. Finds people based on names listed in the phone book. Banyan System's site is rather complete, and it will remove your listing, if you ask.

SOFTWARE—SHAREWARE

Shareware is legitimate. Most of the software you will want for the Internet is shareware or freeware.

Browse CICA Archives
(http://www.nova.edu/Inter-Links/cica/browse.html), (http://www.cica.indiana.edu)   One of the most extensive collections of shareware, fixes, fonts, and other software resources is found at the Center for Innovative Computer Applications at Indiana University, Bloomington. The site is often busy, and many times mirror sites (duplicates at other organizations) are the only way to get at the resources.

McAfee
(http://www.mcafee.com)   Antivirus software available when you need it.

DEC ftp msdos directory
(ftp://gatekeeper.dec.com/pub/micro/msdos)

Exec-PC—World's Largest BBS
(http://execpc.com/lynxindex.html)

Jumbo!—Business
(http://www.jumbo.com/bus)

Microsoft Library
(http://library.microsoft.com)

OAK Software Repository
(http://www.acs.oakland.edu/oak.html)

Welcome to shareware.com
(http://www.shareware.com)

Stroud's CWSApps List—Windows 95/NT Apps
(http://www.wlyn.com/stroud/cwsa.html)

Walnut Creek CD ROM Web, ftp site
(ftp://ftp.cdrom.com)

Windows95.com
(http://www.windows95.com)

Windows Utility Report
(http://www.chorus.cycor.ca/U_report/wwur.html)   Shareware, graphics, FAQs and more.

SOFTWARE—COMMERCIAL

If you need software fixes, updates and add-ons, take a look at the Web sites of leading commercial software vendors.

Accounting: Microsoft Industry Marketing Info

(http://www.microsoft.com/industry)   Microsoft supports its business partners by highlighting their products on these pages of interest to accountants.

Lotus information

(http://www.lotus.com)   Lotus, now part of IBM, makes the most news these days for Lotus Notes, its groupware product that is facing a battle with the Internet itself. Finding information on 1-2-3 is next to impossible (check under SmartSuite). All Lotus products will be Internet enabled.

Microsoft Corporation W

(http://www.microsoft.com)   The place to go for information about Microsoft's products and free Internet software developed by Microsoft.

NetWare Connection Web Site

(http://www.nwconnection.com)   Companies using Novell NetWare may find helpful resources on the pages of *NetWare Connection,* a magazine devoted to Netware and Novell user groups. You'll find archives of their articles, shareware archives, discussion bulletin boards, and links to sites of interest.

Novell

(http://www.novell.com)   Home to the marketing and support of Novell Incorporated, developers of Novell NetWare.

Welcome to WordPerfect (Corel)

(http://www.wordperfect.com/), (http://www.corel.com)   WordPerfect is another office mainstay. Perhaps you didn't know that WordPerfect was bought by Novell and then sold to Corel? You can get up-to-date news, product information, tips from *WordPerfect Magazine,* and join discussion groups for support and tips.

From Here . . .

Chapter 11 covers international issues.

International Issues

If your company conducts business internationally, or if you are interested in expanding your business internationally, you will find a wealth of resources on the Internet. This chapter highlights some sites that may be of interest. It is not meant to be an endorsement of any organization.

The following outline summarizes the contents of this chapter.

- *Professional Society Use:* CPAs, chartered accountants, and management accountants—you will find many resources by and for accountants around the world listed in this section.

- *Internet and Communication:* It is tying people together from around the world. A few things need to be worked out, though. Find out what in this section.

- *Leads and Financing:* This section illustrates many resources for finding international business partners and arranging funding.

- *Coming to an Understanding*: Language and customs are challenges in international operations. This section offers tools to deal with the challenges.

- *Getting Down to Business:* How can you keep up with politics, civil unrest, and hooligans and track down resources for international rules and regulations? This section points you to help.

- *Electronic Commerce:* This section discusses EDI and ISO 9000 resources.

- *More links:* This section lists miscellaneous resources that may be helpful.

PROFESSIONAL SOCIETY USE

If you read professional publications from around the world, you will find greater coverage than in U.S. accounting publications. Most countries have accepted the Internet and computer technology at a far faster pace than U.S. organizations. Perhaps it is the opportunity to get information from the United States years earlier than before. One way or the other, groups in Australia, Canada, Ireland, and the United Kingdom have quickly established themselves on the Internet.

The following lists provide some sites related to accounting around the world.

Canada

Canada is also embracing the information superhighway, also known as L'Autoroute Electronique.

Accountants in Canada Directory
http://www.cusimano.com/dir/accnt/index.html

AccountNet Guide
http://www.morochove.com/netguide

The Bottom Line monthly accounting publication
http://www.butterworths.ca/tbl.htm

Can-AccTech (the accounting technology discussion forum for Canadians):
http://www.morochove.com/canacctech

The Canadian Institute of Chartered Accountants
http://www.cica.ca

CA-Xchange
http://www.cax.org

CCH Canada (lists Canadian tax and accounting sites)
http://www.ca.cch.com/frsub7.html

Certified General Accountants' Association of Canada
http://www.cga-canada.org

The Institute of Chartered Accountants of Ontario
http://www.icao.on.ca

International Federation of Accountants (worldwide accountancy group):
http://www.ifac.org

Montreal Stock Exchange
http://www.mse.org

Revenue Canada (the government department responsible for administering Canadian tax, border, and trade policy):
http://www.revcan.ca

Toronto Stock Exchange
http://www.tse.com

Vancouver Stock Exchange
http://www.vse.com

United Kingdom

The home of accountancy is actively on the Internet.

Accountants through Internet
http://www.netaccountants.com

Chartered Institute of Management Accountants—UK
http://cima.org.uk

Home Page for UK taxes
http://www.open.gov.uk/inrev/irhome.htm

Institute of Chartered Accountants in England and Wales
http://www.icaew.co.uk

Institute of Financial Accountants
http://www.ifa.org.uk

Offshore.net (link to accountants)
http://www.offshore.net/accs.htm

Australia

Australian Society of CPAs
http://www.cpaonline.com.au

Ireland

The Institute of Chartered Accountants in Ireland
http://www.icai.ie

Other Resources

Accounting Web
http://www.accountingweb.co.uk/links/index.html

Hugo Schouten CPA Index
http://www.ozemail.com.au/~dutch

International Accounting Standards Board (International committee to bring into closer conformity global financial accounting and reporting standards)
http://www.rutgers.edu/Accounting/raw/fei/feisite/fei/about/iasc.html

International business resources on the World Wide Web
http://ciber.bus.msu.edu/busres.htm

List of CPA firms—World
http://www.cpafirms.com

INTERNET AND COMMUNICATION

Many companies have found that the Internet is the key to developing relationships with foreign partners. Previously telephone bills and travel time and costs made exploring and maintaining relationships prohibitively expensive. Providing toll-free (800) phone numbers and 24-hour-a-day technical support for international customers can be a burden too heavy for smaller businesses. The Internet explosion has opened new channels of communication between businesses around the world.

At 186,000 miles per second, information can be transferred around the world instantly and inexpensively, breaking down barriers of geography and cost. Support questions can be left and responded to electronically during normal business hours. Time barriers are also broken down by e-mail and other workgroup communication tools.

You can speak and hear each other talk on the Internet using tools like Microsoft's NetMeeting.

Of course, if you want to travel, you will find that all of the major hotel chains and airlines make reservations and scheduling available on the Internet. Microsoft's Expedia (http://expedia.msn.com), Travelocity (http://www.travelocity.com), and any number of other resources will help you book your trips.

If there is a problem with using the Internet for international communication, it is that access to computers and full Internet access can be limited internationally. The costs of Internet access can be high, computers are not as prevalent in the home, and access to on-line services and the Internet is limited outside of the major urban areas. However, America Online's foreign subsidiaries are growing, and other Internet Service Providers are tapping into foreign markets. In some areas of Europe, Internet access is free, as Europeans know the per-minute charges of normal calls can be prohibitive.

LEADS AND FINANCING

In the past, finding a foreign buyer or partner was very difficult. Now many resources are available to find prospective trading partners and to find the financing to make the deal happen. Potential partners for international trade can be found in many places. On USENET (network news), you will find many offers from businesses and organizations looking to make contact with trading partners. Tip clubs for trading leads have sprung up as well. Perhaps the greatest resource is the U.S. government itself, which has many Web sites dedicated to helping U.S. businesses expand their businesses overseas. These sites include:

- Department of Agriculture's Foreign Agriculture Service (FAS Online) (http://www.fas.usda.gov) This site includes information about U.S. exporter assistance, export programs, trade policy, trade data and analysis, foreign market research, and ongoing news releases and product announcements.

- International Trade Administration (http://www.ita.doc.gov/itahome. html) The U.S. Department of Commerce/International Trade Administration (ITA) is dedicated to helping U.S. businesses compete in the global marketplace. It has an extensive site with information about imports and exports, trade statistics, and services.

- The Small Business Administration (http://www.sbaonline.sba.gov) Among the SBA's services to help small businesses expand are counseling by international trade experts, training sessions and publications, and services to link U.S. firms with potential foreign buyers.

- U.S. Census Foreign Trade Status (http://www.census.gov/foreign-trade) The census Bureau offers a wide variety of foreign trade statistics and reports online.

- United States Trade Representative's Home-Page (http://www.ustr.gov) The U.S. Trade Representative represents services from the executive branch to help businesses with foreign trade. The Office of the U.S. Trade Representative (USTR) is responsible for developing and coordinating U.S. international trade, commodity, and direct investment policy, and leading or directing negotiations with other countries on such matters.

- World Bank (http://www.worldbank.org) The World Bank is a primary financing source. There are many other sources of leads and financing, including the Trade Desk at <http://users.aol. com/tradedesk/trade.html>.

COMING TO AN UNDERSTANDING

Do you know what you are getting into? If you have a Web presence reaching out to potential trading partners outside of North America, you may wish to strongly consider localizing your pages for your audiences. If you have more than 1,000 to 1,500 hits a week, it would probably be worth your while to speak in their language and with their customs.

If you have ever tried to tell a joke to someone from another country, you know how much cultures can differ. Yes, there are people who do not know who Michael Jordan is. Banner ads may get you 8 cents per click-through but take up expensive on-line time.

Once you have a lead, you need to be able to understand each other. Language and cultural differences now come to play.

Although English is arguably the language of the Internet (to the chagrin of many), communication often requires the use of an interpreter. Short of hiring your own interpreter, you will find product offerings from real-time translation services to software that integrates with the Internet for rough automatic translations. The U.S. Army maintains a resource of commercial language vendor sites at its home page called LingNet, found at <http://lingnet.army.mil/comm.htm>.

The Alta Vista search engine offers free, easy translation of phrases and Web pages using its Babelfish technology, another reference to *The Hitchhiker's Guide to the Galaxy* (http://babelfish.altavista.digital.com/cgi-bin/translate). Like the hero, you too can have help in reading and translating documents from and to many languages. Want to see roughly what the Accountant's Home Page would look like in French? (See Exhibit 11.1.)

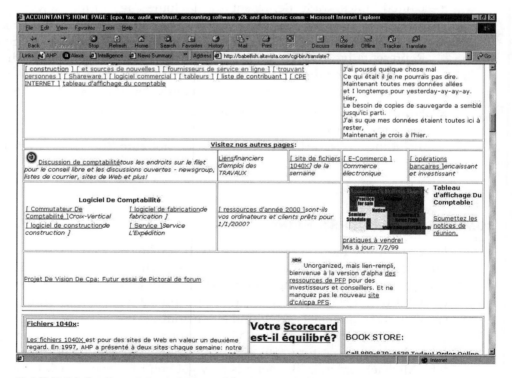

Exhibit 11.1   French translation of Accountant's Home Page.

Can you display your data in your foreign trading partner's or prospects' language? The Unicode group at <http://www.unicode.org> may give you some guidance. It is hard enough to speak in their language. Still, disasters like the introduction of the Chevy Nova into Spanish-speaking culture (nova = "It doesn't run") or Coca Cola into Japan ("Bites the wax tadpole") show some of the problems that arise with language. Also, Spanish in Argentina is not Spanish in Mexico is not Spanish in Spain. Alta Vista's search engine offers free translation services between many major languages through their web site. Note, however, that a professional's services will beat Alta Vista's for translation and may save your dignity.

In addition to language differences, differences in customs can be critical. It is vitally important that businesses understand cultural differences in the international business environment. Among the resources available to help in this area is the Web of Culture at <http://www.webofculture.com>.

It is harder to speak in others' culture. Consider local customs, laws, and even history. Saying one inventor is responsible for an invention when another country credits a local can cause problems. Social and moral issues, history, and religion must be considered for success. What is common one place is scandalous another, as anyone who watches the endless parade of television shows about commercials understands. Help is available from the Localization Industry Standards Association (http://www.lisa.org).

Privacy is a huge issue overseas. Unlike the United States, where everyone seems willing to disclose highly detailed information for the chance for a prize, the European Economic Union is using a strong arm to make sure that the privacy of its citizenry is being respected. Check out I*M Europe (http://www2.echo.lu). Of course, clever European companies can just set up a server in the United States.

If you are successful, you may want foreign customers to buy something. How are you going to get them to pay? Credit cards? Debit cards?

Then there is shipping. Visit the Bureau of Export Administration at <http://www.bxa.doc.gov.>.

GETTING DOWN TO BUSINESS

Doing business internationally is further complicated by economics, political unrest, and differing national rules and regulations. The Internet is a vital resource for breaking through societal and governmental barriers to find new opportunities for business growth.

An extensive set of links, entitled International Law and International Trade Links, has been compiled by Braumiller & Rodriguez, L.L.C., Attorneys. The links provide information about trade oriented to the North

American Free Trade Agreement countries; Asia, Japan, and Australia; Europe and Russia; international trade contacts and leads; U.S. government sites; the United Nations; and more. Their site is at <http://www.exportimport.law>.

A bit of caution is always in order. The *CIA World Factbook* lets you research the economic and political condition of other countries. Many organizations link to the factbook: <http://www.odci.gov/cia/publications/factbook/index.html>. If things are unsettled, you can also review the CIA's Home Page for Kids (http://www.odci.gov).

ELECTRONIC COMMERCE

You can communicate and understand each other. Now you must be able to do business together and share business document with each other efficiently. Two areas you will need help with are ISO 9000 and Electronic Data Interchange (EDI).

Many European companies cannot conduct business with you unless you are certified for ISO 9000. The home of ISO 9000, the International Organization for Standards (ISO), is found on-line at http://www.iso.ch/.

You can find many sources for information about EDI. One excellent source is http://www.harbinger.com.

MORE LINKS

The Octagon Technology Group (Illinois) (http://www.otginc.com) has services for companies hoping to use the Internet for international electronic commerce. Its Web site has a page of links that will be of interest to those doing international business.

The author's Web site (http://www.computercpa.com) has an extensive set of links for accounting and finance, including many that are internationally oriented and EDI/EC related.

From Here . . .

The appendix provides a glossary of terms.

Glossary

@: What goes between a user's name and the domain name in an e-mail address. For example: *eric@computercpa.com.* Pronounced "at."

AUP (acceptable use policy): Refers to policies established to inform and educate how to best use the tools.

ACTIVEX: Microsoft's attempt to create a cross-platform programming language for the Internet.

ACROBAT (from Adobe): A program that lets you prepare documents that, when read with ACROBAT Reader, will look the same on any computer. The IRS lets you pull down forms and publications with Adobe.

ADSL (asymmetric digital subscriber line): A very fast connection to the Internet using standard phone lines. It is asymmetric because the upload and download speeds are not the same.

APPLICATION: A shorter but less clear way of saying *software program.*

ANONYMOUS FTP: Being able to log into a computer with the login name "anonymous" to perform file transfers using the FTP protocol.

ARCHIE: A utility to find files stored on FTP servers.

ARPA: Advanced Research Project Agency, the group that came into being after *Sputnik* and established the need for what has become the Internet.

ASCII (American Standard Code for Information Exchange): One of the simplest methods of storing and transmitting data, ASCII characters are recognizable by most programs and recognizable by people when they appear on the screen.

AUTHENTICATION: Making sure users are who they say they are, using passwords, smart cards, biometrics, or other means.

BANDWIDTH: Used in practice to describe the amount of data that can be transferred over a network connection, or how "big the pipe is."

BIT: Short for "binary digit," the smallest unit of information stored in a computer, corresponding either to 0 or 1, false or true, off or on. Eight bits is a *byte,* 4 bits is a *nibble,* and 2 bits is a quarter. If it were a trinary system, 3 bits would be a tribble.

BOOKMARK: Sometimes known as Favorites, a shortcut to get back to a resource you plan to refer to often.

BPS (bits per second): A measure used most often to describe the speed of data transmission on a modem.

BROWSER: A tool to view the Web, such as Netscape Communicator, Microsoft Internet Explorer, or Opera. Has nothing to do with the fact that people get the browsers for free and never have to pay for them.

CACHE: The use of memory (most often the hard drive) to store the information used by your browser. This saves time when you return to the same site in a session, as the speed of retrieving information from your memory is much faster than over the communications line. Cache can also take up a lot of storage.

CHAT: Talk with other users on a real-time basis.

CLIENT: A computer or software product that uses the services of another system, known as the server. Also the folks that pay us to learn all this stuff.

COOKIES: A way of storing data on your computer, for good or for tracking purposes.

CRACKER: Someone who tries to gain illegal access to computers.

DEDICATED LINE: A communications line that is used solely for one purpose.

DES (data encryption standard): A widely used encryption method on the Internet.

DIAL-UP ACCESS: When a connection must be established routinely because the network connection is not permanent.

DOMAIN NAME: A mnemonic device that makes it easier to use resources on the Internet than if we had to remember a string of 32 bits.

DOMAIN NAME SYSTEM (DNS): A distributed database that correlates mnemonic names into their numeric IP address.

DOWNLOAD: Transfer information from the host to your computer.

E-MAIL: A system of exchanging messages through computer networks using computerized mailboxes and mail servers to handle the flow.

ENCRYPTION: Temporarily changing data so it is unreadable, unless you have the tools to unencrypt that data.

EXTRANET: Involving outside parties, such as customers and vendors, in a system that integrates with your internal systems, using Internet technology.

FAQ (frequently asked questions): A list of basic questions and answers to help newcomers while reducing redundant postings.

FILE INFECTOR VIRUS: The classic virus, it attaches itself to an executable file and passes itself to other computers when that program executes.

FINGER: A utility to find out whether someone is on the Net, and display his or her e-mail address and information the person may wish to make publicly available.

FIREWALL: Hardware and software used to guard an internal network from unauthorized access from the outside and sometimes to limit the internal use of outside resources.

FLAME: To leave really nasty messages to someone else on the Internet. A rash of such messages going back and forth escalates into a flame war.

FREEWARE: Software that may be copied and used freely, but ownership stays with the developer.

FTP (File Transfer Protocol): A standard protocol and utility for moving files across the Internet.

GATEWAY: An intermediary device between disparate networks.

GIF: Pronounced like the peanut butter, a graphical format standard on the Internet.

GRAPHICAL USER INTERFACE (GUI): A program used to assist (and limit) the user when interacting with a computer through the use of windows, icons, menus, and pointing devices, thus promoting the idea that GUIs are for wimps.

GOPHER: A menu-driven search tool, like a table of contents to specific services on or available from a server.

HELPER APPLICATION: A program that works in conjunction with another to add features, such as a plug-in to Netscape to add Adobe Acrobat Support.

HOME PAGE: Literally, the page your browser defaults to; the one that comes up when you start your browser or hit the "Home" icon. In general usage, the main page representing you, your company, or your organization, also known as the *Welcome page*.

HOST: A computer that acts as a server, offering its capabilities to others on the Internet. It may act as a Web host, an FTP host, a gopher host, or offer other services or any combination of services.

HTML (Hypertext Markup Language): It provides hypertext links from a World Wide Web document to different types of data.

HTTP (Hypertext Transfer Protocol): The Internet standard method of communicating Web information.

Hypertext: A means of providing nonlinear movement through a document by being able to jump easily from topic to topic in a document.

INFORMATION SUPERHIGHWAY: The notion of a worldwide system for the exchange of ideas and information in multimedia format. Not synonymous with the Internet, but encompassing it.

INTRANET: The use of Internet software and tools within an organization instead of across organizations.

INTERNET: The world's largest network of networks.

InterNIC: The traditional registration service responsible for assigning domain names.

IP ADDRESS: A 32-bit number (in the format xxx.xxx.xxx.xxx, where xxx <256) that uniquely identifies a location on the Internet. The next generation of IP, IP version 6, will be much larger.

IRC (International Relay Chat): A utility for holding real-time keyboard conversations on-line.

ISDN (Integrated Services Digital Network): A digital line using traditional telephone wires that can offer significantly faster access. Rates vary widely across the country.

ISP (Internet Service Provider): Someone who lets you share his or her connection to the Internet.

LINK: An area that can be clicked to jump to another Web page or access another resource on the Internet.

LISTSERV: One of the major software products used to provide mailing lists, where subscribers have some control over what they receive, how often, and in what format.

Java: SGI's (Sun Microsystems) attempt to provide a cross-platform programming language for the Internet. Java can run on anything from palm devices to UNIX systems.

MACRO VIRUS: The most widespread type of virus today, it does not attach itself to executable files but to Microsoft Office documents. It runs as an automatic macro when the file is opened. Macro viruses are frequently attached to e-mail messages and can be overlooked by antivirus scanners.

MODEM: The hardware that translates between the digital nature of a computer and the analog nature of a phone line; it turns bits into sounds and sounds into bits. ISDN modems are more correctly called *terminal adaptors* because ISDN is a pure digital system. No MOdulation and DEModulation is required.

NETSCAPE: A company bought by America Online; a browser used to view the Internet; a Web site accessed with resources and links to other resources.

NETIQUETTE: The rules of the road to behave properly on the Internet.

NETWORK: Computers communicating with computers.

NEWSGROUP: A forum or conference area where you can read, add, or follow up on topics of mutual interest.

OFF-LINE: Not connected to the Internet; not running.

ON-LINE: Connected to the Internet; running.

ON-LINE SERVICE: A centrally administered computer service offering independent and proprietary content separate from the Internet.

PACKET: A chunk of data.

PDF (portable document file): A document in ACROBAT format. Requires the ACROBAT reader to use.

PLUG-INS: Software that augments the capabilities of the Web browser, such as Shockwave, Flash, and Adobe Acrobat.

PGP (Pretty Good Privacy): A popular encryption tool.

POP (point of presence): A local phone number you can access to get on the Internet; Post Office Protocol for e-mail. POP3 is a popular way to receive mail from the Internet.

POSTING: Sending messages to a newsgroup or discussion group.

POTS (Plain old telephone service): Normal phone lines.

PPP (Point-to-Point Protocol): One of the two most popular ways to connect computer to the Net using a dial-up phone line.

PROTOCOL: A set of standards that describes ways to operate, to ensure compatibility between systems.

RAM (random access memory): The working memory of the computer.

SERVER: A computer providing a server or its resources (access to its hard drives or printer, for example).

SGML: A publishing standard, of which HTML is a subset.

SHAREWARE: Software that may be copied freely, but use beyond a certain time or amount should require a payment to the developer.

SLIP (serial line Internet protocol): one of the two most popular ways to connect computer to the Net using a dial-up phone line.

SNAIL MAIL: Mail sent by the U.S. Postal Service, so called because of the relative speed of delivery of e-mail.

SOURCE DOCUMENT: The unrendered HTML; the text and instruction sent for the browser to display.

SPIDER: Tool that searches web sites and creates an index from the sites it finds. It is a spider because it crawls over the web. Also known as webcrawler.

SPAM: Unwanted and unrequested e-mail.

T-1: A leased line that carries data at 1.544 Megabytes per second.

T-3: A leased line that carries data at 44.746 Megabytes per second.

TCP/IP (Transmission Control Protocol/Internet Protocol): The basic protocols that allow blocks of communication to go from one place to the other on the Net and be understood.

TELNET: A protocol and the utility that lets you log in to a remote computer.

TLA (three-letter acronym): The acronym about acronyms.

TROJAN HORSE: Not a virus in the strictest sense, because it does not reproduce itself; it is payload in a program that seems to serve a desirable end (often games or adult material) but then releases a secret, harmful program.

UPLOAD: Send a file from your computer to another computer.

URL (Uniform Resource Locator): The address of a resource on the Internet.

VERONICA (Very Easy Rodent-Oriented Netwide Index to Computerized Articles): A search tool that looks for text in gopher menus.

VIRUS: A self-replicating program that runs on your computer without your permission. It may do nothing but reproduce and spread to other computers; it may do some slightly annoying things, or it can destroy your data.

WAIS (wide area information servers): The software to index large text files and to search and retrieve documents based on that index.

WEB (short for World Wide Web): A graphical, hypertext-based system of documents that may include text, graphics, photographs, sound, video, and links to other documents and services.

WELCOME PAGE: The front cover for a series of pages on the Web.

WWW (World Wide Web): See WEB.

XML (eXtensible Markup Language): A new way to add tags to text files to create self-describing, cross-platform, machine-readable files that offer new searching and computing capabilities.

Index

Accountant's Home Page, 312
Accounting organizations, 322–325
Accounting software developers, 320–322
AccountingNet, 164–165
AccountMate, 224
ACL, 28
Adobe Acrobat, 85, 128–130
Advanced Software, 224–225
AICPA, 26–27
Alta Vista, 174–175, 352
Amazon.com, 212
America Online, 36, 111
Anet, 49–51
Anonymous FTP, 74
Ask Jeeves, 175
Asymmetric digital subscriber line (ADSL), 96
Attachments, 38–39
Auctions, 208–209
Auditing, 27–29, 238–240
AuditNet Resource List, 178
Authentication, 254

BBBOnline, 270–271
Berners-Lee, Tim, 82
Browsers, 84, 119–127
Business and reference sites, 328–330
Buy.com, 22

Cable modems, 95, 97
Canadian resources, 348
Citrix, 100
CompuServe, 36, 108–110
Computer and technology resources, 330–331
Continuing professional education (CPE), 313
Copernic 99, 194–196
CPA Microcomputer Report, 161
CU-SeeMe, 90

Data Junction, 25–27
Davis, Matt, 284
Deja, 71, 175
Developers of software for CPAs, 319–320
Discussion groups, 55
Domain names, 35–38, 155–157
Double Entries, 51

EBay, 208–209
Edgar, 192
Electronic commerce, 203–243
Electronic Commerce Modeling Language (ECML), 237–238
Electronic Data Interchange (EDI), 10, 14, 229–231, 332–333

Electronic filing, 207–208
Electronic Privacy Information Center
    (EPIC), 267–268
E-mail, 33–47
Encryption, 140
Enterprise Resource Planning (ERP), 10,
    206
European Union and privacy, 259–260
Excite, 36, 85–86, 175, 277–278

Falling through the Net, 8
Faxing, 297–299
FDIC, 210–230
FinanceNet, 52–53, 56–70
Finger, 80
Firewall, 96, 256
Freefind, 138–139
Frequently Asked Questions (FAQs), 71
FTP (file transfer protocol)
    basics, 72–77
    commands, 77

G.Lite, 96
Gates, Bill, 8, 282
Goldmine, 11–12, 44–45, 166–167
Gopher, 83–84, 86–87
Great Plains Software, 225, 240–243

Hitchhiker's Guide to the Galaxy, 171–172
Host, 154–157
HotMail, 36
How to find
    business listings, 183
    hacker sites, 274
    Internet service providers, 186, 342
    mail lists, 187
    maps, 182, 301–302
    new web pages, 184

news, 183–184, 190, 302, 340–342
newsgroups, 188
opinions and discussions, 184
phone numbers, addresses, e-mail,
    182, 343
privacy sites, 275
security sites, 274
HTML, 83
http, 83

Informant, The, 71
INPACT Americas, 286
Instant Messenger, 77–78
Integrated services digital network
    (ISDN), 95
Interactive voice response (IVR), 115
Internal Revenue Service, 207–208
International issues, 347–354
International Relay Chat (IRC), 79–80
International resources
    language and culture, 351–353
    leads and financing, 350–351
Internet
    Benefits, 19–21
    Definition of, 1–6
    free access to, 113
    future of, 21–29
    history of, 18–19
    phones, 89
    relevance, 6–18
    service providers, 111–112
Internet Fraud Watch, 251
Intuit, 141–142, 206–207
Investments, 215–217, 339

Juno, 35, 42

Law and legal resources, 339, 353

Link Exchange, 163
Liszt, 48, 70
Loans, mortgages and credit, 214–215
Lynx, 84

Mailing lists, 47–53, 167–168
Microsoft
   Chat, 81
   FrontPage, 134–136
   Internet Explorer, 23, 119–123
   Media Player, 132–133
   Microsoft Network, 110–111
   NetMeeting, 79
   Office, 12–14
   Outlook Express, 43
   Terminal Server, 100
   VizAct, 136–137
MindSpring, 36
Misc.taxes.moderated, 56
Modem, 94
Mostad and Christensen, 161
MySimon.com, 22, 206, 299
MyTalk.com, 36, 300

Namesecure, 37–38
Net.Medic, 97–99
Net2phone, 90
Netiquette, 72
NetMonitor, 99
Netscape, 43–44, 82, 123–125
Network Solutions, 5, 37
NetZero, 113
News groups, 53–72
Non-repudiation, 255
Northern Light, 176–177

ONEList, 167, 288
Online calendars, 301–302

Online services, 107–108
Open Source, 29
Opera, 125–127
Order entry software for the Internet, 222–228

Palm Connective Device, 11, 101
Patrick, John, 143–145
Payment methods, 232–238
Personal information management, 301–304
Ping, 81
PocketMail, 11, 101
Pointcast, 91–92
Point-to-point protocol (PPP), 103–104
Policies, Internet and e-mail acceptable use, 261–267
Portico, 299–300
Postage, 217–219
Pretty Good Privacy (PGP), 35, 90
Procurement, 220–221
Prodigy, 111
Project management, 305
Publications and publishers, 326–328

Qpass, 234–235
QuickTime, 134

Real, 85, 131–133
ReMarq, 71, 177

Sage Software, 225–226
Search Engine Report, 174
Secure Electronic Transactions (SET), 236
SecurID, 255
Security and privacy, 245–275, 337–338
Shareware, 344

Shell account, 101–103
Shockwave, 85
Shopping 'bots, 206
Small Business Administration, 169–170
Smiles and emoticons, 47
Standards, 228–231
StarOffice, 13, 15
State societies, 324
Submit-It!, 163

T-1 line, 96
T-3 line, 96
Tax resources, 193–194, 325
TCP/IP, 18
Telnet, 87–89
Thomas, 192–193
Threats, 247–248
Trace, 81
TracerLock, 71
Travel, 218–220, 306–307
TRUSTe, 271

U.S. Government resources, 333–335
Unified messaging, 114–118
United Kingdom resources, 349
URL (uniform resource locator), 83
URL-Minder, 162

UWI.com, 25, 128–130

VDOPhone, 90–91
Videoconferencing, 90
Virtual assistants, 116, 299
Viruses, 42, 139–140, 248–249

Walker, Rich, 29–32
Web PrintSmart, 196
Webley, 117–118, 299
WebTrust, 268–274
Whois, 80–81
Wildfire, 115, 117, 299
WinIDEA, 28
Winsock, 105
World Wide Web, 81–84
ws_ftp, 75–77

XML, 22–27

Yahoo!, 177–178, 226–227

Zip file format, 131